PEARSON   ALWAYS LEARNING

Richard Logsdon • Todd Moffett
Tina Eliopulos

Red Rock Reader

Fourth Edition

Pearson Learning Solutions, 501 Boylston Street, Suite 900,
Boston, MA 02116
A Pearson Education Company
www.pearsoned.com

Printed in the United States of America

5 6 7 8 9 10 V0CR 17 16 15 14 13

000200010271291324

JH/JG

ISBN 10: 1-256-67371-4
ISBN 13: 978-1-256-67371-2

COPYRIGHT ACKNOWLEDGMENTS

PREFACE TO *RED ROCK READER*

Welcome to the fourth edition of *Red Rock Reader*. As did the previous editions, this one introduces students to the most valued modes prevalent in college-essay writing. *Red Rock Reader* contains works by well-known professional writers and emerging student voices. Exposing students to both types of writing allows them an avenue toward understanding and appreciating language and composition at multiple levels. The established writer sets the standard and the student writer provides the path. The works of some of these writers initially appeared in *Red Rock Review*, a literary magazine established in 1996. We have selected from *Red Rock Review* essays that we believe illustrate a sophisticated and intelligent application of one or more of the writing modes studied in this reader: description, narration, examples, classification, cause and effect, and so on. New pieces from *National Geographic*, the *New York Times*, and collections by writers such as Steve Martin and James Herriot will further classroom discussions on language, structure, logic, and life events. Additionally, this edition contains a new chapter on literary analysis which will introduce students to the writing strategies they will need in literature courses.

As before, our goal is to encourage students to appreciate the essay as a communication tool, a means for them to make sense of the confusing world around them so they can convey their ideas with the utmost clarity. Thus, moving from description and narration all the way up to argumentation, *Red Rock Reader* is linear in its organization. In fact, the content, organization, and selection of essays have been based upon the theory that to survive in the academic world, students must learn and master those linear forms of writing whose functions, according to Aristotle in *Rhetoric*, are supportive of the persuasive argument, a mode of composition that depends primarily upon logic and only secondarily upon emotion to win its point. Thus, expository modes such as example, comparison and contrast, classification, and cause and effect are treated by Aristotle as well as by the editors of this text as methods of offering proofs that, in turn, ultimately support the premises of the argument.

Our fourth edition would not have been possible without the participation and input of our colleagues at the College of Southern Nevada. These individuals were instrumental in providing us with ideas about classroom activities and readings associated with the *Reader*. We are grateful for their support and for their continued commitment to delivering rigorous and rewarding instruction to our student body each day.

Dr. Richard Logsdon
Todd Moffett
Tina D. Eliopulos
Professors of English, College of Southern Nevada

TABLE OF CONTENTS

CHAPTER ONE

THE WRITING PROCESS

A cartoon in the Writing Center at Tarrant County Junior College showed a first draft of an essay looking imploringly up at a student and crying, "No, no, I'm not good enough for you!" This is a constructive attitude. A first draft is a start and only a start. The full journey—the finished essay or story or book—may take a week or a month or a lifetime to finish. A piece of writing is finished only when the writer finally decides to make no more changes.

An important rule of thumb to follow as both writer and reader is to evaluate the essay's use of *thesis, development and support, organization*, and *mechanics*. These are the four fundamentals of all essay construction. Let's briefly explore each.

THESIS

The thesis is the essay's brain. Without a thesis, even if it is an implied thesis, there is no essay. Four components make up the thesis: *issue, audience, writer*, and *purpose*.

The *issue* is a topic narrowed down for discussion according to the length of the assignment. The issue is derived after the writer has given the topic serious consideration. Usually, writers use any of a number of methods of prewriting to arrive at the issue. Such methods include clustering, mapping, outlining, brainstorming, freewriting, and journal keeping. The issue is carried forth, in one form or another, throughout the entire assignment, giving it unity, coherence, and focus.

The *audience* is the group of people for whom the assignment is written. One audience for a college composition, of course, is the instructor who will read the essay. However, the essay should have a wider audience, well defined and interested in what you have to say about the issue. This wider audience is NOT the "general public"—that is, everyone. The best audience is one that has a clear stake in what you have to say—a specific need for the information you can provide. For example, if you are writing that green, leafy vegetables are good for pregnant women, then your wider audience is pregnant women. Once you are out of the college setting, the professorial audience will disappear, so you will need to learn how to communicate with the wider audience.

The *writer*, obviously, is You. But You as the writer can adopt any number of personas, serious or not, in order to present yourself to your audience. You have many roles to fill in your life, and you can work as one of them when you become the writer. You could be a concerned parent, an angry taxpayer, or an avid football fan. You can even create a persona for yourself—pretend to be LeBron James, or Jennifer Lopez, or SpongeBob— if you feel that adopting such a persona will make you seem more acceptable to your audience. Whoever (or whatever) you pick as your writer, that persona should have a vested interest in the issue being discussed. LeBron James may or may not have a vested interest in the politics of Austria, so choosing him to be the persona for an essay on a parliamentary election in Austria would not be a good fit. LeBron James would have a vested interest in basketball, however, so he would be a good choice of persona to discuss recent issues such as the fall of the Laker dynasty.

The *purpose* of the essay is the reason why the writer would want to communicate to the chosen audience about the issue. Informing and persuading are two general (perhaps too general) purposes one might have. Your own purpose should suit the communication situation at hand. For instance, LeBron James may wish to write about the Laker dynasty to compare it to the one he hopes to begin with the Miami Heat. Jennifer Lopez might want to talk to her fans about how to try out for *American Idol*.

DEVELOPMENT AND SUPPORT

Development and Support are the means of elaborating, explaining, or proving the issue of your paper. This means you must have a thesis clearly in mind when you sit down to write your paper. Without a thesis, any development and support you use will not prove or explain any point you wish to make.

There are several different ways of illustrating or explaining a thesis:

> Description
> Narration
> Example
> Process
> Comparison and Contrast
> Cause and Effect
> Classification and Division
> Definition
> Analogy
> Reporting
> Argumentation
> Quotations/Citing Authorities/Statistics

As you will see, the chapters of this book focus on these methods of developing and supporting a thesis. Examples of these methods of development and support can also be found in the Modes Tables in the back of the book.

These types of development and support can be tailored to meet the needs of the audience to whom you are writing. For example, if your audience is a group of businessmen, and you want to convince them that a different managerial strategy will save their corporation money, then you will probably want to rely on a statistical analysis of the effects your proposed change will cause. Personal experiences in the form of a narrative may not have the information your audience needs. On the other hand, if you are speaking to some ten-year-olds at a summer camp about drug abuse, you will want to keep your ideas and explanations simple. You won't want to cite hard statistics to support a cause and effect analysis but rather tell them what happened to your nine-year-old brother when the police found him carrying a bag of marijuana. A narrative of personal experiences in this case would work better.

Development and support can help you if you are stuck for an idea. Consider trying a type of development and support you haven't used yet in the paper. If you've been using several personal examples and have exhausted your knowledge about the topic, you might think about doing some research in the library or maybe looking at the chain of causes and effects that is connected with your issue. Each new means of development and support that you use can add a paragraph (or even more) to your paper.

When you make a point or state an argument in your paper, you should always ask yourself, "Why?"—Why is this so? Why is this important? Why does this have an effect on my issue? Asking yourself "Why?" will force you to answer "Because," and this answer will in turn force you to rethink your issue using the types of development and support you have at your disposal.

ORGANIZATION

Several levels of organization operate within a paper at once:

> Word-by-word
> Sentence-by-sentence
> Paragraph-by-paragraph
> Overall for paper

Word-by-word organization is sometimes referred to as *syntax* and is usually covered when discussing mechanics. Word-by-word organization is important because the positions of the words can determine the meaning of a sentence. For instance:

> I almost killed seventy people.
> I killed almost seventy people.

These two sentences have the same words in them, but by shifting two of the words, we give them very different meanings.

Word-by-word organization is also affected by grammatical structures such as passive and active verb formations, questions, commands, and dependent and independent clauses. These structures can show the relative importance of the ideas in a sentence or establish a sequence. Look at these three sentences:

> The ball was hit by Tom before it broke the window.
> Tom hit the ball before it broke the window.
> Before it broke the window, Tom hit the ball.

When you put something at the end of a sentence, you are giving it a special stress that you want your readers to notice. These three sentences are saying the same thing, but each is stressing something different about what happens between Tom and the ball. The first sentence, written in passive voice, supplies known information first (the ball was hit by Tom) and new information second (before it hit the window). The second sentence, written in active voice, puts more stress on Tom being the actor. The third sentence, written in active voice but with the dependent clause coming first, reverses the order of the events: now the known information is that the ball hit the window and the new information is that Tom hit the ball.

Sentence-by-sentence organization usually follows some sort of sequence, usually either of time or space. That means when we are telling a story, one event usually follows another event; when telling a friend how to change an oil filter, you tell her what steps she must take from first to last in order to do the job. Each sentence should set forth a step in that process.

Sentence-by-sentence organization can also be determined by the purpose of the sentences within a paragraph. You've probably been told that a paragraph in an essay should begin with some sort of topic sentence and end with a conclusion, with some sentences of explanation or development in between:

> Topic sentence (with transition)
> Narrow down
> Quotation (or example, description, etc.)
> Explanation
> Conclusion

Two paragraphs based on that model might look like this:

> A typical paragraph begins with a topic sentence that sets forward the point to be discussed. The point is narrowed down to a specific instance by means of development and support in the next sentence—or, if a quotation from an outside source will be used to support the point, then this sentence introduces the source of the quotation; as Maxine Hairston and John J. Ruszkiewicz tell their readers, "You have to select [quotations] purposefully, introduce them intelligently, and tailor them to fit your own language" (626). After using a quotation or providing an example, you might explain how the example supports the point you're making. If your point needs no further explanation, you can conclude the paragraph with this sentence and move on to your next point.

> Often, the first sentence of a paragraph will serve as a transition. In that case, you need to signal your reader with one of the transition words or by repeating a key word or by using a synonym for a key word in the previous paragraph. The transition word does not have to appear at the front of the first sentence, but it needs to be present so that you establish the relationship between the paragraphs and signal to

your reader whether you are continuing with a previous idea or introducing a new idea. This transition shows the reader the direction of your paragraph and avoids confusion. Once the point of the second paragraph is explained adequately, then it too can be concluded, and you can move on to the next paragraph.

Scrambling the sentence order of these paragraphs would confuse their meaning because the sentences fulfill specific duties within the paragraphs: to introduce the main idea, to elaborate on the idea, and to finish with the idea while preparing the reader for the next paragraph.

Paragraph-by-paragraph organization is also determined by purpose. Each paragraph should illuminate one idea, and you should move on to another paragraph when you introduce a new idea or change directions within the old one. The paragraphs in this explanation are organized with this thinking in mind: after the paragraph showing the four levels of organization, each paragraph since has developed one of those ideas, with paragraph breaks coming when the next level was introduced or when a new idea about one of the previous levels was mentioned. Sometimes an idea will take more than one paragraph to develop—an idea might take you in one direction, then another. But all of the paragraphs relating to the same central idea should be kept together so that the idea will not be scattered.

One way to keep paragraphs and sentences organized is to use *transitions*. Transitions are like road and street signs: they provide us with directions so that we can arrive at our proper destination. Imagine driving through an unfamiliar city with no streets signs—At which corner do I turn? Am I traveling east or west? Where is the nearest freeway?—and you will understand the difficulty of reading a paper without clear transitions. There are two main ways of providing transitions. The first is by using transitional words and phrases. To understand this method, you need to keep a list of transition words and phrases handy. Some of these are:

Time and sequence: First, first of all, for one thing, one way, second, the third reason, another, another way, also, next, and, in addition, moreover, furthermore, then, after, before, while, meanwhile, now, during, next to, across.

Change of direction/Contrast: But, however, yet, in contrast, still, on the other hand, otherwise, on the contrary.

Illumination: For example, for instance, as an illustration, specifically, such as, like.

Conclusion: Therefore, consequently, thus, then, as a result, in summary, to conclude, last (most) of all, finally. (Langan 43)

By using one of the transitional words or phrases in the first sentence of your paragraphs, you signal to your reader the sequence your thoughts are following and provide a way for him or her to connect the ideas you are developing.

The second method of making transitions is to repeat a key word or idea (or a synonym or a pronoun substituting for that idea) from the previous paragraph in the first sentence of the new paragraph. This paragraph repeated the word *transitions*; this repetition signaled to you that this paragraph was related to the previous one because it was talking about the same topic. It also used the word *second* (a transitional word) to let you know that it was continuing with the list of transitions. You must remember to remind your reader from time to time what direction you are taking and which of your ideas are related, or else your reader will feel as though you have left her stranded in that unfamiliar city. Clear transitions provide signs for your reader to follow.

Overall-for-paper organization incorporates all of the levels mentioned above, but one important consideration will guide you in your choice of how to order your ideas within a paper. You want your ideas to make as much impact upon your reader as possible. This will maintain your reader's interest and make your points more convincing. Three common ways of organizing your paper are by chronology, by relative importance, and by subordination/coordination.

Chronology

If you are reporting a series of events or describing a process or writing about something else that involves a sequence, then the most natural way to organize your paper would be chronologically. This means that the organization of your paper follows the order of the events you're reporting or the process you are describing. George Orwell's "A Hanging" is organized chronologically: he is reporting on the events of a hanging he witnessed in Burma, from the moment a prisoner is brought out of his cell to the final nervous release of tension by the police officers as they have a drink together.

Relative Importance

This method means saving "the best for last"; that is, saving your strongest argument or example or description for last and structuring your essay according to Aristotelian plot structure. Perhaps you've talked about the idea of plot and seen this picture:

This drawing might look like a mountain to you, and that might be a good way to remember it. The first, smaller peak is the *initial conflict,* which sets everything in motion. The long uphill towards the second peak is the *gradual rise in tension* or the *complication.* The top of the second peak is the *climax.* The essay "The Death of the Moth" by Virginia Woolf follows this form: she establishes the initial conflict in the opening paragraph by describing the moth against the backdrop of the vigorous activity proceeding outside; the gradual rise in tension comes as she describes the moth's attempts to escape the window and thus join with that activity; the climax comes when she relates the moth's final valiant struggle to right itself in the face of death. Her most startling and provocative detail is saved until last, and she gradually builds toward it by describing the moth's increasingly heroic fight against a force that can at its whim devour entire cities at a time. Used correctly, this type of organization can pull a reader through an essay by arousing and maintaining her interest. As the writer, you must choose which of your examples will be the most effective at the end and then structure the rest of your examples to lead your reader to it.

Subordination/Coordination

Subordination/Coordination is a method of grouping similar ideas. To use this method when writing your own papers, follow these four steps:

> 1) Make a complete list of the ideas, issues, topics, and/or arguments that you wish to discuss in your paper.
>
> 2) See if any items on the list are related. If they are, group them together (this is coordination) in a list. Above the list, write out the quality that relates the items in the list (this is subordination). Repeat this step until all of the items have been put into lists. For instance, if your list reads
>
> > carrots bread pork
> > cereal orange juice peas
> > beef rice turnips milk
>
> you can align carrots, peas, and turnips under the heading *vegetables;* you can align pork and beef under the heading *meats*; you can align bread, cereal, and rice under the heading *grains;* you can align orange juice and milk under the heading *drinks.*
>
> 3) Find a "title" which describes the common feature(s) of all the lists (this is subordination again). For the example used in step two, you can align all of the lists under the title *foods* or *grocery list.*
>
> 4) Now redraw your lists—with the headings and title included—in an outline form:

Foods

I. Vegetables
    A. Carrots
    B. Peas
    C. Turnips
II. Meats
    A. Pork
    B. Beef
III. Grains
    A. Bread
    B. Cereal
    C. Rice
IV. Drinks
    A. Orange Juice
    B. Milk

You now have a blueprint for your paper. Your title becomes a thesis statement; your headings become sections within the paper; the items under each heading become the topics of individual paragraphs.

The overall organization of a paper can also be influenced by the type(s) of development and support you use to elaborate your thesis. For example, if you are describing an object, you may want to organize the details spatially: move from the top to the bottom of the object, or from the left side to the right, or from front to back. If a car is your object, that would mean starting with the roof and finishing with the underside, or going from the driver's side to the passenger's side, or going from the front bumper to the rear bumper. A description can also be organized by sensory impression: first, by how it looks; then, by how it sounds; then, by how it smells, and so on.

Here are some methods of development and support and the organization patterns that can be used with them:

Cause and Effect

    Centered around key event
    Chronological

Comparison and Contrast

    Alternating
    Continuous

Classification and Division

Subordination/Coordination
Best for last (Relative importance)

Description

Chronological
Spatial
Sensory impression
Best for last

Definition

Definition/example/definition/example
Definition/example/example . . .

Examples

Chronological
Subordination/Coordination
Best for last

Process

Chronological
Spatial
Simple to complex (start with easy steps and move toward more difficult ones)

Reporting

Centered around key event
Chronological
Sensory impression

Argument

Alternating (supporting argument/opposing argument/supporting/opposing)
Continuous (supporting/supporting/opposing/opposing)
Specific to general (inductive)
General to specific (deductive)
Best for last
Background information/opposing view/supporting arguments

Quotations/Citing Authorities/Statistics

>Best for last
>Subordination/Coordination

Specific organizational strategies will be included in the paradigms in the chapters that follow. If you wish, you may use more than one method for organizing your paper; these strategies are not mutually exclusive. The key point to remember when choosing your method, as stated above, is making an impact upon your readers. At all times, you must consider the effect you are trying to create on the audience.

You should also remember that the four levels of organization build upon one another; all four levels must work together to create the greatest impact upon your reader. However, you should wait to consider your paper's organization until you have finished a rough draft and are about to begin another. The ideas presented above will be easier to use when you have something upon the page.

MECHANICS

Mechanics are the nuts and bolts of writing and of preparing your manuscript for submission. You must pay special attention to your instructor's requirements for submitting your essays because those requirements are meant to help make the writing (and the reading) process easier. In particular, you will have to keep in mind six areas: *format of paper, documentation, spelling, punctuation, grammar*, and *sentence construction*.

The *format* of the paper includes directions for putting your name, course, assignment title, and other pertinent information on your manuscript. It also includes directions for margins, paragraph alignment, headers, page numbers, and other details that pertain to the appearance of your text on the page. Many instructors will ask you to follow the Modern Language Association (MLA) guidelines that are explained in most student handbooks. However, many instructors may want you to follow their own method of formatting your assignments. Make sure you understand your instructor's requirements before you sit down to write.

The process of *documentation* applies when your instructor has asked you to write a researched essay or a literary analysis. In either case, you must follow the rules of documentation set out in a style guide such as the *MLA Handbook for Writers of Research Papers* or the *Publication Manual of the American Psychological Association*. These rules will also be set out in most student handbooks. The process of documentation has two main parts: a parenthetical citation that appears in the body paragraphs, and a works cited (or references) list. Please make sure that you understand the documentation rules that your instructor requires as you are writing your essay.

Checking the *spelling* of unfamiliar words, of important vocabulary words, and of words that you frequently misspell should be one of your final tasks when writing your paper. If you work on a computer, your word processor's spell checker is a handy tool— but it is not perfect. You may misspell a word that the spell checker may not recognize as an error. For example, if you type *an* when you meant to type *and*, the spell checker will not see your misspelling as an error because *an* is a word. An extra pass through your assignment—or the eyes of a classmate or friend—may help you catch many spelling mistakes.

Errors of *punctuation, grammar,* and *sentence construction* tend to be the most frustrating for students. You may sense that you have made an error, but you are not sure what that error might be or how to fix it—until you have the assignment handed back with your instructor's marks. Knowing what your instructor is looking for may help you see which errors you commit. Instructors tend to see errors of punctuation, grammar, and sentence construction as belonging to two groups: *frequency errors* and *status errors.*

Frequency errors are those which your instructor sees most often when grading student assignments. Many of these are as simple as a missing comma, but some are as serious as sentence fragments. Following is a list taken from a study conducted by Robert J. Connors and Andrea A. Lunsford in 1988 (qtd. in Noguchi) showing the twenty most frequent punctuation, grammar, and sentence construction errors:

1	No comma after introductory element (presentence modifier, sentence)
2	Vague pronoun reference
3	No comma in compound sentence (independent clause, independent clause)
4	Wrong word
5	No comma in nonrestrictive element
6	Wrong or missing inflected endings (noun/verb)
7	Wrong or missing preposition
8	Comma splice
9	Possessive apostrophe error
10	Tense shift (main verb, auxiliary verb)
11	Unnecessary shift in person (first, second, third person)
12	Sentence fragment (sentence or independent clause)
13	Wrong tense or verb form (main verb, auxiliary verb)
14	Subject-Verb agreement
15	Lack of comma in series
16	Pronoun agreement error
17	Unnecessary comma with restrictive element
18	Run-on or fused sentence
19	Dangling or misplaced modifier
20	Its/It's error

Focusing your attention on the errors that appear at the top of this frequency list may help you to cut down on the number of errors you commit in your own writing. You may also want to look most closely for comma errors, since they appear six times (counting the comma splice). You may wish, therefore, to consult a handbook to learn more about all of these errors.

Status errors are those which stigmatize the writer—that is, mark the writer's social status or educational background—and which elicit the strongest response in a reader. Following is a list taken from a study conducted by Maxine Hairston in 1981 (qtd. in Noguchi) showing the most serious status-marking punctuation, grammar, and sentence construction errors:

Status Marking
Nonstandard verb forms in past or past participle: *we knowed* instead of *we knew*
Lack of subject-verb agreement: *we was* instead of *we were; he don't think* instead of *he doesn't think*
Double negatives: *I don't want no trouble*
Objective pronoun as subject: *Him and me found the dog*
Very Serious
Sentence fragments (sentence or independent clause)
Run-on sentences
Noncapitalization of proper nouns
Would of instead of *would have*
Lack of subject-verb agreement, nonstatus marking
Insertion of comma between verb and complement: *She is, an engineer*
Nonparallelism: *We enjoy hiking, swimming, and to go to the movies*
Faulty adverb forms: *He treats his men bad*
Use of transitive verb *set* for intransitive *sit*: *I set down in the chair*

Again, focusing your attention on the errors that appear on this list may help you to cut down on the errors you commit in your own writing, but you will also be reducing the number of errors that your instructor will see as being the most serious. Comparing this list with the previous one may also give you an idea of which errors you may wish to focus your attention on. As with the previous list, you may wish to consult a handbook to learn more about these errors.

We hope that this brief look into the process of essay writing will help you through your drafting stages. As stated at the outset, the first draft of an essay is not the final draft. You should get into the habit of writing multiple drafts of each assignment so that you will give yourself the chance to form and organize your ideas and to proofread for errors. The following chapters will discuss many writing strategies in more detail.

Works Cited

Hairston, Maxine, and John J. Ruszkiewicz. *The Scott, Foresman Handbook for Writers.* Glenview, Illinois: Scott, Foresman, 1988.

Langan, John. *English Skills with Readings.* 2nd ed. New York: McGraw-Hill, 1991.

Noguchi, Rei R. *Grammar and the Teaching of Writing: Limits and Possibilities.* Urbana, Illinois: NCTE, 1991.

SELECTIONS FROM *THE WRITING LIFE*

BY ANNIE DILLARD

When you write, you lay out a line of words. The line of words is a miner's pick, a woodcarver's gouge, a surgeon's probe. You wield it, and it digs a path you follow. Soon you find yourself deep in new territory. Is it a dead end, or have you located the real subject? You will know tomorrow, or this time next year.

You make the path boldly and follow it fearfully. You go where the path leads. At the end of the path, you find a box canyon. You hammer out reports, dispatch bulletins.

The writing has changed, in your hands, and in a twinkling, from an expression of your notions to an epistemological tool.

The new place interests you because it is not clear. You attend. In your humility, you lay down the words carefully, watching all the angles. Now the earlier writing looks soft and careless. Process is nothing; erase your tracks. The path is not the work. I hope your tracks have grown over; I hope birds ate the crumbs; I hope you will toss it all and not look back.

The line of words is a hammer. You hammer against the walls of your house. You tap the walls, lightly, everywhere. After giving many years' attention to these things, you know what to listen for. Some of the walls are bearing walls; they have to stay, or everything will fall down. Other walls can go with impunity; you can hear the difference. Unfortunately, it is often a bearing wall that has to go. It cannot be helped. There is only one solution, which appalls you, but there it is. Knock it out.

Duck.

Courage utterly opposes the bold hope that this is such fine stuff the work needs it, or the world. Courage, exhausted, stands on bare reality: this writing weakens the work. You must demolish the work and start over. You can save some of the sentences, like bricks. It will be a miracle if you can save some of the paragraphs, no matter how excellent in themselves or hard-won. You can waste a year worrying about it, or you can get it over with now. (Are you a woman, or a mouse?)

The part you must jettison is not only the best-written part; it is also, oddly, that part which was to have been the very point. It is the original key passage, the passage on which the rest was to hang, and from which you yourself drew the courage to begin. Henry James knew it well, and said it best. In his preface to *The Spoils of Poynton*, he pities the writer, in a comical pair of sentences that rises to a howl: "Which is the work in which he hasn't surrendered, under dire difficulty, the best thing he meant to have kept? In which indeed, before the dreadful *done*, doesn't he ask himself what has become of the thing all for the sweet sake of which it was to proceed to that extremity?"

So it is that a writer writes many books. In each book, he intended several urgent and vivid points, many of which he sacrificed as the book's form hardened. "The youth gets together his materials to build a bridge to the moon," Thoreau noted mournfully, "or perchance a palace or temple on the earth, and at length the middle-aged man concludes to build a wood-shed with them." The writer returns to these materials, these passionate subjects, as to unfinished business, for they are his life's work.

It is the beginning of a work that the writer throws away.

A painting covers its tracks. Painters work from the ground up. The latest version of a painting overlays earlier versions, and obliterates them. Writers, on the other hand, work from left to right. The discardable chapters are on the left. The latest version of a literary work begins somewhere in the work's middle and hardens toward the end. The earlier version remains lumpishly on the left; the work's beginning greets the reader with the wrong hand. In those early pages and chapters anyone may find bold leaps to nowhere, read the brave beginnings of dropped themes, hear a tone since abandoned, discover blind alleys, track red herrings, and laboriously learn a setting now false.

Several delusions weaken the writer's resolve to throw away work. If he has read his pages too often, those pages will have a necessary quality, the ring of the inevitable, like poetry known by heart; they will perfectly answer their own familiar rhythms. He will retain them. He may retain those pages if they possess some virtues, such as power in themselves, though they lack the cardinal virtue, which is pertinence to, and unity with, the book's thrust. Sometimes the writer leaves his early chapters in place from gratitude; he cannot contemplate them or read them without feeling again the blessed relief that exalted him when the words first appeared—relief that he was writing anything at all. That beginning served to get him where he was going, after all; surely the reader needs it, too, as groundwork. But no.

Every year the aspiring photographer brought a stack of his best prints to an old, honored photographer, seeking his judgment. Every year the old man studied the prints and painstakingly ordered them into two piles, bad and good. Every year the old man moved a certain landscape print into the bad stack. At length he turned to the young man: "You submit this same landscape every year, and every year I put it on the bad stack. Why do you like it so much?" The young photographer said, "Because I had to climb a mountain to get it."

A cabdriver sang his songs to me, in New York. Some we sang together. He had turned the meter off; he drove around midtown, singing. One long song he sang twice; it was the only dull one. I said, You already sang that one; let's sing something else. And he said, "You don't know how long it took me to get that one together."

How many books do we read from which the writer lacked courage to tie off the umbilical cord? How many gifts do we open from which the writer neglected to remove the price tag? Is it pertinent, is it courteous, for us to learn what it cost the writer personally?

***

To find a honey tree, first catch a bee. Catch a bee when its legs are heavy with pollen; then it is ready for home. It is simple enough to catch a bee on a flower: hold a cup or glass above the bee, and when it flies up, cap the cup with a piece of cardboard.

Carry the bee to a nearby open spot—best an elevated one—release it, and watch where it goes. Keep your eyes on it as long as you can see it, and hie you to that last known place.

Wait there until you see another bee; catch it, release it, and watch. Bee after bee will lead toward the honey tree, until you see the final bee enter the tree. Thoreau describes this process in his journals. So a book leads its writer.

You may wonder how you start, how you catch the first one. What do you use for bait?

You have no choice. One bad winter in the Arctic, and not too long ago, an Algonquin woman and her baby were left alone after everyone else in their winter camp had starved. Ernest Thompson Seton tells it. The woman walked from the camp where everyone had died, and found at a lake a cache. The cache contained one small fishhook. It was simple to rig a line, but she had no bait, and no hope of bait. The baby cried. She took a knife and cut a strip from her own thigh. She fished with the worm of her own flesh and caught a jackfish; she fed the child and herself. Of course she saved the fish gut for bait. She lived alone at the lake, on fish, until spring, when she walked out again and found people. Seton's informant had seen the scar on her thigh.

It takes years to write a book—between two and ten years. Less is so rare as to be statistically insignificant. One American writer has written a dozen major books over six decades. He wrote one of those books, a perfect novel, in three months. He speaks of it, still, with awe, almost whispering. Who wants to offend the spirit that hands out such books?

Faulkner wrote *As I Lay Dying* in six weeks; he claimed he knocked it off in his spare time from a twelve-hour-a-day job performing manual labor. There are other examples from other continents and centuries, just as albinos, assassins, saints, big people, and little people show up from time to time in large populations. Out of a human population on earth of four and a half billion, perhaps twenty people can write a book in a year. Some people lift cars, too. Some people enter weeklong sled-dog races, go over Niagara Falls in barrels, fly planes through the Arc de Triomphe. Some people feel no pain in childbirth. Some people eat cars. There is no call to take human extremes as norms.

***

I do not so much write a book as sit up with it, as with a dying friend. During visiting hours, I enter its room with dread and sympathy for its many disorders. I hold its hand and hope it will get better.

This tender relationship can change in a twinkling. If you skip a visit or two, a work in progress will turn on you.

A work in progress quickly becomes feral. It reverts to a wild state overnight. It is barely domesticated, a mustang on which you one day fastened a halter, but which now you cannot catch. It is a lion you cage in your study. As the work grows, it gets harder to control; it is a lion growing in strength. You must visit it every day and reassert your mastery over it. If you skip a day, you are, quite rightly, afraid to open the door to its room. You enter its room with bravura, holding a chair at the thing and shouting, "Simba!"

***

Push it. Examine all things intensely and relentlessly. Probe and search each object in a piece of art. Do not leave it, do not course over it, as if it were understood, but instead follow it down until you see it in the mystery of its own specificity and strength. Giacometti's drawings and paintings show his bewilderment and persistence. If he had not acknowledged his bewilderment, he would not have persisted. A twentieth-century master of drawing, Rico Lebrun, taught that "the draftsman must aggress; only by persistent assault will the live image capitulate and give up its secret to an unrelenting line." Who but an artist fierce to know—not fierce to seem to know—would suppose that a live image possessed a secret? The artist is willing to give all his or her strength and life to probing with blunt instruments those same secrets no one can describe in any way but with those instruments' faint tracks.

Admire the world for never ending on you—as you would admire an opponent, without taking your eyes from him, or walking away.

One of the few things I know about writing is this: spend it all, shoot it, play it, lose it all, right away, every time. Do not hoard what seems good for a later place in the book, or for another book; give it, give it all, give it now. The impulse to save something good for a better place later is the signal to spend it now. Something more will arise for later, something better. These things fill from behind, from beneath, like well water. Similarly, the impulse to keep to yourself what you have learned is not only shameful, it is destructive. Anything you do not give freely and abundantly becomes lost to you. You open your safe and find ashes.

After Michelangelo died, someone found in his studio a piece of paper on which he had written a note to his apprentice, in the handwriting of his old age: "Draw, Antonio, draw, Antonio, draw and do not waste time."

STUDY QUESTIONS for selections from *The Writing Life*

COMPREHENSION

1. What do you think is Dillard's main concern about the process of writing? About the writer? Why does she say "Process is nothing" when in fact the entire passage is a description of the process, which apparently she takes very seriously?
2. Define *epistemological, feral, bravura,* and *capitulate.*

DEVELOPMENT AND ORGANIZATION

1. Dillard has a number of very short paragraphs—one even a single word. Does she use these brief paragraphs to develop ideas or to provide transitions? Or does she have other purposes for them?
2. Refer to the list of types of development and support and determine what kinds Dillard uses in this essay.
3. Pick a quotation that Dillard uses in the essay. How does this quotation support the paragraph's controlling idea? Is this quotation actually about the process of writing or does it say something about another activity?

STYLE AND TECHNIQUE

1. If there is one quality in Dillard's writing that stands out above all others, it may well be her skillful use of metaphors and similes from the natural world to explain human experience. Take the following ideas and discuss the application of each to the experience of writing.

   a. Building a house.
   b. Taking photographs.
   c. Singing songs.
   d. Finding a honey tree.
   e. Fishing with a strip of one's own flesh.
   f. Eating a car.
   g. Taming a lion.
   h. Drawing pictures.

2. Do any other metaphors or similes regarding writing seem to fit your experience? Try imitating Dillard's method and explain something about writing in terms of your own response.
3. Dillard frequently uses the second-person pronoun ("you") in this essay. What effect does her use of this pronoun have on the essay?
4. List five sentences in which Dillard issues commands. When do they occur? Why do you think she uses them?

TEN-MINUTE TOPICS

1. Describe your own writing process. Why do you write and how do you go about it?
2. If you were allowed to write another paragraph after the final one of this selection, what would you write? Keep in mind what appears here is an excerpt from a longer work.

CHAPTER TWO

DESCRIPTION

DEFINITION

Usually written to convey a dominant impression of a person, place, or thing, description is characterized by the use of concrete details; these are words that appeal to sight, sound, taste, touch, and/or smell. For instance, in the following paragraph, the writer uses such detail to describe a turtle on a beach:

> Her shell, half green and covered with barnacles, was four feet long, three feet wide, and one and a half feet tall. Seaweed and plankton clung to the rough-textured, hexagon-patterned shell. We ran our hands on the surface of it, and a mysterious phosphorescent green glow appeared.

Description often paints a picture; accordingly, this piece is highly visual, relying upon "half green," "covered with barnacles," "seaweed and plankton," "rough-textured," "hexagon-patterned," and "phosphorescent green glow" to enable us to see the turtle and ultimately to convey the writer's sense of wonder.

APPLICATION

When we write a lengthy description, we must arrange the concrete details in some logical order: left to right, right to left, near to far, far to near, and so on. In the following passage from his short story "The Secret Sharer," Joseph Conrad selects and arranges his descriptive details to convey the dominant impression of isolation:

> On my right hand there were lines of fishing stakes resembling a mysterious system of half-submerged bamboo fences, incomprehensible in its division of the domain of tropical fishes, and crazy of aspect as if abandoned for ever by some nomad tribe of fishermen now gone to the other end of the ocean; for there was no sign of human habitation as far as the eye could reach. To the left a group of barren islets, suggesting ruins of stone walls, towers, and blockhouses, had its foundations set in a blue sea that itself looked solid, so still and stable did it lie below my feet; even the track of light from the westering sun shone smoothly, without that animated glitter which tells of an imperceptible ripple. And when I turned my head to take a parting glance at the tug which had just left us anchored outside the bar, I saw the straight line of the flat shore joined to the stable sea, edge to edge, with a perfect and unmarked

closeness, in one levelled floor half brown, half blue under the enormous dome of the sky. Corresponding in their insignificance to the islets of the sea, two small clumps of trees, one on each side of the only fault in the impeccable joint, marked the mouth of the river Meinam we had just left on the first preparatory stage of our homeward journey; and, far back on the inland level, a larger and loftier mass, the grove surrounding the great Paknam pagoda, was the only thing on which the eye could rest from the vain task of exploring the monotonous sweep of the horizon.

First of all, Conrad has given us a visual impression of this ocean setting with such words and phrases as "lines of fishing stakes," "half-submerged bamboo fences," "group of barren islets" and "blue sea." Further, Conrad wants to bring out the terrific isolation that the narrator is feeling with such words and phrases as "mysterious system," "incomprehensible," "abandoned for ever," "no sign of human habitation," "barren islet," "ruins of stone walls," and so on. Finally, Conrad reveals a logical arrangement of details with such transitions as "On my right hand," "to the left," and "far back." Such directions, of course, make the passage easier to follow.

Conrad's passage is a good example of what we might call *subjective* description: that is, its descriptive details convey an emotional response on the part of the writer. But some description is *objective*, conveying—or seeming to convey—almost no emotion. Most weather reports contain objective description: "The wind is blowing out of the northwest at forty-five miles per hour tonight. Since noon, the temperature has dropped to twenty-one degrees. Snow is expected at the higher elevations of Mount Charleston with freezing rain expected at the lower elevations." Ernest Hemingway is a master at writing descriptions that seem, on the surface, very objective. Consider the following passage from his novel *The Sun Also Rises:*

> It was a warm spring night and I sat at a table on the terrace of the Napolitain after Robert had gone, watching it get dark and the electric signs come on, and the red and green stop-and-go traffic-signal, and the crowd going by, and the horse-cabs clippety-clopping along at the edge of the solid taxi traffic, and the *poules* going by, singly and in pairs, looking for the evening meal. I watched a good-looking girl walk past the table and watched her go up the street and lost sight of her, and watched another, and then saw the first one coming back again. She went by once more and I caught her eye, and she came over and sat down at the table. The waiter came up.

The only slightly subjective phrase in the entire description is "good-looking girl."

Besides arranging the descriptive details logically, both Conrad and Hemingway have also done something else: they have selected only a few sensory details while leaving out most of the objects that the world offers the eyes, ears, nose, tongue, and fingertips. Both passages entirely omit references to the senses of taste and smell. If an odor of dead fish pervaded the Conrad landscape, the author preferred not to record the fact. And while including sound and temperature in his description, Hemingway tells nothing of the odors emanating from the crowds of people or of the taste of the evening meals. Good writers choose their details in order to support and not interfere with the dominant impression, or impressions, that they seek to convey.

PARADIGM

When writing the descriptive essay, keep in mind the following paradigm, which establishes only very general guidelines:

> **Introduction: Use descriptive details to set mood and focus upon person, place, or thing to be described.**

> **Body: Create picture and convey impression/mood/feeling with concrete details arranged in some logical order (e.g., left to right, right to left, near to far, etc.)**

> **Conclusion: Summarize the dominant impression or offer a final image, message, or judgment.**

SUMMARY

Most description, of course, tends to be more subjective than objective. When we write our descriptions, we must be sure to use concrete details, details that appeal to sight, sound, taste, touch, and/or smell. Further, we must be sure to arrange our concrete details in some logical order. Finally, we should seek, through our description, to convey some sort of dominant impression of the object being described.

MY SECRET PLACE

BY JESSIE M. PHILSON (student)

The jagged rocks cut a slash in the side of the black patent leather shoes I was wearing, and I looked down, half expecting to see blood, the pain bringing tears to my eyes. I swore and continued my climb towards the end of the jetty. An occasional rough, oversized wave would send salty spray up over the rocks and into my face to mingle with the salt in my tears that had finally come, not from the pain in my foot but the deeper pain inside me. I slipped and stumbled, but I stubbornly continued until I reached the other side of the unmanned lighthouse that perched precariously at the end of the jetty.

I sat down between two huge boulders smoothed by the wind and constant pounding of the waves at high tide. I was sheltered from the wind and the tide was low so that even the strongest waves were several feet below my refuge. How often I had come here as a child, to dream, to be alone and to think. I had always felt safe here in this place that some people called dangerous. As I curled up between the boulders, I noticed that I had lost the heel from one of my shoes, and my nylons were shredded. I took off my shoes and nylons and then, as I had done as a child, I pulled my legs up under me and hid far back between the huge rock arms of my boulder chair.

There, hidden from the world, I could see, through a small wind hole, the beach for miles. It was deserted except for a few seagulls, sweeping and diving in flight, and sandpipers, running as if on wheels along the water's edge, stopping only to dip their beaks into the sand in search of a tasty morsel.

The ocean was dark today, since the clouds blocked out most of the sun. As the waves hit the rocks below me, I tried to see pictures in the white foam, as some people see pictures in the clouds, or gypsies see pictures in tea leaves. I imagined I saw a large bird, flying high in an empty sky, but before I could really make it out, it looked more like a horse, running wildly in an open field, mane flying, and then it was gone as the tide pulled the foam away and another wave brought new pictures to decipher. I stared at the waves and became almost hypnotized by their movement.

I loved the ocean and her moods. I could feel her strength, and today I needed her to share some of that strength with me. She seemed to share my mood as she appeared dark and sad, swirling and undecided, with an occasional angry wave crashing against the rocks. I remembered days when she had seemed smooth and cold and emotionless as I had been accused of being in the past few days. I remembered when she had been angry and out of control just before a Northeasterner. How I wished I could explode in anger! Maybe then the pain would go away. I thought about how beautiful she was when the sun came up over the horizon and her waves danced and glistened in the colors of a new day or when the moon was low and she undulated and swayed in her evening dress of yellows and golds.

I sat there for an eternity of memories and suddenly realized that the tide was beginning to rise. I glanced at my watch, but the crystal was broken and it had stopped, probably some time during my climb to the end of the jetty. The watch was a gift from him, and now the tears came again. This time they seemed to wash away some of the pain, and as I tasted the salty moisture, I felt that somehow the ocean was sharing my pain and perhaps could take it away from me. Though many of my thoughts were not rational, it seemed she looked darker and stronger at that moment.

I suddenly seemed more calm and rational and realized I must go home. I had forgotten that family and people who cared about me would be worried at my unannounced disappearance and were probably looking for me. I looked up the beach and saw a patrol car slowly driving along the water's edge, heading towards the jetty. They could not see me, but I knew I must leave my secret place.

I put on my shoes and started to climb back over the jetty. The rising tide was now much higher on the rocks, but the heavy spray felt good as I clambered over the path of rocks I knew so well. I waved at the patrol car so they would know I was okay. I looked back at my friend, the ocean, as if she could give me one last bit of her strength. I would need help to make it through the funeral.

STUDY QUESTIONS for "My Secret Place"

COMPREHENSION

1. What is the situation that prompted the experience that Philson writes about? Why do you think that she retreated to her "secret place"? Find details from the essay to support your answer.
2. Is there any special significance in the fact that Philson goes to a place that she knew as a child? If so, what is it?
3. A current psychiatrist, also a best-selling author, argues for the necessity of the kind of suffering that results from the pain of continual self-examination; such self-examination, he argues, promotes emotional and spiritual growth. Is Philson's essay one that reveals, in any way, this kind of self-examination? Do you believe that Philson experienced any "growth" as a result of the pain that she experienced during the ordeal she records in her essay? Explain.

DEVELOPMENT AND ORGANIZATION

1. To what senses does Philson mainly appeal in her selection of concrete details?
2. Comment upon the effectiveness—or ineffectiveness—of the opening paragraph. Why, for instance, does she begin by focusing upon physical pain? Is it possible that the physical pain is intended to correspond with an inward pain? If so, explain.
3. Discuss the nature of the inner struggle, or conflict, that Philson experiences as she retreats to her "secret place." What details in the essay help bring out or suggest the nature of this conflict?
4. Philson's essay is heavily descriptive. But because it records an event that takes place in time, it can also be considered a narrative. Many narratives reveal a change occurring in the main character—a change in thought, feeling, and/or behavior. Does Philson, in her essay, reveal herself going through any sort of change from the beginning to the ending of the essay? If so, what is the nature of this change?

STYLE AND TECHNIQUE

1. What dominant impression/mood does Philson seek to convey of her "secret place" by the ocean? Does she seek to convey one or several related impressions? Explain your answer. What words and phrases most effectively help Philson to convey this impression—or these interrelated impressions?
2. Philson writes in paragraph four, "I imagined I saw a large bird, flying high into the empty sky." Do you think that the bird symbolizes anything for Philson? If so, what? Can you find any other symbols in the essay?

TEN-MINUTE TOPICS

1. Describe a place that represents escape for you and include details using several of the senses. You may include a narrative framework based on an incident in your life if you wish.
2. Describe an object you own that represents a person in your life. Explain why the object has this significance. Do other people view this object in the same way? Or do they perhaps see the object as insignificant?

THE DEATH OF THE MOTH

BY VIRGINIA WOOLF

Moths that fly by day are not properly to be called moths; they do not excite that pleasant sense of dark autumn nights and ivy-blossom which the commonest yellow-underwing asleep in the shadow of the curtain never fails to rouse in us. They are hybrid creatures, neither gay like butterflies nor somber like their own species. Nevertheless the present specimen, with his narrow hay-colored wings, fringed with a tassel of the same color, seemed to be content with life. It was a pleasant morning, mid-September, mild, benignant, yet with a keener breath than that of the summer months. The plough was already scoring the field opposite the window, and where the share had been, the earth was pressed flat and gleamed with moisture. Such vigor came rolling in from the fields and the down beyond that it was difficult to keep the eyes strictly turned upon the book. The rooks too were keeping one of their annual festivities; soaring round the tree tops until it looked as if a vast net with thousands of black knots in it had been cast up into the air; which, after a few moments, sank slowly down upon the trees until every twig seemed to have a knot at the end of it. Then, suddenly, the net would be thrown into the air again in a wider circle this time, with the utmost clamor and vociferation, as though to be thrown into the air and settle slowly down upon the treetops were a tremendously exciting experience.

The same energy which inspired the rooks, the ploughmen, the horses, and even, it seemed, the lean bare-backed downs, sent the moth fluttering from side to side of his square of the window-pane. One could not help watching him. One was, indeed, conscious of a queer feeling of pity for him. The possibilities of pleasure seemed that morning so enormous and so various that to have only a moth's part in life, and a day moth's at that, appeared a hard fate, and his zest in enjoying his meager opportunities to the full, pathetic. He flew vigorously to one corner of his compartment, and, after waiting there a second, flew across to the other. What remained for him but to fly to a third corner and then to a fourth? That was all he could do, in spite of the size of the downs, the width of the sky, the far-off smoke of the houses, and the romantic voice, now and then, of a steamer out at sea. What he could do he did. Watching him, it seemed as if a fiber, very thin but pure, of the enormous energy of the world had been thrust into his frail and diminutive body. As often as he crossed the pane, I could fancy that a thread of vital light became visible. He was little or nothing but life.

Yet, because he was so small, and so simple a form of the energy that was rolling in at the open window and driving its way through so many narrow and intricate corridors in my own brain and in those of other human beings, there was something marvelous as well as pathetic about him. It was as if someone had taken a tiny bead of pure life and decking it as lightly as possible with down and feathers, had set it dancing and zigzagging to show us the true nature of life. Thus displayed one could not get over the strangeness of it. One is apt to forget all about life, seeing it humped and bossed and garnished and cumbered so that it has to move with the greatest circumspection and dignity. Again, the thought of all that life might have been had he been born in any other shape caused one to view his simple activities with a kind of pity.

After a time, tired by his dancing apparently, he settled on the window ledge in the sun, and, the queer spectacle being at an end, I forgot about him. Then, looking up, my eye was caught by him. He was trying to resume his dancing, but seemed either so stiff or so awkward that he could only flutter to the bottom of the windowpane; and when he tried to fly across it he failed. Being intent on other matters I watched these futile attempts for a time without thinking, unconsciously waiting for him to resume his flight, as one waits for a machine, that has stopped momentarily, to start again without considering the reason of its failure. After perhaps a seventh attempt he slipped from the wooden ledge and fell, fluttering his wings, onto his back on the windowsill. The helplessness of his attitude roused me. It flashed upon me that he was in difficulties; he could no longer raise himself; his legs struggled vainly. But, as I stretched out a pencil, meaning to help him right himself, it came over me that the failure and awkwardness were the approach of death. I laid the pencil down again.

The legs agitated themselves once more. I looked as if for the enemy against which he struggled. I looked out of doors. What had happened there? Presumably it was midday, and work in the fields had stopped. Stillness and quiet had replaced the previous animation. The birds had taken themselves off to feed in the brooks. The horses stood still. Yet the power was there all the same, massed outside, indifferent, impersonal, not attending to anything in particular. Somehow it was opposed to the little hay-colored moth. It was useless to try to do anything. One could only watch the extraordinary efforts made by those tiny legs against an oncoming doom which could, had it chosen, have submerged an entire city, not merely a city, but masses of human beings; nothing, I knew, had any chance against death. Nevertheless after a pause of exhaustion the legs fluttered again. It was superb, this last protest, and so frantic that he succeeded at last in righting himself. One's sympathies, of course, were all on the side of life. Also, when there was nobody to care or to know, this gigantic effort on the part of an insignificant little moth, against a power of such magnitude, to retain what no one else valued or desired to keep, moved one strangely. Again, somehow, one saw life, a pure bead. I lifted the pencil again, useless though I knew it to be. But even as I did so, the unmistakable tokens of death showed themselves. The body relaxed, and instantly grew stiff. The struggle was over. The insignificant little creature now knew death. As I looked at the dead moth, this minute wayside triumph of so great a force over so mean an antagonist filled me with wonder. Just as life had been strange a few minutes before, so death was now as strange. The moth having righted himself now lay most decently and uncomplainingly composed. O yes, he seemed to say, death is stronger than I am.

STUDY QUESTIONS for "The Death of the Moth"

COMPREHENSION

1. What is the essay's thesis? Is it implied or explicit? Write it down.

2. According to the narrator, why are day moths inaccurately named? Be specific.
3. What is more important to the narrator and to the moth: the quest for life or the acceptance of death? Explain.

DEVELOPMENT AND ORGANIZATION

1. Examine the essay's organization. Are the events arranged in chronological (linear) order? Or does Woolf use flashbacks? Or a combination of both? Explain her method of organization. What effect does the organization have on the narrative's intent?
2. What time of year (season) is it in the essay? What details does Woolf use to bring the season alive for us? What does the season have to do with the themes of this essay?

STYLE AND TECHNIQUE

1. Identify four words whose meanings were unknown to you prior to reading "The Death of the Moth." Write down each word's dictionary definition. How do the denotative and connotative meanings of each word contribute to the mood and tone of the essay?
2. What is the purpose of the use of the words *forget* and *forgot* in paragraphs three and four? Is their use ironic since the moth's presence causes the narrator to be reminded of an important truth?
3. What's the significance of the "open window" in paragraph three? Why is it important to both the narrator and to the moth?

TEN-MINUTE TOPICS

1. Write a brief narrative about an object or animal you've observed. Your subject's behavior should symbolize some characteristic of you and/or your society.
2. Take a topic that has a large scope—as death does in Woolf's essay—and try to represent it in an everyday or seemingly insignificant object or activity, as Woolf does with the moth.

IN THE GRASS

BY WILLIAM G. FRASER

My evil twin brother Randall lives in a tangle of willows over there across the interstate. He is devoutly antisocial—bordering on misanthropic—and deeply strange. According to legend, no one has ever seen him eat or sleep, and no picture of him has ever been successfully developed.

Me, I live over here, in this apartment complex built around a parking lot where fully one-third of the cars sit on a flat tire (or two), slowly bleeding oil and antifreeze onto the rotten asphalt. I've got my own eccentricities, but I do like to eat and sleep, and my mother still has my baby pictures hanging on her wall.

Randall's hideout is what I call a remnant zone—an oddly shaped bit of mixed-grass prairie that urban sprawl somehow stepped over on its march to the horizon. A determined seeker can still turn one up here and there. I don't suppose they are what the academic outdoor-persons would call "ecologically viable" and most of them aren't even pretty, but Randall finds them quite hospitable. He must. He's been living in them for years.

When the developers come back around to stuff video stores and hamburger joints into the spots they missed on their first pass, Randall folds his canvas and moves on. Most times, I'm able to warn him. I'm an engineer and a surveyor and part of my job is to hammer orange-tipped wooden stakes into the remnant zones to mark the corners of progress in the making.

"You have to go," I'll say to him. "The excavation contractors will be out next week."

Randall will stub out his cigarette, strip the remaining tobacco from the butt, and put it back in the leather pouch he keeps tucked inside his greasy army surplus jacket.

I know what he's going to say. Close enough anyway. But I sit there in whatever hobo camp I find him in, with my own bony butt perched on a stump or a milk crate like a pelican roosting in the rain, and wait for him to take his shot.

"One of us—is a fool," he says. Or words to that effect.

I look down at the grass. I don't care to duel with him much any more.

"Just don't be here." I tell him. "They'll put you in jail."

"And you won't come and get me out?"

"You never know," I might say.

He is shadowing my movements. I know it and he knows it, but we don't talk about it. Sometimes at first light, I go out on my balcony and look across the six lanes of traffic that divide my world from his and I can see the smoke from his cooking fire still hanging in the air. (He puts his fire out at sunrise to avoid attracting attention.)

Every now and again, I go over there to see how he's doing. We sit by his stream and drink warm beer. His spot isn't really too bad when the willows aren't in bloom—when they are my allergies go crazy. The embankment blocks out most of the highway noise and you can hear the birds. An old cow path leads in there through the grass. That's mostly what grows in the remnant zones, just grass.

What I mean is I've been thinking lately that it all comes down to that. The differences between me and him, the distance from one side of the highway to the other—are in the grass.

Things were different once, back before the split. Then the two of us might have enjoyed a splendid afternoon lolling around in the grass, watching the clouds. Now, on my worst days, I think about putting a match to the margins of his leftover patch of prairie and burning him out. And it's all because of a breach of perspective regarding grass.

I guess I don't expect that herbaceous contention to be self-evident and I don't really know if I can explain—in the sense of building up the chronological sequence of causally related events that passes for history and makes for sound sleep. But there are a few pieces of context that might shed some light on this particular Siamese-sibling feud.

To start with, the remnant zone Randall lives in now is maybe 120 acres or so. Two natural streams come together near the middle. They appear from and disappear into concrete culverts at the borders. This parcel features a nice stand of mature cottonwoods, a wetland with muskrat and waterfowl, and the willow thicket in which Randall cleared an 8 x 10-foot canvas-roofed square to call home. His spot is beside the smaller stream, which runs even when the larger one dries up. I told him that is probably due to a leaking sewer, but Randall doesn't listen to me.

He seems quite proud of a wicker chair with no legs that he liberated from one of the dumpsters in my parking lot here. He sets it on the stream bank and calls his little cave in the willows his "waterfront estate."

"You can't live like this forever," I tell him.

Randall jabs at his glasses and grunts in the evident satisfaction that tells you he's got you where he wants you, rhetorically speaking.

"I'm not going to."

"What are you going to do?"

"Go to hell," he says triumphantly. "Right along with you."

He pays no rent, no taxes, and not much heed.

The apartment I live in now is 740 square feet, three flights up. My balcony is about the same size as my bathtub and has a warped and rotting plywood floor. When my neighbors drive around the parking lot with the bass-boosters on their car stereos set on pulverize, my sliding glass door rattles. (I can only surmise that their bodies must be impervious to low-frequency vibrations.) Twice a week at 5 a.m., a man in a giant, prehistoric-looking truck comes to empty the trash dumpsters. But they are nearly always full—mostly of broken furniture, plastic pop bottles, and cardboard cartons from electronic toys.

In good weather, I sit out on the balcony and have a beer at sunset. But it never really gets dark here. The floodlights see to that, even though half of them have been shot out.

Randall makes it a point to avoid the sprawl zones except when he is forced to forage. But late one night a month or so back, he came over to see me. The visit went badly from the start. He knocked and I looked out through the peephole. He was staring at me with his eyes wide and his index fingers hooked in the corners of his stretched-out mouth.

I took a minute to consider pretending I wasn't home. When I opened the door, he was looking down at the floor across the landing, where my neighbor had dropped a disposable diaper that she apparently didn't want stinking up her apartment until she got time to take out the trash.

"Nice touch," Randall said. He turned it over with the toe of his boot. "This what you call the fruits of civilization?"

"What are you doing here?"

He looked at me like he really didn't think he needed a reason.

"I thought you might want to take me moonlight bowling," he said. "I hear it's the latest thing with the singles set."

I pay $675/month rent, plus utilities, and tend to obsess.

Randall and I are about the same size and shape. In a police description we would both fit into the "average height, medium build" category. The clearest difference—to the eye—is our hair. Mine is graying and very short. His trails off his balding head and down his back in an unevenly woven braid normally held together at the end by a garbage bag twist-tie. He sports a wild and often matted beard and he smokes when he can get tobacco. I shave regularly and never took to cigarettes. We both wear glasses. Mine are the ultrathin, plastic variety. He prefers the old-fashioned thick glass kind. They ride his hawklike beak at an odd angle and he habitually jabs them back into place with the tip of his middle finger—the last joint of which is missing due to an unfortunate attempt to befriend a barracuda by hand-feeding him soggy cheese doodles.

Time was, we both did silly shit like that. For my part, I blame that on the grass too.

Perhaps then—now—a few moments of history in narrative.

My first clear recollection of the allure of grass comes from a time when I was lapsing into unconsciousness from the sudden loss of blood. I had been struck directly in the forehead by the edge of a metal swing on which my sister had been riding. The resulting gash was quite large and bled profusely, so I'm told. That accident happened something more than forty years ago now, and I still have a faint scar to document the occasion.

About halfway between the swing set and the side door of our house—to which I instinctively headed to summon the omnipotent healing powers of the Mother figure—was a small depression approximating the size and shape of a large doggie bed. Due, I suppose, to its tendency to retain water, the grass in that spot always grew greener, thicker, and softer than the rest—which barely earned the label of "lawn" as applied in the postwar subdivision world.

As my mother reached the door and saw my blood-soaked face and shirt, I reached the cool, green margins of that shallow oasis in the crabgrass and chickweed. She tells me she screamed. I only remember floating down into that lusciously fragrant, welcoming green bowl and curling up in a realm of comfort so sublime as to remain unsurpassed in subsequent experience.

It occurs to me now that I must have left bloodstains in that grass. That my father may have seen them the next time he mowed the lawn and maybe he thought about how easily a child could die there. But I don't remember that either. I do know that a few years later my father bought a second car. He had the driveway expanded and paved with asphalt to accommodate it. From then on, he parked with his front wheels straddling the spot where I fell.

By the time I entered the skirmish and hormone zone of the teenage years, the task of mowing the lawn fell to me. Grass became a loathsome form of vegetation that demanded attention when much better things cried out to be done. The mowing was a hot and miserable task, and the dust and flying shreds of grass made me sneeze until I couldn't breathe. My eyes itched and swelled so badly I had to grope my way into the bathroom and run cold water on my face until I could see again.

When he came home from work, my father would get out of the car, look around at the freshly cut lawn and say, "You forgot to trim along the fence."

Skipping ahead a bit, but remaining within the limits of a long time ago—I am at my tenth high school reunion, drinking too much with people I haven't seen in years and didn't particularly like when I saw them every day, although I wouldn't have admitted it then.

"I knew I was an adult," someone says too loudly, "when I had to buy a goddamn lawnmower." (Badly-acted reluctant homeowner takes deep swig of watery gin and tonic.)

"I always hated cutting the fucking grass." (General Hilarity enters from stage right.)

Ah, men. Right on. Roll another one.

I admit it. In around that interval somewhere the term grass took on a whole new meaning, and a whole bunch of synonyms. Pot. Weed. Dope. Mary Jane. Reefer. To name a few. And the episodes from that era that survive in some semblance of clarity do so despite diligent and resourceful efforts to blur them into a blue and fragrant haze.

In that time, what began as a beckoning place of rest for the wounded transcended its adolescent role as a harvest of drudgery and respiratory irritation and transmuted into an avenue of escape and the basis for a fragile form of social cohesion. The idea seems comical now, and profoundly childish, but back in the Nixonian era, potheads enjoyed a sense of community.

"Want to get stoned?" would be the question.

"Does a bear shit in the woods?" would be the answer.

Pull up a piece of floor, and don't be afraid to doze off. You're among friends.

In this time—way up forward here in the now—the subdivisions are full of folks staying up late watching murder and mayhem on TV and feeling a sharp lack of that very same sense of community. Because toking your way down the road to peace and love was an idea that couldn't survive, but that doesn't necessarily mean it was a bad idea.

That's what I think. Randall thinks otherwise. Our roads diverged back there in the hazy time somewhere. Randall never believed a few whacked-out college kids sticking flowers in rifle barrels meant anything compared to the bullets those rifles fired. He always thought human beings were fundamentally small-minded and vicious. I burned a bale of grass trying to convince myself otherwise. He walked off into the grass to try and find a way to face the world dead-on.

Randall went feral.

I got a haircut, wrote a résumé, and went out looking for suitable employment.

It took awhile but I got one job. And then another. And another. Town to town, apartment to apartment. The only thing that never changed was the grass, and the work. Land Development Engineering they call it. Simple really. You start with the little wooden stakes with the orange tips, progress through the bulldozers, backhoes, cement trucks, lumber trucks, framers, roofers, electricians, plumbers, and painters. Last but not least, you bring in the landscapers to roll out a carpet of new sod over the scalped skull of Mother Earth and, poof. Another patch of worthless prairie starts generating property taxes for the county commissioners to squander on gambling junkets to Las Vegas and lobbying trips to Capitol Hill.

As Randall might put it.

I say it ain't bad work if you can get it.

Eventually, I gave up smoking grass, no longer needed to cut it, and lost my faith in its ability to catch me when I fainted. But it is always there. The grass doesn't give up. Pave it over and it pushes up through the cracks. Burn it and it only grows greener.

Which brings me back to how I've been thinking lately that it all comes down to grass. Maybe what I meant was that in simple terms of survival, if you go back to the dawn of time, right after the evolution of the angiosperm, and take away the grasses—thus eliminating their domesticated derivatives like wheat, corn, rice, and oats—the mammals on this planet don't stand any more chance of survival than an honest politician in Chicago.

What scares me is that I'm starting to suspect this notion of us all being beholden to the grass is pretty close to what Randall has been trying to tell me all along.

He gave me a book once titled *Let the Mountains Talk, Let the Rivers Run.* Underneath that he had scrawled out in black magic marker, "But Most of All, Let the Fucking Grass Grow." At the time, I chalked his editorial comment up to another one of his psychotic tangents. Now I'm not so sure. Because when you think about it, to the rancher, the dairyman, and the shepherd (to name a few), grass is—in a very direct sense—life; their bread and meat. And to an awful lot of people in the world, grass is shelter too—either as thatch for a roof or a binder in mud bricks for walls. And if you think of the earth as a coyote like the one that dens over there in Randall's remnant zone, then grass is her coat, her fur, the thing that shields her from the absolute cold of space. Without it, her nakedness would be obscene, and deadly.

To my bosses, grass is just that fuzzy sort of parasite that grows on vacant lots; the stuff they scrape off before they get down to feeding, the way a beggar trims the moldy crust off of a discarded slice of bread.

The split in perspective there is about as wide as the Grand Canyon. It's certainly enough to make you think twice about walking across it.

I'm not sure why I'm suffering from this attack of the doubts, unless maybe it's because the economics of land use has got Randall running short on alternatives. The maps and the stakes are sitting here on my dining room table. I was supposed to mark the road cuts today. Instead I walked over there at dawn carrying a pound of beef jerky, a six pack, and a sack of 100% additive-free tobacco.

Randall was drinking his morning coffee when I stepped through the willows. The big tin can he boils it in was still sitting on the embers from the fire, steaming.

He offered me a cup. I refused. His cowboy coffee goes down like drain cleaner.

"Hate to see you so early," Randall said.

"Why's that?" I took a seat.

"Because you're so damn wide awake."

"You're awake," I told him. "What's the difference?"

Randall thought about that for a while. Or at least he stared into his coffee and *appeared* to be thinking about it. Then he looked at me, and I met his scrutiny halfway.

"I'm awake to watch the morning," he said. "You're awake to rearrange a little piece of the world before lunch. *That's* the difference."

I watched the suspicious trickle of water in his streambed push its way through a tuft of slim, wiry grass that blocked its path.

"Randall," I said. "Have I ever told you what a colossal pain in the ass you are?"

Randall dumped the rest of his coffee into his mouth, sloshed it around, and spit a slurry of grounds into the water.

"Not more than two or three hundred times," he answered.

He picked up the organic tobacco, opened it, and rolled a smoke. He stuck it on his lower lip and let it hang there unlit while he watched me watch the water carry away the coffee grounds.

"Why don't you give it up?" I asked.

"Thanks," he said.

I thought he was thanking me for the tobacco. "You shouldn't thank me for supporting your bad habits," I told him.

"I wasn't," he answered. "I meant that's why I won't give it up."

"What is?"

"Thanks is."

"What the hell are you talking about, Randall?"

"I'm talking about the fact that you haven't thanked me yet. For not supporting your bad habits. When you do, I'll think about letting you off."

"Jesus. Give it a rest, will you?"

And he did. He lit his cigarette and sat there smoking it, and I sat there watching two very large red ants shove each other back and forth in the space of about an inch or so on the tree stump between my legs. It was some kind of death struggle the two giants were intent on playing out while four or five small black ants harassed the combatants by nipping at their flanks. At least it appeared that's what was going on.

I never did see how it ended.

"You came to tell me I have to get out of here, didn't you?"

"Yes," I said.

"Well, the answer is no."

"What do you mean 'no'?"

"I mean no. It's not a complicated concept. No. I am not going anywhere."

"You don't have a choice," I told him. "In three months this spot will be buried ten feet under the Kmart parking lot. Face it. It's over."

Randall got up, rinsed his cup in the stream, and put it back in the crate with his cooking things. Then he picked up his wicker chair. He grabbed it from behind and stood with his hands under the front edge of the seat, the upright back braced against his chest. Then he squeezed. He raised the pressure slowly and deliberately. His arms started to bulge and strain as the creaking protests of the dying chair changed to a scattering of sharp snaps. He squeezed harder. The muscles along his jaw quivered under the tension. He groaned like a man in the last spasm of passion that heralds the release, and the brittle, worn-out chair snapped and shattered and fell to the ground around his feet.

He dropped the fragments that remained in his hands.

"It hasn't started yet," he said. "But it will."

I don't recall how long he stood there, but the freeze-frame lasted long enough for me to realize it is entirely possible that he is stone crazy. And it is equally possible that I am.

He often says one of us is a madman. He never says which one.

When he did move, he went out through the tunnellike entrance to his thicket and came back with two stalks of grass, each about three feet long and carrying a large seed head on the drooping end. He peeled the bottom of his and stuck the exposed fresh shoot in his mouth. It glistened with moisture drawn up from under the earth.

He handed me the other shoot and told me to chew on it on my walk home.

"It purifies the blood and stimulates the mind," were his exact words.

So I took it and peeled it and stuck it in my mouth, and it tasted sharp and sweet and smelled like youth and blood.

Then I headed up the path, along the embankment, and across the highway to my own half of the world. That route is strewn with odd bits of transportation trash. The very ground beneath your feet on that path consists mostly of shards of glass, shreds of plastic, and the gritty black dust that comes from pavement and spinning tires grinding each other up. The air you breathe on that walk is not air. You inhale only the diluted exhaust gasses of internal combustion. It is a journey on which it is difficult to think, or reflect.

But I chewed Randall's grass and a few things occurred to me. First, a lawn is to grass what a poodle is to a coyote—fussy and ornamental vs. wild and elemental—only an idiot could confuse them. Second, the interstate highway system is only a temporary blight on the eternity of grass. Because, third, humans hold no dominion over the grasses; we live by their good graces.

In time, they will reduce all our grand works to ruins.

None of which helps even a little bit with the decision I have to make. Do I refuse to drive in the stakes? Do I tell the owners that my evil twin has gone completely around the bend and is likely to do about anything to protect the grass growing on the dirt they need to hold up their shopping center? Do I try to explain?

On my walk home today, my chewed-grass-enhanced observations seemed revelatory, but grass has led me down that path before. I always woke up to find that the glittering bits of insight scribbled down in the arms of Mother Mary were but drivel in the light of day.

So I don't know what I'm going to do yet. I have all night to think about it.

"Zip," Randall says. "That's what you got. Diddly squat."

My fondest longing is to let myself sink into the cool, luxuriant, green grass—like a poodle with a hole in its head.

But the traffic is light tonight and the parking lot is quiet. So I can hear him without having to squint my ears. I will pull up a chair and we will talk and maybe drink a little. I'd like to think we could be a team again, like the old days. It's no good with him squatting out there in his thicket in the dark and waiting for doom to come rumbling over the horizon, and me standing here in this dilapidated plywood box, looking out at the parking lot and hoping for salvation to drive up and blow its trumpet.

It's time, I think. Time to go wait on the bridge.

I will walk to the middle and meet him there. I will shake his hand in greeting.

And when one of us speaks, the other might listen.

STUDY QUESTIONS for "In the Grass"

COMPREHENSION

1. What causes the split in the brothers' relationship?
2. The narrator identifies four moments of his "history" with grass beginning with paragraph thirty-six. What are these four moments? Why are these moments important to the narrator's awareness of himself, his family, and his society?
3. Ultimately, what importance does the narrator ascribe to grass? Does his opinion of it coincide with Randall's? In what way does the essay's point of view make it difficult for the reader to answer this question?

DEVELOPMENT AND ORGANIZATION

1. Why does the narrator refer to his brother Randall as "evil" in the essay's opening paragraph? Does the description of him and of the relationship between the brothers that appears throughout the essay show him as evil? What is the effect of this word choice?
2. In what ways are the brothers different? Pay particular attention to the narrator's discussion of his hair and Randall's hair.
3. Look closely at the essay's last nine paragraphs. How does the narrator decide to resolve his conflict with his brother? Is it ironic that the narrator is the one "hoping for salvation" while Randall is "waiting for doom"?

STYLE AND TECHNIQUE

1. Late in the essay, the narrator describes two large ants struggling with each other. How is this struggle a metaphor of the brothers' relationship?
2. What tone does the author create? What specific words and phrases does he use to create this tone?

TEN-MINUTE TOPICS

1. Examine your relationship with a family member who is seemingly different from you. Make sure that you describe any people, places, and objects involved with strong sensory details.
2. Examine a natural object that gives you some insight into how life works. Describe the object and explain the insight it gives you.
3. The narrator's reference to the ants may also be an allusion to the Henry David Thoreau essay "The Battle of the Ants," included later in this textbook. Read Thoreau's essay and list any similarities you see.

FROM "MAPS OF WATER HOLES," CHAPTER ONE OF
THE SECRET KNOWLEDGE OF WATER
BY CRAIG CHILDS

Cabeza Prieta, Arizona
February-March

The desert breathed and then went silent at the first mention of nightfall, a kind of quiet that comes only at the edge of the earth. The last small winds broke apart, rolling down unrelated washes like pearls off a snapped necklace. Then came stars. And a crescent moon. And a desert strung in every direction, iridescent indigo in the west where the sun had just set, black in the east.

I walked west, toward an escarpment on the horizon barely into Arizona from the Mexican border. In evening silhouettes, these sere, isolated mountains had the look of tall ships strewn about the desert. Between were gulfs of open land furrowed with slight washes. Within the washes were the dimpled tracks of black-tailed jackrabbits and kangaroo rats, and within them the curled parchment of bursage leaves left by a wind gone somewhere else.

Across the flats I heard only the hushing sound of my boots through sand, then the sharper sound of my boots through the broken granite above the washes. The hum of one of the stray breezes through thousands of saguaro cactus needles. The sound of creosote leaves scratching the brim of my hat. At night it is best to walk through the desert with a hat held in the hand, pushed forward to block the thorns and sharp spines of occasional unseen plants. Almost everything alive out here is armored with some barb, spike, or poison quill. From the years that I did not carry my hat, the back of my right hand is scarred as if it had been offered to a furious cat.

Tonight the moon, a waxing crescent thin as an eyelash, would not give enough light for shadows. I used it as a reference, walking directly toward it, carrying on my back all of the gear needed to resupply a base camp fifteen miles out, and the gear to supply the lesser camps beyond that. I had come to map water holes, working on a project for the US Fish and Wildlife Service. The agency wanted to know what kind of water hid among these mountains, in some of the driest land in the Western Hemisphere. There are years when rain never falls, and sometimes the water holes contain nothing but rainwater that is twelve or sixteen months old, if they hold anything at all.

To find the water, I took thirty-seven days to traverse a single mountain range, hunting in its cracks and canyons. I carried simple measuring tools along with a device that communicates with satellites to record latitude and longitude of whatever water I found, perhaps a quart of evaporating rainwater in a rock depression. With my coordinates recorded, I placed small red marks on the map, showing one water hole, then the next.

This survey area was chosen not for any special characteristics, or a promise of water, but because it looked as arid and embattled as any of the mountains out here. Now and then I would return to my truck, which was parked beside a wash, off a long-winded road made of sand. There I would refill my supplies and cache them in the desert beyond. As I found water from the outlying natural cisterns, I was able to drink and extend deeper into the range, until I had recorded lifelines of water holes leading from my base camp into nowhere.

The final product of this work would go to the files of Cabeza Prieta National Wildlife Refuge. The refuge is managed primarily for desert bighorn sheep that supposedly thrive on these quarts. There are those people who worry for the sheep, who believe water should be shipped into the desert during early-summer droughts so that the sheep can maintain an "optimum" population, so that they can fill their range. There are also those who believe that after ten thousand years of seeking water, sheep do not require our aid.

While out walking through these canyons, below summits sharp as ice picks, I have heard sheep clattering among rocks but have rarely been able to get close enough to see their eyes. I have lifted their discarded bones and horns, turned them in my hand, and studied their tracks near water holes. One morning I watched a group of four rams carefully pick through steep talus. I waited above, crouched shirtless in shade, observing their choices, how their hooves negotiated each small rock. I tried to decipher their boldness and indecision, learning how an animal must behave in this landscape. The fourth ram, the youngest, waited until the others were out of sight before making its own mistakes, then backtracking. This made me smile, made me rest easier.

My personal reasons for mapping water holes here had little to do with bighorn sheep. I came to put a story back together and recover parts that had been lost. The story, when it was complete, would have told of secret water in a desperately ragged place, would have shown the route to safely cross from one end of Cabeza Prieta to the other. I wanted to understand water in a land this dry. Within the 860,000 acres of this refuge, only one spring exists. It is a bare, dripping spring, yet is enough to have bestowed the entire mountain range in which it sits with the name *Agua Dulce*. Sweet Water.

The desert cities have their cement aqueducts to siphon distant rivers, and holes are drilled into ten-thousand-year-old banks of groundwater. Familiarity with scattered water holes has become obsolete, left only for the bighorn sheep. Words are now missing from the story of ephemeral waters, severing critical pieces of information. Many people have died while crossing this desert, regardless of their reasons for being here. They died because the story was forgotten.

This country is not idle. The mountains are bitterly seared. Rising a couple thousand feet off the floor, they are offset by swaths of bulged, rolling desert, called *bajadas*, that take days to cross. As I walked on this night of the crescent moon, the bajada unfurled to the horizons to the north and south. Here and there it was intercepted by farther mountains, each an island, or a chain, or a misshapen monstrosity bursting straight from the ground.

On long night walks like this, brushing through plants and walking up and down against the grain of dry, north-flowing washes, I told myself stories, recounting whatever I remembered about the place. Stories gave the land definition at night, as the mountains vanished around me. Sometimes I would speak the stories out loud to break the loneliness. A particular one came from a site about eight miles straight ahead of me. An archaeologist making a sweep of the area found among assemblages of prehistoric potsherds two .45-caliber Colt cartridges, manufactured by the Winchester Repeating Arms Company. They had probably been discharged onto the ground in the early 1900s. The two cartridges had been rammed together, making a small, enclosed capsule. Inside this capsule was a note that read, "Was it worth it?"

So I invented scenarios, tried to imagine what the message meant. Death or desperation or gold that was never found or somebody like myself pushing the edges of the desert only to be confronted with this question in the end.

Just south of these two cartridges, in six hundred square miles of lava flows, cinder cones, and dune seas, ten forty-pound boulders were found butted against one another to form a perfect southeast-to-northwest line. It is not possible to tell if it was constructed hundreds or thousands of years ago, but it was done, for whatever reason, by strenuous human labor. I told myself stories about this. Perhaps they levered the boulders with wooden saguaro ribs tied together, rolling them from miles away. For what? To appease certain gods? To reinvent the mountains? To invite the rain with a signal that could be seen from the clouds?

In another place each small rock on the ground had been cleared, revealing the pale belly of earth in a line six feet wide and seven hundred feet long without deviation. There are other, more ornate sites: geometric designs hundreds of feet in length, with mazes and inner circles that can be seen as a whole only from an airplane. I have seen in one of these stone clearings the life-size and accurate image of a horse, probably a sixteenth-century Spanish horse as seen by an indigenous artist, while around it ran a web of exposed lines radiating into the landscape.

In the mountain range ahead of me, a Spanish missionary of the Franciscan order came through in the 1700s, querying local inhabitants about the mounds of horns and bones from bighorn sheep he found erected near the water holes. He was talking to the people called the Hia C'ed O'odham, known as the Sand People by the Spanish. Without offering further explanation, the people gave him a simple answer. The horns and bones had been placed to keep the wind from leaving the country.

Stories everywhere. This is the place where people came to hold on to the wind. It is where they brought expectations that were rammed into rifle shells. In the coming dark, the desert grew richer with stories. And I became more alone. I knew of a small group of archaeologists with a work site about a four- or five-day walk southwest of here. Probably a few illegal immigrants were coming up from the border, but not through here, where people die from exposure and thirst. So I figured I was the only person for thirty to eighty miles in any direction. This left a kind of openness and remoteness that made merely breathing feel obscene. A friend once traveled with me here and as we walked the perimeter of one of these ranges, he said the vastness reminded him of the Arctic, up by the Brooks Range where great basins of tundra lie between distant and imposing mountains, where there is no human artifact. I nodded at the time, realizing a sensation I had not yet been able to place.

Humans are absent here because they die. One document records the death of four hundred people here by 1900, many of whom were traveling from Mexico to the California goldfields. More have died since. Within view of several distant mountains, a family had been memorialized by black pieces of basalt arranged to form the numeral 8, telling how many family members perished. Sixty-five graves surround one of the better-known watering sites, presumably from the times that the holes went dry. Most victims died of dehydration and exposure, but occasional reports concerned those who drowned, too weak from thirst to climb out of the deep stone water holes into which they had plunged.

There are more recent deaths, those of illegal immigrants from Mexico, who come seeking jobs picking watermelons or cleaning houses. These people walk out in small groups, some of them from the tropics, never having seen the desert. They hire a person, a *coyote*, who deposits them across the border and points the way to Interstate 8. Each carries a gallon plastic milk jug filled with water, which in the summer lasts a few hours. The walk takes many days and they live maybe until the afternoon of the second or third day, their tracks of discarded belongings and empty milk jugs signaling insanity. Some of their milk jugs are, in fact, found half-full beside their bodies, skin taut to bursting. This story repeats itself every year.

As in stories I have heard from Mount Everest, where bodies of climbers are dispersed among glaciers, bodies here are turned to bones and spread across the sand and gravel and in the rocks. The bones are uncounted and unburied, scattered like offerings. It is perhaps these bones, rather than those of bighorns, that now prevent the wind from leaving the country.

Coming close to the horizon, the moon appeared to move quickly. As it fell into the mountains of Cabeza Prieta, it described ridges as splintered as dry wood broken over a knee. For a moment, all that remained in the sky was the watermark stain of the moon's dark side. Then it set, leaving this hysterical swarm of stars. I chose certain constellations and followed them, my hat still extended in my hand.

There were good places to sleep. There were open flats where the ground curved slightly, barren of most plants. I could lie on one of these flats with my eyes open, the earth presenting me to the sky as if I were a newborn or a sacrifice. I chose instead a narrow wash, one barely depressed so that the wind had to bend down to find me. I protected myself beneath a creosote bush on ripples of wash sand. This is where I slept, in a country littered with arcane rock symbols, and death, and rumors of water.

STUDY QUESTIONS for "Maps of Water Holes"

COMPREHENSION

1. Why was Childs exploring this desert? For whom was he working?
2. What are the some of the interesting things Childs finds in the desert? What stories does he create to explain their existence?
3. What are some of the influences of Spanish culture that Childs encounters?
4. Why is it so important for Childs to emphasize his isolation in the desert?

DEVELOPMENT AND ORGANIZATION

1. To which senses does Childs appeal most strongly in his descriptions? Why did he choose to appeal to those senses and not to some others?
2. Childs intersperses present-time action (things that he's doing) with recollections of historical events, past experiences, and stories from scientists and other explorers. Why does he do this? What would this chapter be like if he had simply described what he himself was doing?
3. Childs spends a portion of the chapter describing bighorn sheep. What is the significance of the sheep to the desert? What details does Childs notice about them?
4. Childs draws attention to the plight of illegal immigrants who face the desert he is exploring. Why does he include this information? How does it shape your view of the landscape?

STYLE AND TECHNIQUE

1. At one point, Childs states, "Humans are absent here because they die." How effective is this direct statement? Why do you think he makes it? What follows from it?
2. Childs titles this chapter "Maps of Water Holes"; how much time does he spend talking about maps and water? How much water does he actually find?
3. Childs ends this portion of the chapter by searching for a place to sleep, and he spends some time making a decision. Why does Childs end the portion in this manner? How effective is this choice?

TEN-MINUTE TOPICS

1. Think of a time when you were by yourself in a natural setting. Describe the place, the time of year, and the weather. What were you doing, and what dangers did you have to plan for? What equipment, if any, did you bring with you?
2. Think of a time when you ran out of a necessary supply (food, water, medicine, etc.). What was the supply, and where were you at the time? What physical or emotional change did you feel because of the missing supply? What danger did you face? How were you finally able to obtain another supply?
3. Write your own description of a desert setting. What plants and animals inhabit it? How far off are the closest people? Which time of day and weather conditions would be the most favorable? Which would be the least?

ODE TO MY CAR

BY STEVEN WAGONER (student)

Everyone looks forward to getting his first car. The freedom of mobility and independence bring delight to every young adult. It represents a milestone on the road of life, a road he can now drive down instead of walk. However, that delightful feeling can come to a screeching halt when that first car was spawned in hell, much like my first set of wheels.

Said car was a 1982 Chevy Cavalier. It came into my possession through my Uncle Larry who drove into town unannounced one day shortly after my sixteenth birthday. He was out of money, out of gas, and full of sob stories. Somehow he scammed my dad into trading our 1989 Volkswagen Jetta for his 1982 Cavalier. Then the sneaky weasel drove off into the sunset.

It was a sorry piece of machinery. The faded blue paint was peeling away in sheets exposing the rusted metal underneath. Still, I was content; an ugly car was far superior to having no car at all. The first logical thing to do was to assess the situation and see exactly what repairs were needed. With a set of wrenches in hand and armed with my limited knowledge of automotive technology, I began to examine the car. I sat down in the driver's seat and went through a mental checklist of all the characteristics a normal functioning car should have.

I could tell this was going to be an incredible amount of work. The interior was dirty and smelled like a mix of hot garbage and noxious fumes. The dashboard was cracked and sunbeaten, and the upholstery was stained and unraveling at the seams. The first mechanical discrepancy I observed was that the driver's side window would not roll up. That was a simple fix. I removed the inner door panel with a screwdriver and set the window back on the track allowing it to roll up and down smoothly. I was willing to overlook some of these problems so long as the thing would get me from point A to point B.

I inserted the key into the ignition and cranked it over. Alas, the engine drank huge thirsty gulps of gasoline in an attempt to rumble to life but instead sputtered, choked, and then drowned to death. This was not good at all. I opened the hood and peered down into the grease-coated engine compartment. The rat's nest of tangled wires under the hood looked as though they could unravel with spring-loaded force or simply burst into an electrical fire at any moment. I could see that the carburetor was dirty, and this was likely the cause of the flooding. After a few minutes the engine turned over and was now purring like a kitten. Enthusiasm ran through my veins like a sugar high.

There I sat, like a lab monkey ready to be shot into outer space; I reached down and pulled the gear lever into drive. As the car began to roll forward, I could hear the eerie screeching and grinding sounds of worn metal parts rotating against each other; the volume of the quandary only intensified with acceleration. The worn-out shock absorbers made the ride horribly rough; each speed bump and pothole felt like a rollercoaster ride.

Suddenly, the car dipped into an exceptionally deep pothole, knocking the driver's side window off of the track and into the metal doorframe with a crash. The window, made of tempered glass, was now a thousand tiny cubes in my lap. The blast of cool air entering the passenger compartment was a like a breath of fresh air, though.

As I made my way to the nearest service station, the engine went into arrhythmia, and a smoky bluish haze engulfed the car. I was beginning to think the broken window was the least of my worries. Just yards away from the Texaco, the tired engine block fractured like tectonic plates in a devastating earthquake. In a matter of moments the car was reduced to a salvage yard on wheels.

The brief lifespan of the Cavalier was not in vain, however. Its carcass was eventually donated to the Green River Fire Department for extrication training. The car was crushed to half its original size and was then dismembered by the Jaws of Life. It died so that others may live.

I do not regret that I owned the car. Even though my father referred to it as the Chariot of the Anti-Christ, it was still my first and favorite set of wheels. Besides, there is nothing wrong with bumming a ride down the road of life until you find yourself a newer and more dependable car.

STUDY QUESTIONS for "Ode to My Car"

COMPREHENSION

1. What is the thesis of this essay? If it is explicit, write it out word for word and give the number of the paragraph in which it appears. If it is implicit, summarize it in about twenty-five words.
2. What was the writer's first sign that the "new" car was going to be trouble for him?
3. What is the writer's opinion of the car now, in recollection?

DEVELOPMENT AND ORGANIZATION

1. Wagoner has arranged his essay into ten paragraphs. Why do you think he has used that many? Do you think he has too many? Too few? Why?
2. Though this essay is listed among the descriptive essays, Wagoner makes use of the narrative and the process modes, too. What evidence do you see of the narrative mode? Of the process? You might want to look at the headnotes for chapters three and five.
3. Look closely at the first sentence of each paragraph. What methods does Wagoner use to make transitions from paragraph to paragraph, based upon these sentences? You might want to look again at the section on organization in chapter one.

STYLE AND TECHNIQUE

1. The writer uses several skillful metaphors and concrete details. What are three of the most striking, in your view? What makes them so interesting? In what way do they give you a word picture of what the writer is describing?
2. Why do you think Wagoner titled this essay an "ode"? What is an ode? Is this title appropriate for the subject matter of the essay?

3. Wagoner makes use of semicolons throughout the essay. What is a semicolon? How are they normally used? Where do they occur in this essay? Does Wagoner use them appropriately?

TEN-MINUTE TOPICS

1. Describe your own first car. What was it? What were the circumstances surrounding your acquisition of it? What shape was it in when you got it? How long did it last?
2. Write about a time a friend or acquaintance talked you into a trade. What did you give up? What did you get in return? Was it something you really wanted? Did you regret giving up what you had to begin with?

CHAPTER THREE

NARRATION

DEFINITION

Whereas descriptive writing can make time stand still as it gathers its sensory impressions, sometimes for several paragraphs, narrative writing relies on the flow of time from moment to moment. Frequently, a narrative may be introduced or interrupted by a descriptive passage. But the narrative itself is a chronological sequence of events. Sometimes the flow of events is leisurely, sometimes rapid; sometimes the normal sequence is changed, as when the writer uses a flashback—an earlier series of events that illuminates the main action. Although late nineteenth and early twentieth century writers such as Proust, Joyce, Woolf, and Faulkner may have experimented with stories that are held together more by association than by strict chronology, a traditional narrative is almost always dominated in its organization by the ceaseless flow of time.

APPLICATION

The personal narrative is a kind of writing that, recently, has developed into a nonfiction art form. Beyond the mere recording of action, good narration generally must make use of description. Further, the general function of this kind of writing is to fulfill the purpose that late nineteenth century English writer Joseph Conrad addresses in one of his prefaces:

> My task which I am trying to achieve is, by the power of the written word to make you hear, to make you feel—it is, before all, to make you see. That—and no more, and it is everything. If I succeed, you shall find there according to your deserts: encouragement, consolation, fear, charm—all you demand—and, perhaps, also that glimpse of truth for which you have forgotten to ask.
>
> To snatch in a moment of courage, from the remorseless rush of time, a passing phase of life, is only the beginning of the task. The task approached in tenderness and faith is to hold up unquestioningly, without choice and without fear, the rescued fragment before all eyes in the light of a sincere mood. It is to show its vibration, its color, its form; and through its movement, its form, and its color, reveal the substance of its truth—disclose its inspiring secret: the stress and passion within the core of each convincing moment.

Like Annie Dillard, Conrad emphasizes that writing is a passionate act that requires courage and commitment. And while he acknowledges that the writer's aim is also to articulate the truth of the human experience, Conrad underscores the importance of using details appealing to the senses—concrete or descriptive detail—to achieve the task that he sets before us all: the capturing of truth.

In the above passage, Conrad manages to touch upon another aspect of writing that applies not only to his own fiction but to all writing, fiction and nonfiction, and that is the importance of audience. Too often, in composing an essay, we ignore the needs, at times even the demands, of the audience, preferring instead to concentrate on overall organization, paragraph structure, and sentence correctness. Certainly, we should make sure that our essays are tightly organized, and that our paragraphs and sentences are structured correctly; but we must also keep in mind that in our writing we are addressing an audience, in this case made of at least two components: your instructor and, more importantly, the larger group of people (which shall be referred to as the primary audience) who would benefit from or find interest in your essay. Too often as we write, we make little effort to engage and maintain the primary audience's interest. As Italian post-modernist Umberto Eco has noted in his collection *Six Walks in the Fictional Woods*, an understanding of our audience—in this case, an awareness of what the reader expects from a good narrative—contributes greatly to the shape and word selection of the entire essay. In short, audience helps shape the essay.

So how is a narrative put together? What is your instructor—as well as the primary audience—likely to be looking for? The introduction to a standard narrative may consist of one or more paragraphs and generally establishes setting, situation, and tone or mood.

These elements are present in Wade Cruse's essay titled "The Vegetable Patch":

> I was sitting in the rear of the bus as usual, the last seat on the left. Every day I would catch the three o'clock bus home from Ed White Junior High School. Every day I sat in that same seat. My family and I were stationed at Tachikawa Air Force Base in Japan. Every day, Monday through Friday, I would take that bus home and every day I endured. The bus route took us by a vegetable patch, not just any vegetable patch but probably the foulest smelling one in Asia, possibly the world. It always smelled the same regardless of the weather (although in the summer it may have been worse). I suppose when I started riding the bus, I sat in the back in order to avoid that stench for as long as I could. Just before we'd come to it, I'd pinch my nostrils together and close my eyes to keep them from tearing.

In this passage, Cruse briefly establishes setting: he's on the three o'clock bus heading home from junior high near an Air Force base in Japan. Further, he conveys tone, or mood, through the repetition of "every day"; that is, he finds the ride home boring—nothing different ever happens.

In the body of the narrative, a problem is often introduced, followed by the development of action. This development of action may focus upon a relationship or upon conflict—say between the main character and nature. With this in mind, read the next two paragraphs of "The Vegetable Patch":

> At the Kazu Shichi stop a very old man boarded the bus. He was Korean and looked to be anywhere from seventy to one hundred years old. I was proud that I could identify him as Korean but I wondered what he was doing there, in Japan I mean. The Japanese hate the Koreans fervidly. He hobbled down the aisle looking for a seat. The bus was packed. Most of the passengers were Japanese and wouldn't give up their seats for a Korean no matter how old or frail he was. I held no animosities towards the Koreans so I offered him mine. As he sat down he said something to me in his language. I suppose he was thanking me. I was glad he took it because he didn't look strong enough to stand up for any length of time.
>
> We came to the patch two stops later and four more Japanese boarded. Because I was occupied, trying to keep my balance, I couldn't perform my nose-holding ritual. I did manage to close my eyes, but it didn't help much.

In these two paragraphs, Cruse introduces a situation to which he responds with compassion: the boarding of an old Korean man. And, as the conflict between the Japanese passengers and the old man is suggested, so too is a relationship established between Cruse and the Korean: "As he sat down he said something to me in his language. I suppose he was thanking me. I was glad he took it because he didn't look strong enough to stand up for any length of time."

The body of a narrative, whether it develops a conflict or a relationship or both, often leads to a climax, the turning point of the story. In the following paragraph from Cruse's narrative, the climax is almost understated:

> The bus soon reached the base's gate and most of the passengers had gotten off. I had regained a seat, and the Korean was still in mine. One of the guards boarded to check ID cards. I fumbled through my wallet, found mine, and showed it to him. He nodded and passed by me to the Korean. I looked back. The old man was sleeping peacefully. I remember thinking it was a shame that the guard would wake him up. At first he just stood there, waiting for him to wake up I guess. Nothing happened. He tapped him gently on the shoulder. Still nothing. Then he looked at me and back at the Korean. This time he shook him, gently at first, then more vigorously. Nothing. He felt for a pulse in the Korean's neck. "Dead," he said to no one in particular. He went up to the bus driver and whispered something before getting off the bus. I stared at the body of the dead Korean.

The striking thing about this passage is the way in which the narrator Cruse responds to the death. The boy's shock is registered in one concise sentence: "I stared at the body of the dead Korean." Although we are not told, we can probably assume from this narration that this was the first time that Cruse had come face to face with the death of someone with whom he had established a relationship, however brief.

The conclusion to a narrative generally wraps up any loose ends. In a personal experience essay, the student may choose to use the final paragraph(s) to summarize the impact or significance of the experience. The final line and conclusion to "The Vegetable Patch" suggests that Cruse is still numbed by the experience and is not sure what to make of the old man's death: "The last thing I remember was the driver telling us in English first and then Japanese to get off the bus." Further, this final line helps convey the essay's theme: death can be an unpredictable, numbing experience.

It may be argued that the language of Cruse's essay is too general, that he should have used more concrete detail. However, to overwhelm the reader with descriptive detail would work against the objective, Hemingwayesque style that Cruse uses in order to convey to the reader the impression that, at the time it occurred, the old man's death left him speechless and emotionally deadened. In all probability, Cruse is telling us that he felt nothing. While Cruse does use concrete details, he does so sparingly for a very good reason.

PARADIGM

When writing the narrative, whether you are relating a personal experience or making up a fictional story, keep in mind the following paradigm, which establishes only very general guidelines:

Introduction
1. **Grab the reader's attention.**
2. **Introduce the setting and the situation.**
3. **Introduce central character(s).**
4. **Establish point of view.**

Body paragraphs (generally more than one)
1. **Introduce a problem or crisis.**
2. **Develop the conflict: internal, external, or both.**
3. **Build to a climax or turning point, where conflicts are resolved for or against the main character.**

Conclusion
1. **Bring the narrative to a satisfying close.**
2. **Clarify the outcome of preceding events (how main character is affected).**
3. **Keep in mind that there may be no neat tying together of loose ends.**

SUMMARY

The kind of narrative that your instructor is likely to ask you to write is the personal experience, the structure of which resembles that of a short story. Don't worry about whether your instructor will find your essay interesting or not. Almost any personal experience essay can be effective if you remember to follow certain guidelines. For one thing, select a significant event that occurred in a specific place in a specific time. For instance, it wouldn't do to write a 500-word essay on your three-week summer vacation in the Pacific Northwest. It would be better to focus on a specific happening in a specific time—for instance, the Saturday night you went bar-hopping in Bend, Oregon, and wound up at a tent revival where your life was dramatically changed. Finally, be sure to make use of concrete, descriptive writing, the purpose of which is, according to Joseph Conrad is "to make you hear, to make you feel—it is, before all, to make you see. That—and no more, and it is everything."

SALVATION

BY LANGSTON HUGHES

I was saved from sin when I was going on thirteen. But not really saved. It happened like this. There was a big revival at my Auntie Reed's church. Every night for weeks there had been much preaching, singing, praying, and shouting, and some very hardened sinners had been brought to Christ, and the membership of the church had grown by leaps and bounds. Then just before the revival ended, they held a special meeting for children, "to bring the young lambs to the fold." My aunt spoke of it for days ahead. That night I was escorted to the front row and placed on the mourners' bench with all the other young sinners, who had not yet been brought to Jesus.

My aunt told me that when you were saved you saw a light, and something happened to you inside! And Jesus came into your life! And God was with you from then on! She said you could see and hear and feel Jesus in your soul. I believed her. I had heard a great many old people say the same thing and it seemed to me they ought to know. So I sat there calmly in the hot, crowded church, waiting for Jesus to come to me.

The preacher preached a wonderful rhythmical sermon, all moans and shouts and lonely cries and dire pictures of hell, and then he sang a song about the ninety and nine safe in the fold, but one little lamb was left out in the cold. Then he said: "Won't you come? Won't you come to Jesus? Young lambs, won't you come?" And he held out his arms to all us young sinners there on the mourners' bench. And the little girls cried. And some of them jumped up and went to Jesus right away. But most of us just sat there.

A great many old people came and knelt around us and prayed, old women with jet-black faces and braided hair, old men with work-gnarled hands. And the church sang a song about the lower lights are burning, some poor sinners to be saved. And the whole building rocked with prayer and song.

Still I kept waiting to *see* Jesus.

Finally, all the young people had gone to the altar and were saved, but one boy and me. He was a rounder's son named Westley. Westley and I were surrounded by sisters and deacons praying. It was very hot in the church and getting late now. Finally Westley said to me in a whisper: "God damn! I'm tired o' sitting here. Let's get up and be saved." So he got up and was saved.

Then I was left all alone on the mourners' bench. My aunt came and knelt at my knees and cried, while prayers and songs swirled all around me in the little church. The whole congregation prayed for me alone, in a mighty wail of moans and voices. And I kept waiting serenely for Jesus, waiting, waiting—but he didn't come. I wanted to see him, but nothing happened to me. Nothing! I wanted something to happen to me, but nothing happened.

I heard the songs and the minister saying: "Why don't you come? My dear child, why don't you come to Jesus? Jesus is waiting for you. He wants you. Why don't you come? Sister Reed, what is the child's name?

"Langston," my aunt sobbed.

"Langston, why don't you come? Why don't you come and be saved? Oh, Lamb of God! Why don't you come?"

Now it was really getting late. I began to be ashamed of myself, holding everything up so long. I began to wonder what God thought about Westley, who certainly hadn't seen Jesus either but who was now sitting proudly on the platform, swinging his knickerbockered legs and grinning down at me, surrounded by deacons, and old women on their knees praying. God had not struck Westley dead for taking his name in vain or for lying in the temple. So I decided that maybe to save further trouble, I'd better lie, too, and say that Jesus had come, and get up and be saved.

So I got up.

Suddenly the whole room broke into a sea of shouting, as they saw me rise. Waves of rejoicing swept the place. Women leaped in the air. My aunt threw her arms around me. The minister took me by the hand and led me to the platform.

When things quieted down, in a hushed silence, punctuated by a few ecstatic "Amens," all the new young lambs were blessed in the name of God. Then joyous singing filled the room.

That night, for the last time in my life but one—for I was a big boy twelve years old—I cried. I cried, in bed alone, and couldn't stop. I buried my head under the quilts, but my aunt heard me. She woke up and told my uncle I was crying because the Holy Ghost had come into my life and because I had seen Jesus. But I was really crying because I couldn't bear to tell her that I had lied, that I had deceived everybody in the church, and I hadn't seen Jesus, and that now I didn't believe there was a Jesus any more, since he didn't come to help me.

STUDY QUESTIONS for "Salvation"

COMPREHENSION

1. In what sense was the young Hughes "saved from sin . . . but not really saved"?
2. Why does the young Hughes go forward to be "saved"?
3. Discuss the significance of the final paragraph. How has the boy's perception of being saved changed? How is he ultimately affected by the revival?
4. What is the theme of this narrative?
5. What does the young boy think is going to happen to him during the revival? What in fact does occur?
6. What is the nature of the conflict that the boy experiences? Is it internal or external? What details in the story intensify the conflict?

DEVELOPMENT AND ORGANIZATION

1. Where does the writer make effective use of concrete details? What is gained in this essay by making use of concrete details?
2. What details prove especially helpful in establishing setting for this narrative?

3. How much does Hughes reveal of himself in the opening paragraphs? Should he have revealed more, such as the specific town or city in which the church meeting occurred and/or his parents' occupations? Why or why not?
4. Define climax as a literary term. At what point does the climax occur in this piece? Where are the conflicts resolved?

STYLE AND TECHNIQUE

1. Hughes's essay contains two one-sentence paragraphs: "Still I kept waiting to *see* Jesus" and "So I got up." Should Hughes have combined these short paragraphs with the longer ones either preceding or following them? Explain your answer.
2. What is the point of view used in this narrative: that of an adolescent or that of an adult recalling an adolescent event? Find proof to support your answer.
3. What is the effect upon the young Hughes, as well as upon the reader, of Westley's comment, "God damn! I'm tired o' sitting here. Let's get up and be saved"? Why does Hughes include Westley in the narration?

TEN-MINUTE TOPICS

1. Narrate a turning-point experience from your early life in which your beliefs and/or values were deeply affected.
2. Describe a time when peer pressure made you do something you did not want to do. What were the causes and the effects of your action?

A HANGING

BY GEORGE ORWELL

It was in Burma, a sodden morning of the rains. A sickly light, like yellow tinfoil, was slanting over the high walls into the jail yard. We were waiting outside the condemned cells, a row of sheds fronted with double bars, like small animal cages. Each cell measured about ten feet by ten and was quite bare within except for a plank bed and a pot for drinking water. In some of them brown silent men were squatting at the inner bars, with their blankets draped round them. These were the condemned men, due to be hanged within the next week or two.

One prisoner had been brought out of his cell. He was a Hindu, a puny wisp of a man, with a shaven head and vague liquid eyes. He had a thick, sprouting moustache, absurdly too big for his body, rather like the moustache of a comic man on the films. Six tall Indian warders were guarding him and getting him ready for the gallows. Two of them stood by with rifles and fixed bayonets, while the others handcuffed him, passed a chain through his handcuffs and fixed it to their belts, and lashed his arms tight to his sides. They crowded very close about him, with their hands always on him in a careful, caressing grip, as though all the while feeling him to make sure he was there. It was like men handling a fish which is still alive and may jump back into the water. But he stood quite unresisting, yielding his arms limply to the ropes, as though he hardly noticed what was happening.

Eight o'clock struck and a bugle call, desolately thin in the wet air, floated from the distant barracks. The superintendent of the jail, who was standing apart from the rest of us, moodily prodding the gravel with his stick, raised his head at the sound. He was an army doctor, with a gray toothbrush moustache and a gruff voice. "For God's sake hurry up, Francis," he said irritably. "The man ought to have been dead by this time. Aren't you ready yet?"

Francis, the head jailer, a fat Dravidian in a white drill suit and gold spectacles, waved his black hand. "Yes sir, yes sir," he bubbled. "All iss satisfactorily prepared. The hangman iss waiting. We shall proceed."

"Well, quick march, then. The prisoners can't get their breakfast till this job's over."

We set out for the gallows. Two warders marched on either side of the prisoner, with their rifles at the slope; two others marched close against him, gripping him by the arm and shoulder, as though at once pushing and supporting him. The rest of us, magistrates and the like, followed behind. Suddenly, when we had gone ten yards, the procession stopped short without any order or warning. A dreadful thing had happened—a dog, come goodness knows whence, had appeared in the yard. It came bounding among us with a loud volley of barks, and leapt round us wagging its whole body, wild with glee at finding so many human beings together. It was a large woolly dog, half Airedale, half pariah. For a moment it pranced round us, and then, before anyone could stop it, it had made a dash for the prisoner and, jumping up, tried to lick his face. Everyone stood aghast, too taken aback even to grab at the dog.

"Who let that bloody brute in here?" said the superintendent angrily. "Catch it, someone!"

A warder, detached from the escort, charged clumsily after the dog, but it danced and gamboled just out of his reach, taking everything as part of the game. A young Eurasian jailer picked up a handful of gravel and tried to stone the dog away, but it dodged the stones and came after us again. Its yaps echoed from the jail walls. The prisoner, in the grasp of two warders, looked on incuriously, as though this was another formality of the hanging. It was several minutes before someone managed to catch the dog. Then we put my handkerchief through its collar and moved off once more, with the dog still straining and whimpering.

It was about forty yards to the gallows. I watched the bare brown back of the prisoner marching in front of me. He walked clumsily with his bound arms, but quite steadily, with that bobbing gait of the Indian who never straightens his knees. At each step his muscles slid neatly into place, the lock of hair on his scalp danced up and down, his feet printed themselves on the wet gravel. And once, in spite of the men who gripped him by each shoulder, he stepped slightly aside to avoid a puddle on the path.

It is curious, but till that moment I had never realized what it means to destroy a healthy, conscious man. When I saw the prisoner step aside to avoid the puddle I saw the mystery, the unspeakable wrongness, of cutting a life short when it is in full tide. This man was not dying, he was alive just as we are alive. All the organs of his body were working—bowels digesting food, skin renewing itself, nails growing, tissues forming— all toiling away in solemn foolery. His nails would still be growing when he stood on the drop, when he was falling through the air with a tenth of a second to live. His eyes saw the yellow gravel and the gray walls, and his brain still remembered, foresaw, reasoned— reasoned even about puddles. He and we were a party of men walking together, seeing, hearing, feeling, understanding the same world; and in two minutes, with a sudden snap, one of us would be gone—one mind less, one world less.

The gallows stood in a small yard, separate from the main grounds of the prison, and overgrown with tall prickly weeds. It was a brick erection like three sides of a shed, with planking on top, and above that two beams and a crossbar with the rope dangling. The hangman, a gray-haired convict in the white uniform of the prison, was waiting beside his machine. He greeted us with a servile crouch as we entered. At a word from Francis the two warders, gripping the prisoner more closely than ever, half led, half pushed him to the gallows and helped him clumsily up the ladder. Then the hangman climbed up and fixed the rope round the prisoner's neck.

We stood waiting, five yards away. The warders had formed in a rough circle round the gallows. And then, when the noose was fixed, the prisoner began crying out to his god. It was a high, reiterated cry of "Ram! Ram! Ram! Ram!", not urgent and fearful like a prayer or a cry for help, but steady, rhythmical, almost like the tolling of a bell. The dog answered the sound with a whine. The hangman, still standing on the gallows, produced a small cotton bag like a flour bag and drew it down over the prisoner's face. But the sound, muffled by the cloth, still persisted, over and over again: "Ram! Ram! Ram! Ram! Ram!"

The hangman climbed down and stood ready, holding the lever. Minutes seemed to pass. The steady, muffled crying from the prisoner went on and on, "Ram! Ram! Ram!" never faltering for an instant. The superintendent, his head on his chest, was slowly poking the ground with his stick; perhaps he was counting the cries, allowing the prisoner a fixed number—fifty, perhaps, or a hundred. Everyone had changed color. The Indians had gone gray like bad coffee, and one or two of the bayonets were wavering. We looked at the lashed, hooded man on the drop, and listened to his cries—each cry another second of life; the same thought was in all our minds: oh, kill him quickly, get it over, stop that abominable noise!

Suddenly the superintendent made up his mind. Throwing up his head he made a swift motion with his stick. "Chalo!" he shouted almost fiercely.

There was a clanking noise, and then dead silence. The prisoner had vanished, and the rope was twisting on itself. I let go of the dog, and it galloped immediately to the back of the gallows; but when it got there it stopped short, barked, and then retreated into a corner of the yard, where it stood among the weeds, looking timorously out at us. We went round the gallows to inspect the prisoner's body. He was dangling with his toes pointed straight downward, very slowly revolving, as dead as a stone.

The superintendent reached out with his stick and poked the bare brown body; it oscillated slightly. "He's all right," said the superintendent. He backed out from under the gallows, and blew out a deep breath. The moody look had gone out of his face quite suddenly. He glanced at his wristwatch. "Eight minutes past eight. Well, that's all for this morning, thank God."

The warders unfixed bayonets and marched away. The dog, sobered and conscious of having misbehaved itself, slipped after them. We walked out of the gallows yard, past the condemned cells with their waiting prisoners, into the big central yard of the prison. These convicts, under the command of warders armed with lathis, were already receiving their breakfast. They squatted in long rows, each man holding a tin pannikin, while two warders with buckets marched round ladling out rice; it seemed quite a homely, jolly scene, after the hanging. An enormous relief had come upon us now that the job was done. One felt an impulse to sing, to break into a run, to snigger. All at once everyone began chattering gaily.

The Eurasian boy walking beside me nodded toward the way we had come, with a knowing smile: "Do you know, sir, our friend [he meant the dead man] when he heard his appeal had been dismissed, he pissed on the floor of his cell. From fright.—Kindly take one of my cigarettes, sir. Do you not admire my new silver case, sir? From the boxwallah, two rupees eight annas. Classy European style."

Several people laughed—at what, nobody seemed certain.

Francis was walking by the superintendent, talking garrulously: "Well, sir, all hass passed off with the utmost satisfactoriness. It was all finished—flick! like that. It is not always so—oah, no! I have known cases where the doctor wass obliged to go beneath the gallows and pull the prissoner's legs to ensure decease. Most disagreeable!"

"Wriggling about, eh? That's bad," said the superintendent.

"Ach, sir, it iss worse when they become refractory! One man, I recall, clung to the bars of hiss cage when we went to take him out. You will scarcely credit, sir, that it took six warders to dislodge him, three pulling at each leg. We reasoned with him. 'My dear fellow,' we said, 'think of all the pain and trouble you are causing to us!' But no, he would not listen! Ach, he wass very troublesome!"

I found that I was laughing quite loudly. Everyone was laughing. Even the superintendent grinned in a tolerant way. "You'd better all come out and have a drink," he said quite genially. "I've got a bottle of whisky in the car. We could do with it."

We went through the big double gates of the prison into the road. "Pulling at his legs!" exclaimed a Burmese magistrate suddenly, and burst into a loud chuckling. We all began laughing again. At that moment Francis's anecdote seemed extraordinarily funny. We all had a drink together, native and European alike, quite amicably. The dead man was a hundred yards away.

STUDY QUESTIONS for "A Hanging"

COMPREHENSION

1. What is the purpose of this narrative? Why do you think Orwell wrote it: to entertain, to inform or impart insight, or to convey strong feeling? Be specific—e.g., if he wrote the essay to convey insight, what insight into human behavior does he communicate through his writing?
2. Of what significance is the appearance of the dog? What does the dog do that is so upsetting? What does the behavior of the dog contribute to Orwell's own development of thought as he participates in the hanging ritual?
3. Of what significance is the fact that the prisoner sidesteps the puddle? What impact does this action have on the young Orwell? In what paragraph does Orwell focus upon the emotional and intellectual impact of the prisoner's sidestepping the puddle?
4. How do the behavior of the dog and the action of the condemned man prepare us for the insight that Orwell shares with the reader in paragraph ten?
5. What do you believe is the central conflict of this narrative? Is it external or internal? Are there other conflicts present in this narrative?
6. What is the climactic scene or moment of this narrative? In other words, where is the emotional high point—or turning point—in this essay?

DEVELOPMENT AND ORGANIZATION

1. What details contribute to bringing out the conflict in the essay?
2. In his opening paragraph, what sort of an impression does Orwell try to create through selection and arrangement of concrete/descriptive details?
3. Which details of the opening paragraph do you find the most striking? Why?
4. How did Orwell feel on this particular day? How do you know? Which details of Orwell's description of setting and situation reveal what he is thinking and feeling?
5. Reread the description of the actual execution. What do the descriptive details reveal about how Orwell and the other observers were affected by the hanging? Which details prove especially effective in revealing the emotional state of those observing the event?

6. How do you think that Orwell felt about his participation in the execution? What details in the narrative can you find to support your answer?

STYLE AND TECHNIQUE

1. Discuss the characterization of each of the following characters: the superintendent, Francis, the hangman, the Eurasian boy with the cigarettes. What details prove helpful in revealing something about these characters? What do we learn, although briefly, of each one?
2. Why does Orwell use so many details to reveal the character of the prisoner and so few details to reveal the other characters?

TEN-MINUTE TOPICS

1. Write about an event which gave you an awareness of other people, or of yourself, or of the nature of an institution or organization, greater than you had before the event.
2. Write about a time you were faced with a repugnant task. What was the task? Did you choose to complete it or not? What were the consequences of your choice?
3. Write about how we judge those individuals who are responsible for completing tasks that many deem repugnant.

HOMECOMING AND REGRETS

BY FRANK BRUNI

Above Rome's pale yellow and dusky orange buildings, the sky somehow looks bluer than it does almost anywhere else. Did I take proper note of that when I saw it all the time? When it was the canopy over my waking, my working and the all-consuming, all-distracting tedium of daily life?

I worry I didn't. And I wonder how, during the two years when I called Rome home and wandered frequently through the Villa Borghese park, I never noticed an especially lush, shady patch near the Galleria Borghese that I stumbled across recently, on a return trip. Like the sky's vividness, the discovery unsettled me. So did the regular peal of church bells, a music that must have been the soundtrack of my past but that I remembered only vaguely. It seems I failed to hear it—to listen—back then.

This is the stretch of the calendar, from Thanksgiving through New Year's, when many of us revisit the places we've left behind. These journeys can be difficult, and I don't mean the brawls over the overhead bin. Nor do I mean what Thomas Wolfe did when he contemplated the messiness of going home again, stirring up resentments and confronting how much we—and it—have changed.

What weighs on me is the opposite: how much everything has no doubt stayed the same, coupled with the recognition that I didn't appreciate or really even examine it before. The sorrow lies there.

About a year ago I visited Chapel Hill, NC, where I went to college, for the first time since I graduated in 1986. I ran an old running route, just to see if it conformed to my memories.

It did, in that I knew exactly where to turn and how soon the next juncture would come along. Then again it didn't, because what I encountered along the way—the columned rotunda to my left, the storybook quadrangle to my right—had a grace and even a majesty I'd never registered before. I felt location envy, about a location I'd inhabited for no fewer than four years.

And with each stride I grew more disappointed in myself, and angrier, for having missed or at least ignored so much of this when it more or less belonged to me and was there for the taking. College was when I first, and last, had Joni Mitchell in my head, so I was well acquainted with the refrain of "Big Yellow Taxi" and its deceptively chirpy insistence that "you don't know what you've got till it's gone." But I turned a deaf ear to the song's message as surely as I turned a blind eye to the arboretum beside the campus planetarium, though it, too, skirted the route of my runs.

My friend J. says that I shouldn't beat up on myself, and makes the excellent point that we're not only older and wiser when we circle back to our former homes but we're also, even more crucially, unencumbered guests able to take their measure and siphon off their pleasures in a way we couldn't before.

But it's also true that we're often just plain oblivious to the scenery right in front of us. By being closest, it's farthest away.

I'm not talking about obvious, monumental stuff. More than half of my New York friends haven't been to the Metropolitan Museum of Art in five years or bothered with the Empire State Building in twenty. But they know full well that they're denying themselves glorious art and a God's-eye view; it's a conscious decision, made with the belief that they can always treat themselves later. That's a foolishness all its own.

I'm talking about subtle, incidental blessings that are strangely invisible to us. My friend N. realized that there was a towering, flowering Schefflera plant in front of her childhood home in California only after she'd moved to New York and begun coveting one in a Manhattan store, which wanted $500 for it.

I've met a half dozen people on my Manhattan block who have never set foot inside the corner bakery, Levain, which makes what might be the best chocolate chip cookies in the city. And it's not because these neighbors of mine are dieting. A few of them don't even know the bakery's there, though there are lines out the door some weekends.

I doubt any of the food got by me when I lived in Rome. Food seldom does. But too much else did. On my recent stay my companion halted in his tracks one afternoon to point out the heart-tugging perfection of the square we were in. It was the Piazza di Sant'Ignazio, one long side of which is traced by elaborately curved eighteenth-century buildings that evoke a rococo chest of drawers. I'd zoomed through it repeatedly years ago. And never once lingered.

On this occasion I did. And then, my lesson learned, I stopped by again the next morning, before I headed to the airport and lost the precious chance.

STUDY QUESTIONS for "Homecoming and Regrets"

COMPREHENSION

1. What is the "significant event" that triggers this essay? What unease does it cause within the author?
2. Why does Bruni get so angry with himself as he is running in Chapel Hill?
3. What sorts of things do New Yorkers ignore or put off doing? Are these things important in your opinion? Why or why not?

DEVELOPMENT AND ORGANIZATION

1. Bruni begins and ends his essay in Rome. Why does he do so? What final detail does he add to the essay by making this return?
2. Bruni makes reference to the song "Big Yellow Taxi." Find a copy of the lyrics, read through them, and determine why the song's message is relevant to what he is saying in this essay.
3. How much of the essay comes from Bruni's own personal experience, and how much of it comes from the experience of friends and acquaintances? Where does Bruni place each kind of experience, early or late in the essay?

STYLE AND TECHNIQUE

1. Bruni waits until the third paragraph to state what could be his thesis. What is this thesis, and why does he wait until this point to present it? How would the essay have changed if he had begun the essay with it?
2. Why doesn't Bruni use the full names of his friends? What does he gain by keeping them anonymous?
3. Find the longest sentence in the essay. How many words does it have? How many clauses does it have in it? What kind of clauses are they?

TEN-MINUTE TOPICS

1. Describe a time when you returned to a place where you once had lived. How different was the place? What new things had appeared? What old things had disappeared? What were your feelings upon seeing those changes?
2. Describe a place you have visited. What sort of things did you do, and what did you see? How different is your choice of activities when you are on vacation compared to when you are at home?
3. Describe a place or an object you can see only in the area where you live. What is it? What makes it unique? Do you visit it very often yourself? Why or why not?

THE TRUE NATURE OF BALLET

BY CARON JONARD (student)

The perception of ballet dancers as being hard workers who are graceful in movement and gracious in character is accurate, but so much more is not understood. Dancers are also athletes who endure countless physical injuries, have short-lived careers, and live with uncertainty and rejection in an unpredictable, highly competitive industry.

In looking back on my dance history, I can recall numerous examples of concealing physical pain. I often had blisters on my toes and heels that, when I walked, stung as though hot pokers were stabbing into my flesh. I remember the feeling of cramming my throbbing, blistered feet into point shoes which were so hard and tight that I would have almost preferred to grate my already raw skin against a rough cement wall. I could barely even stand; I had to hobble to my place on the studio floor. But when the music started, I was expected to smile and delicately twirl my way through forty-eight minutes of torturous hell. I found the strength to oblige. When it was over: I took off my shoes, swabbed the blood off my feet, carefully placed Dr. Scholl's oval moleskin discs over each toe (to cushion and cradle the sores), put my shoes back on, wiped away the tears which had swelled in my eyes, and positioned myself on the dance floor to rehearse the second act.

Another time, I was on an injury hiatus when an audition came up for a performing arts college I was hoping to attend. I had broken my ankle while at ballet camp in Cuba, and the doctors there made no effort to immobilize it. Within two weeks, I fell and severely twisted the same ankle. It was while recovering from this double injury that my audition took place. The swelling had reduced enough for me to put a shoe on, and I could finally bear some weight on that side of my body. The pain was excruciating, but somehow I managed to pull through with flying colors. Although I fell once while landing on my hurt foot from a grand leap, the instructors were impressed by my talent and my ability to perform under such circumstances. I was eagerly welcomed to the school.

The high rate of injury, the intense strain of training, and the rigorous schedule of performing have caused the average retirement age of dancers to plummet to the late twenties or early thirties. While performers such as Madonna and Baryshnikov have successfully bridged the gap between dance and mainstream entertainment, most are relegated to live out their days teaching others to love to dance or finding jobs in mainstream society. In fact, there is a nonprofit organization, Career Transition for Dancers, which provides free counseling and other necessary resources to help retired dancers decide upon their new paths. The minimum eligible age requirement of twenty-seven can be waived for someone with seven years of paid dance employment.

Some are lucky enough to have enjoyed relatively pain-free careers in dance, at least in the physical sense. The emotional stress, however, can be just as crippling. In New York, for example, every opening in a dance show has hundreds of talented young professionals vying for the position. The competition is fierce. My friends and I used to jam our toes into the two-inch gap under the piano and slide our bottoms along the floor until out legs were straight and our feet felt like their bones would snap. We were driven to boost our appeal, and having the perfect arch was a good start. We would also endlessly slide into reverse angle splits by placing one foot on the barre (which stood approximately waist level) and forcing our already flexible legs into unnatural, two hundred degree or more, extensions. After all, if our arabesques weren't higher than the other thousands of teenaged girls', we would never stand a chance.

Luckily, due to my low percentage of body fat, I had not yet begun my journey into womanhood. I had no experience with the weight gain and fat distribution that led the majority of my peers down the road to anorexia nervosa, a frightening condition brought about by the expectation that dancers should weigh at least thirty pounds less than the American Medical Association's healthy weight standards suggest.

Finally, for those who are fortunate enough to have the talent and body type to land a coveted spot in a reputable show, there is no guarantee that the show, "must," as they say, "go on." In Las Vegas, the home of Siegfried and Roy's Mirage review, the show was shut down suddenly and indefinitely by Roy's freak accident with a tiger. The large production show had been a Strip staple for thirteen years and had just been signed into a lifetime contract. Now, hundreds of workers are left without employment; more than sixty of them are dancers who, because of age and the town's limited opportunities, will not likely find another dancing gig.

A back injury put an end to my dance career when I was twenty. Now, as I'm approaching forty, my young daughter aspires to be a ballerina. The passion is in her blood; even though she's never taken a class, I can see the spark in her eyes as she twirls about the house. That spark tells me she will be driven to starve and torture herself to meet the unrealistic industry standards of beauty and grace. As I witness in her what I once so strongly felt, I am filled with excitement and nostalgia. More than that, though, I am filled with the fear of a mother who knows the pain, the disappointment, and the heartache that lie ahead for my precious little girl.

STUDY QUESTIONS for "The True Nature of Ballet"

COMPREHENSION

1. According to Jonard, what are the truths of ballet? Be specific.
2. What is the life span of a dancer?
3. What obstacles do most dancers endure? Be specific.

DEVELOPMENT AND ORGANIZATION

1. Does Jonard use her personal experience in a thoughtful fashion? Explain.
2. Where does she make use of concrete details and allusions? What is the benefit of using such in a narrative essay?
3. Jonard mentions the Siegfried and Roy show toward the end of the essay. What was this show? Why does she refer to it? Is her reference effective?

STYLE AND TECHNIQUE

1. What is the writer's attitude towards her subject matter? Does she have conflicting emotions about ballet?
2. How effective is Jonard's introduction in capturing your attention? What has she done to make this introduction—and the essay that follows—interesting?
3. How effective is Jonard's concluding paragraph? Does it serve as an adequate bridge between her examples of ballet as a sport of joy and pain?
4. Who is the essay's intended audience? Can this essay inform someone who does not share Jonard's knowledge of dance?

TEN-MINUTE TOPICS

1. Pick a sport you are familiar with and discuss the training it requires.
2. Discuss a sport that is largely glamorized and discuss the rigor involved in doing it well.
3. Discuss how dance as an art form has evolved and changed over the years.

I WAS YOUNG, HAD HAIR, AND WENT TO WAR

BY H. LEE BARNES

I read too many stories of small lives in search of understanding something so vague it hardly seems a problem, if indeed it exists at all, and I wonder why these writers don't have messier lives or at least messier minds. Are their lives and minds as sterile as their prose is clean? What experience do they hit the water with when the fire is at their backs? The fact of experience may not stir a smooth, easy psycho-fictive drama that leads to a nice, neat epiphany, but experiences, especially those worth having, are rarely smooth and rarely internal. They are rather internalized, become perhaps obsessions.

I was young, had hair, and went to war. No experience since has been as forceful or as immediate or genuine. Thirty years later it is an after ring, an irritant, a vibration that gives tone to everything I write, but there is one moment that slips irresistibly into my consciousness. The moment lives by itself, forms and recasts itself in the fiction, nonfiction, and poetry I've written. In part, this is it:

> I stand on a mound atop my camp, Tra Bong, a bare swell of red earth, cut by trenches and surrounded by three barriers of barbed wire. Monsoon clouds stalk landward up the fertile valley, which in sunlight is emerald and shimmering with rice paddies where water lies so still you can walk the berms and see trees and sky reflected precisely on the surface. But now everything is leaden, and colorless except the red clay, which slurries in the trenches like molten rust. I watch one hundred Vietnamese soldiers march away from the camp led by four Americans, one my captain, two my friends, Brownie and Jacobson, and the last Riffschnelder, who is due to rotate out of country in weeks. Him I barely know. There are reasons I cannot write this image out of my life, try though I may. First, all of the Americans died. Second, I was supposed to go on the operation and Brown died in my place. Third, it was an ill-advised mission. Fourth, I saw a beetle crawl out of a bullet hole in Jacobson's forehead. Fifth, Captain Fewell's body was never recovered, but his head was discovered months later in a Buddhist pagoda where he'd been decapitated. I along with a handful of others survived to try and make sense of our buddies' deaths and to speculate, I especially, on that most profound and most dread of questions: Why me? (Or, if you prefer: Why not me?)

All experience orders up opposing questions, and roughly the same lame answers, and despite the impact of this particular experience, more than fifteen years lapsed before I began writing about Vietnam. The first manuscript, a novel, went through a round of rejections, some complimentary, most standard, before I wrote away from that subject. Twelve years would pass before Vietnam again found space in my writing. When it did, it became the force behind a novel manuscript, a novella, seven short stories and an ongoing string of poems, all written in two years. Obsession.

Of course I didn't realize it was an obsession until Alberto Ríos, who teaches graduate writing at ASU, told me of a seminar he conducts called "Obsessions." The concept is to take a particular image, work it and rework it for an entire semester, following whatever direction it takes. The method, even as he described it to me, resounded with truth, for as a way to develop an honest dialogue with experience, the writer must, I think, be a bit obsessed. This, it seems, is approximately what I've experienced in writing about Vietnam. It isn't the fact or the truth of the experience I wish to capture, but the intensity and effect. Poe was right on this count: The writer should write toward effect. Roderick Usher, crushed under the weight of his house, took the full force of it in front of his friend's eyes. In "Gunning for Ho" Bruce Stoner used explosives and a television camera to negate the problem of distance. The narrators (survivors) are compelled to tell the story. The plots are (quite by accident) parallel but the experiences that impel the stories are dissimilar and thus details are quite different. Each experience has its own frequency. I don't know what inspired Poe, but I drew upon the experience of climbing mountains into Laos, of being in the Tra Bong Valley, of seeing friends die, of witnessing and engaging in youthful macho behavior. Plot limits stories; experience limits the writer but creates a uniqueness of vision.

In both "Gunning for Ho" and "Cat in the Cage" I use the image of a prisoner carried in a bamboo cage. This was an actual condition some captured Americans, particularly pilots and Special Forces troopers, endured. Though I never experienced it, I was indoctrinated to the possibility of suffering such mistreatment if captured. I, by being in proximity to where such things happened, experienced the fright. I best relate this to a woman I know who suffers nightmares about rape, all manner of violations. I'll not venture into the psychology of her phobia, but I know with certainty she has experienced the terror of rape. Must a woman be raped to feel the fear or imagine the indignities involved?

Along with the actual and imagined experience, my writing includes use of the collective experience, which includes history and social setting. This is the hard part of writing stories about Vietnam; here is where gender and age, where bias and assumption, where "other" experiences and myths and stereotypes emerge. I know from rejections that accompany my Vietnam stories (and there are many) that women generally, particularly young women, can't enter into the narratives. The stories, simply put, meter out too high on the testosterone scale—men, Vietnam, death. The collective experience of women readers from my generation seems rooted in antiwar marches or loss of family or friends and the women's movement (and those are their stories); the younger ones' reactions are likely linked to *Rambo* and bad-movie dates with pimply-cheeked kids who were raised watching cartoon warriors (and those are their stories). Women and men alike associate Vietnam with My Lai, napalm, heroin addiction and racism. It's so easy to view it from these perspectives, to give it your own slant. (In fact My Lai was an aberration, but atrocities committed by the Viet Cong and North Vietnamese on Montagnard and South Vietnamese were commonplace and part of a political strategy).

Recently I read of a Navy corpsman who served with the Marines at Hue. He'd crawled out into enemy fire to carry wounded Marines to safety or to administer aid and gather ammunition. Though wounded several times, he'd continued to go out and had saved several Marines. He was so badly shot up that he was thought to be dead and was set aside with the dead while the wounded were evacuated. Somehow he lived through his wounds and drifted into obscurity. Over twenty-five years later he was recognized by one of the Marines who'd witnessed his courage on that violent day. Others came forward to testify to this man's selfless acts of courage. Thirty years after the battle, he was awarded the Congressional Medal of Honor. This speaks of old-fashioned heroism, but in a way speaks also of the collective experience I mentioned, the one that is somehow counter to the greater consciousness of the literary establishment. The corpsman's story isn't one day at Hue or a ceremony during which the president of the United States drapes a medal over a hero's neck; it is the thousands of days in between and the tomorrow he faces.

I like the splash and the ripples that move the boat, the sudden surprise when a fish jumps unexpectedly. I feed off what is incomprehensible. I want a continuing dialogue with the boy who stood atop that mound of red clay and watched his friends march down a valley to their deaths. He raises the questions that start the process (for these are my stories).

STUDY QUESTIONS for "I Was Young, Had Hair, and Went to War"

COMPREHENSION

1. What is the central idea expressed in the essay? Does Barnes express this idea in a clearly stated thesis, or does he imply it? If the former, write out the thesis as it appears in the text, and identify by number the paragraph in which it appears; if the latter, summarize the central idea in fifteen words.
2. Barnes seems to direct a portion of his essay toward an audience of women. Why does he target women specifically in that passage? What misapprehensions on their part does he point out?
3. Why is the idea of Obsession important to Barnes? How does it affect his writing?
4. What is Barnes's purpose for writing this essay?

DEVELOPMENT AND ORGANIZATION

1. How closely does Barnes's essay follow the methods of organization set forth in the paradigm for the narration essay? Does he use any other plan for organizing his essay in conjunction with (or instead of) the paradigm?
2. Look again at Barnes's description of his Tra Bong experience. Which details are the most interesting? Which are the most disturbing? Why does he resort to making a list at the end of the description?
3. Barnes relates the story of the Navy corpsman toward the end of the essay. What does it say about the experience of war? Why do you think he included this story?

STYLE AND TECHNIQUE

1. What is the style of this essay: formal, informal, conversational? What is Barnes's tone: serious, nostalgic, regretful? What words and phrases does Barnes use to create the essay's style and tone? How do they affect our perception of Barnes as the writer? Why do you think Barnes writes in this style and in this tone?
2. Look at the essay's fourth paragraph (beginning with "Of course"). Count the number of sentences in the paragraph. Now count the number of dependent clauses and independent clauses. What is the ratio of clauses to sentences? Of dependent clauses to sentences? Of independent clauses to sentences? Of dependent clauses to independent clauses?

TEN-MINUTE TOPICS

1. Think about the best day you have ever had. What events or conditions led up to that day? What were some of the effects of that day?
2. What is a "story" you have to tell about a war? How do you view any of the wars your generation has lived through? Look again at how Barnes describes "'other' experiences and myths and stereotypes" in paragraph six before responding.

CHAPTER FOUR
EXAMPLES

DEFINITION

With this chapter, we shall begin studying several types of expository essay: example, process, classification, division, comparison and contrast, cause and effect, analogy, and definition. Regardless of the type of expository essay we are studying, we must keep in mind a general format: introduction, body, and conclusion. While many accomplished writers do take liberties with this format, all begin with an understanding of the essay's basic requirements:

The Introduction

In a traditional expository essay, the introduction generally works to (1) capture the reader's attention, (2) introduce the topic, (3) establish the tone (the writer's attitude towards the subject matter), and (4) present the thesis. Generally, the thesis is offered as a direct statement, but in some essays it may be merely strongly implied.

The Body

The thesis in turn must be supported by the body paragraphs, which in turn must be unified, coherent, logically arranged, and well developed. These are four of the most important criteria involved in writing any essay.

Let's consider what these terms mean. A paragraph is *unified* if all its sentences support the topic idea; an essay has unity if all parts support the thesis. Further, the composition is *coherent* if the writer establishes clear connections or relationships between sentences. Clear connections, as we shall see throughout this text, are established in several ways: by using traditional transitions such as *however, moreover, furthermore, finally, on the contrary*, and so on; by repeating key words and phrases, often taken from the thesis; by using pronouns to refer back to nouns; and by using parallel sentence structures—that is, sentences that are structured alike. Along with this, we can say that a paragraph is coherent if it contains sentences that are *logically arranged*. Like the larger essay, a good paragraph will contain sentences that are arranged in logical order: left to right, right to left, far to near, or near to far in the case of description; chronologically, in the case of narrative; and from the least important detail to the most important detail in exposition. And finally in most essays, the body paragraphs should be reasonably *well developed*. Often, body paragraphs are developed using specific and/or concrete details, which even in an expository essay may be presented as description or narration.

The Conclusion

The conclusion, of course, brings the essay to a close, and the writer can use several techniques to do this: repeat the thesis (in different words), summarize main points in the body of the essay, take a broader view, challenge the reader, end with a striking quote or statistic, and so on. Of course, in writing an effective conclusion, the student must learn what the instructor wants. For instance, one instructor may prefer a conclusion that goes a bit beyond a mere restatement of the thesis and/or a summary of main ideas; too often, the use of this summary/restatement technique signals the writer's desire to exit the essay as soon as possible. Because students are engaged in college-level writing, instructors often prefer conclusions that take a broader view of the topic, thereby challenging the reader to think and grow intellectually.

APPLICATION

To get a better grasp of the expository mode, let's examine parts of two examples essays. One of the most fundamental elements in all expository writing, an example is an illustration used to clarify a general statement. According to Aristotle, the examples essay is the most basic form of inductive argument, to be studied later in the text.

In the opening paragraph to his essay, eighteenth-century English writer Samuel Johnson uses an example to introduce his thesis as well as to introduce the topic, the tendency to name people after animals:

> It is common to distinguish men by names of animals which they are supposed to resemble. Thus a hero is frequently termed a lion, and a statesman a fox, an extortioner gains the appellation of vulture, and a fop the title of monkey. There is also among various anomalies of character, which a survey of the world exhibits, a species of beings in human form, which may be properly marked out as the screech-owls of mankind.

In this paragraph, the examples are "lion," "fox," "vulture," and "monkey," all labels used to distinguish men. As he uses the first sentence to introduce the general topic—naming men after the animals that they resemble—Dr. Johnson also adopts a formal though satirical *tone*; that is, he is making fun not only of this process of naming but, more importantly, of all humanity. Along with this, the choice of words and labels that are either ennobling or demeaning—"lion," "fox," and "vulture"—contribute immensely to the tone and are intended by Johnson to pull the potentially amused reader into the essay. In his final sentence, Johnson states his *thesis*, which he is obliged to illustrate in the body of his essay with examples.

It should be noted as well that Dr. Johnson displays, in all the paragraphs of this essay, an awareness of and understanding of his audience. When Johnson wrote this particular piece in the eighteenth century, numerous journals were appearing on the British literary scene, particularly in London. The tone and word choice of even the first paragraph suggests Dr. Johnson's keen awareness that his audience is highly intelligent, extremely literate, and quite capable of appreciating the tongue-in-cheek sarcasm that saturates his composition.

In the following two paragraphs, we see the example that Johnson has used to support his thesis concerning "screech-owls":

> I have now known Suspirius fifty-eight years and four months, and have never yet passed an hour with him in which he has not made some attack upon my quiet. When we were first acquainted, his great topic was the misery of youth without riches, and whenever we walked out together he solaced me with a long enumeration of pleasures, which, as they were beyond the reach of my fortune, were without the verge of my desires, and which I should never have considered as the objects of a wish, had not his unseasonable representations placed them in my sight.

> Another of his topics is the neglect of merit, with which he never fails to amuse every man whom he sees not eminently fortunate. If he meets with a young officer, he always informs him of gentlemen whose personal courage is unquestioned, and whose military skill qualifies them to command armies, that have, notwithstanding all their merit, grown old with subaltern commissions. For a genius in the church, he is always provided with a curacy for life. The lawyer he informs of many men of great parts and deep study, who have never had an opportunity to speak in the courts. And meeting Serenus the physician, "Ah, doctor": says he, "what? A-foot still, when so many blockheads are rattling their chariots? I told you seven years ago that you would never meet with encouragement, and I hope you will now take more notice, when I tell you that your Greek, and your diligence, and your honesty, will never enable you to live like yonder apothecary, who prescribes to his own shop, and laughs at the physician."

Along with eighteenth-century British writers Richard Steele and Joseph Addison, Dr. Johnson helped develop the form of the essay studied today as the expository mode. In the above two paragraphs, he provides examples within an example. His primary example, Suspirius (quite possibly a pseudonym for Johnson himself), illustrates the character of a "screech-owl." Within the framework of this one example, Johnson gives us specific examples of topics about which Suspirius complains: youth without riches and unrecognized merit. One step further, Johnson even provides two situations to illustrate his point concerning Suspirius.

We should see, at this point, that the movement in this remarkably coherent excerpt is towards greater specificity: Dr. Johnson begins with a general introduction of the topic, moves to a specific statement of thesis, gives us a particular example of the character of the "screech-owl"—Suspirius—and finally gives us even more specific examples to enable us to see Suspirius. Johnson's essay provides a remarkable and amusing illustration of how to use examples. Logically, Johnson moves the reader from the general to the specific.

Now let's turn to a more recent examples essay. "The View from Here" by Vickie Smith relies upon well-developed examples to reinforce its thesis. Here is the opening paragraph from Smith's essay:

> "If the teachers and school administrators were as concerned about teaching as they are about pay raises and benefits maybe more of our children would know how to read and write," remarked my neighbor the other day, and I'm sure she believed her statement to be true. She wanted to believe it was true. Why? One of the reasons could be that by placing the responsibility in the hands of the school and its teachers she is releasing herself from being blamed for her own child's lack of education. How she *wants* to perceive the situation greatly influences how she *will* perceive it. This method of carefully choosing and interpreting information is called selective perception—or in other words, people tend to believe what they want to believe.

Let's examine what the writer has done here. To begin, Smith attempts to engage the reader—to capture the reader's attention—by directly quoting her neighbor. The effectiveness of this particular opening is that many readers are likely to agree with the neighbor's statement. Certainly Smith knows this as she moves on to build her introductory paragraph—and, as we shall see, her entire essay—in response to this statement.

(Too many student writers are content with using the introduction to introduce the topic and present the thesis. And frequently such introductions are flat and uninteresting simply because the writer has failed to acknowledge his or her audience, to incorporate details that establish a larger ideological framework in which to understand the main point of the essay, and to create for that audience the impression that the essay that follows is worth reading. Smith's introduction clearly offers more.)

Beyond grabbing the reader's attention, Vickie Smith clearly introduces her topic in her opening paragraph; even before she uses the phrase "selective perception," the reader has a pretty good idea of what the essay is about. Just as importantly, Smith establishes her tone—in this case casual and somewhat satiric—and in so doing, she also adopts a role, giving the reader the impression that she is someone who is intelligent, thoughtful, and capable of seeing a situation from several different angles. In the final sentence, she states her thesis—"people tend to believe what they want to believe"—which requires *proofs* in the form of *examples*.

Now let's look at the first body paragraph. Not only does this paragraph clearly support, or illustrate, the thesis; as well, it is unified, coherent, logically put together, and well developed. Here is the paragraph:

> I was confronted by a fine example of this last week. I had missed the recent presidential debate but was filled in by a friend. He reenacted some of the conversation for me and explained how each candidate had responded. Very exuberantly, he detailed how poorly Newt Gingrich came across, particularly how vicious Gingrich had seemed in comparison with a confident and "on the ball" Mitt Romney. Not until school the next morning did I realize how influential was the fact that my friend is from Massachusetts and a Romney supporter. Sitting in my first class, I overheard people behind me discussing the debate. It became obvious very quickly that they were Gingrich supporters, as they enthusiastically praised the former speaker's fine performance, then whole-heartedly set about degrading not only Romney's candidacy but also his personality, saying he was laughable and dull. Had all these people watched the same debate? Of course they had, but through the process of selective perception each group had unconsciously selected what data best fit its needs and that's what they'd chosen to remember.

This paragraph is very well put-together. For one thing, it is tightly unified: every statement clearly supports the topic idea, which is stated in the final sentence: "Each group had unconsciously selected what data best fit its needs and that's what they'd chosen to remember." Further, the paragraph is well developed; Smith illustrates her paragraph's central idea (and the thesis as well) by relating an event that occurred during school. Her example, in fact, implies a brief narration—and keep in mind that we can use narration and description to clarify points in our expository essays. Beyond this, the sentences are arranged logically, in both a chronological and a climactic order: that is, in her example, Smith records an event that took place in time, but she also builds to the paragraph's most important statement. Finally, the paragraph is coherent. Effortlessly, Smith establishes connections between sentences. For instance, the pronoun *this* of her opening statement "I was confronted by a fine example of this last week" connects this paragraph to the previous one. She uses the pronoun *he* in sentences three and four to refer back to *friend* in sentence two. In the fifth sentence, Smith again uses the noun *friend*. By repeating keywords and using pronouns, Smith easily establishes connections between the sentences. The use of the transitional phrase *Of course* towards the end of the paragraph further reinforces this piece's coherence, signaling that the sentence that follows is a response to the question, "Had all these people watched the same debate?"

A good conclusion to an expository essay can do a number of things. As explained above, it can restate the thesis in different words; it can summarize the main points of the essay; it can take a broader view; it can challenge the reader; or it can end with a startling statement. Let's see what Smith does:

> This position of parallax is the spot from which we make our value judgments and decisions. Thus, where we "are at" in social, economic, and political terms is a very decisive factor in forming our ideals. We

strengthen and build on these ideals as we sift through daily information in search of reinforcement for our preconceived views, rejecting or ignoring those views that contradict our own. This is how we make decisions, important decisions such as who our friends are and whom we want for president, as well as the not-so-important decisions like what to eat for dinner or what color socks to wear. It is the natural process of forming likes and dislikes: nothing is absolutely neutral, and there is no such thing as an unbiased opinion.

As you can see, this conclusion does far more than simply restate the thesis and summarize the essay's main points, techniques often used by students who are looking for a fast exit from an essay they tired of writing long before the final paragraph. In this essay, Smith is not only taking a broader view of her topic by applying the essay's ideas and examples to all aspects of our existence; she is challenging the readers to acknowledge that most of their opinions are biased, and she thus encourages the reader to grow intellectually.

The examples essay is only one form of exposition. However, because it represents inductive logic in its most basic form, we need to regard the examples essay as the foundation not only for other expository forms but for the argumentative essay.

PARADIGM

When putting together the examples essay, keep in mind the following paradigm. Bear in mind that a good introduction (or conclusion) may consist of more than one paragraph, just as the body may go beyond three paragraphs.

Introduction
1. **Engage the reader's attention.**
2. **Introduce topic.**
3. **Establish tone.**
4. **Present thesis.**

First Body Paragraph
1. **Topic sentence introducing example.**
2. **Supporting details.**

Second Body Paragraph
1. **Topic sentence introducing example.**
2. **Supporting details.**

Third Body Paragraph
    1. Topic sentence introducing example.
    2. Supporting details.

Conclusion (options)
    1. Summarize main points and restate thesis.
    2. Offer a final image, message, or judgment.
    3. Take a broader view.
    4. End with quotation.
    5. End with striking statistic.
    6. Challenge the reader.
    7. Something else.

SUMMARY

In his classic work *Rhetoric*, Aristotle acknowledged the use of examples as the most fundamental form of inductive reasoning, which requires the use of specific proofs to support general assertions—and it is upon the effectiveness of its proofs, often synonymous with examples, that a persuasive argument depends. Beyond this, examples represent perhaps the most fundamental and important method of developing an expository essay; indeed, most other expository essays—certainly, comparison and contrast, classification, cause and effect, and definition—frequently could benefit from a selective use of examples for the purpose of clarity.

Whether brief or developed, examples can make the thesis—or central argument—of our essays more vivid, more interesting, and more relevant. While we may draw from books, newspapers, magazines, or TV, the best source for lively examples often remains our own personal experience.

THE CAREFUL WAY TO CLEAN EARS

BY NANCY C. SOMMERMAN (student)

Daily bombardment of semi-useful information sets the mind a-spin. The compulsive reader dutifully skims every word, becoming highly susceptible to the ailment known as *info-glut*.

For example, instructions for the use of Q-Tips are stated on their container:

> *Hold swab firmly and use a soft touch. Stroke swab gently around the outer surfaces of the ear, without entering the ear canal.*

Might a waxen-eared consumer have known this without instruction? Did he purchase the packet on a whim, hoping to discover a use for cotton swabs? Nonsense.

Bits and pieces of superfluous print abound.

Behold the hand lotion container: "Shake well with cap on." Leave the cap on to shake. That would never have occurred to the luckless owner of chapped, split, and dry hands. By following directions, one finds not only that his supply of lotion lasts longer but that one can avoid mysterious grease spots on the ceiling.

The Band-Aid wrapper advises, "Remove the protective covering from strip and apply." Any fool knows Band-Aids stick better when unwrapped.

Check the shampoo label: "Wet hair. Lather gently. Rinse thoroughly." Who would ever think to rinse? One often sees nonreaders walking around with a mass of lather on their heads.

Printed trivia is not limited to the medicine cabinet.

The automobile dashboard features eight or more gauges, some of which convey information that the driver could live without. The computerized readout is an electronic marvel, which checks six of the auto's systems and is designed to flash red on malfunction. Car zipping along at 65 mph, the warning light flashes: jockey to slow lane; drive onto shoulder and stop. One discovers that the windshield washer fluid is low. There are only four hundred and twenty-eight squirts left. Whew! An emergency waylaid. That was a close one.

Relax a minute. Smoke a cigarette. Glaring from the Bic lighter package: "Hold away from face to light the lighter." Darn! Another amusement ruined. I always enjoy shoving the lighter up one nostril before I light it.

Stop at Wendy's for a snack and to rest the eyes. Not a chance! The place mat features eating instructions—short essays on "How to Build a Burrito" and "The Well-Dressed Salad."

The printed word serves to instruct, educate, and edify. By paying attention to all print, a reader can learn that spiral notebooks instruct one on the tearing out of pages; that matchbooks say, "Close cover before striking." The attentive consumer is overwhelmed: "Open sides first"; "Break seal and lift"; "This side up"; "Line forms here"; and, of course, the all-time favorite, "Use other door."

Instructions, directions, orders, advice—the words buzz around one's head like gnats on a summer's eve. Where will it end?

Relief, at last? Here sits the coffee maker with only one switch and two words: "On" and "Off." Even this is one word too many.

Escape is impossible.

"Be all you can be—READ."

The pitiful compulsive reader finds himself afflicted with a chronic case of info-glut.

STUDY QUESTIONS for "The Careful Way to Clean Ears"

COMPREHENSION

1. What is Sommerman's thesis? How many times does it appear in the essay?
2. The title of the essay is taken directly from a Q-Tips package. Is it an appropriate title? Why or why not?
3. What was the first indication for you that this essay was humorous rather than wholly serious? On the other hand, is there seriousness behind the humor? And is all good humorous writing essentially making a serious point?

DEVELOPMENT AND ORGANIZATION

1. The writer occasionally contrasts readers and nonreaders, as in the shampoo example. What is the effect of the contrast?
2. Why, in paragraphs ten and fourteen, does the writer bring in positive generalizations about reading?

STYLE AND TECHNIQUE

1. In your own words, explain what Sommerman means by the made-up word *info-glut*.
2. Many sentences in this essay are very short, five words or fewer. What impression do you get from these short sentences?
3. This essay uses a large number of different examples rather than a few examples developed in detail. How does this method affect the reader? Does the essay, in fact, produce almost the same effect on the reader that the reader's "info-glutted" environment is said to produce? Might the same thing be said about the large number of paragraphs?
4. A number of sentence fragments, some consisting of only one word, are used in the essay; are they justified? Do they produce any lack of clarity for the reader?

TEN-MINUTE TOPICS

1. Using examples, write about things we have but don't need.

2. Write about a time you discovered a product label that had directions that assumed that people do not have common sense. What was the product? Where did you find it? How was it to be used? What did the directions say? What would have been the consequences (humorous, of course) if the people had not followed the directions?

3. Write about a time when you observed someone *not* following a set of directions. Be sure to describe the product and its intended purpose. What was the outcome of the individual's failure to read and comprehend?

A YEAR RUINED BY SLEAZE

BY DAVE BARRY

It was the kind of year that made a person look back fondly on the gulf oil spill.

Granted, the oil spill was bad. But it did not result in a high-decibel, weeks-long national conversation about a bulge in a congressman's underpants. Which is exactly what we had in the Festival of Sleaze that was 2011. Remember? There were days when you could not escape The Bulge. At dinnertime, parents of young children had to be constantly ready to hurl themselves in front of their TV screens, for fear that it would suddenly appear on the news in high definition. For a brief (Har!) period, The Bulge was more famous than Justin Bieber.

And when, at last, we were done with The Bulge, and we were able to turn our attention to the presidential election, and the important issues facing us, as a nation, in these troubled times, it turned out that the main issue, to judge by quantity of press coverage, was: groping.

So finally, repelled by the drainage ditch that our political system has become, we turned for escape to an institution that represents all that is pure and wholesome and decent in America today: college football.

That was when we started to have fond memories of the oil spill.

I'm not saying that the entire year was ruined by sleaze. It was also ruined by other bad things. This was a year in which journalism was pretty much completely replaced by tweeting. It was a year in which a significant earthquake struck Washington, yet failed to destroy a single federal agency. It was a year in which the nation was subjected to a seemingly endless barrage of highly publicized pronouncements from Charlie Sheen, a man who, where you have a central nervous system, has a Magic 8-Ball. This was a year in which the cast members of *Jersey Shore* went to Italy and then—in an inexcusable lapse of border security—were allowed to return.

But all of these developments, unfortunate as they were, would not by themselves have made 2011 truly awful. What made it truly awful was the economy, which, for what felt like the seventeenth straight year, continued to stagger around like a zombie on crack. Nothing seemed to help. President Obama, whose instinctive reaction to pretty much everything that happens, including sunrise, is to deliver a nationally televised address, delivered numerous nationally televised addresses on the economy, but somehow these did not do the trick. Neither did the approximately 37 million words emitted by the approximately 249 Republican-presidential-contender televised debates, out of which the single most memorable statement made was, quote: "Oops."

As the year wore on, frustration finally boiled over in the form of the Occupy Various Random Spaces movement, wherein people who were sick and tired of a lot of stuff finally got off their butts and started working for meaningful change via direct action in the form of sitting around and forming multiple committees and drumming and not directly issuing any specific demands but definitely having a lot of strongly held views for and against a wide variety of things. Incredibly, even this did not bring about meaningful change. The economy remained wretched, especially unemployment, which got so bad that many Americans gave up even trying to work. Congress, for example.

Were there any positive developments in 2011? Yes:

• Osama bin Laden, Moammar Gaddafi and the New York Yankees all suffered major setbacks.

• Kim Kardashian finally found her lifetime soul mate for nearly 2½ months.

• Despite a prophecy by revered Christian radio lunatic Harold Camping, the world did not end on May 21.

Come to think of it, that last development wasn't totally positive, not when we consider all the other things that happened in 2011. In case you've blotted it out, let's take one last look back, through squinted eyelids, at this train wreck of a year, starting with . . .

JANUARY

. . . which sees a change of power in the House of Representatives, as outgoing Democratic Speaker Nancy Pelosi hands the gavel over to Republican John Boehner, who, in the new spirit of Washington bipartisanship, has it checked for explosives.

In the State of the Union address, President Obama calls on Congress to improve the nation's crumbling infrastructure. He is interrupted 79 times by applause, and four times by falling chunks of the Capitol ceiling. In other Washington action, Chinese President Hu Jintao is honored at a White House dinner for 225 luminaries, who dine on prime rib accompanied by 17,000 little plastic packets of soy sauce. As the official state gift from the United States, President Obama presents Hu with a six-pack of Bud Light, this being the only American product the White House staff can find that is not manufactured in China.

The month's biggest story is a tragedy in Tucson, where a man opens fire on a meet-and-greet being held by US Rep. Gabrielle Giffords. The accused shooter turns out to be a mentally unstable loner with a history of drug use; there is no evidence that his actions had anything to do with uncivil political rhetoric. So naturally the blame for the tragedy is immediately placed on: uncivil political rhetoric. This results in a nationwide spasm of civil political rhetoric lasting about two hours, after which everybody returns to uncivil political rhetoric, which has been the norm in the United States for two centuries.

In Egypt, demonstrators take to the streets to protest the three-decade regime of President Hosni Mubarak following revelations that "Hosni Mubarak" can be rearranged to spell "A Bum Honks Air." The movement continues to grow in . . .

FEBRUARY

. . . when "Arab Spring" antigovernment demonstrations spread from Egypt to Yemen, then to Iraq, then to Libya, and finally—in a development long feared by the US government—to the volatile streets of Madison, Wis., where thousands of protesters occupy the state capitol to dramatize the fact that it's warmer in there than outside. As the protests escalate, 14 Democratic Wisconsin state legislators flee to Illinois, where they barricade themselves in a hotel and, after a heated four-hour debate, decide, by a 7 to 4 vote with three abstentions, to order room service.

In other national news, a massive snowstorm paralyzes the Midwest, forcing a shutdown of Chicago's O'Hare Airport after more than a dozen planes are attacked by yetis. President Obama responds with a nationally televised speech pointing out that the storm was caused by a weather system inherited from a previous administration.

In Europe, the economic crisis continues to worsen, especially in Greece, which has been operating under a financial model in which the government spends approximately $150 billion a year while taking in revenue totaling $336.50 from the lone Greek taxpayer, an Athens businessman who plans to retire in April. Greece has been making up the shortfall by charging everything to a MasterCard account that the Greek government applied for—in what some critics consider a questionable financial practice—using the name "Germany."

In a historic episode of the TV quiz show *Jeopardy!*, two human champions are swiftly dispatched by an IBM supercomputer named Watson, which combines an encyclopedic knowledge of a wide range of subjects with the ability to launch a 60,000-volt surge of electricity 25 feet.

On Broadway, the troubled musical *Spider-Man: Turn Off the Dark* suffers a setback when three actors and 11 audience members are injured in what the producers describe as a "catastrophic spandex failure."

In sports, two storied NFL franchises, the Pittsburgh Steelers and the Green Bay Packers, meet in Super Bowl XLV, a tense, back-and-forth battle won at the last minute, in a true shocker, by Watson the IBM supercomputer.

Speaking of shocking, in . . .

MARCH

. . . the European economic crisis worsens still further as Moody's downgrades its credit rating for Spain following the discovery that the Spanish government, having run completely out of money, secretly sold the Pyrenees to China and is now separated from France only by traffic cones.

In domestic news, the renegade Wisconsin Democratic state legislators are finally captured in a late-night raid by the elite Wisconsin State Parliamentarian SWAT team, which knocks down the legislators' hotel room door using a 200-pound, steel-reinforced edition of Robert's Rules of Order. The SWAT team then subdues the legislators using what one source describes as "a series of extremely aggressive cloture votes."

On the national political front, Newt Gingrich, responding to a groundswell of encouragement from the voices in his head, reveals that he is considering seeking the Republican presidential nomination. He quickly gains the support of the voter who had been leaning toward Ross Perot.

In tech news, Apple, with much fanfare, unveils the latest model of its hugely popular iPad tablet computer. The new model, called the iPad 2, is similar to the original iPad but—in yet another example of the brilliant customer-pleasing innovation that Apple has become famous for—has a "2" after it. Apple enthusiasts line up by the thousands to buy the new model, even as excitement builds for the next iPad, which, according to rumors swirling around an excited Apple fan community, will feature a "3."

The troubled musical *Spider-Man: Turn Off the Dark* suffers yet another setback when four orchestra musicians are killed by what producers describe as a "freak clarinet accident." Responding to the tragedy, President Obama delivers a nationally televised address, expressing his personal sympathy and noting that Republicans in Congress have repeatedly blocked the administration's proposed $37 billion Federal Department of Woodwind Safety, which would create literally dozens of jobs.

In sports, National Football League team owners lock out the players after negotiations break down over the issue of—in the words of NFL Commissioner Roger Goodell—"locker rooms being littered with reeking jockstraps the size of hammocks."

Speaking of negotiations, in . . .

APRIL

. . . a major crisis is barely avoided when Congress, after frantic negotiations, reaches a last-minute agreement on the federal budget, thereby averting a government shutdown that would have had a devastating effect on the ability of Congress to continue spending insanely more money than it actually has.

Meanwhile the economic outlook remains troubling, as Federal Reserve Chairman Ben Bernanke, in a rare news conference, consumes an entire bottle of gin. Things are even worse in Europe, where Moody's announces that it has officially downgraded Greece's credit rating from "poor" to "rat mucus" following the discovery that the Acropolis has been repossessed.

On the political front, the field of Republican contenders considering running for presidential nomination continues to expand with the addition of Ron Paul, Rick Santorum and Gary Johnson, all of whom pose a serious threat to gain traction with the Gingrich voter. Donald Trump reveals that he, too, is considering running for president, spurred by a sincere and passionate desire for attention. Trump makes headlines when he appears to side with the "birther" movement, questioning whether Barack Obama is in fact a natural-born US citizen. Under growing pressure to respond, the White House finally releases a certified copy of a long-form birth certificate that appears to prove conclusively that Donald Trump is Belgian. Also, biologically female.

Meanwhile the troubled musical *Spider-Man: Turn Off the Dark* suffers yet another setback when the actor playing Peter Parker, the young man who develops superpowers after being bitten by a radioactive spider, is bitten by an actual radioactive spider. Unfortunately, instead of superpowers, he develops a world-class case of diarrhea, which makes for what the show's producers describe as "some audience unpleasantness during the flying scenes."

But the month ends on a joyous note as millions of TV viewers around the world watch Prince William and Catherine Middleton, two young people widely hailed for their down-to-earth likability and common touch, get married in a wedding costing the equivalent of the gross domestic product of Somalia.

Speaking of joyous, in . . .

MAY

. . . the big story takes place in Abbottabad, Pakistan, where Osama bin Laden, enjoying a quiet evening chilling in his compound with his various wives and children and porn stash, receives an unexpected drop-in visit from a team of Navy SEALs. After due consideration of bin Laden's legal rights, the SEALs convert him into Purina brand Shark Chow; he is then laid to rest in a solemn ceremony concluding upon impact with the Indian Ocean at a terminal velocity of 125 miles per hour.

While Americans celebrate, the prime minister of Pakistan declares that his nation (a) is very upset about the raid and (b) had no earthly idea that the world's most wanted terrorist had been living in a major Pakistani city in a large high-walled compound with a mailbox that said BIN LADEN.

"As God is my witness," states the prime minister, "we thought that place was a Walmart."

In domestic affairs, Arnold Schwarzenegger reveals that he fathered the child of a member of his household staff; incredibly, he does not follow this up by announcing that he will seek the Republican presidential nomination. Herman Cain, however, does enter the GOP race, promising to reach out to as many . . . No, wait, let's rephrase that: Promising to take firm positions on . . . No, sorry, how about: Promising to appeal to a broad . . . Okay, never mind. Former Minnesota governor Tim Pawlenty also announces his candidacy, but winds up withdrawing from the race about midway through his announcement speech when he realizes that his staff has fallen asleep.

Meanwhile, followers of Christian radio broadcaster Harold Camping prepare for the Rapture, which Camping has prophesized will occur at 6 p.m. May 21. But the fateful hour comes and goes without incident, except in New York City, where, in yet another setback for the troubled production of *Spider-Man: Turn Off the Dark*, the entire cast is sucked through the theater ceiling, never to be seen again.

As the month draws to a close, a Twitter account belonging to Anthony Weiner—a feisty, ambitious Democratic up-and-comer who managed to get elected to Congress despite looking like a nocturnal rodent that somehow got a full-body wax and acquired a gym membership—tweets a link to a photograph of a pair of briefs containing what appears to be a congressional member rarin' to filibuster, if you catch my drift. This member immediately captivates the nation, although, surprisingly, President Obama fails to deliver a nationally televised address about it. The drama continues to build in . . .

JUNE

. . . when Weiner denies that he sent the photo, although he admits he cannot say "with certitude" whether the member is or is not his. He finally confesses to sending the photo, and, as the pressure on him to resign becomes overwhelming, he is left with no choice but to declare his intention to seek the Republican presidential nomination.

No, I'm kidding. Weiner resigns and takes a full-time position in the private sector admiring himself in the mirror.

Meanwhile the Republican field does in fact continue to grow as Michele Bachmann, Rick Santorum, Mitt Romney, the late Sonny Bono and somebody calling himself "Jon Huntsman" all enter the race, bringing the Republican contender total to roughly 125.

In Washington, Congress is under mounting pressure to do something about the pesky federal debt, which continues to mount as a result of the fact that the government continues to spend insanely more money than it actually has. Congress, after carefully weighing its three options—stop spending so much money; get some more money somehow; or implement some combination of options one and two—decides to go with option four: continue to do nothing while engaging in relentlessly hyperpartisan gasbaggery. Incredibly, this does not solve the debt problem.

The economic crisis is even worse in Europe, where the Greek government sends out an e-mail to everybody in its address book claiming it was mugged in London and needs its friends to wire it some emergency cash so it can get home. This prompts Moody's to change Greece's credit rating to, quote, "a word we can't say, but trust us, it's worse than rat mucus."

But perhaps the month's most disturbing development takes place in the Middle East when Iran, which is believed to be close to developing nuclear weapons, test-fires 14 missiles, including some capable of threatening US interests, as becomes clear when one of them plunges through the theater roof during a matinee performance of the troubled musical *Spider-Man: Turn Off the Dark*.

Speaking of disturbing, in . . .

JULY

. . . the eyeballs of the nation are riveted on Orlando, where Casey Anthony is on trial on charges of being an attractive young woman who is definitely guilty of murder, according to millions of deeply concerned individuals watching on TV. The trial becomes an obsession for hundreds of people who are not in any way connected to the victim, Caylee Anthony, but are so distraught over her death that they feel compelled to travel to Orlando and lurk around the courthouse expressing anguish, as opposed to doing something that might actually help one of the many living children who are at risk but who, unfortunately for them, are not featured on TV. In a shocking verdict, Anthony is acquitted of murder and set free, only to be attacked outside the courtroom and have large clumps of her hair yanked out by outraged prominent TV legal harpy Nancy Grace.

Speaking of drama: In Washington, as the deadline for raising the federal debt limit nears, Congress and the Obama administration work themselves into a frenzy trying to figure out what to do about the fact that the government is spending insanely more money than it actually has. After hours of intense negotiations, several walkouts, countless press releases and of course a nationally televised address by the president, the Democrats and the Republicans are finally able to announce, at the last possible minute, that they have hammered out a historic agreement under which the government will continue to spend insanely more money than it actually has while a very special congressional committee— A SUPER committee!—comes up with a plan, by a later date, that will solve this pesky problem once and for all. Everybody involved heaves a sigh of relief and basks in the feeling of satisfaction that comes from handling yet another crisis, Washington-style.

But things are not so rosy in Europe, where the debt crisis continues to worsen with the revelation that Greece has sold the naming rights to itself and will henceforth be officially known as the Republic of Burger King. In response, Moody's lowers Greece's bond rating to the point where it is no longer represented by words or letters, just a brownish stain on the rating document.

In England, the News Corp. media empire comes under scrutiny for alleged phone hacking when an investigation reveals that calls to Queen Elizabeth's private mobile number are being answered by Rupert Murdoch speaking in a high-pitched voice.

On a positive note, NFL owners and players are finally able to settle their dispute, thereby averting the very real danger that millions of fantasy football enthusiasts would be forced to develop lives.

Speaking of threats, in . . .

AUGUST

. . . Standard & Poor's makes good on its threat to downgrade the US credit rating, noting that the federal government, in making fiscal decisions, is exhibiting "the IQ of a turnip." Meanwhile Wall Street becomes increasingly jittery as investors react to Federal Reserve Board Chairman Bernanke's surprise announcement that his personal retirement portfolio consists entirely of assault rifles.

With the stock market in a steep nosedive, economic growth stagnant and unemployment relentlessly high, the White House, moving swiftly to prevent panic, reassures a worried nation that President Obama will once again be vacationing on Martha's Vineyard, where he will recharge his batteries in preparation for what White House press secretary Jay Carney promises will be "a real humdinger of a nationally televised address."

In political news, Texas Gov. Rick Perry announces that he will seek the Republican nomination with a goal of "restoring the fundamental American right to life, liberty and a third thing." But the early GOP leader is Michele Bachmann, who scores a decisive victory in the crucial Ames, Iowa, Straw Poll, garnering a total of 11 votes, narrowly edging out Ron Paul and a heifer named Widget. In what will become a pattern for GOP front-runners, Bachmann's candidacy immediately sinks like an anvil in a duck pond.

Abroad, a wave of riots sweeps across England as thousands of protesters take to the streets of London and other major cities to strike a blow against racism and social injustice by stealing consumer electronics and designer sneakers.

As the end of the month nears, a rare 5.8-magnitude earthquake, with its epicenter in Virginia, rattles the East Coast, shaking buildings from South Carolina to Maine but causing little damage, except in New York, where a theatrical set depicting a building topples over onto the cast of *Spider-Man: Turn Off the Dark*. The producers, determined to escape the bad luck that has haunted the current theater, move the entire production to New Jersey, which unfortunately turns out to be directly in the path of Hurricane Irene.

Speaking of disasters, in . . .

SEPTEMBER

. . . the worsening European debt crisis worsens still further when Italy, desperate for revenue, establishes a National Tip Jar. As markets plunge, the International Monetary Fund, seeking to prevent worldwide investor panic, announces that it will henceforth be supplementing its income by selling Herbalife.

In domestic news, President Obama returns from his Martha's Vineyard getaway refreshed and ready to tackle the job he was elected by the American people to do: seek reelection. Focusing on unemployment, the president delivers a nationally televised address laying out his plan for creating jobs, which consists of traveling around the nation tirelessly delivering job-creation addresses until it's time for another presidential getaway.

Meanwhile on the Republican side, Herman Cain surges to the top of the pile with his "9-9-9" plan, which combines the quality of being easy to remember with the quality of being something that nobody thinks will ever actually happen. Seeking to regain momentum, Rick Perry also comes out with a tax plan, but he can remember only the first two nines. Adding spice to the mix, Mitt Romney unexpectedly exhibits a lifelike facial expression but is quickly subdued by his advisers.

In what is seen as a sign of public disenchantment with the political process, voters in New York's Ninth Congressional District, choosing a replacement for disgraced Rep. Anthony Weiner, elect Anthony Soprano, despite the fact that he is a fictional character and not even Jewish.

Disenchantment is also apparent in New York's Zuccotti Park with the birth of the Occupy Wall Street movement, a gathering of individuals who seek to focus the nation's attention, laserlike, on the problems of income inequality, greed, corporations, student loans, hunger, mortgages, health care, deforestation, unemployment, political corruption, racism, gender discrimination, lack of tents, consumerism, global climate change, banks, poverty, people wanting to tell other people where and when they can and cannot drum, fossil fuels, showers, immigration, animal rights, Internet access, capitalism and many other issues that will not be resolved until people finally wake up, get off their butts and start seriously engaging in long-term urban camping.

As the month draws to a close, an anxious world looks to the skies, as a NASA satellite weighing more than six tons goes into an uncontrolled reentry, breaking into fiery pieces that hurtle toward Earth but fortunately come down at sea, where they do no damage other than sinking a passenger ship that had been chartered for a recuperation cruise for the surviving cast members of *Spider-Man: Turn Off the Dark*.

The downward trend continues in . . .

OCTOBER

. . . which sees yet another troubling development in the world economic crisis when an International Monetary Fund audit of the 27-nation European Union reveals that 11 of the nations are missing. "Also," states the audit report, "the nation claiming to be Slovakia is in fact Belize using a fake ID." Meanwhile in Greece, thousands of rioters take to the streets of Athens to protest a tough new government austerity program that would sharply reduce the per diem rioter allowance.

In Arab Spring developments, Libyan strongperson and lunatic Moammar Gaddafi steps down and receives an enthusiastic sendoff from his countrymen, who then carry him, amid much festivity, to his retirement freezer.

On the domestic protest front, Occupy Wall Street spreads to many more cities, its initially vague goals now replaced by a clear sense of purpose as occupiers focus on the single issue that is most important to the 99 percent: bathrooms. Some cities seek to shut down the protests, but the occupiers vow to remain until there is a reawakening of the national consciousness. Or, winter.

Attorney General Eric Holder announces that the FBI has uncovered a plot by Iran to commit acts of terror in the United States, including assassinating the Saudi ambassador, bombing the Israeli Embassy, and—most chillingly—providing funding for traveling productions of *Spider-Man: Turn Off the Dark.*

On the political front, Sarah Palin announces that she will not seek the Republican presidential nomination, noting that the GOP field is "already funny enough."

In technology news, Apple releases the iPhone that comes after the iPhone 4, which was rumored to be named the "5," but which instead is named—talk about innovation—the "4S." It is of course a huge hit with Apple fans, who, upon purchasing it, immediately form new lines outside Apple stores to await the next breakthrough iPhone, preliminarily rumored to be named the "4.7."

In sports, one of the most exciting World Series in history is won by some team other than the New York Yankees.

Humanity reaches a major milestone as the United Nations estimates that the population of the Earth has reached 7 billion people, every single one of whom sends you irritating e-mails inviting you to join something called LinkedIn.

The month ends on a tragic note when Kim Kardashian, who only 72 days earlier had a fairy-tale $10 million wedding to the love of her life, professional basketball player whatshisname, files for divorce, citing irreconcilable differences in height. "Also," she states in the filing documents, "I am a total slut."

Speaking of fairy tales, in . . .

NOVEMBER

. . . the congressional Supercommittee, after months of pondering what to do about the fact that the federal government is spending insanely more money than it actually has, announces that, in the true "can-do" bipartisan Washington spirit, it is giving up. This means the government will continue spending insanely more money than it actually has until 2013, at which time there are supposed to be automatic spending cuts, except Congress would never let that happen, and even if it did happen, the federal government would still be spending insanely more money than it actually has.

Undaunted, Democratic and Republican leaders move forward with the vital work of blaming each other. As it becomes clear that Congress will do nothing, a visibly frowning President Obama delivers a nationally televised address in which he vows to, quote, "continue reading whatever it says here on the teleprompter."

Speaking of the many benefits provided by the federal government: As Thanksgiving approaches, the Department of Homeland Security, having apparently handled all the other terrorist threats, issues a warning, including a scary video, on the dangers of: turkey fryers. I am not making this item up.

Abroad, the worsening Greek economic crisis forces Prime Minister George Papandreou to resign, leading to the formation of a new coalition government headed—in what some economists view as a troubling sign—by Bernie Madoff.

In domestic politics, the Republican Party is rocked by polls showing that 43 percent of all likely voters—nearly 55 million people—claim to have been sexually harassed by Herman Cain. With Rick Perry stumbling and Mitt Romney continuing to generate the excitement level of a dump fire, the GOP front-runner becomes none other than that fresh-faced, no-baggage, anti-establishment Washington outsider . . . Newt Gingrich!

Speaking of extraterrestrial phenomena: Astronomers watch closely as an asteroid 1,300 feet across hurtles extremely close to Earth. Incredibly—NASA calls it "a one in a billion chance"—the asteroid fails to hit anyone or anything connected with *Spider-Man: Turn Off the Dark*.

In business news, GM, responding to fears that the Chevy Volt might be prone to catch fire, issues a message to the six American consumers who have actually purchased Volts, assuring them that the car is "completely safe" and "should never be parked near buildings." American Airlines files for Chapter 11 bankruptcy, but assures its passengers that "normal flight operations will remain just as screwed up as before."

The month ends on a reflective note as Americans pause to observe Thanksgiving very much as the Pilgrims did in 1621, by pepper-spraying each other at malls.

Speaking of pausing, in . . .

DECEMBER

. . . Herman Cain announces that he is suspending his presidential campaign so he can go home and spend more time sleeping in his basement. This leaves the Republicans with essentially a two-man race between Gingrich and Romney, which means it's only a matter of time before we start hearing the name "Bob Dole."

The US Postal Service, facing huge losses, announces a cost-cutting plan under which it will start delivering first-class mail "to totally random addresses." The resulting savings will enable the USPS "to continue providing every American household with a minimum of 145 pounds of junk mail per week."

Meanwhile, in a vindication for the Department of Homeland Security, alert passengers aboard a United Airlines flight foil an apparent terrorist attack when they subdue a man attempting to deep-fry a turkey in economy class. After the plane makes an emergency landing, the man is removed by federal agents, who confirm that he was carrying not only cranberry sauce, but "enough stuffing to choke a buffalo."

Abroad, the member nations of the European Union, in a last-ditch effort to avoid an economic meltdown, announce that they are replacing the euro with a new unit of currency, the "pean," the exchange rate for which will be linked to the phases of the moon. The goal, according to the EU announcement, is "to cause American tourists to become even more confused than they already are." The plan starts paying dividends immediately as a pair of elderly ladies from Indianapolis purchase two croissants at a Paris cafe for six peans and wind up leaving the equivalent of a $3,780 tip.

The economic outlook is also brighter in Washington, where congressional leaders, still working night and day to find a solution to the problem of the federal government spending insanely more money than it actually has, announce that they have a bold new plan: They will form another committee. But this one will be even better than the Supercommittee, because it will be a SuperDUPERcommittee, and it will possess what House and Senate leaders describe, in a joint statement, as "magical powers."

So the nation is clearly in good hands, and as the troubled year finally comes to an end, throngs of New Year's revelers, hoping for better times to come, gather in Times Square to watch the descent of the famous illuminated ball, followed by the rise of what appears to be a mushroom cloud from the direction of *Spider-Man: Turn Off the Dark*.

But there's no need to worry: The president is planning a nationally televised address. So everything will be fine. Happy new year.

STUDY QUESTIONS for "A Year Ruined by Sleaze"

COMPREHENSION

1. What replaced journalism in 2011?
2. What made 2011 "truly awful"?
3. What is President Obama's "instinctive reaction" to nearly every event?
4. What did Nancy Pelosi hand over to John Boehner and why?
5. Who is Watson?
6. What did not happen on May 21, 2011?
7. What fell from the sky?

DEVELOPMENT AND ORGANIZATION

1. Which events and individuals are referenced in multiple months? What does their presence say about the year 2011?

2. What is Standard and Poor's? Moody's? The International Monetary Fund? A supercommittee? In your definitions for each, offer its real purpose or function, not Barry's exaggerated sense of it.
3. Discuss the real problems and issues behind each of the following:
   a. Greece's economic failure.
   b. *Spider-Man: Turn Off the Dark*'s production troubles.
   c. The NFL lockout.
4. Barry organizes this piece chronologically—month by month. What other method could he have chosen? (Look closely at the overall-for-paper organization patterns discussed in chapter one.) Would another method have been more effective? Why or why not?

STYLE AND TECHNIQUE

1. Barry uses exaggeration and hyperbole throughout his account of 2011. Find three examples of such usage.
2. Barry also uses repetition in this account. What words does he repeat? What is the effect of each of these repetitions?
3. In this piece, Barry appears to both manufacture quotes from sources and present them accurately. Identify three examples of each by writing out each quote and labeling them as fact or fiction.

TEN-MINUTE TOPICS

1. How have the events, people, and issues listed in this piece changed since its publication?
2. Pick any notable year from your own life and go through it event by event. What was the net effect of that year on your life?
3. Discuss the use of humor when reporting serious issues. How much humor is appropriate? You may draw on Dave Barry and J. Patrick Coolican as examples.

TEMPORARY INSANITY

BY KARENMARY PENN

With my teaching income gone for the summer, and my budgeting skills being what they are, I have been compelled to rejoin the ranks of those unsung heroes of the American workforce: the temps. You might think there would be some appeal in leapfrogging from company to company, job to job, meeting new people and learning new things. Indeed, temping might be interesting in the upper echelons of the Vegas business community, but for the $9 an hour wage apes, it ain't all bubbles and sunshine. Sometimes, temps have to rebel.

The word "temp," I have decided, is a euphemism for the person hired by a company to do a job the dimmest bulb on their payroll doesn't feel like doing. I had this epiphany while working in a mailroom, stuffing brochures into pre-addressed envelopes handed to me by telemarketers working the phones in the next room. Whenever some pigeon bit on their timeshare spiel, I assembled a packet of information to be mailed. To me, the pace of the mailroom was similar to that of a cricket match, but for my slightly cross-eyed "supervisor," Marsha, the slightest backlog of envelopes threw her into a sweaty tailspin of incompetence. During these times, I'd notice blood spattered on the postage meter, check my own fingertips, then tell Marsha to put on another Band-Aid. Paper cuts are the carpal tunnel syndrome of the mailroom.

Another temp gig had me dressing models for a small fashion show. My model was a beautiful young woman who, folded in half, could have easily fit into my right pant leg. She and several other models dressed, paraded coolly across a stage, and then sprinted into a staging area where temps waited, ready to tear one set of clothes off and put another one on, making sure the models all had the right shoes and bags for each outfit. I felt like we were playing with life-sized Barbies.

Another time I was called to fill in for an executive secretary. There were three secretaries for two executives. One woman was a former temp from my agency, who asked me about my other temp jobs, in the furtive manner of a convict who hasn't breathed free air in years. The other woman was pushing 50 but had a prissy, sycophantic quality—brought out by the presence of any man in a suit—which gave me chills. There was barely enough work for one person, let alone three, and the most stimulating thing I did for that corporation was buy gyros at lunchtime for the two executives. I stood in line at the Daily Chicken thinking, "I have an advanced degree. I shouldn't be doing fast food runs for money." (In petty defiance, I stuffed all of their change into the tip jar.)

Being a temp is like being a member of a lower work caste. It's as if, in a former life, you were a business owner who treated your employees so badly that the work gods saw to it that you were reborn as a Cubicle Untouchable. When you go to a new office as a temp, people oftentimes refuse to look at you. They won't learn your name. Perhaps these people got attached to another temp, who stepped on a land mine. Perhaps they have post temp stress disorder.

The only people who understand the horror of temporary work are other temps. Instant bonds develop between two temps working together, because usually the other temp is the only other person in the building aware of how truly weird a given company is. Occasionally, I get saddled with co-temps who are either crackling with industriousness or so openly slothful that I'm amazed that they feel comfortable accepting a paycheck. The latter type is more interesting to watch, because the lazy ones are most often "temp terrorists," who are not above clogging their PC's desktop folders with cyber porn, or tampering with the formulas in the electronic spreadsheets, or stealing anything not bolted down.

A temp I met, hired to personalize rejection letters for some 960 applicants who applied for a single job (which she later learned went to a VP's niece), deleted the hard drive on her computer after completing her assignment, then calmly had her timecard signed by a manager. I hate to admit it, but after my initial horror at hearing what she'd done, I admired her. So, when I got called back to stuff envelopes for another week with Marsha, I wrote "Help! I'm being held captive in the mailroom at —!" on some Post-its. I sealed them in envelopes along with glossy brochures, then ran everything through the postage meter, undetected. I was a temporary anarchist, and it felt good.

STUDY QUESTIONS for "Temporary Insanity"

COMPREHENSION

1. What is the thesis statement of this essay? If it is the last sentence of the first paragraph, then how can the writer justify taking so long to reach the point of rebellion, implied in the concluding paragraph?
2. What is the nature of Penn's audience? On the basis of her essay, make a profile of the audience that she seems to have in mind.
3. Why do temps have to rebel? What do you learn of this occupation from the examples?
4. Use a dictionary to look up the following words: *euphemism* (paragraph 2), *epiphany* (paragraph 2), *furtive* (paragraph 4), *slothful* (paragraph 6), and *anarchist* (paragraph 7).

DEVELOPMENT AND ORGANIZATION

1. How does Penn achieve a sense of coherence in this essay? Which of the following techniques does she use to enable the reader to see connections between paragraphs: repetition of key words and phrases, use of pronouns, use of transitional words and phrases?
2. How does the use of one or more of these techniques contribute to the essay's overall sense of unity?
3. Are the body paragraphs logically organized? You may notice that Penn devotes her first three body paragraphs to providing examples and the next two to articulating her thoughts and feelings about being a temp. Would the essay have been as effective had she first articulated what it means to be a temp and then provided the examples? Explain.

STYLE AND TECHNIQUE

1. What style does Penn adopt in writing this essay: formal, informal, or conversational? On your own, determine what kind of style each one of these terms designates and decide which one most accurately applies to "Temporary Insanity."
2. What is the tone of Penn's essay, that is, her attitude towards her subject matter? Is she serious, somber, comic, sarcastic, neutral, or something else? Find words and phrases that help establish tone.
3. Many English composition instructors will tell their students not to use the first-person pronoun *I* in an essay. Yet, as you can see, Penn makes frequent use of the first-person pronoun throughout this piece. When is it acceptable to use the first-person pronoun in your writing? Why is it a necessary selection in this essay? What would be a suitable alternative?
4. Comment upon the effectiveness of the introductory paragraph. How successful is Penn in engaging the reader's attention and creating the impression that her essay is worth reading? How has she accomplished this?
5. Comment upon the effectiveness of the concluding paragraph. Does this paragraph bring the essay to a satisfactory close? If so, how does it manage to do this?

TEN-MINUTE TOPICS

1. Use examples to illustrate the unpleasantness of doing a specific kind of work.
2. Have you ever broken a rule to establish your individuality? Describe the circumstances.
3. What, in your opinion, is rewarding work? Be specific.

BLACK MEN AND PUBLIC SPACE

BY BRENT STAPLES

My first victim was a woman—white, well dressed, probably in her late twenties. I came upon her late one evening on a deserted street in Hyde Park, a relatively affluent neighborhood in an otherwise mean, impoverished section of Chicago. As I swung onto the avenue behind her, there seemed to be a discreet, uninflammatory distance between us. Not so. She cast back a worried glance. To her, the youngish black man—a broad six feet two inches with a beard and billowing hair, both hands shoved into the pockets of a bulky military jacket—seemed menacingly close. After a few more quick glimpses, she picked up her pace and was soon running in earnest. Within seconds she disappeared into a cross street.

That was more than a decade ago. I was twenty-two years old, a graduate student newly arrived at the University of Chicago. It was in the echo of that terrified woman's footfalls that I first began to know the unwieldy inheritance I'd come into—the ability to alter public space in ugly ways. It was clear that she thought herself the quarry of a mugger, a rapist, or worse. Suffering a bout of insomnia, however, I was stalking sleep, not defenseless wayfarers. As a softy who is scarcely able to take a knife to a raw chicken—let alone hold one to a person's throat—I was surprised, embarrassed, and dismayed all at once. Her flight made me feel like an accomplice in tyranny. It also made it clear that I was indistinguishable from the muggers who occasionally seeped into the area from the surrounding ghetto. That first encounter, and those that followed, signified that a vast, unnerving gulf lay between nighttime pedestrians—particularly women—and me. And I soon gathered that being perceived as dangerous is a hazard in itself. I only needed to turn a corner into a dicey situation, or crowd some frightened, armed person in a foyer somewhere, or make an errant move after being pulled over by a policeman. Where fear and weapons meet—and they often do in urban America—there is always the possibility of death.

In that first year, my first away from my hometown, I was to become thoroughly familiar with the language of fear. At dark, shadowy intersections, I could cross in front of a car stopped at a traffic light and elicit the *thunk, thunk, thunk, thunk* of the driver—black, white, male, or female—hammering down the door locks. On less traveled streets after dark, I grew accustomed to but never comfortable with people crossing to the other side of the street rather than pass me. Then there were the standard unpleasantries with policemen, doormen, bouncers, cabdrivers, and others whose business it is to screen out troublesome individuals *before* there is any nastiness.

I moved to New York nearly two years ago and I have remained an avid night walker. In central Manhattan, the near-constant crowd cover minimizes tense one-on-one street encounters. Elsewhere—in SoHo, for example, where sidewalks are narrow and tightly spaced buildings shut out the sky—things can get very taut indeed.

After dark, on the warrenlike streets of Brooklyn where I live, I often see women who fear the worst from me. They seem to have set their faces on neutral, and with their purse straps strung across their chests bandoleer-style, they forge ahead as though bracing themselves against being tackled. I understand, of course, that the danger they perceive is not a hallucination. Women are particularly vulnerable to street violence, and young black males are drastically overrepresented among the perpetrators of that violence. Yet these truths are no solace against the kind of alienation that comes of being ever the suspect, a fearsome entity with whom pedestrians avoid making eye contact.

It is not altogether clear to me how I reached the ripe old age of twenty-two without being conscious of the lethality nighttime pedestrians attributed to me. Perhaps it was because in Chester, Pennsylvania, the small, angry industrial town where I came of age in the 1960s, I was scarcely noticeable against a backdrop of gang warfare, street knifings, and murders. I grew up one of the good boys, had perhaps a half-dozen fistfights. In retrospect, my shyness of combat has clear sources.

As a boy, I saw countless tough guys locked away; I have since buried several, too. They were babies, really—a teenage cousin, a brother of twenty-two, a childhood friend in his mid-twenties—all gone down in episodes of bravado played out in the streets. I came to doubt the virtues of intimidation early on. I chose, perhaps unconsciously, to remain a shadow—timid, but a survivor.

The fearsomeness mistakenly attributed to me in public places often has a perilous flavor. The most frightening of these confusions occurred in the late 1970s and early 1980s, when I worked as a journalist in Chicago. One day, rushing into the office of a magazine I was writing for with a deadline story in hand, I was mistaken for a burglar. The office manager called security and, with an ad hoc posse, pursued me through the labyrinthine halls, nearly to my editor's door. I had no way of proving who I was. I could only move briskly toward the company of someone who knew me.

Another time I was on assignment for a local paper and killing time before an interview. I entered a jewelry store on the city's affluent Near North Side. The proprietor excused herself and returned with an enormous red Doberman pinscher straining at the end of a leash. She stood, the dog extended toward me, silent to my questions, her eyes bulging nearly out of her head. I took a cursory look around, nodded, and bade her good night.

Relatively speaking, however, I never fared as badly as another black male journalist. He went to nearby Waukegan, Illinois, a couple of summers ago to work on a story about a murderer who was born there. Mistaking the reporter for the killer, police officers hauled him from his car at gunpoint and but for his press credentials would probably have tried to book him. Such episodes are not uncommon. Black men trade tales like this all the time.

Over the years, I learned to smother the rage I felt at so often being taken for a criminal. Not to do so would surely have led to madness. I now take precautions to make myself less threatening. I move about with care, particularly late in the evening. I give a wide berth to nervous people on subway platforms during the wee hours, particularly when I have exchanged business clothes for jeans. If I happen to be entering a building behind some people who appear skittish, I may walk by, letting them clear the lobby before I return, so as not to seem to be following them. I have been calm and extremely congenial on those rare occasions when I've been pulled over by the police.

And on late-evening constitutionals I employ what has proved to be an excellent tension-reducing measure: I whistle melodies from Beethoven and Vivaldi and the more popular classical composers. Even steely New Yorkers hunching toward nighttime destinations seem to relax, and occasionally they even join in the tune. Virtually everybody seems to sense that a mugger wouldn't be warbling bright, sunny selections from Vivaldi's *Four Seasons*. It is my equivalent of the cowbell that hikers wear when they know they are in bear country.

STUDY QUESTIONS for "Black Men and Public Space"

COMPREHENSION

1. What is the central idea expressed in the essay? Does Staples express this idea in a clearly stated thesis, or does he imply it? If the former, write out the thesis as it appears in the text, and identify by number the paragraph in which it appears; if the latter, summarize the central idea in fifteen words.
2. What is the source of the apprehension Staples creates in others? What is the most "frightening" of the "confusions" he has encountered? Who is affected most by the encounters: Staples, or the people he meets?
3. How does Staples deal with the treatment he has received from those who perceive him as a threat? What success has he had with his countermeasures?
4. What audience do you think Staples had in mind as he wrote this essay? What words and phrases support your conclusion?
5. What is Staples's purpose for writing this essay?

DEVELOPMENT AND ORGANIZATION

1. What kinds of examples does Staples use to develop and support his central idea? How well do his examples develop his central idea?
2. How closely does Staples's essay follow the method of organization set forth in the paradigm for the example essay? Does he use any other plan for organizing his examples in conjunction with (or instead of) the paradigm?
3. What effect does the essay's first sentence create? What is our impression of the author based upon that first sentence and upon the events he relates in the first paragraph? What is our impression of the author after reading the second paragraph?

STYLE AND TECHNIQUE

1. Staples uses the words *perpetrators, minimizes, proprietor, labyrinthine, ad hoc,* and *uninflammatory* in his essay. Look up these words in a standard desk dictionary and determine which languages these words came from. How do these words affect the tone and the style of the essay? Why does Staples use them? Do they affect our perception of him as the writer?

2. Count the number of sentences in the essay. Now count the number of paragraphs. What is the ratio of the two numbers? Compare the same ratio in a recent essay that you yourself have written. Are the numbers the same?

TEN-MINUTE TOPICS

1. Write about a time when you were perceived in a manner that was very different from how you perceive yourself. Use specific examples to show what treatment you received from others and what response(s) you made to that treatment.
2. Have you ever been perceived as threatening? Write about the circumstances surrounding that time.

HEY, RENO: CRY IT OUT WITH A TIRE FIRE AND A KEG

BY J. PATRICK COOLICAN

I feel a bit of guilt making fun of Reno, which has recently endured an air show crash and a bad fire.

But Reno gives me no choice, being so Reno and all.

In the new Muppet movie, Reno appears as a sad sack dump for Fozzie Bear's failed solo career. The TV show *Reno 911* has long mocked the city's police department, and to add insult to injury, the show isn't even filmed in Reno—where this week two bins of Toys for Tots were stolen from a Walmart only to be returned.

And then on *Saturday Night Live* last week, Weekend Update host Seth Meyers had this to say: "According to a new list, the least happiest city in America is St. Petersburg, Fla. But that's only because Reno, Nevada, finally killed itself." (Las Vegas is actually the suicide capital of America, but moving on . . .)

Well, Reno is fighting back!

Some genius in an editors' meeting of the *Reno Gazette-Journal* decided he'd had enough. (Somehow I know it was a he.) The paper asked its readers to contribute to an "open letter to Seth Meyers" that will be published Sunday from the people of Reno, a city known for the purity of its methamphetamine.

"It just needs to be funny," says the newspaper of Reno, where the five food groups are venison, fish, berries, beer and Marlboro Reds.

Here are some examples the editors provided:

- Seth Meyers: Making David Spade look macho since 2001.
- Hey Seth, washing Tina Fey's Mercedes is not the same as "I worked with Tina Fey at *SNL*."
- Wow, Seth Meyers made fun of Donald Trump. Even Donald Trump makes fun of Donald Trump.

The problem here is that these aren't funny. In fact, the whole flaw in this plan, as I noted on Twitter on Tuesday, is that Seth Meyers is funny. Whereas the people of Reno—where the dirt flooring of the homes serves for both sleeping and eating—and the editors of the *Reno Gazette-Journal* are not funny.

If they were funny, they wouldn't be living in Reno, where we all hope girls will be permitted to go to school someday. They'd be in New York City getting paid to be funny. (Same goes with me, s'pose.)

Then after they got famous they'd come back to Reno and be VIPs at the Reno Rodeo and be served Reno's famous delicacy—equine tartare.

No, see, there's nothing more Podunk, nothing more Reno, than shaking your fist at the big-city snob, who I assure you doesn't know or care.

Do you think it ever worked for Cleveland? Just ignore the guff and get busy bringing modern conveniences like electric light and running water—preferably fluoridated water—to the good people of Reno, whose outhouses are filling to capacity as we speak.

In fact, the editors might take note of Brian Duggan, the paper's city reporter, who takes a far more droll and knowing tone to the recent cultural embarrassments.

He suggests an excellent motto: At least we're not Detroit. (Reno may have to fight Vegas for that one.)

Or better yet, make lemonade out of lemons, or in terms Reno would understand, make "purdy" flowers out of manure. When Gene Weingarten of the *Washington Post* named Battle Mountain the "armpit of America," the rural Nevada town ran with it. In 2003, Old Spice sponsored the city's new event, the "Festival of the Pit."

Is there an equivalent for Reno and its marker as the "saddest city in America"? A "Festival of Sadness"? Perhaps a film festival celebrating—or mourning?—the movies of Ingmar Bergman? Sorry, I forgot who I was dealing with. Just get some kegs and start a tire fire and call it a party.

Finally, I'll stipulate that there's nothing more suspect and pathetic than the metro columnist for one failing city making fun of another (smaller) failing city. Reno readers: Let us have it. In the comments, tell us why you hate Vegas.

STUDY QUESTIONS for "Hey, Reno: Cry It Out with a Tire Fire and a Keg"

COMPREHENSION

1. List three concrete examples of Reno's negative image as presented in the media.
2. According to Coolican, what is the problem with the reader contributions to the *Gazette-Journal*'s open letter to Seth Myers?
3. What was the "Festival of the Pit"?

DEVELOPMENT AND ORGANIZATION

1. Identify three of Coolican's pop culture references. In using them, does he show any more sophistication than do the people of Reno?
2. What types of paragraph transitions does Coolican employ? Where might better transitions be needed?
3. What social issues are indirectly presented in this piece?

STYLE AND TECHNIQUE

1. Identify examples of Coolican's use of parenthetical statements (appearing in parentheses). Why does he use this technique? Is it effective?
2. Identify examples of Coolican's use of clichés. Do they work? If so, why?
3. What are some of the attributes Coolican gives to Reno? Why so many? What do they reveal?

TEN-MINUTE TOPICS

1. Defend Reno against Coolican's remarks, or defend another town that is commonly the butt of jokes.
2. Create your picture of a town lacking broad appeal. Use humor to make valid points. You may even use the prompt Coolican offers in his last sentence.
3. Can humor go too far with disparaging remarks? Identify a time when someone trying to be funny went too far with his or her comments.
4. Can humor cause individuals to look more closely at their own behavior or that of others? Give some examples.

CHAPTER FIVE
PROCESS

DEFINITION

In our society, in which the creation, processing, and distribution of information is a major activity, we are inundated with processes. Examples of *directional processes*, telling us how to do something, abound. Instructions on how to tune a car's engine, how to operate a home computer, how to operate an automatic bank teller, and how to repair an air conditioning system constitute directional processes. Similarly, self-help books flooding the market and telling us how to win through intimidation, how to improve our sex lives, how to make friends and influence people, and how to pray are all directional processes.

We can also recognize many examples of an *informational process*, which explains how something came about. Thus, accounts relating how the West was won, how the earth was created, how a baby develops in the womb and is born, how a bill is passed through Congress, how a drug like cocaine affects the body, and how the Saint Louis Cardinals won the 2011 World Series are informational processes. An informational process, therefore, may be historical, biological, chemical, social, and so on, and tells us not how to do something but how something came or comes about.

APPLICATION

To get a better grasp of this essay, let's take a look at a composition by student Michael Crowder. Titled "How to Apprehend a Shoplifter at Target," the essay's primary audience is the person who is looking at a career, however brief, as a store detective at Target. Since the members of this audience will represent a wide range and level of educational experiences, Crowder writes an essay that is very detailed and direct. In his introduction, for instance, note that his thesis—the last sentence—is very specific:

> Correctly apprehending a shoplifter at Target is very important for the store's profit margin. If done incorrectly, many problems may occur; for example, the shoplifter may get away with the stolen merchandise, charges could be filed against the store for harassing an innocent person, or the shoplifter could be released from charges because improper procedures were followed in apprehending him. To fulfill procedure requirements, you must have the following items ready and available: a security badge, a pair of handcuffs, a pen, an arrest form, and a filing cabinet. Even with these materials, a proper apprehension depends on your ability to follow instructions. Correctly apprehending a male shoplifter can be accomplished in five

steps: (1) locating a potential shoplifter, (2) following the subject without being noticed, (3) stopping the shoplifter, (4) completing the paperwork, and (5) notifying the police.

The thesis is factored—broken down into specific parts—and tells the reader that five body paragraphs are to follow, each to elaborate on one of the steps. Further, while Crowder doesn't seem to make the same effort to engage the reader's attention, that, say, Vickie Smith does in "The View from Here," we need to consider that he probably didn't have to. For one, the topic itself—apprehending a shoplifter—may generate sufficient interest by itself even among those who are not looking forward to working at Target. Too, Crowder seems to have a captive audience in mind; their interest in becoming a store detective at Target obligates them to read—or listen.

Beyond this, Crowder very clearly introduces his topic, in the very first sentence, so that we know immediately what the essay is going to be about. Finally, Crowder uses the introduction to establish an objective, even slightly authoritarian tone that he maintains throughout the essay; and that tone reinforces the role of teacher/store detective that Crowder adopts to address his audience. Note as well that the language of the introduction is a mixture of the general and the specific. The opening general statement, for instance, is followed by a second sentence providing specific examples.

The first body paragraph of Crowder's essay is as detailed and precise as the introduction:

> In the first and perhaps the hardest step, locate a potential shoplifter. To accomplish this successfully, go to the most probable area for shoplifting to occur. The electronics section is common because it has many expensive items that are small enough to conceal easily. Once you've established a vulnerable area, look for people who seem nervous and often look around as if they have something to hide. Also, keep an eye on persons who look at one product for a long time and continually pick it up and set it back down when someone walks by. While observing the suspect, stay out of his sight. He may see you and leave. Although his departure from the store may stop him from shoplifting now, he will probably come back later to commit the crime. Use shelves and large objects to keep out of sight. Only after you see that the shoplifter has concealed the merchandise should you begin the next step.

This is a coherent paragraph. Crowder uses not only transitional expressions such as *first*, *also*, and *although* to establish connections between sentences; he as well uses pronouns such as *this*, *it*, *his*, and *he*. Reinforcing the paragraph's coherence is the logical arrangement of details: sentences break this first step in apprehending a shoplifter into a kind of mini-process following a chronological order. Finally, to enable his reader to visualize this procedure, Crowder refers to the electronics section as an example of where in the store one might find a shoplifter; and he briefly describes the potential shoplifter as one who will "look at one product for a long time and continually pick it up and set it back down when someone walks by."

The four body paragraphs that follow are developed in the same fashion.

The paragraph concluding this essay is very brief, perhaps a bit too much so. But it does maintain the objective, almost authoritarian tone. Further, as it refers back to the thesis, it does leave the reader with the impression that the essay is now complete:

> It is important that all of the steps are followed strictly. Any deviations from them can result in unnecessary difficulties. However, following them can make you a successful Target security officer. If you are successful, you can expect to apprehend about one shoplifter each day you work.

Of course, given his immediate audience and the situation that prompted the writing of the essay, Crowder may not need to do anything in his conclusion beyond sounding a warning and emphasizing the effectiveness of following the process he has just explained. Keep in mind that the style and content of any essay are largely shaped by the audience, or the writer's awareness of the audience.

Not all process essays need be as objective as Crowder's. Consider, for instance, Nikka Jolly's essay "The Lock," an informational process written to a much more general audience. In this piece, Jolly uses narration and description to allow the reader to see the process: how she broke out of a Mexican jail.

> Each morning, a guard slid a bowl of greasy soup and a dirty spoon under the bars and into my cell. One day, I saw the image of my friend's lock picking tools in the handle of the dirty spoon. Using the rough concrete floor of the cell as a grinding stone, I filed the metal handle of the spoon into the tools that I needed. I could attempt to use these tools only under the cover of darkness.
>
> I became a creature of the night. A blind woman learning Braille, I explored the pegs within the tiny space with my metal probe. At the end of the week, I knew that my master lock had five pegs within its bowels. Each peg demanded a gentle touch to caress it into the proper position. Yet this was not enough. The lock required me to become the perfect lover. The tool in one hand must tease the pegs into place while the tool in the other hand must hold the exact pressure necessary to entice the pegs to stay put long enough for the lock to open up.
>
> Night after night, I struggled, often resorting first to abusive force in my frustration, finally to lack of attention due to fatigue. Over the weeks as my anguish became almost unbearable, my fingers sometimes bled, and my tears seemed to wash the surface of the lock clean. On the thirty-eighth night, I painstakingly bent the hooked end of my probe and kissed the lock for luck. Slipping the tools into place, I counted.

One long peg in place and holding—number two peg, short, hard to find—okay—third peg, a delightful child willing to obey—fourth and fifth pegs, so identical in length, so hard to maneuver. Then, at that moment, without a sound the lock opened.

A well-written piece, Jolly's process-narrative incorporates a number of descriptive details—"bowl of greasy soup," "dirty spoon," and "concrete floor," to name a few—that enable the reader not only to see her working to open the lock but to feel the anguish behind her attempts to gain her freedom.

There is a final point to keep in mind. When writing a process essay, the student should remember that effectively written processes often make use of transitional devices that emphasize the relationship between two sentences or even two paragraphs. As pointed out in the discussion of Crowder's essay, transitional devices include repeating pronouns that refer back to nouns, repeating key words and phrases (such as "apprehending a shoplifter"), and making selective use of transitional words and phrases such as *first, next, then, however, in addition to, consequently, finally,* and so on. In the following excerpt from her essay "How to Make a Terrarium," Nancy Bubel uses transitions to indicate direction and progression:

> Begin by putting down a base of several layers as follows, remembering that each layer serves a purpose. First, put down a mat of moss to absorb moisture and form an attractive lining. Then pour sand or fine gravel over the moss to promote proper drainage and prevent water logging. Next, scatter a handful of charcoal pieces over the gravel to prevent the soil from souring. . . .

As we can see, the writer uses the transitions *first, then,* and *next* to point out the sequential relationships joining the sentences of this brief paragraph.

PARADIGM

When you write your process essay, keep in mind the following paradigm. Like the one offered at the end of the explanation of the examples essay, this paradigm is offered only as a guide. A good introduction (or conclusion) may consist of more than one paragraph, just as body paragraphs may number more than three.

Introduction
1. **Engage the reader's interest.**
2. **Introduce topic.**
3. **Establish tone.**
4. **Present thesis.**

First Body Paragraph
    1. Use topic sentence to state first step or phase.
    2. Add detail to support opening statement.

Second Body Paragraph
    1. Use topic sentence to state second step or phase.
    2. Add supporting detail.

Third Body Paragraph
    1. Use topic sentence to state third step or phase.
    2. Add supporting detail.

Fourth Body Paragraph
    1. Topic sentence . . .
    2. Supporting detail . . .

Conclusion (options)
    1. Summarize main points and restate thesis.
    2. Offer a final image, message, or judgment.
    3. Take a broader view.
    4. End with quotation.
    5. End with striking statistic.
    6. Challenge the reader.
    7. Something else.

SUMMARY

When seeking a topic for your process essay, remember that there are two kinds of processes from which to choose: the directional, telling the reader how to do something; and the informational, telling the reader how something came about. Also, remember to include all the essential stages of the process about which you are writing. Finally, choose a topic with which you are thoroughly familiar, one into which you can incorporate your own perceptions, impressions, and experience.

MY FIRST CONK

BY MALCOLM X

Shorty soon decided that my hair was finally long enough to be conked. He had promised to school me in how to beat the barbershops' three- and four-dollar price by making up congolene, and then conking ourselves.

I took the little list of ingredients he had printed out for me, and went to a grocery store, where I got a can of Red Devil lye, two eggs, and two medium-sized white potatoes. Then at a drugstore near the poolroom, I asked for a large jar of Vaseline, a large bar of soap, a large-toothed comb and a fine-toothed comb, one of those rubber hoses with a metal spray-head, a rubber apron, and a pair of gloves.

"Going to lay on that first conk?" the drugstore man asked me. I proudly told him, grinning, "Right!"

Shorty paid six dollars a week for a room in his cousin's shabby apartment. His cousin wasn't at home. "It's like the pad's mine, he spends so much time with his woman," Shorty said. "Now, you watch me—"

He peeled the potatoes and thin-sliced them into a quart-sized Mason fruit jar, then started stirring them with a wooden spoon as he gradually poured in a little over half the can of lye. "Never use a metal spoon; the lye will turn it black," he told me.

A jellylike, starchy-looking glop resulted from the lye and potatoes, and Shorty broke in the two eggs, stirring real fast—his own conk and dark face bent down close. The congolene turned pale-yellowish. "Feel the jar," Shorty said. I cupped my hand against the outside, and snatched it away. "Damn right, it's hot, that's the lye," he said. "So you know it's going to burn when I comb it in—it burns bad. But the longer you can stand it, the straighter the hair."

He made me sit down, and he tied the string of the new rubber apron tightly around my neck, and combed up my bush of hair. Then, from the big Vaseline jar, he took a handful and massaged it hard all through my hair and into the scalp. He also thickly Vaselined my neck, ears and forehead. "When I get to washing out your head, be sure to tell me anywhere you feel any little stinging," Shorty warned me, washing his hands, then pulling on the rubber gloves, and tying on his own rubber apron. "You always got to remember that any congolene left in burns a sore into your head."

The congolene just felt warm when Shorty started combing it in. But then my head caught fire.

I gritted my teeth and tried to pull the sides of the kitchen table together. The comb felt as if it was raking my skin off.

My eyes watered, my nose was running. I couldn't stand it any longer; I bolted to the washbasin. I was cursing Shorty with every name I could think of when he got the spray going and started soap lathering my head.

He lathered and spray-rinsed, lathered and spray-rinsed, maybe ten or twelve times, each time gradually closing the hot-water faucet, until the rinse was cold, and that helped some.

"You feel any stinging spots?"

"No," I managed to say. My knees were trembling.

"Sit back down, then. I think we got it all out okay."

The flame came back as Shorty, with a thick towel, started drying my head, rubbing hard. "*Easy, man, easy!*" I kept shouting.

"The first time's always worst. You get used to it better before long. You took it real good, homeboy. You got a good conk."

When Shorty let me stand up and see in the mirror, my hair hung down in limp, damp strings. My scalp still flamed, but not as badly; I could bear it. He draped the towel around my shoulders, over my rubber apron, and began again Vaselining my hair.

I could feel him combing, straight back, first the big comb, then the fine-tooth one.

Then, he was using a razor, very delicately, on the back of my neck. Then, finally, shaping the sideburns.

My first view in the mirror blotted out the hurting. I'd seen some pretty conks, but when it's the first time, on your *own* head, the transformation, after the lifetime of kinks, is staggering.

The mirror reflected Shorty behind me. We both were grinning and sweating. And on top of my head was this thick, smooth sheen of shining red hair—real red—as straight as any white man's.

How ridiculous I was! Stupid enough to stand there simply lost in admiration of my hair now looking "white," reflected in the mirror in Shorty's room. I vowed that I'd never again be without a conk, and I never was for many years.

This was my first really big step toward self-degradation: when I endured all of that pain, literally burning my flesh to have it look like a white man's hair. I had joined that multitude of Negro men and women in America who are brainwashed into believing that the black people are "inferior"—and white people "superior"—that they will even violate and mutilate their God-created bodies to try to look "pretty" by white standards.

Look around today, in every small town and big city, from two-bit catfish and soda-pop joints into the "integrated" lobby of the Waldorf-Astoria, and you'll see conks on black men. And you'll see black women wearing these green and pink and purple and red and platinum-blond wigs. They're all more ridiculous than a slapstick comedy. It makes you wonder if the Negro has completely lost his sense of identity, lost touch with himself.

You'll see the conk worn by many, many so-called "upper class" Negroes, and, as much as I hate to say it about them, on all too many Negro entertainers. One of the reasons that I've especially admired some of them, like Lionel Hampton and Sidney Poitier, among others, is that they have kept their natural hair and fought to the top. I admire any Negro man who has never had himself conked, or who has had the sense to get rid of it—as I finally did.

I don't know which kind of self-defacing conk is the greater shame—the one you'll see on the heads of the black so-called "middle class" and "upper class," who ought to know better, or the one you'll see on the heads of the poorest, most downtrodden, ignorant black men. I mean the legal-minimum-wage ghetto-dwelling kind of Negro, as I was when I got my first one. It's generally among these poor fools that you'll see a black kerchief over the man's head, like Aunt Jemima; he's trying to make his conk last longer, between trips to the barbershop. Only for special occasions is this kerchief-protected conk exposed—to show off how "sharp" and "hip" its owner is. The ironic thing is that I have never heard any woman, white or black, express any admiration for a conk. Of course, any white woman with a black man isn't thinking about his hair. But I don't see how on earth a black woman with any race pride could walk down the street with any black man wearing a conk—the emblem of his shame that he is black.

To my own shame, when I say all of this, I'm talking first of all about myself—because you can't show me any Negro who ever conked more faithfully than I did. I'm speaking from personal experience when I say of any black man who conks today, or any white-wigged black woman, that if they gave the brains in their heads just half as much attention as they do their hair, they would be a thousand times better off.

STUDY QUESTIONS for "My First Conk"

COMPREHENSION

1. What is the thesis of this essay? If it is explicit, write it out word for word and give the number of the paragraph in which it appears. If it is implicit, summarize it in about twenty-five words.
2. Why did African Americans conk their hair? Why did the writer begin to conk his? What is the writer's opinion of conks at the end of the essay?
3. What does the conk say about the status of African Americans at the time that Malcolm X wrote this essay?

DEVELOPMENT AND ORGANIZATION

1. Malcolm X takes us step by step through the process of conking his hair. What are the steps? Is this a directional or an informational process? How can you tell?
2. In what way does Malcolm X make his transition from the description of the conk to his commentary on conking itself? When does the transition take place?
3. What is the equivalent of the conk for African American women, as described by Malcolm X? What is his opinion of what these women do? What do they look like? What does Malcolm X say these men and women should spend their time doing?

STYLE AND TECHNIQUE

1. Look closely at paragraphs 1-21 and then paragraphs 22-27. In which group do you see longer paragraphs? In which do you see shorter? Why do you see longer paragraphs in the one group and shorter ones in the other?
2. Malcolm X uses the word *shame* in the last two paragraphs. Why? What is your opinion of him when he uses the word *shame* to describe himself?

3. What audience is Malcolm X attempting to reach with this essay? In what ways does he do so? How effective are his techniques? In other words, if his target audience read this essay, would they be convinced of the validity of his point of view?

Ten-Minute Topics

1. Write about something you did to fit into a group. What did you do? Were you forced to do it, or did you do it voluntarily? Did anyone help you? What was the outcome? Did completing this action give you what you had expected?
2. Describe something you did when you were younger—some habit or practice—that you no longer do now. Why did you do it when you were younger? Why did you stop? In what way did stopping change your view about yourself?
3. Describe a process that you go through to change your appearance. Why do you do it? Is it a necessary process? How do you feel about yourself after you finish with the process?

THE SPIDER AND THE WASP

BY ALEXANDER PETRUNKEVITCH

To hold its own in the struggle for existence, every species of animal must have a regular source of food, and if it happens to live on other animals, its survival may be very delicately balanced. The hunter cannot exist without the hunted; if the latter should perish from the earth, the former would, too. When the hunted also prey on some of the hunters, the matter may become complicated.

This is nowhere better illustrated than in the insect world. Think of the complexity of a situation such as the following: There is a certain wasp, *Pimpla inquisitor*, whose larvae feed on the larvae of the tussock moth. *Pimpla* larvae in turn serve as food for the larvae of a second wasp, and the latter in their turn nourish still a third wasp. What subtle balance between fertility and mortality must exist in the case of each of these four species to prevent the extinction of all of them! An excess of mortality over fertility in a single member of the group would ultimately wipe out all four.

This is not a unique case. The two great orders of insects, Hymenoptera and Diptera, are full of such examples of interrelationship. And the spiders (which are not insects but members of a separate order of arthropods) also are killers and victims of insects.

The picture is complicated by the fact that those species which are carnivorous in the larval stage have to be provided with animal food by a vegetarian mother. The survival of the young depends on the mother's correct choice of food which she does not eat herself.

In the feeding and safeguarding of their progeny the insects and spiders exhibit some interesting analogies to reasoning and some crass examples of blind instinct. The case I propose to describe here is that of the tarantula spiders and their archenemy, the digger wasps of the genus *Pepsis*. It is a classic example of what looks like intelligence pitted against instinct—a strange situation in which the victim, though fully able to defend itself, submits unwittingly to its destruction.

Most tarantulas live in the tropics, but several species occur in the temperate zone and a few are common in the southern US. Some varieties are large and have powerful fangs with which they can inflict a deep wound. These formidable-looking spiders do not, however, attack man; you can hold one in your hand, if you are gentle, without being bitten. Their bite is dangerous only to insects and small mammals such as mice; for a man it is no worse than a hornet's sting.

Tarantulas customarily live in deep cylindrical burrows, from which they emerge at dusk and into which they retire at dawn. Mature males wander about after dark in search of females and occasionally stray into houses. After mating, the male dies in a few weeks, but a female lives much longer and can mate several years in succession. In a Paris museum is a tropical specimen which is said to have been living in captivity for 25 years.

A fertilized female tarantula lays from 200 to 400 eggs at a time; thus it is possible for a single tarantula to produce several thousand young. She takes no care of them beyond weaving a cocoon of silk to enclose the eggs. After they hatch, the young walk away, find convenient places in which to dig their burrows, and spend the rest of their lives in solitude. Tarantulas feed mostly on insects and millipedes. Once their appetite is appeased, they digest the food for several days before eating again. Their sight is poor, being limited to sensing a change in the intensity of light and to the perception of moving objects. They apparently have little or no sense of hearing, for a hungry tarantula will pay no attention to a loudly chirping cricket placed in its cage unless the insect happens to touch one of its legs.

But all spiders, and especially hairy ones, have an extremely delicate sense of touch. Laboratory experiments prove that tarantulas can distinguish three types of touch: pressure against the body wall, stroking of the body hair, and riffling of certain very fine hairs on the leg called trichobothria. Pressure against the body, by a finger or the end of a pencil, causes the tarantula to move off slowly for a short distance. The touch excites no defensive response unless the approach is from above, where the spider can see the motion, in which case it rises on its hind legs, lifts its front legs, opens its fangs, and holds this threatening posture as long as the object continues to move. When the motion stops, the spider drops back to the ground, remains quiet for a few seconds, and then moves slowly away.

The entire body of a tarantula, especially its legs, is thickly clothed with hair. Some of it is short and woolly, some long and stiff. Touching this body hair produces one of two distinct reactions. When the spider is hungry, it responds with an immediate and swift attack. At the touch of a cricket's antennae the tarantula seizes the insect so swiftly that a motion picture taken at the rate of 64 frames per second shows only the result, not the process of capture. But when the spider is not hungry, the stimulation of its hair merely causes it to shake the touched limb. An insect can walk under its hairy belly unharmed.

The trichobothria, very fine hairs growing from disklike membranes of the legs, were once thought to be the spider's hearing organs, but we now know that they have nothing to do with sound. They are sensitive only to air movement. A light breeze makes them vibrate slowly without disturbing the common hair. When one blows gently on the trichobothria, the tarantula reacts with a quick jerk of its four front legs. If the front and hind legs are stimulated at the same time, the spider makes a sudden jump. The reaction is quite independent of the state of its appetite.

These three tactile responses—to pressure on the body wall, to moving of the common hair, and to flexing of the trichobothria—are so different from one another that there is no possibility of confusing them. They serve the tarantula adequately for most of its needs and enable it to avoid most annoyances and dangers. But they fail the spider completely when it meets its deadly enemy, the digger wasp *Pepsis*.

These solitary wasps are beautiful and formidable creatures. Most species are either a deep shiny blue all over, or deep blue with rusty wings. The largest have a wingspan of about four inches. They live on nectar. When excited, they give off a pungent odor—a warning that they are ready to attack. The sting is much worse than that of a bee or common wasp, and the pain and swelling last longer. In the adult stage the wasp lives only a few months. The female produces but a few eggs, one at a time in intervals of two or three days. For each egg the mother must provide one adult tarantula, alive but paralyzed. The tarantula must be of the correct species to nourish the larva. The mother wasp attaches the egg to the paralyzed spider's abdomen. Upon hatching from the egg, the larva is many hundreds of times smaller than its living but helpless victim. It eats no other food and drinks no water. By the time it has finished the single gargantuan meal and become ready for wasphood, nothing remains of the tarantula but its indigestible chitinous skeleton.

The mother wasp goes tarantula-hunting when the egg in her ovary is almost ready to be laid. Flying low over the ground late on a sunny afternoon, the wasp looks for its victim or for the mouth of a tarantula burrow, a round hole edged by a bit of silk. The sex of the spider makes no difference, but the mother is highly discriminating as to species. Each species of *Pepsis* requires a certain species of tarantula, and the wasp will not attack the wrong species. In a cage with a tarantula which is not its normal prey, the wasp avoids the spider, and is usually killed by it in the night.

Yet when a wasp finds the correct species, it is the other way about. To identify the species the wasp apparently must explore the spider with her antennae. The tarantula shows an amazing tolerance to this exploration. The wasp crawls under it and walks over it without evoking any hostile response. The molestation is so great and so persistent that the tarantula often rises on all eight legs, as if it were on stilts. It may stand this way for several minutes. Meanwhile the wasp, having satisfied itself that the victim is of the right species, moves off a few inches to dig the spider's grave. Working vigorously with legs and jaws, it excavates a hole 8 to 10 inches deep with a diameter slightly larger than the spider's girth. Now and again the wasp pops out of the hole to make sure that the spider is still there.

When the grave is finished, the wasp returns to the tarantula to complete her ghastly enterprise. First she feels it all over once more with her antennae. Then her behavior becomes more aggressive. She bends her abdomen, protruding her sting, and searches for the soft membrane at the point where the spider's leg joins its body—the only spot where she can penetrate the horny skeleton. From time to time, as the exasperated spider slowly shifts around, the wasp turns on her back and slides along with the aid of her wings, trying to get under the tarantula for a shot at the vital spot. During all this maneuvering, which can last for several minutes, the tarantula makes no move to save itself. Finally the wasp corners it against some obstruction and grasps one of its legs in her powerful jaws. Now at last the harassed spider tries a desperate but vain defense. The two contestants roll over and over on the ground. It is a terrifying sight and the outcome is always the same. The wasp finally manages to thrust her sting into the soft spot and holds it there for a few seconds while she pumps in the poison. Almost immediately the tarantula falls paralyzed on its back. Its legs stop twitching; its heart stops beating. Yet it is not dead, as is shown by the fact that if taken from the wasp it can be restored to some sensitivity by being kept in a moist chamber for several months.

After paralyzing the tarantula, the wasp cleans herself by dragging her body along the ground and rubbing her feet, sucks the drop of blood oozing from the wound of the spider's abdomen, then grabs a leg of the flabby, helpless animal in her jaws and drags it down to the bottom of the grave. She stays there for many minutes, sometimes for several hours, and what she does all that time in the dark we do not know. Eventually she lays her egg and attaches it to the side of the spider's abdomen with a sticky secretion. Then she emerges, fills the grave with soil carried bit by bit in her jaws, and finally tramples the ground all around to hide any trace of the grave from prowlers. Then she flies away, leaving her descendant safely started in life.

In all this the behavior of the wasp evidently is qualitatively different from that of the spider. The wasp acts like an intelligent animal. This is not to say that instinct plays no part or that she reasons as man does. But her actions are to the point; they are not automatic and can be modified to fit the situation. We do not know for certain how she identifies the tarantula—probably it is by some olfactory or chemo-tactile sense—but she does it purposefully and does not blindly tackle a wrong species.

On the other hand, the tarantula's behavior shows only confusion. Evidently the wasp's pawing gives it no pleasure, for it tries to move away. That the wasp is not simulating sexual stimulation is certain, because male and female tarantulas react in the same way to its advances. That the spider is not anesthetized by some odorless secretion is easily shown by blowing lightly at the tarantula and making it jump suddenly. What, then, makes the tarantula behave as stupidly as it does?

No clear, simple answer is available. Possibly the stimulation by the wasp's antennae is masked by a heavier pressure on the spider's body, so that it reacts as when prodded by a pencil. But the explanation may be much more complex. Initiative in attack is not in the nature of tarantulas; most species fight only when cornered so that escape is impossible. Their inherited patterns of behavior apparently prompt them to avoid problems rather than attack them. For example, spiders always weave their webs in three dimensions, and when a spider finds that there is insufficient space to attach certain threads in the third dimension, it leaves the place and seeks another, instead of finishing the web in a single plane. This urge to escape seems to arise under all circumstances, in all phases of life, and to take the place of reasoning. For a spider to change the pattern of its web is as impossible as for an inexperienced man to build a bridge across a chasm obstructing his way.

In a way the instinctive urge to escape is not only easier but more efficient than reasoning. The tarantula does exactly what is most efficient in all cases except in an encounter with a ruthless and determined attacker dependent for the existence of her own species on killing as many tarantulas as she can lay eggs. Perhaps in this case the spider follows its usual pattern of trying to escape, instead of seizing and killing the wasp, because it is not aware of its danger. In any case, the survival of the tarantula species as a whole is protected by the fact that the spider is much more fertile than the wasp.

STUDY QUESTIONS for "The Spider and the Wasp"

COMPREHENSION

1. What kind of process is illustrated by Petrunkevitch's essay: directional or informational?
2. What general idea—or thesis—does the author wish to illustrate by describing this process

involving the spider and the wasp? Where is this main idea expressed?

3. Who is Petrunkevitch's intended audience? Fellow scientists and university professors? The average person? How do you know?
4. Why did Petrunkevitch write this essay? What was he trying to accomplish?
5. Did you enjoy reading this essay? Why or why not?

DEVELOPMENT AND ORGANIZATION

1. What are the various steps or states involved in the process?
2. Discuss the function of paragraphs two through fourteen in relation to the actual process that follows. What do these paragraphs contribute to the essay? Why are they necessary?
3. Where does the writer make use of descriptive detail? What are some of the more striking descriptive details that Petrunkevitch uses? What is gained by using descriptive details in this essay? Are they necessary?
4. Could the process that Petrunkevitch relates also be considered a narration? What elements does this selection contain that allow us to associate it with narrative writing?
5. What other patterns of developing an essay does the writer make use of? Where, for instance, does the writer make use of comparison and contrast? Where does he include a definition? Does Petrunkevitch use any other patterns?
6. Does the use of these different patterns interfere with the actual process that Petrunkevitch relates in the second half of the essay? What allows for the working together of sections containing comparison and contrast and definition with a process which makes use of narration and description? In other words, what holds together these different patterns of writing?
7. Identify the various transitions or linking devices that Petrunkevitch uses to join his paragraphs and make the essay coherent.

STYLE AND TECHNIQUE

1. What is the tone that Petrunkevitch adopts in writing this essay? That is, what is his attitude towards his subject matter? How do you know? Find passages to support your answer.
2. Is this essay written in a subjective/impressionistic style or in an objective style? Does the essay represent a combination of both styles? Explain your answer.

TEN-MINUTE TOPICS

1. Describe a process from the natural world that you find fascinating. Consider, for example, the process by which dogs get acquainted, or by which cats stalk a mouse. Describe it as an outsider would—even, perhaps, as an alien from another galaxy, if you enjoy science fiction.

2. Describe a process from the realm of human interaction. Consider, for example, the process by which small children get ready for school, or the one by which you got accustomed to a new job. Again, describe it as an outsider would.

CHAPTER ONE FROM *ALL CREATURES GREAT AND SMALL*

BY JAMES HERRIOT

They didn't say anything about this in the books, I thought, as the snow blew in through the gaping doorway and settled on my naked back.

I lay face down on the cobbled floor in a pool of nameless muck, my arm deep inside the straining cow, my feet scrabbling for a toe hold between the stones. I was stripped to the waist and the snow mingled with the dirt and the dried blood on my body. I could see nothing outside the circle of flickering light thrown by the smoky oil lamp which the farmer held over me.

No, there wasn't a word in the books about searching for your ropes and instruments in the shadows; about trying to keep clean in a half bucket of tepid water; about the cobbles digging into your chest. Nor about the slow numbing of the arms, the creeping paralysis of the muscles as the fingers tried to work against the cow's powerful expulsive efforts.

There was no mention anywhere of the gradual exhaustion, the feeling of futility and the little far-off voice of panic.

My mind went back to that picture in the obstetrics book. A cow standing in the middle of a gleaming floor while a sleek veterinary surgeon in a spotless parturition overall inserted his arm to a polite distance. He was relaxed and smiling, the farmer and his helpers were smiling, even the cow was smiling. There was no dirt or blood or sweat anywhere.

That man in the picture had just finished an excellent lunch and had moved next door to do a bit of calving just for the sheer pleasure of it, as a kind of dessert. He hadn't crawled shivering from his bed at two o'clock in the morning and bumped over twelve miles of frozen snow, staring sleepily ahead till the lonely farm showed in the headlights. He hadn't climbed half a mile of white fell-side to the doorless barn where his patient lay.

I tried to wriggle my way an extra inch inside the cow. The calf's head was back and I was painfully pushing a thin, looped rope towards its lower jaw with my finger tips. All the time my arm was being squeezed between the calf and the bony pelvis. With every straining effort from the cow the pressure became almost unbearable, then she would relax and I would push the rope another inch. I wondered how long I would be able to keep this up. If I didn't snare that jaw soon I would never get the calf away. I groaned, set my teeth and reached forward again.

Another little flurry of snow blew in and I could almost hear the flakes sizzling on my sweating back. There was sweat on my forehead too, and it trickled into my eyes as I pushed.

There is always a time at a bad calving when you begin to wonder if you will ever win the battle. I had reached this stage.

Little speeches began to flit through my brain. "Perhaps it would be better to slaughter this cow. Her pelvis is so small and narrow that I can't see a calf coming through," or "She's a good fat animal and really of the beef type, so don't you think it would pay you better to get the butcher?" or perhaps "This is a very bad presentation. In a roomy cow it would be simple enough to bring the head round but in this case it is just about impossible."

Of course, I could have delivered the calf by embryotomy—by passing a wire over the neck and sawing off the head. So many of these occasions ended with the floor strewn with heads, legs, heaps of intestines. There were thick textbooks devoted to the countless ways you could cut up a calf.

But none of it was any good here, because this calf was alive. At my furthest stretch I had got my finger as far as the commissure of the mouth and had been startled by a twitch of the little creature's tongue. It was unexpected because calves in this position are usually dead, asphyxiated by the acute flexion of the neck and the pressure of the dam's powerful contractions. But this one had a spark of life in it and if it came out it would have to be in one piece.

I went over to my bucket of water, cold now and bloody, and silently soaped my arms. Then I lay down again, feeling the cobbles harder than ever against my chest. I worked my toes between the stones, shook the sweat from my eyes and for the hundredth time thrust an arm that felt like spaghetti into the cow; alongside the little dry legs of the calf, like sandpaper tearing against my flesh, then to the bend in the neck and so to the ear and then, agonizingly, along the side of the face towards the lower jaw which had become my major goal in life.

It was incredible that I had been doing this for nearly two hours; fighting as my strength ebbed to push a little noose round that jaw. I had tried everything else—repelling a leg, gentle traction with a blunt hook in the eye socket, but I was back to the noose.

It had been a miserable session all through. The farmer, Mr. Dinsdale, was a long, sad, silent man of few words who always seemed to be expecting the worst to happen. He had a long, sad, silent son with him and the two of them had watched my efforts with deepening gloom.

But worst of all had been Uncle. When I had first entered the hillside barn I had been surprised to see a little bright-eyed old man in a pork pie hat settling down comfortably on a bale of straw. He was filling his pipe and clearly looking forward to the entertainment.

"Now then, young man," he cried in the nasal twang of West Riding. "I'm Mr. Dinsdale's brother. I farm over in Listondale."

I put down my equipment and nodded. "How do you do? My name is Herriot."

The old man looked me over, piercingly. "My vet is Mr. Broomfield. Expect you'll have heard of him—everybody knows him, I reckon. Wonderful man, Mr. Broomfield, especially at calving. Do you know, I've never seen 'im beat yet."

I managed a wan smile. Any other time I would have been delighted to hear how good my colleague was, but somehow not now, not now. In fact, the words set a mournful little bell tolling inside me.

"No, I'm afraid I don't know Mr. Broomfield," I said, taking off my jacket and, more reluctantly, peeling my shirt over my head. "But I haven't been around these parts very long."

Uncle was aghast. "You don't know him! Well you're the only one as doesn't. They think the world of him in Listondale, I can tell you." He lapsed into a shocked silence and applied a match to his pipe. Then he shot a glance at my goose-pimpled torso. "Strips like a boxer does Mr. Broomfield. Never seen such muscles on a man."

A wave of weakness coursed sluggishly over me. I felt suddenly leaden-footed and inadequate. As I began to lay out my ropes and instruments on a clean towel the old man spoke again.

"And how long have you been qualified, may I ask?"

"Oh, about seven months."

"Seven months!" Uncle smiled indulgently, tamped down his tobacco and blew out a cloud of rank, blue smoke. "Well, there's nowt like a bit of experience, I always says. Mr. Broomfield's been doing my work now for over ten years and he really knows what he's about. No, you can 'ave your book learning. Give me experience every time."

I tipped some antiseptic into the bucket and lathered my arms carefully. I knelt behind the cow.

"Mr. Broomfield always puts some special lubricating oils on his arms first," Uncle said, pulling contentedly on his pipe. "He says you get infection of the womb if you just use soap and water."

I made my first exploration. It was the burdened moment all vets go through when they first put their hand into a cow. Within seconds I would know whether I would be putting on my jacket in fifteen minutes or whether I had hours of hard labour ahead of me.

I was going to be unlucky this time; it was a nasty presentation. Head back and no room at all; more like being inside an undeveloped heifer than a second calver. And she was bone dry—the "waters" must have come away from her hours ago. She had been running out on the high fields and had started to calve a week before her time; that was why they had had to bring her into this half-ruined barn. Anyway, it would be a long time before I saw my bed again.

"Well now, what have you found, young man?" Uncle's penetrating voice cut through the silence. "Head back, eh? You won't have much trouble, then. I've seen Mr. Broomfield do 'em like that—he turns calf right round and brings it out back legs first."

I had heard this sort of nonsense before. A short time in practice had taught me that all farmers were experts with other farmers' livestock. When their own animals were in trouble they tended to rush to the phone for the vet, but with their neighbors' they were confident, knowledgeable and full of helpful advice. And another phenomenon I had observed was that their advice was usually regarded as more valuable than the vet's. Like now, for instance; Uncle was obviously an accepted sage and the Dinsdales listened with deference to everything he said.

"Another way with a job like this," continued Uncle, "is to get a few strong chaps with ropes and pull the thing out, head back and all."

I gasped as I felt my way around. "I'm afraid it's impossible to turn a calf completely round in this small space. And to pull it out without bringing the head round would certainly break the mother's pelvis."

The Dinsdales narrowed their eyes. Clearly they thought I was hedging in the face of Uncle's superior knowledge.

And now, two hours later, defeat was just round the corner. I was just about whacked. I had rolled and grovelled on the filthy cobbles while the Dinsdales watched me in morose silence and Uncle kept up a non-stop stream of comment. Uncle, his ruddy face glowing with delight, his little eyes sparkling, hadn't had such a happy night for years. His long trek up the hillside had been repaid a hundredfold. His vitality was undiminished; he had enjoyed every minute.

As I lay there, eyes closed, face stiff with dirt, mouth hanging open, Uncle took his pipe in his hand and leaned forward on his straw bale. "You're about beat, young man," he said with deep satisfaction. "Well, I've never seen Mr. Broomfield beat but he's had a lot of experience. And what's more, he's strong, really strong. That's one man you couldn't tire."

Rage flooded through me like a draught of strong spirit. The right thing to do, of course, would be to get up, tip the bucket of bloody water over Uncle's head, run down the hill and drive away; away from Yorkshire, from Uncle, from the Dinsdales, from this cow.

Instead, I clenched my teeth, braced my legs and pushed with everything I had; and with a sensation of disbelief I felt my noose slide over the sharp little incisor teeth and into the calf's mouth. Gingerly, muttering a prayer, I pulled on the thin rope with my left hand and felt the slipknot tighten. I had hold of that lower jaw.

At last I could start doing something. "Now hold this rope, Mr. Dinsdale, and just keep a gentle tension on it. I'm going to repel the calf and if you pull steadily at the same time, the head ought to come round."

"What if the rope comes off?" asked Uncle hopefully.

I didn't answer. I put my hand in against the calf's shoulder and began to push against the cow's contractions. I felt the small body moving away from me. "Now a steady pull, Mr. Dinsdale, without jerking." And to myself, "Oh God, don't let it slip off."

The head was coming round. I could feel the neck straightening against my arm, then the ear touched my elbow. I let go the shoulder and grabbed the little muzzle. Keeping the teeth away from the vaginal wall with my hand, I guided the head till it was resting where it should be, on the fore limbs.

Quickly I extended the noose till it reached behind the ears. "Now pull on the head as she strains."

"Nay, you should pull on the legs now," cried Uncle.

"Pull on the bloody head rope, I tell you!" I bellowed at the top of my voice and felt immediately better as Uncle retired, offended, to his bale.

With traction the head was brought out and the rest of the body followed easily. The little animal lay motionless on the cobbles, eyes glassy and unseeing, tongue blue and grossly swollen.

"It'll be dead. Bound to be," grunted Uncle, returning to the attack.

I cleared the mucus from the mouth, blew hard down the throat and began artificial respiration. After a few pressures on the ribs, the calf gave a gasp and the eyelids flickered. Then it started to inhale and one leg jerked.

Uncle took off his hat and scratched his head in disbelief. "By gaw, it's alive. I'd have thowt it'd sure to be dead after you'd messed about all that time." A lot of the fire had gone out of him and his pipe hung down empty from his lips.

"I know what this little fellow wants," I said. I grasped the calf by its fore legs and pulled it up to its mother's head. The cow was stretched out on her side, her head extended wearily along the rough floor. Her ribs heaved, her eyes were almost closed; she looked past caring about anything. Then she felt the calf's body against her face and there was a transformation; her eyes opened wide and her muzzle began a snuffling exploration of the new object. Her interest grew with every sniff and she struggled on to her chest, nosing and probing all over the calf, rumbling deep in her chest. Then she began to lick him methodically. Nature provides the perfect stimulant massage for a time like this and the little creature arched his back as the coarse papillae on the tongue dragged along his skin. Within a minute he was shaking his head and trying to sit up.

I grinned. This was the bit I liked. The little miracle. I felt it was something that would never grow stale no matter how often I saw it. I cleaned as much of the dried blood and filth from my body as I could, but most of it had caked on my skin and not even my finger nails would move it. It would have to wait for the hot bath at home. Pulling my shirt over my head, I felt as though I had been beaten for a long time with a thick stick. Every muscle ached. My mouth was dried out, my lips almost sticking together.

A long, sad figure hovered near. "How about a drink?" asked Mr. Dinsdale.

I could feel my grimy face cracking into an incredulous smile. A vision of hot tea well laced with whisky swam before me. "That's very kind of you, Mr. Dinsdale, I'd love a drink. It's been a hard two hours."

"Nay," said Mr. Dinsdale looking at me steadily, "I meant for the cow."

I began to babble. "Oh yes, of course, certainly, by all means give her a drink. She must be very thirsty. It'll do her good. Certainly, certainly, give her a drink."

I gathered up my tackle and stumbled out of the barn. On the moor it was still dark and a bitter wind whipped over the snow, stinging my eyes. As I plodded down the slope, Uncle's voice, strident and undefeated, reached me for the last time.

"Mr. Broomfield doesn't believe in giving a drink after calving. Says it chills the stomach."

STUDY QUESTIONS for Chapter One of *All Creatures Great and Small*

COMPREHENSION

1. What process is the author attempting to complete in this chapter? What is preventing him from completing this task?
2. What is the setting of this scene? Why is it important for us to know the time, the location of the barn, and the weather conditions?

3. Why does the narrator begin to babble at the end, when Mr. Dinsdale asks about giving the cow a drink?

DEVELOPMENT AND ORGANIZATION

1. Herriot starts the chapter in the present time, while he is still trying to deliver the cow, and then returns us to the events leading up to that moment. Why does he start us where he does? What would this process gain or lose if he were to give us the events in chronological order?
2. Why is Uncle present at the birth? Why does he contrast the main character with Mr. Broomfield? What does Uncle's presence add to the chapter's atmosphere? How can we characterize him by the way he acts and speaks?
3. Why does Herriot allow Uncle to get in the last word of the chapter? How do Uncle's words affect the mood of the ending?
4. Which steps of the birth does Herriot describe in the most detail? What details does he use? In what ways do they depart from what he learned in his books?

STYLE AND TECHNIQUE

1. Herriot records the speech of the farmers in their dialect by altering the spellings of certain words and by using contractions. Why does he do this? What sense do you get of the characters because of it?
2. In the sentence "As I lay there, eyes closed, face stiff with dirt, mouth hanging open, Uncle took his pipe in his hand and leaned forward on his straw bale," what sort of constructions are "eyes closed," "face stiff with dirt," and "mouth hanging open"? What do they tell us about the main character? Why do we see these phrases at this moment in the chapter?
3. Herriot uses the medical terms of birthing, such as "presentation" and "parturition," throughout the chapter. Why does he do so? How do these terms contrast with the language used in the rest of the chapter?

TEN-MINUTE TOPICS

1. Describe a time when a process went wrong. What were you doing? What went wrong? What did you have to do to correct the problem? Was the problem corrected?
2. Describe a time you had a conflict with someone about the steps to take to complete a process. What was the process? Who was the other person? What steps did you want to follow, and what steps did the other person wish to follow? Whose steps were finally followed, and what was the result?

HPV VACCINE FOR BOYS? YES AND MAYBE NOT

BY DANIEL AKST

In September, prompted by one of the Republican presidential debates, I wrote a column about the foolishness of scaring people away from having their teenagers vaccinated against human papillomavirus.

The vaccine has mostly been administered to girls, who are at greatest risk of the various HPV cancers. But it works in boys, too. So my wife and I decided to have our sons vaccinated.

That was the easy part. The hard part was penetrating the maddening opaqueness and expense of the fragmented American health care system, which may be effective at treating dire diseases, but has shortened my life by making my blood boil at every encounter.

All we wanted was to have our boys vaccinated. They're the right age. We have health insurance. We can afford some out-of-pocket expenses. Getting them the shots would even benefit society: First, by protecting others from HPV, and second, by protecting others from the cost of treating my sons someday if they got an HPV-related ailment. Health care in this country, remember, is a heavily shared expense.

Yet trying to do the right thing for our boys and everyone else has involved considerable hair tearing. First we learned that our outrageously expensive health insurance doesn't cover the Gardasil vaccine for boys. Fine, I thought; we'll pay for it. How much can three shots cost?

Well, $900, or $1,800 for my twins—which seemed outlandish. Ah, but we could pay with pretax dollars from our "flexible spending account," thereby foisting a bunch of the expense on the taxpayers. What the heck, employer-paid health insurance premiums do the same thing by being tax-deductible. But we didn't have that much money in the account.

Luckily, I discovered the federal Vaccines for Children program, which covers shots for kids lacking insurance or with insurance that doesn't cover a vaccine. (Neither our pediatrician or insurer mentioned it.) VFC, presumably, gets a better deal than $900.

Back to the pediatrician. Are you a VFC provider? Yup. OK, great, let's have the shots.

Not so fast. Gardasil for boys isn't covered by VFC, the doctor's office said, after transferring me around a bit. But the VFC Web site says it is, and so does the Centers for Disease Control and Prevention, VFC's parent agency. Merck, the maker of Gardasil, agreed.

As it turns out, VFC does cover Gardasil for boys, but won't pay for the shots at a normal VFC provider. No, you have to go to "the department of health," our doctor's office said. Whose department of health? Not clear.

So I tracked down the regional VFC administrator, at the state Department of Health in Albany, who said VFC-paid Gardasil for "underinsured" kids can only be had "at a Federally Qualified Health Center."

I'll spare you a blow-by-blow account of every phone call, web search and email.

Suffice to say that the amount of time and energy this has consumed—without a single shot having been fired, so to speak—is ridiculous. The whole episode perfectly encapsulates so much of what is wrong with our health-care system, which can thwart even the best informed, insured and intentioned of individuals.

And my sons still aren't vaccinated—the Federally Qualified Health Centers are far from our home. (Visit findahealthcenter.hrsa.gov to find one.) But recently the Advisory Committee on Immunization Practices, which advises the CDC, recommended that boys get Gardasil just like girls. So maybe, soon, our health insurance will cover it. Or not.

No wonder so many kids are still unvaccinated. One can only hope their cancer treatment, if they need it later in life, isn't so difficult to obtain.

STUDY QUESTIONS for "HPV Vaccine for Boys? Yes and Maybe Not"

COMPREHENSION

1. What are two of the benefits of vaccinating boys for HPV?
2. What is the Vaccines for Children program?
3. What is the cost of the HPV vaccine for the uninsured?

DEVELOPMENT AND ORGANIZATION

1. List in chronological order the roadblocks the writer faced in acquiring the vaccines.
2. What are some of the long-term effects of the failure to vaccinate? From these, develop an additional paragraph for the essay.
3. What is the role of the pediatrician in this process? Is his lack of control in the matter surprising?

STYLE AND TECHNIQUE

1. What is the writer's tone? In what ways does it enter the essay?
2. Akst poses numerous questions to his reader. Is this an effective technique? Which questions are best? Which are worst?
3. What types of transitions does Akst use between paragraphs? You may want to review an earlier discussion on transitions before answering.

TEN-MINUTE TOPICS

1. Describe a roadblock you've faced as a result of government (national, state, county, city, etc.) rules.
2. Describe a ridiculous law or rule you've encountered at work, at school, with the government, or in some other venue.

3. Discuss the hypocrisy of how differently the medical field treats men (boys) and women (girls).
4. Discuss the relationship between pharmaceutical companies and medical care and treatment.

WRITING IS EASY!

BY STEVE MARTIN

Writing is one of the most easy, pain-free, and happy ways to pass the time in all the arts. For example, right now I am sitting in my rose garden and typing on my new computer. Each rose represents a story, so I'm never at a loss for *what* to write. I just look deep into the heart of the rose and read its story and write it down through *typing*, which I enjoy anyway. I could be typing "kjfiu joewmv jiw" and would enjoy it as much as typing words that actually make sense. I simply relish the movement of my fingers on the keys. Sometimes, it is true, agony visits the head of a writer. At these moments, I stop writing and relax with a coffee at my favorite restaurant, knowing that words can be changed, rethought, fiddled with, and, of course, ultimately denied. Painters don't have that luxury. If they go to a coffee shop, their paint dries into a hard mass.

Location, Location, Location

I would recommend to writers that they live in California, because here they can look up at the blue sky in between those moments of looking into the heart of a rose. I feel sorry for writers—and there are some pretty famous ones—who live in places like South America and Czechoslovakia, where I imagine it gets pretty dreary. These writers are easy to spot. Their books are often depressing and filled with disease and negativity. If you're going to write about disease, I would suggest that California is the place to do it. Dwarfism is never funny, but look at the result when it was dealt with out here in California. Seven happy dwarfs. Can you imagine seven dwarfs in Czechoslovakia? You would get seven melancholic dwarfs at best, seven melancholic dwarfs with no handicapped-parking spaces.

Love in the Time of Cholera: Why It's a Bad Title

I admit that "Love in the Time of . . ." is a great title, so far. You're reading along, you're happy, it's about love, I like the way the word *time* comes in there, something nice in the association of *love* and *time*, like a new word almost, *lovetime*: nice, nice feeling. Suddenly, the morbid *Cholera* appears. I was happy till then. "Love in the Time of Oozing Sores and Pustules" is probably an earlier, rejected title of this book, written in a rat-infested tree house on an old Smith-Corona. This writer, whoever he is, could have used a couple of weeks in Pacific Daylight Time.

I did a little experiment. I decided to take the following disheartening passage, which was no doubt written in some depressing place, and attempt to rewrite it under the influence of California:

> Most people deceive themselves with a pair of faiths: they believe in *eternal memory* (of people, things, deeds, nations) and in *redressibility*

(of deeds, mistakes, sins, wrongs). Both are false faiths. In reality the opposite is true: everything will be forgotten and nothing will be redressed. (Milan Kundera)

Sitting in my garden, as the bees glide from flower to flower, I let the above paragraph filter through my mind. The following new paragraph emerged:

> I feel pretty,
> Oh so pretty,
> I feel pretty and witty and bright.

Kundera was just too wordy. Sometimes the delete key is your greatest friend.

Writer's Block: A Myth

Writer's block is a fancy term made up by whiners so they can have an excuse to drink alcohol. Sure a writer can get stuck for a while, but when that happens to real authors, they simply go out and get an "as told to." The alternative is to hire yourself as an "as heard from," thus taking all the credit. It is also much easier to write when you have someone to "bounce" with. This is someone to sit in a room with and exchange ideas. It is good if the last name of the person you choose to bounce with is Salinger. I know a certain early-twentieth-century French writer, whose initials were M. P., who could have used a good bounce person. If he had, his title might have been the more correct "Remembering Past Things" instead of the clumsy one he used. The other trick I use when I have a momentary stoppage is virtually foolproof, and I'm happy to pass it along. Go to an already published novel and find a sentence you absolutely adore. Copy it down in your manuscript. Usually that sentence will lead you naturally to another sentence; pretty soon your own ideas will start to flow. If they don't, copy down the next sentence. You can safely use up to three sentences of someone else's work—unless they're friends; then you can use two. The odds of being found out are very slim, and even if you are, there's no jail time.

Creating Memorable Characters

Nothing will make your writing soar more than a memorable character. If there is a memorable character, the reader will keep going back to the book, picking it up, turning it over in his hands, hefting it, and tossing it into the air. Here is an example of the jazzy uplift that vivid characters can offer:

Some guys were standing around when in came this guy.

You are now on your way to creating a memorable character. You have set him up as being a guy, and with that come all the reader's ideas of what a guy is. Soon you will liven your character by using an adjective:

But this guy was no ordinary guy, he was a red guy.

This character, the red guy, has now popped into the reader's imagination. He is a full-blown person, with hopes and dreams, just like the reader. Especially if the reader is a red guy. Now you might want to give the character a trait. You can inform the reader of the character trait in one of two ways. First, simply say what that trait is—for example, "but this red guy was different from most red guys, this red guy liked frappés." The other is rooted in action—have the red guy walk up to a bar and order a frappé, as in:

"What'll you have, red guy?"
"I'll have a frappé."

Once you have mastered these two concepts, vivid character writing combined with adjectives, you are on your way to becoming the next Shakespeare's brother. And don't forget to copyright any ideas you have that might be original. You don't want to be caught standing by helplessly while your familiar "red guy" steps up to a bar in a frappé commercial.

Writing Dialogue

Many very fine writers are intimidated when they have to write the way people really talk. Actually it's quite easy. Simply lower your IQ by fifty and start typing!

Subject Matter

Because topics are in such short supply, I have provided a few for writers who may be suffering in the darker climes. File some of these away, and look through them during the suicidal winter months:

"Naked Belligerent Panties": This is a good sexy title with a lot of promise.

How about a diet book that suggests your free radicals *don't* enter ketosis unless your insulin levels have been carbo-charged?

Something about how waves at the beach just keep coming and coming and how amazing it is (I smell a bestseller here).

"Visions of Melancholy from a Fast-Moving Train": Some foreign writer is right now rushing to his keyboard, ready to pound on it like Horowitz. However, this title is a phony string of words with no meaning and would send your poor book to the "Artsy" section of Barnes and Noble, where—guess what—it would languish, be remaindered, and die.

A Word to Avoid

"Dagnabbit" will never get you anywhere with the Booker Prize people. Lose it.

Getting Published

I have two observations about publishers:

1. Nowadays, they can be either male or female.
2. They love to be referred to by the appropriate pronoun. If your publisher is male, refer to him as "he." If your publisher is female, "she" is considered more correct. Once you have established a rapport, "Babe" is also acceptable for either sex.

Once you have determined your pronoun usage, you are ready to "schmooze" your publisher. Let's say your favorite author is Dante. Call Dante's publisher and say you'd like to invite them both for lunch. If the assistant says something like "But Dante's dead," be sympathetic and say, "Please accept my condolences." Once at lunch, remember never to be moody. Publishers like up, happy writers, although it's impressive to suddenly sweep your arm slowly across the lunch table, dumping all the plates and food onto the floor, while shouting "Sic Semper Tyrannis!"

A Demonstration of Actual Writing

It's easy to talk about writing and even easier to do it. Watch:

> Call me Ishmael. It was cold, very cold, here in the mountain town of Kilimanjaroville.© I could hear a bell. It was tolling. I knew exactly for who it was tolling, too. It was tolling for me, Ishmael Twist,© a red guy who likes frappé. [Author's note: I am now stuck. I walk over to a rose and look into its heart.] That's right, Ishmael Twist.©

Finally, I can't overstress the importance of having a powerful closing sentence.

STUDY QUESTIONS for "Writing Is Easy!"

COMPREHENSION

1. Why, according to the narrator of this piece, is the process of writing so easy? What step would make writing easier for just about everyone?
2. What is a Smith-Corona? Why would using one make the process of writing more difficult?

3. What are the techniques for creating memorable characters? Is the sample character created by the narrator memorable to you? Why or why not?

DEVELOPMENT AND ORGANIZATION

1. The piece is divided by headings into sections that cover different aspects of the writing process. How effectively are the sections organized? Do they in fact cover the most useful or most important steps in the process?
2. Several examples illustrate the steps of the process being described. How well do the examples illustrate these steps? Which are most effective? Which are least?
3. The sample of writing that appears in the demonstration at the end includes allusions to four different literary works (including one that appears elsewhere in this reader). What are the four works, and who are the authors? Is the passage an effective and engaging piece of writing?

STYLE AND TECHNIQUE

1. Martin writes with a high level of irony in this piece. Where are the most ironic passages? What words imply most strongly the ironic tone?
2. Martin, the author, also adopts a persona—a narrator—by whom the essay is written. What evidence can you find that allows you to perceive a difference between the narrator and the author?
3. The tip that the narrator passes along for avoiding writer's block, copying down sentences from an already published novel, is actually a form of plagiarism that could get a writer into serious trouble (despite the narrator's claims). Why would Martin allow the narrator to voice such a suggestion?
4. How effective is the closing sentence? Does it do what the sentence implies it should do?

TEN-MINUTE TOPICS

1. Create a character using the techniques set forth in Martin's process.
2. Take one of the subject matter suggestions and try to work it into a story.
3. The narrator implies that the writer's setting (where he or she works) may influence what a writer writes. Find different places in your home, or in the neighborhood where you live, and try writing in each one of them. Do you notice a difference?

CHAPTER SIX

COMPARISON and CONTRAST

DEFINITION

One of the most common ways of organizing information is comparison or contrast. For example, if interested in buying a Mac or a PC, we would compare the features— ease of use, variety of software, capability and reliability of hardware, etc.—before choosing. Similarly, when we shop to buy a new car and narrow our choice down to two automobiles, we automatically contrast horsepower, repair records, handling ease, overall construction, and so on. And if we have just moved to Las Vegas from, say, Boise, Idaho, we may find ourselves comparing the two cities in terms of size, recreational opportunities for children and adults, cleanliness of the environment, the quality of primary and secondary education, and so on. Consciously or unconsciously, then, we probably compare and contrast on a daily basis.

First, we need to distinguish comparison from contrast. When we *compare*, we point out similarities between two things. Thus, in comparing cats with dogs, we notice that they both have a strong affinity for human beings, a tendency to defend their territory against intruders, a carnivorous diet, and a tendency to take over a household if given half a chance. When we *contrast*, on the other hand, we stress the differences between two objects. Accordingly, in contrasting cats and dogs, we can point out that while cats largely care for themselves, demanding only food, water, and a clean litter box, dogs expect a great deal more, including a daily walk and frequent bathing; that while both cats and dogs will fight off animals intruding into their territory, only dogs will attack human intruders; and that while cats do most of their damage to our furniture with their claws, dogs do most of theirs with their teeth. Comparison, then, emphasizes likenesses while contrast stresses differences.

APPLICATION

To write a comparison or contrast essay—or one using both methods—we must select two objects from the same category. It wouldn't do, for instance, to compare the price of ice cream today with the price of meat ten years ago. Though both objects are foods, one is a dessert and the other a main course. Similarly, it wouldn't do to contrast the way a refrigerator works with the process of making a movie. Such an exercise would be meaningless, if not altogether ludicrous. We must select the parts of our topic from the same category: thus, we could compare or contrast two dogs, two countries, two cities, two bosses, two fashions, and so on.

Having selected our topic, we must establish clear bases for our comparison or contrast—that is, the points along which our comparison or contrast is to be developed. Thus, if we are contrasting Professor A and Professor B, we might do so on the bases of their knowledge of the subject matter, their personal appearance, and their ability to inspire students. These are the points along which the hypothetical essay will be developed. A rough outline might look something like this:

> Tentative thesis: While they both teach at the same university and received degrees from the same graduate school, Professor A and Professor B differ dramatically in their knowledge of their subject matter, their personal appearance, and their ability to inspire students.

> I. Brief educational background.
> A. Professor A.
> B. Professor B.
> II. Knowledge of subject matter.
> A. Professor A.
> B. Professor B.
> III. Personal appearance.
> A. Professor A.
> B. Professor B.
> IV. Ability to inspire students.
> A. Professor A.
> B. Professor B.

In the actual essay, we would use examples, taken from what we've seen and what we know of each professor, to illustrate the points made about the two educators. Further, in the larger written paper, points I through IV would correspond to four paragraph divisions of the body. Too, the writing of the comparison and contrast should reveal to the reader that the writer's intent, beyond satisfying simple requirement of form, is to prove the superiority of one professor over another. As Aristotle suggests in his *Rhetoric*, a good comparison and contrast goes beyond similarities and differences and reveals that one item is better than or preferable to the other. All exposition, Aristotle suggests, is a form of argumentation.

When setting up a comparison and contrast essay, the student needs to keep in mind that two patterns of logical development are available and that these patterns may be used independently of one another or interchangeably. For instance, the outline above suggests that the hypothetical essay about Professor A and Professor B will be organized according to the alternating pattern: ABABAB. However, perhaps with less effect, the comparisons and the contrasts could be set up according to the continuous pattern of AAABBB. The resulting outline would look something like this:

> Tentative thesis: While they both teach at the same university and received degrees from the same graduate school, Professor A and Professor B differ dramatically in their knowledge of their subject matter, their personal appearance, and their ability to inspire students.

I. Professor A.
    A. Academic background.
    B. Knowledge of subject matter.
    C. Personal appearance.
    D. Ability to inspire.
II. Professor B.
    A. Academic background.
    B. Knowledge of subject matter.
    C. Personal appearance.
    D. Ability to inspire.

The problem with using the continuous pattern to contrast the professors is worth noting: by the time the student begins explaining Professor B's personal appearance or ability to inspire his or her students, the reader is likely to have forgotten the points made about Professor A's appearance and abilities. In selecting a pattern of development, therefore, the student should select the one that, given the subject matter, is most logical and coherent.

Thus, while the alternating pattern may be most appropriate for most comparisons and contrasts, the continuous pattern often works well with essays that rely heavily upon description. For instance, if a student is contrasting the way his or her best friend looks today with the way that same friend looked twenty-five years ago (description would have to be used), the continuous pattern would be the most effective. Indeed, the following paragraphs, a before-and-after description, rely upon the continuous pattern:

> Rodney had undergone a radical change. I remembered him as a person who dressed to the hilt—you know, not a hair out of place, three-piece suit, matching tie, spit-shined shoes. At one time, he was very talkative and argumentative. In the several college courses we took together, he sat near the front, never missing his professor's words, even disputing their theories at times. Our Psych 101 professor, for instance, in a burst of rage, told Rodney to shut up for one hour or leave the class. Of course, Rodney left the class.
>
> The person who stood before me now bore little resemblance to the Rodney I had known. Balding and potbellied, he wore a gray foodstained sweatshirt, fading blue jeans with the left knee torn, and a pair of worn-out glossy brown street shoes. Moreover, he had withdrawn to the darkest corner of the room, where I was now standing before him, and as far as I could gather from the people seated around him, he had not spoken a word all night. "Rodney," I wanted to ask him in private, "what in the world has happened to you?"

The bases here are two: appearance and spirit. That is, over the years, Rodney has changed dramatically in appearance and in spirit. The effectiveness of this contrast has much to do with the writer's use of example and concrete detail, both of which enable the reader to visualize the changes in Rodney. For instance, the reference to the incident in the Psych 101 class illustrates Rodney's argumentative nature. And the descriptive words, such as "three-piece suit," "matching tie," "spit-shined shoes," "gray food-stained sweatshirt," help the reader to actually see Rodney and therefore understand the writer's consternation over realizing how his old friend must have changed.

Now let's examine a student essay in some depth in order to get a better handle upon the continuous and alternating patterns. In the following paragraphs from his essay "Hamilton vs. Jefferson" (modeled after Bruce Catton's famous "Grant and Lee"), student Greg Randall uses three brief paragraphs to introduce the items, or people, that he is going to contrast.

> "The rich had advantages of character. . . . Their vices could be considered more favorable to the prosperity of the state than those of the indigent."
>
> "All men are equal in right, regardless of both wealth and status, and . . . government is the servant, not the master, of human beings."
>
> With these words, Alexander Hamilton and Thomas Jefferson exposed the fundamental differences in their philosophies. Although both men had a long and faithful history of service to America, these differences were aggravated as they both tried to shape the destiny of their fledgling country.

Randall engages our interest and introduces the topic with two direct quotes. Note that the thesis, the last sentence, suggests that Randall is going to begin the body of his essay by pointing out a similarity ("both . . . had a long and faithful history of service to America") and then move to the differences separating these two men.

Here are the first two body paragraphs. Following the AAABBB or continuous pattern of development, Randall incorporates specific detail into each paragraph in order to bring out both men's service to their country:

> Alexander Hamilton was born in the West Indies on January 11, 1755. He was the illegitimate son of Rachel Faucett and James Hamilton. Abandoned by his father, he went to work at age twelve with two New York merchants on the island and showed immediate promise. In 1774, he was sent on a scholarship to King's College, which later became Columbia University. During the Revolutionary War, Hamilton became a lieutenant colonel and trusted aide-de-camp to General George Washington. He became a military hero of great personal courage and valor, particularly distinguishing himself at the Battle of Monmotte. After the war, he was a leader at the Annapolis Convention, calling for a strong national government. He served as a member of the New York delegation to the Constitutional Convention

in Philadelphia. Along with John Jay and James Madison, he authored *The Federalist Papers*, still considered to be a masterpiece on constitutional interpretation. While serving as the first secretary of treasury under President Washington, Hamilton was instrumental in creating a national bank.

Thomas Jefferson was born in Virginia on April 13, 1743, into one of the most prominent families in that colony. He was educated at the College of William and Mary and admitted to the bar in 1767. At the age of twenty-five, he was elected to the Virginia House of Burgess. In 1776, he wrote The Declaration of Independence, a document that years later still inspires people all over the world. During the Revolutionary War, he served as governor of Virginia. After the war, he succeeded Ben Franklin as minister to France. Jefferson was the first secretary of state under President Washington. In 1796, he became vice president, and in 1800, president, serving eight years and adding immense territory to the US through the Louisiana Purchase. An avid bibliophile, Jefferson donated his private library to the government. This collection was the beginning of the present-day Library of Congress.

Note also in these two paragraphs that the writer has clearly established bases of commonality: date and place of birth, educational background, service to country during Revolutionary War, and service to country after Revolutionary War. Clearly, Randall employs the continuous, or AAABBB pattern; that is, he covers the four points mentioned below first as they relate to Hamilton and then as they relate to Jefferson. A rough outline may look something like this:

    I. Hamilton.
        A. Date and place of birth.
        B. Educational background.
        C. Service during War.
        D. Service after War.
    II. Jefferson.
        A. Date and place of birth.
        B. Educational background.
        C. Service during War.
        D. Service after War.

Had Randall used the alternating, or ABABAB, pattern, the result would likely have been a series of short, choppy paragraphs.

In the remainder of his essay, Randall uses the alternating pattern to emphasize some fundamental differences between the two men. Here are the next four paragraphs:

Hamilton had a very pessimistic view of human nature and a low opinion of the ability of the common man to govern himself. He said our form of government should be "republic only in a technical sense that a life-tenured chief executive would be elected indirectly and not be hereditary; while replacing the House of Lords would be a life-tenured elective senate." He believed that the national government should have broad powers and to that end advocated a liberal interpretation of the Constitution. He felt that the Constitution did not go far enough and said, "I own it is my opinion . . . that the present government is not that which will answer the ends of society by giving stability and protection to its rights, and that it will probably be found expedient to go into the British form."

Thomas Jefferson, though not blind to the foibles of human nature, believed that the average man was quite capable of conducting the affairs of government. He was very suspicious of a strong central government and felt that it could, through the efforts of an elite few, thwart the will of the majority. He felt that "government cannot be trusted to the rulers of the people alone." To that end, he favored a very narrow interpretation of the powers of the federal government under the Constitution. He felt that the Constitution went too far.

The first clash of opposing philosophies came over Shay's Rebellion in 1786, when farmers in Massachusetts rebelled against foreclosure, forcing judges out of their courtrooms and freeing debtors. This alarmed Hamilton, who saw it as proof of the need for a strong central government that could deal harshly with such rebellion. Jefferson, on the other hand, said, "The tree of liberty must be refreshed from time to time with the blood of patriots and tyrants." He saw continuing popular revolution as a good thing.

Hamilton and Jefferson also clashed over the Bill of Rights. Hamilton believed that there was no need for a specific Bill of Rights, since the government was already limited enough in its powers. However, Jefferson believed that the Bill of Rights was too important to rely solely on inference and the good faith of the government. They—the Rights—should be written down in the Constitution.

In these four body paragraphs, which do become a bit general, the student-writer very clearly establishes his bases of contrast: differing political philosophies, responses to Shay's Rebellion, and responses to the Bill of Rights. His use of the alternating ABABAB pattern suggests the following tentative outline:

III. Political philosophies.
   A. Hamilton.
   B. Jefferson.

IV. Shay's Rebellion.
    A. Hamilton.
    B. Jefferson.
V. Bill of Rights.
    A. Hamilton.
    B. Jefferson.

Note also that, to give his essay a greater sense of coherence, Randall makes intelligent use of such transitions as *although, on the other hand,* and *however.*

In his concluding paragraph, Randall uses just enough detail to emphasize differences that grew almost paradoxically from the status into which each man was born:

> So, the two men had opposing philosophies which colored their actions on behalf of the new government. The lowborn Hamilton came to represent the moneyed interests and government by the elite few, while Jefferson, to the manor born, championed the cause of the common man. Perhaps we are better off today because each was able to check the more radical impulses of the other.

In the final sentence, Randall is challenging the reader to take a broader view of his topic and to consider how the differences separating these two men, Alexander Hamilton and Thomas Jefferson, continue to affect and shape our country today.

PARADIGM

When you are putting together your comparison and contrast essay, keep in mind the following paradigms. The first is the alternating, or ABABAB; the second is the continuous, or AAABBB.

Alternating (ABABAB)

Introductory paragraph
    1. Engage the reader's interest.
    2. Introduce topic.
    3. Establish tone.
    4. Present thesis.

First Body Paragraph
    1. Use topic sentence to introduce first similarity or difference.
    2. Give examples/proofs.
        a. Item A.
        b. Item B.

Second Body Paragraph
    1. Use topic sentence to mention second similarity or difference.
    2. Give examples/proofs.
        a. Item A.
        b. Item B.

Third Body Paragraph
    1. Use topic sentence to mention third similarity or difference.
    2. Give examples/proofs.
        a. Item A.
        b. Item B.

Conclusion (options)
    1. Summarize main points and restate thesis.
    2. Offer a final image, message, or judgment.
    3. Take a broader view.
    4. End with quotation.
    5. End with striking statistic.
    6. Challenge the reader.
    7. Something else.

Continuous (AAABBB)

Introductory paragraph
    1. Engage reader's interest.
    2. Introduce topic.
    3. Establish tone.
    4. Present thesis.

First section of body
    1. Introduce item A.
    2. Proofs/description.
        a. First basis of comparison or contrast.
        b. Second basis.
        c. Third basis.

Second section of body
1. Introduce item B.
2. Proofs/description.
    a. First basis of comparison or contrast.
    b. Second basis.
    c. Third basis.

Conclusion (options)
1. Summarize main points and restate thesis.
2. Offer a final image, message, or judgment.
3. Take a broader view.
4. End with quotation.
5. End with striking statistic.
6. Challenge the reader.
7. Something else.

SUMMARY

Whichever pattern we use, we must make sure to establish clear bases for our comparison or contrast; we must clarify the essential ways in which the two parts of our topic are similar to or are different from each other. Thus, if we are contrasting two automobiles and we mention something about the horsepower of one car, we must say something about the horsepower of the other. If we say something about one car's engine size, we must refer to the other car's.

Ultimately, of course, we use comparison and contrast to support a thesis statement. And as we develop our comparisons or contrasts in support of our thesis, we can draw our information from the books and magazines that we read. Remember, though, that the best source from which to draw information that we use to support a thesis is our own unique experience.

TWO WAYS OF SEEING A RIVER

BY MARK TWAIN

Now when I had mastered the language of this water and had come to know every trifling feature that bordered the great river as familiarly as I know the letters of the alphabet, I had made a valuable acquisition. But I had lost something, too. I had lost something which could never be restored to me while I lived. All the grace, the beauty, the poetry, had gone out of the majestic river! I still kept in mind a certain wonderful sunset which I witnessed when steamboating was new to me. A broad expanse of the river was turned to blood; in the middle distance the red hue brightened into gold, through which a solitary log came floating, black and conspicuous; in one place a long, slanting mark lay sparkling upon the water; in another the surface was broken by boiling, tumbling rings that were as many-tinted as an opal; where the ruddy flush was faintest was a smooth spot that was covered with graceful circles and radiating lines, ever so delicately traced; the shore on our left was densely wooded, and the somber shadow that fell from this forest was broken in one place by a long, ruffled trail that shone like silver; and high above the forest wall a clean-stemmed dead tree waved a single leafy bough that glowed like a flame in the unobstructed splendor that was flowing from the sun. There were graceful curves, reflected images, woody heights, soft distances, and over the whole scene, far and near, the dissolving lights drifted steadily, enriching it every passing moment with new marvels of coloring.

I stood like one bewitched. I drank it in, in a speechless rapture. The world was new to me and I had never seen anything like this at home. But as I have said, a day came when I began to cease from noting the glories and the charms which the moon and the sun and the twilight wrought upon the river's face; another day came when I ceased altogether to note them. Then, if that sunset scene had been repeated, I should have looked upon it without rapture and should have commented upon it inwardly after this fashion: "This sun means that we are going to have a wind tomorrow; that floating log means that the river is rising, small thanks to it; that slanting mark on the water refers to a bluff reef which is going to kill somebody's steamboat one of these nights, if it keeps on stretching out like that; those tumbling 'boils' show a dissolving bar and a changing channel there; the lines and circles in the slick water over yonder are a warning that the troublesome place is shoaling up dangerously; that silver streak in the shadow of the forest is the 'break' from a new snag and he has located himself in the very best place he could have found to fish for steamboats; that tall dead tree, with a single living branch, is not going to last long, and then how is a body ever going to get through this blind place at night without the friendly old landmark?"

No, the romance and beauty were all gone from the river. All the value any feature of it had for me was the amount of usefulness it could furnish toward compassing the safe piloting of a steamboat. Since those days, I have pitied doctors from my heart. What does the lovely flush in a beauty's cheek mean to a doctor but a "break" that ripples above some deadly disease? Are not all her visible charms sown thick with what are to him the signs and symbols of hidden decay? Does he ever see her beauty at all, or doesn't he simply view her professionally and comment upon her unwholesome condition all to himself? And doesn't he sometimes wonder whether he has gained most or lost most by learning his trade?

STUDY QUESTIONS for "Two Ways of Seeing a River"

COMPREHENSION

1. Account for the fact that, to Mark Twain the river captain, "all the grace, the beauty, the poetry, had gone out of the majestic river."
2. How did Twain's perception of the river change?
3. In your own words, state the main idea of this essay.

DEVELOPMENT AND ORGANIZATION

1. Where in the essay does Twain make use of concrete/descriptive detail?
2. Where does Twain make use of objective description, that is, description that is technical, even scientific? Where does he use subjective description, description that conveys personal impressions? What dominant impression does he manage to convey with each description?
3. Discuss the organization of detail in Twain's two descriptions. Is the organization of detail random, or is there a pattern to it?
4. What pattern of organizing this contrast does Twain use: continuous or alternating? Explain what would be gained or lost by employing the other method.
5. What is the function of paragraph three? Would the essay be as effective without it? Why, in this paragraph, does Twain refer to his pity for doctors? How has he become like a doctor?

STYLE AND TECHNIQUE

1. Discuss the shift in point of view that accompanies the transition from subjective to objective description.
2. Count the number of words in paragraph one; then count the number in paragraph two. Now count the number of sentences in the two paragraphs. Which paragraph has a higher ratio of words per sentence?
3. In which description of the river does Twain use the most colors? In which does he use the most nouns? The most adjectives? The most linking verbs? The most adverbs?

TEN-MINUTE TOPICS

1. Contrast your initial romantic impression of a certain setting or scene with your later, more objective, perhaps more realistic impression of the same scene or setting.

2. Contrast your initial impression of a person with a later impression of the same person. What has changed? What has stayed the same?

WHEN WOMEN SHOP, EXPECTATIONS USUALLY OUT OF STOCK

BY GINA BARRECA

I wanted to buy a T-shirt saying DOES THIS T-SHIRT MAKE ME LOOK FAT?—except it was too small.

It was my most recent low self-esteem holiday shopping moment. Women have a lot of low self-esteem shopping moments thrust upon them by smart-alecky store mirrors and inner demons.

This is especially true when the mirrors are positioned under hideous fluorescent lighting, thereby giving our flesh the seductive texture of pot cheese and our skin the greenish glow of Area 51. Under such conditions, women like Natalie Portman catch themselves looking bucktoothed and cross-eyed. Had Kim Kardashian glimpsed herself unawares in a bad full-length mirror at Kohl's, she would have stayed married, fearful that no other guy would ever look at her.

This explains why, if you observe women trying on shoes, for example, you'll see us playing with our hair when we look in the mirror. We're trying on shoes but not looking at our feet. It's as if smoothing our bangs will somehow make a pair of ankle boots look better. We'll fluff our ponytail when buying a bracelet. Female CIA officers probably tuck a stray lock or two behind their ears when trying on hazmat suits. This is all part of an elaborate effort to distract ourselves while attempting to preserve a semblance of composure and self-reliance.

Is it such a surprise, really? After all, there's not much we can do about our jaw line or height, not, at least, before somebody else sneaks into the mirror in front of us.

Men don't do this. Men don't torture themselves this way. Most straight men, for example, have never even tried on a T-shirt.

They walk into Odd Lot, Job Lot or some other store with "Lot" in the title, go directly to the bin where 2,000 blue shirts are folded by size, hold one up to the light, look at it, say "It's big enough. It'll fit." They then buy four of them and leave.

They're dressed for the year.

The only time guys are forced to go out and buy new T-shirts is after some woman has discarded the T-shirts they've had since high school, the ones with the gaping, shredded holes under the armpits. When they discover the loss of these garments, they become as histrionic as Hamlet when he discovered his mother married his uncle.

Men do not perform acts of self-assessment, self-actualization, atonement, penance or exorcism during their shopping trips. That's because men see stores as, well, "stores" and not shrines or palaces of judgment. For men, stores are places where products are available for purchase, and some of these products are designed just for them.

Women, in contrast, want to fit ourselves into the shapes and sizes we're told we should be. Women also try to be worthy of the item we want to purchase. This kind of insecurity has, I believe, kept us from being elected to the highest of political offices: Deep down inside, an intelligent and accomplished woman can still wonder whether she is good enough for a Chanel suit.

This is sad. This is a woman who will not be trusted to make decisions concerning the tactical use of nuclear weaponry.

We need to do better. We need to stop trying to fit ourselves into the world and start making sure the world begins to fit us.

Just think about how many women you've heard announce, especially around this time of year, "Ooh, I want to fit into a size 10, a size 6, a sub-zero by New Year's!"

You've never heard a guy say "I want to be a 42 short by Christmas."

Men practice self-acceptance. That's why it's difficult to insult men. You can say to a man "Fred, I personally will buy you a new jacket so I don't have to see that particular herringbone pattern anymore," and Fred, with a grin, will reply "Bought it in '92. Still fits. I can't button it, but still." He's not upset. He sees your remark as a compliment.

Apparently some men feel about their wardrobe the way they feel about a stack of 30-year Treasury bills: The less they do with it, the better.

Let's celebrate the season by banishing inner demons and ignoring unflattering mirrors. After all, they're no reflection on us.

STUDY QUESTIONS for "When Women Shop, Expectations Usually out of Stock"

COMPREHENSION

1. What time of year prompts the most self-examination? Why?
2. What is a "palace of judgment"?
3. Who shops at stores with "Lot" in their name? Why?

DEVELOPMENT AND ORGANIZATION

1. What traits does Barreca use to create a basis of comparison?
2. If you could revise one paragraph of this piece, which one would you choose and why?
3. How do the introductory and concluding paragraphs complement one another?

STYLE AND TECHNIQUE

1. How does the use of the first-person "I" affect your understanding of Barreca's stance?
2. Are the women mentioned in the article effective examples of her thesis? Should Barreca have named any male celebrities?
3. Discuss the writer's use of the mirror. Why is it an important symbol in this article? How does its history connect to this essay?

TEN-MINUTE TOPICS

1. Create a list of ways to achieve self-acceptance. Have you tried any of these yourself? If so, pick one and contrast how you were before and how you were after you tried this method. If not, pick one you would most likely try. How do you view yourself now? What effects would you hope it had on you?

2. Describe an environment (place, atmosphere, group of people) where you feel most comfortable. Then describe one where you feel least comfortable. Compare and contrast the reasons for these contrary feelings.

3. Describe in detail a man or a woman you know who possesses the behavior traits Barreca identifies.

THE TWO POLITICAL MOONS

BY DAVID BROOKS

In 1951, Samuel Lubell invented the concept of the political solar system. At any moment, he wrote, there is a Sun Party (the majority party, which drives the agenda) and a Moon Party (the minority party, which shines by reflecting the solar rays).

During Franklin Roosevelt's era, Democrats were the Sun Party. During Ronald Reagan's, Republicans were. Then, between 1996 and 2004, the two parties were tied. We lived in a 50-50 nation in which the overall party vote totals barely budged five elections in a row. It seemed then that we were in a moment of transition, waiting for the next Sun Party to emerge.

But something strange happened. No party took the lead. According to data today, both parties have become minority parties simultaneously. We are living in the era of two moons and no sun.

It used to be that the parties were on a seesaw: If the ratings of one dropped, then the ratings of the other rose. But now the two parties have record-low approval ratings together. Neither party has been able to rally the country behind its vision of government.

Ronald Brownstein summarized the underlying topography recently in *The National Journal*: "In Allstate/*National Journal* Heartland Monitor polls over the past two years, up to 40 percent of Americans have consistently expressed support for the conservative view that government is more the problem than the solution for the nation's challenges; about another 30 percent have backed the Democratic view that government must take an active role in the economy; and the remaining 30 percent are agnostic. They are open to government activism in theory but skeptical it will help them in practice."

In these circumstances, both parties have developed minority mentalities. The Republicans feel oppressed by the cultural establishment, and Democrats feel oppressed by the corporate establishment. They embrace the mental habits that have always been adopted by those who feel themselves resisting the onslaught of a dominant culture.

Their main fear is that they will lose their identity and cohesion if their members compromise with the larger world. They erect clear and rigid boundaries separating themselves from their enemies. In a hostile world, they erect rules and pledges and become hypervigilant about deviationism. They are more interested in protecting their special interests than converting outsiders. They slowly encase themselves in an epistemic cocoon.

The Democrat and Republican parties used to contain serious internal debates—between moderate and conservative Republicans, between New Democrats and liberals. Neither party does now.

The Democratic and Republican parties used to promote skilled coalition builders. Now the American parties have come to resemble the ideologically coherent European ones.

The Democrats talk and look like a conventional liberal party (some liberals, who represent, at most, 30 percent of the country, are disappointed because President Obama hasn't ushered in a *Huffington Post* paradise). Meanwhile, many Republicans flock to Herman Cain or Newt Gingrich because they are more interested in having a leader who can take on the mainstream news media than in having one who can plausibly govern. Grover Norquist's tax pledge isn't really about public policy; it's a chastity belt Republican politicians wear to show that they haven't been defiled by the Washington culture.

The era of the two moons is a volatile era. Independent voters are trapped in a cycle of sour rejectionism—voting against whichever of the two options they dislike most at the moment. The shift between the 2008 election, when voters rejected Republicans, and the 2010 election, when voters rejected Democrats, was as big as any shift in recent history.

Sometimes voters even reject both parties on the same day. In Ohio this month [November 2011], for example, voters rejected the main fiscal policy of the Republican governor. On the same ballot, by 31 points, they rejected health care reform, the main initiative of their Democratic president.

In policy terms, the era of the two moons is an era of stagnation. Each party is too weak to push its own agenda and too encased by its own cocoon to agree to a hybrid. The supercommittee failed for this reason. Members of the supercommittee actually took some brave steps outside party orthodoxy (Republicans embraced progressive tax increases, Democrats flirted with spending cuts), but these were baby steps, insufficient to change the alignment.

In normal circumstances, minority parties suffer a series of electoral defeats and then they modernize. But in the era of the two moons, the parties enjoy periodic election victories they don't deserve, which only re-enforce their worst habits.

So it's hard to see how we get out of this, unless some third force emerges, which wedges itself into one of the two parties, or unless we have a devastating fiscal crisis—a brutal cleansing flood, after which the sun will shine again.

STUDY QUESTIONS for "The Two Political Moons"

COMPREHENSION

1. Who coined the term "Sun Party"? What did he mean by the phrase?
2. By whom do the two political parties (Democrats and Republicans) "feel oppressed"?
3. Why can't either party effectively further its agenda?

DEVELOPMENT AND ORGANIZATION

1. Brooks repeats the phrase "used to" to present points of comparison and contrast. What does the phrase imply? Where do these instances occur? Why are the points important?

2. What concrete examples does Brooks use to support his primary points? Which points warrant more examples?
3. Offer two or three current examples of moon stagnation that could be effectively added to this article.

STYLE AND TECHNIQUE

1. Identify four words in the article whose meanings are unknown to you. Look them up in a dictionary and write out their primary definitions.
2. What words and images suggest that our two moons are creating an unhealthy political environment? Be specific.
3. Identify and list the transitions used between the paragraphs.

TEN-MINUTE TOPICS

1. Create a list of achievements (or failures) made by the Democrats or the Republicans; then discuss the consequences of these achievements (or failures) on the American public.
2. Discuss an individual or group who has attempted to challenge the stagnation created by the Democrats and the Republicans.
3. Compare and contrast the political system of another country to that of America.

A GUIDE TO INEQUALITY IN AMERICA

BY DAVID BROOKS

Foreign tourists are coming up to me on the streets and asking, "David, you have so many different kinds of inequality in your country. How can I tell which are socially acceptable and which are not?"

This is an excellent question. I will provide you with a guide to the American inequality map to help you avoid embarrassment.

Academic inequality is socially acceptable. It is perfectly fine to demonstrate that you are in the academic top 1 percent by wearing a Princeton, Harvard or Stanford sweatshirt.

Ancestor inequality is not socially acceptable. It is not permissible to go around bragging that your family came over on the Mayflower and that you are descended from generations of Throgmorton-Winthrops who bequeathed a legacy of good breeding and fine manners.

Fitness inequality is acceptable. It is perfectly fine to wear tight workout sweats to show the world that pilates have given you buns of steel. These sorts of displays are welcomed as evidence of your commendable self-discipline and reproductive merit.

Moral fitness inequality is unacceptable. It is out of bounds to boast of your superior chastity, integrity, honor or honesty. Instead, one must respect the fact that we are all morally equal, though our behavior and ethical tastes may differ.

Sports inequality is acceptable. It is normal to wear a Yankees jersey, an LSU T-shirt or the emblem of any big budget team. The fact that your favorite sports franchise regularly grounds opponents into dust is a signal of your overall prowess.

Church inequality is unacceptable. It would be uncouth to wear a Baptist or Catholic or Jewish jersey to signal that people of your faith are closer to God. It is wrong to look down on other faiths on the grounds that their creeds are erroneous.

Income inequality is acceptable. If you are a star baseball player, it is socially acceptable to sell your services for $25 million per year (after all, you have to do what's best for your family). If you are a star CEO, it's no longer quite polite to receive an $18 million compensation package, but everybody who can still does it.

Spending inequality is less acceptable. If you make $1 billion, it helps to go to work in jeans and black T-shirts. It helps to live in Omaha and eat in diners. If you make $200,000 a year, it is acceptable to spend money on any room previously used by servants, like the kitchen, but it is vulgar to spend on any adult toy that might give superficial pleasure, like a Maserati.

Technological inequality is acceptable. If you are the sort of person who understands the latest hardware and software advances, who knows the latest apps, it is acceptable to lord your superior connoisseurship over the aged relics who do not understand these things.

Cultural inequality is unacceptable. If you are the sort of person who attends opera or enjoys Ibsen plays, it is not acceptable to believe that you have a more refined sensibility than people who like Lady Gaga, Ke$ha or graffiti.

Status inequality is acceptable for college teachers. Universities exist within a finely gradated status structure, with certain schools like Brown clearly more elite than other schools. University departments are carefully ranked and compete for superiority.

Status inequality is unacceptable for high school teachers. Teachers at this level strongly resist being ranked. It would be loathsome to have one's department competing with other departments in nearby schools.

Beer inequality is on the way down. There used to be a high status difference between microbrews and regular old Budweiser. In academic jargon, beer had a high Gini Coefficient. But as microbrews went mainstream, these status differences diminished.

Cupcake inequality is on the way up. People will stand for hours outside of gourmet cupcake stores even though there are other adequate cupcakes on offer with no waiting at nearby Safeways.

Travel inequality is acceptable. It is perfectly normal to have separate check-in lines and boarding procedures for airline patrons who have achieved Gold, Platinum, Double Ruby or Sun God status.

Supermarket inequality is unacceptable. It would not be permissible to have separate checkout lines at the grocery store for obese frequent buyers who consume a lot of Twinkies.

Jock inequality is unacceptable if your kid is an average performer on his or her youth soccer team. If your kid is a star, then his or her accomplishments validate your entire existence.

Vocation inequality is acceptable so long as you don't talk about it. Surgeons have more prestige than valet parkers, but we do not acknowledge this. On the other hand, ethnic inequality—believing one group is better than another—is unacceptable (this is one of our culture's highest achievements).

Dear visitor, we are a democratic, egalitarian people who spend our days desperately trying to climb over each other. Have a nice stay.

STUDY QUESTIONS for "A Guide to Inequality in America"

COMPREHENSION

1. Which types of inequality are both acceptable and unacceptable?
2. Why is beer inequality on the way down?
3. Why, in the case of spending inequality, is it acceptable to live in Omaha and eat in diners?

DEVELOPMENT AND ORGANIZATION

1. Pick three paragraphs and support their controlling ideas with two or three additional examples.
2. Write out on a separate sheet of paper the first word of paragraphs 3-21. What do these words tell us about American behavior? How do you fit into or go against these generalizations?
3. Why is it acceptable (or is it?) for Brooks not to use clear paragraph transitions in this article?

STYLE AND TECHNIQUE

1. Why does Brooks choose to end (rather than begin) his article with a salutation?
2. Where are there examples of sarcasm? Is its use effective?
3. How does pop culture influence Brooks's findings?
4. After reading both of Brooks's articles ("The Two Political Moons," "A Guide to Inequality in America"), compare and contrast the writing styles he uses in these pieces.

TEN-MINUTE TOPICS

1. Name and describe three additional types of socially acceptable and unacceptable inequality. Support each with a concrete example.
2. Compare or contrast the inequalities given here with those of another culture or country. What do your findings tell you about that culture or country?
3. Using at least half of the words you listed in question 2 of the Development and Organization section above, write a poem about inequality in America.

CHAPTER SEVEN

CAUSE and EFFECT

DEFINITION

Cause and effect analysis is a pattern to which we have been frequently exposed as students. In sociology class, for instance, we may have been asked to consider why we hold certain beliefs and why we discriminate against certain types of people. In our history classes, we may have studied the causes behind the Revolutionary War, the Civil War, or the rise of power in Germany of the Third Reich. In a political science class, we may have studied the effect of a certain legislative act upon the people of the United States. And in philosophy class, we may have examined the effect of Christianity upon the development of Western thought. Thus, when we speak of *causes*, we are looking for reasons to explain a certain behavior, act, relationship, or phenomenon. When we focus upon *effects*, we are looking for consequences or results.

APPLICATION

Structurally, the cause and effect essay follows the expository format used in most of the other compositions. However, when we write such an essay, we must decide whether we are going to deal primarily with causes or effects. In the following editorial the writer seeks the main cause of the San Diego massacre of July 1984 in which twenty-one people were killed at a McDonald's restaurant:

> Critics are used to saying these are troubled times. Troubled, because amid the bountiful life most people enjoy, there is sorrow so profound that only through violence can it be expressed.
>
> James Oliver Huberty, who shot 21 innocent people dead and wounded another 20, was not that eccentric an American. But somewhere, somehow, something went awry.
>
> The San Diego carnage could have happened anywhere. But the likelihood of it happening in the United States is greater simply because the country has failed to live up to its lofty ideals. In a society where success is paramount, there is never really a retreat for the loser, except the abyss of his mind. In a society which glorifies the individual . . . the guilt of failure is borne by the person.
>
> Many have gone to the US . . . in pursuit of a dream. When the dream sours, what is left but the bitterness whose consequence is misdirected hatred? There are those, like Huberty, who cannot root themselves to something permanent and secure in the lotus land. . . . To them the only time they feel the sense of purpose and power is the moment, with guns and knives in their hands, they can destroy lives. . . . .

America indulges in its glories and its promises. But, alas, these men are on the outside, looking in with envy and rancor, and so long as they cannot attain what they want in the mainstream, they shall exercise the only avenue to success they know—a chapter in the annals of blood baths. . . .

America is at peace, but an undeclared war is waging every minute in the troubled souls lost in the land of plenty and of hopes. (Reprinted by permission of *Honolulu Advertiser*)

In the first two paragraphs, the writer introduces a situation or incident that requires some sort of explanation. He thus ends his introduction that directs us to seek a reason for the massacre: "But somewhere, somehow, something went awry." In a lengthier and therefore more in-depth essay, one could have considered a number of other possible causes contributing to Huberty's violent outburst, such as chronic depression, an argument with his wife, a history of unemployment, being bullied as a child and adolescent, and so on. Were we to briefly outline these hypothetical causes and arrange them in a logical order, the result may look something like this:

Thesis: A statement suggesting that Huberty's action can be understood as the end result of a life gone sour.

   I. First body paragraph.
      A. Cause: being bullied as a child and adolescent.
      B. Examples/proofs.
  II. Second body paragraph.
      A. Cause: lengthy history of employment difficulties.
      B. Examples/proofs.
 III. Third body paragraph.
      A. Cause: chronic depression.
      B. Examples/proofs.
 IV. Fourth body paragraph.
      A. Cause: argument and separation from wife.
      B. Examples/proofs.

While you can incorporate both causes and effects into the body of an essay (as Joan Didion does in an essay included in this chapter), most students find it easier to concentrate either upon cause or upon effect, not upon both. Accordingly, while the Huberty outline emphasizes causes, in the following excerpts from his essay "Of Studies," English Renaissance scientist and author Sir Francis Bacon emphasizes the effects of studying:

Studies serve for delight, for ornament, and for ability. Their chief use for delight, is in privateness and retiring; for ornament, is in discourse; and for ability, is in the judgment and disposition of business. For expert men can execute, and perhaps judge of particulars, one by one; but the general counsels, and the plots and marshalling of affairs, comes best from those that are learned. To spend too much time in studies is sloth; to use them too much for ornament, is affectation; to make judgment wholly by their rules, is the humor of a scholar. They perfect nature, and are perfected by experience: for natural abilities are like natural plants, that need pruning by study; and studies themselves do give forth directions too much at large, except they be bounded in by experience.

Here, Bacon is encouraging his own students by emphasizing the benefits, or effects, of studying. To paraphrase the rather difficult language of this passage, study in the privacy of one's chamber or room brings delight and enjoyment to the student; in other words, studying can be fun. Bacon goes on to say that if we study, we can gain enough knowledge to hold our ground in any "discourse," or conversation with others; studying therefore makes us knowledgeable. Finally, studying sharpens our mental acumen, our abilities, as we are required to use our judgment or reveal our character in the carrying out of business in our professional lives.

Note as well that Bacon warns against too much study, the results (again, effects) of which may be several: "sloth," or laziness; "affectation," revealed when we use what we have learned in our studies simply to show off and impress others; and, finally, a kind of narrow-mindedness, which comes from the scholar's decision to cut himself or herself off from the rest of the world. Bacon ends this paragraph by pointing to the main effect, or gain, of studies: studies, modified by actual life experiences, help perfect one's nature.

Later, in the same essay, Bacon gives examples of the benefits (or effects) resulting from specific fields of study: "Histories make men wise; poets[,] witty; the mathematics[,] subtle; natural philosophy[,] deep; moral[,] grave; logic and rhetoric[,] able to contend." In short, the study of history brings wisdom; studying mathematics enables one to draw fine distinctions and differences; the study of natural philosophy brings intellectual, emotional, and spiritual depth to the scholar; the study of morality makes one serious; and finally logic and rhetoric prepare one for a legal career involving arguing cases before a court.

For a final example of how to construct a cause and effect essay, let's look at excerpts from a student piece. In his essay, student Robert Marynow focuses upon the Beatle phenomenon:

When the jet carrying the Beatles touched down in New York City on the seventh of February, 1964, America and its people were forever changed. Nearly overnight the Beatles' music swept the country, exhilarating millions of teenagers. Concerts were complete pandemonium, full of shrieking so loud that they made even a jet plane inaudible.

Besides their music, the Beatles' personalities had a great impact on Americans, from changing many people's attitudes towards political issues to affecting how Americans dressed and cut their hair. Why were the Beatles such a phenomenon in America? The three major reasons were probably their unique music, their fresh image, and the historic occasion of their arrival in America.

Marynow has ended his introduction with a specific and concise thesis informing the reader that in the body of his essay, he is going to elaborate upon the three primary factors (causes) contributing to the Beatles' popularity. Here is his first body paragraph:

The Beatles brought a new sound to America. Though the Beatles' early material was greatly influenced by such great artists as Chuck Berry, Elvis Presley, and Buddy Holly, they were moved towards creating their own innovative sound. Their music combined the English folk sound with America's black rhythm and blues. So when the Beatles made their first appearance on the *Ed Sullivan Show*, Americans knew that they were experiencing a new kind of music, one that sounded familiar yet foreign. It was spirited, energetic music everyone could associate with, songs about love and life. By 1970, the Beatles' music became so popular that they had sold over 200 million singles.

The subsequent body paragraphs discuss, in the order in which the causes were arranged in the thesis, the Beatles' image and the historic occasion of their arrival. Finally, rather than summarizing the three chief causes behind the Beatles' popularity, Marynow makes a single statement emphasizing this group's terrific impact: "After more than forty years, the Beatles' popularity remains strong, proving that the genius of the Beatles is timeless."

PARADIGM

Writing the cause and effect essay is an exercise in logic. When you do write the cause and effect essay, you will find it helpful to keep in mind the following paradigms. Given the probable length of this essay, you should focus either upon illustrating the causes contributing to a specific effect or, conversely, upon discussing the effects proceeding from a specific cause.

Emphasis on Causes

Introduction
1. **Engage reader's interest.**
2. **Introduce topic.**
3. **Establish tone.**
4. **Present thesis, stating the causes of a certain phenomenon.**

First Body Paragraph
1. State cause.
2. Elaborate in specific and/or concrete detail.

Second Body Paragraph
1. State cause.
2. Elaborate in specific and/or concrete detail.

Third Body Paragraph
1. State cause.
2. Elaborate in specific and/or concrete detail.

Conclusion (options)
1. Summarize main points and restate thesis.
2. Offer a final image, message, or judgment.
3. Take a broader view.
4. End with quotation.
5. End with striking statistic.
6. Challenge the reader.
7. Something else.

Emphasis on Effects

Introduction
1. Engage reader's interest.
2. Introduce topic.
3. Establish tone.
4. Present thesis, in this case, the effects of a certain phenomenon.

First Body Paragraph
1. State effect.
2. Elaborate using specific and/or concrete details.

Second Body Paragraph
1. State effect.
2. Elaborate using specific and/or concrete details.

Third Body Paragraph
1. State effect.
2. Elaborate using specific and/or concrete details.

Conclusion (options)
1. Summarize main points and restate thesis.
2. Offer a final image, message, or judgment.
3. Take a broader view.
4. End with quotation.
5. End with striking statistic.
6. Challenge the reader.
7. Something else.

SUMMARY

One thing to be on guard for when we write the cause and effect essay is the *post hoc ergo propter hoc* fallacy (after this, therefore because of this). Often, when two events occur at proximate points in time, we wrongly tend to blame the second event upon the first. Thus, during the 2012 presidential election, President Obama was repeatedly blamed for having caused the enormous deficit under which this country was suffering; admittedly, he may have contributed to the deficit, but we must also keep in mind that when Obama took office in 2008 the country was already in the grip of a growing deficit. As another political example, when Richard Nixon took his office as president in 1968, a time when turmoil over Vietnam was at its peak, he was blamed for the war in Vietnam as well as for many domestic problems that he inherited but did not necessarily cause—in short, Nixon may have been a victim of faulty cause and effect reasoning. Thus, before we jump to a hasty conclusion and assume that one event is the cause of another, because both occurred at approximately the same period of time, we should examine all of the circumstances that could have contributed to the phenomenon in question.

HOW ABOUT BETTER PARENTS?

BY THOMAS L. FRIEDMAN

In recent years, we've been treated to reams of op-ed articles about how we need better teachers in our public schools and, if only the teachers' unions would go away, our kids would score like Singapore's on the big international tests. There's no question that a great teacher can make a huge difference in a student's achievement, and we need to recruit, train and reward more such teachers. But here's what some new studies are also showing: We need better parents. Parents more focused on their children's education can also make a huge difference in a student's achievement.

How do we know? Every three years, the Organization for Economic Cooperation and Development, or OECD, conducts exams as part of the Program for International Student Assessment, or PISA, which tests fifteen-year-olds in the world's leading industrialized nations on their reading comprehension and ability to use what they've learned in math and science to solve real problems—the most important skills for succeeding in college and life. America's fifteen-year-olds have not been distinguishing themselves in the PISA exams compared with students in Singapore, Finland and Shanghai.

To better understand why some students thrive taking the PISA tests and others do not, Andreas Schleicher, who oversees the exams for the OECD, was encouraged by the OECD countries to look beyond the classrooms. So starting with four countries in 2006, and then adding fourteen more in 2009, the PISA team went to the parents of 5,000 students and interviewed them "about how they raised their kids and then compared that with the test results" for each of those years, Schleicher explained to me. Two weeks ago, the PISA team published the three main findings of its study:

"Fifteen-year-old students whose parents often read books with them during their first year of primary school show markedly higher scores in PISA 2009 than students whose parents read with them infrequently or not at all. The performance advantage among students whose parents read to them in their early school years is evident regardless of the family's socioeconomic background. Parents' engagement with their fifteen-year-olds is strongly associated with better performance in PISA."

Schleicher explained to me that "just asking your child how was their school day and showing genuine interest in the learning that they are doing can have the same impact as hours of private tutoring. It is something every parent can do, no matter what their education level or social background."

For instance, the PISA study revealed that "students whose parents reported that they had read a book with their child 'every day or almost every day' or 'once or twice a week' during the first year of primary school have markedly higher scores in PISA 2009 than students whose parents reported that they had read a book with their child 'never or almost never' or only 'once or twice a month.' On average, the score difference is 25 points, the equivalent of well over half a school year."

Yes, students from more well-to-do households are more likely to have more involved parents. "However," the PISA team found, "even when comparing students of similar socioeconomic backgrounds, those students whose parents regularly read books to them when they were in the first year of primary school score 14 points higher, on average, than students whose parents did not."

The kind of parental involvement matters, as well. "For example," the PISA study noted, "on average, the score point difference in reading that is associated with parental involvement is largest when parents read a book with their child, when they talk about things they have done during the day, and when they tell stories to their children." The score point difference is smallest when parental involvement takes the form of simply playing with their children.

These PISA findings were echoed in a recent study by the National School Boards Association's Center for Public Education, and written up by the center's director, Patte Barth, in the latest issue of the *American School Board Journal*.

The study, called "Back to School: How Parent Involvement Affects Student Achievement," found something "somewhat surprising," wrote Barth: "Parent involvement can take many forms, but only a few of them relate to higher student performance. Of those that work, parental actions that support children's learning at home are most likely to have an impact on academic achievement at school.

"Monitoring homework; making sure children get to school; rewarding their efforts and talking up the idea of going to college. These parent actions are linked to better attendance, grades, test scores, and preparation for college," Barth wrote. "The study found that getting parents involved with their children's learning at home is a more powerful driver of achievement than parents attending PTA and school board meetings, volunteering in classrooms, participating in fund-raising, and showing up at back-to-school nights."

To be sure, there is no substitute for a good teacher. There is nothing more valuable than great classroom instruction. But let's stop putting the whole burden on teachers. We also need better parents. Better parents can make every teacher more effective.

STUDY QUESTIONS for "How About Better Parents?"

COMPREHENSION

1. What is the thesis, or central argument, of Friedman's essay? Where does he state it?
2. Friedman refers to two factors that play an important role in our children's education. What are they? Exactly how much influence do they have over students?
3. From what study does Friedman quote the most often, and what information does he quote from it?

DEVELOPMENT AND ORGANIZATION

1. What transitions does Friedman use between paragraphs? Where specifically does he signal that he is introducing a different cause or effect?
2. Friedman enumerates more than one way in which a parent can influence a student's success at school. What actions does he list? What exactly are their effects?
3. Take a look at the headnotes to the reporting chapter later in this book. Which methods of reporting does he use? What sort of reporting does Friedman rely on the most? Could he have used another type just as effectively? Which type? How could he have used it?

STYLE AND TECHNIQUE

1. Whether expository or argumentative, an essay must conform to certain principles: thesis, development and support, and organization (review the explanations of these terms in chapter one). Is Friedman's essay focused, developed, and well organized? Explain your answer.
2. When we write an argumentative essay, we should at some point acknowledge and respond to the opposition. Does Friedman do this? Where?
3. Does the final paragraph bring this essay to a satisfactory close? Why or why not?

TEN-MINUTE TOPICS

1. Can you think of any other factors, besides those named in this article, that might contribute to the poor performance by students? What are they, and how do they affect students? What can be done to lessen their influence?
2. Write about a time in the classroom that a teacher had a large effect on you. What class was it? What was the subject matter? What grade were you in? What exactly did you learn that day? How has that lesson influenced you since?
3. What factors in your own schooling have hindered you the most? Which have helped the most? After listing the factors, explain exactly how they have hindered or helped you.

LOS ANGELES NOTEBOOK

BY JOAN DIDION

There is something uneasy in the Los Angeles air this afternoon, some unnatural stillness, some tension. What it means is that tonight a Santa Ana will begin to blow, a hot wind from the northeast whining down through the Cajon and San Gorgonio Passes, blowing up sandstorms out along Route 66, drying the hills and the nerves to the flash point. For a few days now we will see smoke back in the canyons, and hear sirens in the night. I have neither heard nor read that a Santa Ana is due, but I know it, and almost everyone I have seen today knows it too. We know it because we feel it. The baby frets. The maid sulks. I rekindle a waning argument with the telephone company, then cut my losses and lie down, given over to whatever it is in the air. To live with the Santa Ana is to accept, consciously or unconsciously, a deeply mechanistic view of human behavior.

I recall being told, when I first moved to Los Angeles and was living on an isolated beach, that the Indians would throw themselves into the sea when the bad wind blew. I could see why. The Pacific turned ominously glossy during a Santa Ana period, and one woke in the night troubled not only by the peacocks screaming in the olive trees but by the eerie absence of surf. The heat was surreal. The sky had a yellow cast, the kind of light sometimes called "earthquake weather." My only neighbor would not come out of her house for days, and there were no lights at night, and her husband roamed the place with a machete. One day he would tell me that he had heard a trespasser, the next a rattlesnake.

"On nights like that," Raymond Chandler once wrote about the Santa Ana, "every booze party ends in a fight. Meek little wives feel the edge of the carving knife and study their husbands' necks. Anything can happen." That was the kind of wind it was. I did not know then that there was any basis for the effect it had on all of us, but it turns out to be another of those cases in which science bears out folk wisdom. The Santa Ana, which is named for one of the canyons it rushes through, is a *foehn* wind, like the *foehn* of Austria and Switzerland and the *hamsin* of Israel. There are a number of persistent malevolent winds, perhaps the best known of which are the mistral of France and the Mediterranean sirocco, but a *foehn* wind has distinct characteristics: it occurs on the leeward slope of a mountain range and, although the air begins as a cold mass, it is warmed as it comes down the mountain and appears finally as a hot dry wind. Whenever and wherever a *foehn* blows, doctors hear about headaches and nausea and allergies, about "nervousness," about "depression." In Los Angeles some teachers do not attempt to conduct formal classes during a Santa Ana, because the children become unmanageable. In Switzerland the suicide rate goes up during the *foehn*, and in the courts of some Swiss cantons the wind is considered a mitigating circumstance for crime. Surgeons are said to watch the wind, because blood does not clot normally during a *foehn*. A few years ago an Israeli physicist discovered that not only during such winds, but for the ten or twelve hours which precede them, the air carries an unusually high ratio of positive to negative ions. No one seems to know exactly why that should be; some talk about friction and others suggest solar disturbances. In any case the positive ions are there, and what an excess of positive ions does, in the simplest terms, is make people unhappy. One cannot get much more mechanistic than that.

Easterners commonly complain that there is no "weather" at all in Southern California, that the days and the seasons slip by relentlessly, numbingly bland. That is quite misleading. In fact the climate is characterized by infrequent but violent extremes: two periods of torrential subtropical rains which continue for weeks and wash out the hills and send subdivisions sliding toward the sea; about twenty scattered days a year of the Santa Ana, which, with its incendiary dryness, invariably means fire. At the first prediction of a Santa Ana, the Forest Service flies men and equipment from northern California into the southern forests, and the Los Angeles Fire Department cancels its ordinary non-firefighting routines. The Santa Ana caused Malibu to burn the way it did in 1956, and Bel Air in 1961, and Santa Barbara in 1964. In the winter of 1966-67 eleven men were killed fighting a Santa Ana fire that spread through the San Gabriel Mountains.

Just to watch the front-page news out of Los Angeles during a Santa Ana is to get very close to what it is about the place. The longest single Santa Ana period in recent years was in 1957, and it lasted not the usual three or four days but fourteen days, from November 21 until December 4. On the first day 25,000 acres of the San Gabriel Mountains were burning, with gusts reaching 100 miles an hour. In town, the wind reached Force 12, or hurricane force, on the Beaufort Scale; oil derricks were toppled and people ordered off the downtown streets to avoid injury from flying objects. On November 22 the fire in the San Gabriels was out of control. On November 24 six people were killed in automobile accidents, and by the end of the week the Los Angeles Times was keeping a box score of traffic deaths. On November 26 a prominent Pasadena attorney, depressed about money, shot and killed his wife, their two sons, and himself. On November 27 a South Gate divorcée, twenty-two, was murdered and thrown from a moving car. On November 30 the San Gabriel fire was still out of control, and the wind in town was blowing eighty miles an hour. On the first day of December four people died violently, and on the third the wind began to break.

It is hard for people who have not lived in Los Angeles to realize how radically the Santa Ana figures in the local imagination. The city burning is Los Angeles's deepest image of itself: Nathaniel West perceived that, in The Day of the Locust; and at the time of the 1965 Watts riots what struck the imagination most indelibly were the fires. For days one could drive the Harbor Freeway and see the city on fire, just as we had always known it would be in the end. Los Angeles weather is the weather of catastrophe, of apocalypse, and, just as the reliably long and bitter winters of New England determine the way life is lived there, so the violence and the unpredictability of the Santa Ana affect the entire quality of life in Los Angeles, accentuate its impermanence, its unreliability. The wind shows us how close to the edge we are.

STUDY QUESTIONS for "Los Angeles Notebook"

COMPREHENSION

1. What is the thesis of this essay? Where does she state her thesis?
2. What are some of the effects of the Santa Ana wind, according to Didion? In which paragraphs does she focus upon effects?
3. How, according to the first paragraph, does Didion know that a Santa Ana is due in the L. A. area?
4. What does Didion mean, when she writes at the end of her first paragraph, "To live with the Santa Ana is to accept, consciously or unconsciously, a deeply mechanistic view of human behavior"?

DEVELOPMENT AND ORGANIZATION

1. How does this essay use cause and effect reasoning?
2. Where does Didion make use of concrete/descriptive detail in her essay? What is gained by using descriptive detail in this essay?
3. According to the essay, what is the scientific basis for the effect that the Santa Ana has upon the area and its people? In what paragraph does Didion provide the scientific explanation?
4. Where does Didion make use of examples? What is the benefit of using examples in this essay?
5. Where does she make use of facts and statistics? What is gained by incorporating these elements into her essay?

STYLE AND TECHNIQUE

1. Discuss the opening sentence of the essay: how has it succeeded in capturing your attention?
2. Didion seems to draw an analogy between the weather and the Los Angeles lifestyle. What analogy is she drawing? How does it contrast with the impression that Easterners have of Los Angeles's weather?

TEN-MINUTE TOPICS

1. Write about the causes or effects of some natural phenomenon in the area where you live.
2. Write about a natural disaster you may have lived through—a hurricane, tornado, blizzard, forest fire, and so on—and how it affected your life.
3. Write your own "Los Angeles Story"—about Los Angeles, or about another city.

BASEBALL: MYTH AND LEGEND

BY TODD SCOTT MOFFETT

Until I die, I will prefer baseball to any other American sport. My love for baseball started in childhood, when I could listen to either the Dodgers or the Angels on the radio. So much of the sport's power comes from anticipation, not from action: you wait for the pitcher to throw, you wait for the batter to swing; ball, strike, foul ball after foul ball; and then resolution—walk, strikeout, fly ball, groundout, sacrifice, base hit. The medium of radio worked best with my anticipation, for the radio let me imagine the movements of the pitcher, the batter, and the fielders, and it let me hear the crowd, who waited with as much anxiety as I did. The radio also allowed me to learn. During the tense lulls between pitches, the announcers brought up statistics, streaks, and lore ("Baylor is batting three-forty-five with men in scoring position"; "Joyner is hitting over four hundred for the month of April"; "Downing pitched Aaron's record-breaker, and now he faces the Phillies' hottest hitter") that made me aware of the players and forces at work during these critical moments. The information not only heightened the tension but also gave me the history of the game. No other sport can be so reflective about its own history while being broadcast.

Baseball's self-reflective character, especially as seen in its obsession with numbers, has been noted by many commentators. Every outcome of every play can be categorized and stored as a statistic, and these statistics, due to the static nature of the game, can be used to compare the players of all generations. But during the magical seasons when players strive for seasonal or career records, statistics become living things—quarry, prey—and the players themselves become hunters. Willingly or not, the players chase down these statistics, and for the fan, the excitement of the chase adds itself to the magic of the comparison. Again, I think of my childhood when a player makes his run at a record. We had a hill so steep and long in my hometown that no one would dare to skateboard down it. But then someone would shout, "Look! Tommy's trying to skate the hill!" And every child within running distance would flock to the hill to see Tommy make his run. That's the excitement a fan feels when a ballplayer braves a hallowed record. Will he make it? Will he not? And if he crashes, how bloody will it be?

But there is no greater comparison, and no greater hunt, than during seasons with home run chases. The number sixty-one will immediately light up any group of baseball fans, and a slugger who has thirty home runs by the All-Star break cannot escape its mystique. No other sport has such a record; the only other that approaches it in difficulty is the 2,000 yards-per-season barrier for a running back in football. But because this milestone was achieved only after the growth of the football season to fourteen and then to sixteen games—the equivalent of making the baseball season two hundred games long—it has nowhere near the weight of glory and history associated with it. It cannot be used as a measuring stick for any of the great running backs—Jim Brown, Bronko Nagurski—who played in the twelve-game era. It does not unite the generations as does the home run record. Despite the shift from a 154-game to a 162-game schedule, Mark

McGwire, Ken Griffey, Jr., Sammy Sosa, Roger Maris, and Babe Ruth will forever be measured against one another—and against the players of the future—for their ability to hit the most home runs in a single season.

To some fans, though, the home run record—or any record, for that matter—is far more important than the chase. The record becomes some sort of monolith, a cathedral, that no one can approach without angering the gods. I don't like this attitude. To immortalize a record is to kill the incentive of the players who chase the record: Why chase down immortality if all it will do is destroy them? It becomes a device not for comparing but for belittling the efforts of all those who must live in its shadow. Hence the backlash against players like Aaron, Maris, and Ripken, who dared to topple the monoliths. The record setters, Ruth and Gehrig, were not gods, but men, and taking their records out of the realm of mortals defaces the human qualities of the men who set them. No, let the records live among men, and if a ballplayer is fortunate enough to catch one, let him release it for the next generation to catch.

I use the hunting metaphor deliberately. Baseball has many levels of meaning, one of which is mythological. A myth expresses the world view and the beliefs of a people, and baseball is a quintessential mode of American self-expression, peppering our language with metaphors and providing us a means of transmitting our values to cultures worldwide. (Particularly interesting is that Lewis and Clark engaged the Indians in a primitive form of "base ball" during their expedition and that baseball has flourished among nations we have warred with: Cuba, Vietnam, Korea, and Japan). Baseball as American myth draws from a primitive source—the myth of the frontier. And at the center of the frontier myth stands the hunter, the man who crosses the frontier, back and forth, between the known and the foreign, the safe and the dangerous, the city and the wilderness. As explained by Richard Slotkin in his book *Regeneration through Violence: The Mythology of the American Frontier, 1600-1860*, the lore of Daniel Boone comprises the first great body of mythmaking in American literature. For the first three hundred and fifty years of its existence, the Euro-American civilization confronted a wilderness with many guises—mountain range, desert, forest, and Indian savage. The hunter represented American Literature's first successful attempt to define our culture's relationship with that wilderness.

I believe that baseball is a modern descendant of this myth. The actual frontier has disappeared, legislated out of existence by Congress in 1890, but the mythic frontier lives on in baseball. In the place of the frontier, we have the outfield wall, which separates the Known World from the Other World. This distinction between the known and the unknown, the real world and the magical, is portrayed most dramatically in the movie *Field of Dreams*. From the cornfields bordering the outfield come the ghosts of the players, and into the cornfields disappears the writer Terence Mann, who journeys on a quest unknown to us. That cornfield also suggests ancient vegetation mythologies and rites, ancient powers of life-giving potency, that open up several avenues of exploration beyond our scope here.

But a simple trip to a normal playing field will also show us the legacy of the frontier myth in baseball. If you stand at home plate and look down the foul lines, the field does not end, as does the football field or the basketball court. Those two playing surfaces are completely surrounded; they turn in upon themselves, goals facing one another. (It says something ominous about our culture that each of these new pastimes in turn has brought us to a smaller playing field.) The baseball field is never surrounded. It carries the eyes far beyond the confines of the park. The foul lines stretch into the sky, into eternity, thrust there by the poles. All the universe becomes part of the playing field—as seen at Wrigley Field, where fans can watch from the surrounding buildings and chase down the longest of the home runs, and as seen at the new retro baseball stadiums, which allow fans a view of the cityscapes beyond the outfield seats. As suggested above, that greater universe beyond the outfield wall represents the unknown, the otherworldly, the dangerous, the wilderness, to which only the strongest of men can journey. Inside the outfield wall is the known limit of the American continent, presented in much the same scope as it must have appeared to the earliest colonists and explorers. The infield represents the semi-tamed pastoral community, with outposts set at its farthest reaches. Home, and safety, is represented in the tiniest corner of the playing field.

And in the place of the hunter we have the batter. Like the hunter, the batter must leave the safety of home (after an initiatory struggle with the pitcher), explore the continent, and return home with what he has discovered. Even when he first approaches home plate, the batter resembles the hunter, bat slung like a spear or rifle or bow over his shoulder. The great slayer, the great killer of the batter, is the baseball, which the batter must avoid at all costs. The baseball put in play forces the nine guardians (or bears, or wolves, or Indians) to retrieve it in time to use its deadly powers on the runners, before they can reach the safety of the bases. But the great paradox of the game is that the deeper the ball travels into the field, toward the wilderness, the quicker the runners can return home to safety. And stemming from this paradox comes the great power of the home run hitter. By hitting the ball over the fence, into the wilderness, he reaches into the realm of the unknown, into that great beyond, and receives not only the power to return home, but the power to redeem any runner stranded in the outposts before him. He redeems us, the audience, as well, spinning our flaxen anticipation into gold. Thus we revere the home run hitter more than the singles hitter—who knows what the single season singles record is?—because he takes us into the magic realm, the ancient realm of life-potency, banishes all the obstacles set before us, and allows us to partake in a great mystery.

His action represents the suspension of time. Baseball by its very nature is without temporal boundaries, being the only major sport played without a clock. But each home run hit, because it reaches into the eternal realm beyond the outfield wall, recalls another home run, and another before that, and another. Each home run hitter recalls the one before him, and the one before him. Quick—what are the greatest moments in World Series history? Almost all are home runs: Jim Leyritz's home run in the 1996 World Series recalls Joe Carter's home run in 1993, recalls Gibson's in 1988, recalls Reggie's three shots in the late 1970s, recalls Fisk's in 1975, recalls Mazeroski's in 1960, recalls

Ruth's famous called shot in the 1930s. The home runs are not merely repetitions of one another; because they partake of the same mystery and tap into the same life energy, they become one and the same act and thereby unite each hitter, and each person who watches him hit, in the same ceremony of tension and anticipation released. Thus the ease by which we make our comparisons: when time stops, comparisons begin.

As I write this, the great home run chase of 1998 is heading into its final weeks. Babe Ruth, in the follow-through of his mighty swing, is on the cover of the latest *Sports Illustrated*. Mark McGwire and Sammy Sosa seek the life force that lies beyond the outfield wall and with each home run hit bring some of its energy back to us. It is an energy I cherish as a fan, an energy that has brought enthusiasm to millions—an energy that only baseball can bring. Here's proof: back in May, my wife and some friends and I went to Qualcomm Park to see the Cards play the Padres. Twenty thousand fans came early to see Mark McGwire take batting practice, and several fans cheered when he hit his twenty-seventh home run in the first inning. And we didn't even need radios.

STUDY QUESTIONS for "Baseball: Myth and Legend"

COMPREHENSION

1. What is baseball to Moffett? State the answer in your own words.
2. Discuss what Moffett means when he makes the following statements:
   a. "Baseball's self-reflective character, especially as seen in its obsession with numbers, has been noted by many commentators."
   b. "The record becomes some sort of monolith, a cathedral, that no one can approach without angering the gods."
   c. "Baseball has many levels of meaning, one of which is mythological."
   d. "[The home run hitter's] action represents a suspension of time. Baseball by its very nature is without temporal boundaries, being the only major sport played without a clock."

DEVELOPMENT AND ORGANIZATION

1. Is the thesis of this essay directly stated or implied? If directly stated, in what paragraph does it appear? If implied, write the thesis in your own words.
2. Discuss Moffett's composition as a cause-and-effect essay. Does he emphasize causes or effects? What are they?
3. What other modes studied in this text does the writer use in defining baseball? Where, for instance, does he make use of analogy? How many analogies does he use? Where does he use examples? What is gained through the use of examples? Where does he use comparison and contrast?
4. Where does the writer make use of specific details—that is, words and phrases that answer the questions *who? what? when? where? how much?* Why is it a good idea to use specific details in our writing?

STYLE AND TECHNIQUE

1. What is the tone of the essay? What is the writer's attitude towards sports records? About baseball?
2. How effective is Moffett's introduction in capturing your attention? What has he done to make this introduction—and the essay that follows—interesting?
3. What words and details in the introduction help draw the reader into this essay?
4. What does Moffett do in his conclusion: restate the thesis, summarize the main points, take a broader view, or something else? How effective is Moffett's concluding paragraph? How does this paragraph create the impression that the essay is complete?

TEN-MINUTE TOPICS

1. Describe the effects of your favorite sport, hobby, or other activity on your life. How often do you engage in the activity? How much time do you spend when you engage with it? How does it make you feel? What do others think of your activity?
2. Describe the effects of a particular sport on the American lifestyle. How does that sport engage its fans? What do fans do to celebrate their sport? What happens to those fans when something negative (a big loss, a scandal) occurs?
3. This essay was written before Barry Bonds set the home run record in 2001—and before the steroid scandal tarnished the baseball records set during the late 1990s and the early 2000s. Write a paragraph for this essay—or an essay in response to Moffett's—in which you take those two factors into account.

MY WOOD

BY E. M. FORSTER

A few years ago I wrote a book which dealt in part with the difficulties of the English in India. Feeling that they would have had no difficulties in India themselves, the Americans read the book freely. The more they read it the better it made them feel, and a check to the author was the result. I bought a wood with the check. It is not a large wood—it contains scarcely any trees, and it is intersected, blast it, by a public footpath. Still, it is the first property that I have owned, so it is right that other people should participate in my shame, and should ask themselves, in accents that will vary in horror, this very important question: What is the effect of property upon the character? Don't let's touch economics; the effect of private ownership upon the community as a whole is another question—a more important question, perhaps, but another one. Let's keep to psychology. If you own things, what's their effect on you? What's the effect on me of my wood?

In the first place, it makes me feel heavy. Property does have this effect. Property produces men of weight, and it was a man of weight who failed to get into the Kingdom of Heaven. He was not wicked, that unfortunate millionaire in the parable, he was only stout; he stuck out in front, not to mention behind, and as he wedged himself this way and that in the crystalline entrance and bruised his well-fed flanks, he saw beneath him a comparatively slim camel passing through the eye of a needle and being woven into the robe of God. The Gospels all through couple stoutness and slowness. They point out what is perfectly obvious, yet seldom realized: that if you have a lot of things you cannot move about a lot, that furniture requires dusting, dusters require servants, servants require insurance stamps, and the whole tangle of them makes you think twice before you accept an invitation to dinner or go for a bathe in the Jordan. Sometimes the Gospels proceed further and say with Tolstoy that property is sinful; they approach the difficult ground of asceticism here, where I cannot follow them. But as to the immediate effects of property on people, they just show straightforward logic. It produces men of weight. Men of weight cannot, by definition, move like the lightning from the East unto the West, and the ascent of a fourteen-stone[1] bishop into a pulpit is thus the exact antithesis of the coming of the Son of Man. My wood makes me feel heavy.

In the second place, it makes me feel it ought to be larger.

The other day I heard a twig snap in it. I was annoyed at first, for I thought that someone was blackberrying, and depreciating the value of the undergrowth. On coming nearer, I saw it was not a man who had trodden on the twig and snapped it, but a bird, and I felt pleased. My bird. The bird was not equally pleased. Ignoring the relation between us, it took fright as soon as it saw the shape of my face, and flew straight over the boundary hedge into a field, the property of Mrs. Henessy, where it sat down with a loud squawk. It had become Mrs. Henessy's bird. Something seemed grossly amiss here,

---

[1] A stone, an English unit of weight, is fourteen pounds; therefore, a fourteen-stone bishop would weigh 196 pounds.

something that would not have occurred had the wood been larger. I could not afford to buy Mrs. Henessy out, I dared not murder her, and limitations of this sort beset me on every side. Ahab did not want that vineyard—he only needed it to round off his property, preparatory to plotting a new curve—and all the land around my wood has become necessary to me in order to round off the wood. A boundary protects. But—poor little thing—the boundary ought in its turn to be protected. Noises on the edge of it. Children throw stones. A little more, and then a little more, until we reach the sea. Happy Canute! Happier Alexander! And after all, why should even the world be the limit of possession? A rocket containing a Union Jack, will, it is hoped, be shortly fired at the moon. Mars. Sirius. Beyond which . . . But these immensities ended by saddening me. I could not suppose that my wood was the destined nucleus of universal dominion—it is so very small and contains no mineral wealth beyond the blackberries. Nor was I comforted when Mrs. Henessy's bird took alarm for the second time and flew clean away from us all, under the belief that it belonged to itself.

In the third place, property makes its owner feel that he ought to do something to it. Yet he isn't sure what. A restlessness comes over him, a vague sense that he has a personality to express—the same sense which, without any vagueness, leads the artist to an act of creation. Sometimes I think I will cut down such trees as remain in the wood, at other times I want to fill up the gaps between them with new trees. Both impulses are pretentious and empty. They are not honest movements towards money-making or beauty. They spring from a foolish desire to express myself and from an inability to enjoy what I have got. Creation, property, enjoyment form a sinister trinity in the human mind. Creation and enjoyment are both very, very good, yet they are often unattainable without a material basis, and at such moments property pushes itself in as a substitute, saying, "Accept me instead—I'm good enough for all three." It is not enough. It is, as Shakespeare said of lust, "The expense of spirit in a waste of shame": it is "Before, a joy proposed; behind, a dream." Yet we don't know how to shun it. It is forced on us by our economic system as the alternative to starvation. It is also forced on us by an internal defect in the soul, by the feeling that in property may lie the germs of self-development and of exquisite or heroic deeds. Our life on earth is, and ought to be, material and carnal. But we have not yet learned to manage our materialism and carnality properly; they are still entangled with the desire for ownership, where (in the words of Dante) "Possession is one with loss."

And this brings us to our fourth and final point: the blackberries.

Blackberries are not plentiful in this meager grove, but they are easily seen from the public footpath which traverses it, and all too easily gathered. Foxgloves, too—people will pull up the foxgloves, and ladies of an educational tendency even grub for toadstools to show them on the Monday in class. Other ladies, less educated, roll down the bracken in the arms of their gentlemen friends. There is paper, there are tins. Pray, does my wood belong to me or doesn't it? And, if it does, should I not own it best by allowing no one else to walk there? There is a wood near Lyme Regis, also cursed by a public footpath, where the owner has not hesitated on this point. He has built high stone walls each side of the path, and has spanned it by bridges, so that the public circulate like termites while he gorges on the blackberries unseen. He really does own his wood, this able chap. Dives in Hell did pretty well, but the gulf dividing him from Lazarus could be traversed by vision, and nothing traverses it here. And perhaps I shall come to this in time. I shall wall in and fence out until I really taste the sweets of property. Enormously stout, endlessly avaricious, pseudo-creative, intensely selfish, I shall weave upon my forehead the quadruple crown of possession until those nasty Bolshies come and take it off again and thrust me aside into the outer darkness.

STUDY QUESTIONS for "My Wood"

COMPREHENSION

1. Why did Forster write this essay? What do you think is his overriding purpose? Is it to talk about owning a wood, a piece of land containing many trees, or does he have something else in mind? Explain.
2. Who is Forster's primary audience? That is, for whom is the essay initially written? What are some of the characteristics of this audience? How do you know?
3. Does the essay contain a direct statement of thesis?

DEVELOPMENT AND ORGANIZATION

1. In the body paragraphs of this essay, does Forster focus primarily upon causes or effects? Explain.
2. Does Forster arrange the body paragraphs in any kind of logical order? Would the essay have been just as effective, for instance, if he had put the last paragraph second or third in the essay? Why or why not?
3. Where does Forster make effective use of example to illustrate how owning the wood has altered him?
4. In this essay, Forster frequently alludes to figures in the Bible and/or in Western history. Where does he do this, and why? How do the references to these people contribute to Forster's overall purpose?

STYLE AND TECHNIQUE

1. What tone does Forster adopt: high, middle, or low? Why?
2. What sort of impression of himself is Forster trying to convey to the reader? Is Forster to be taken seriously, for instance, when he appears to choose the great outer darkness—permanent isolation from God—at the end of his essay?
3. Can you find any sentence in which Forster refers to the specific ways in which he has been influenced by owning this wood? If so, where is this statement? What is gained by putting this statement where you have found it?

TEN-MINUTE TOPICS

1. Write about the effects of owning something else such as a car or a house. You may write it in the tone that Forster uses in his essay above, or you may try for a different tone. Remember to use specific details when describing the possession under consideration.
2. Why do you suppose people want more than they have? Write down any number of causes and then speculate on what these causes will lead to.
3. What is ownership? Define it. How does it shape you and others you know?

CHAPTER EIGHT

CLASSIFICATION and DIVISION

DEFINITION

Classification and division are two more methods of organizing our thoughts and impressions. Whereas *classification* requires us to break a group of things into two or more classes or categories, *division* requires us to break one thing into its component parts. Classification, therefore, always deals with a group of things and represents a pattern of organization with which we are, consciously or unconsciously, familiar. For instance, a little league baseball coach might classify opposing teams into at least three categories, based upon their levels of skill: the good teams, which win through good pitching, good fielding, and good hitting; the average teams, which likely contain an uneven balance of hitting, pitching, and fielding; and the weak teams, which are generally characterized by glaring weakness in at least one important area of the game. Division, on the other hand, always deals with one thing. Thus, to analyze a short story, we use division, breaking the work into component parts: plot, setting, character, point of view, conflict, and so on. Again, to explain how to write an essay, we use division as we break the composition into introduction, body, and conclusion. To explain how the federal government works, we would need to discuss in great detail the function of each of its components: the congressional, the presidential, and the judicial.

APPLICATION—CLASSIFICATION

Our first task in developing a classification essay is to select a group of things that, once a basis is established, can be sorted into classes. The topics are numerous: friends, teachers, students, games, movies, songs, shoes, comic strips, restaurants, salespeople, dogs, cats, and so on. Thus, teachers could be broken into four classes on the basis of their knowledge of the subject matter; conceivably, we could have the following groups: (1) teachers who have an excellent background in the topic they are teaching, (2) teachers who have an adequate background in the course's topic, (3) teachers who seem to have little background in the topic, and (4) teachers who apparently have no background.

In her essay "The Cat's Meow," student Teresa Cannon breaks cats into three categories, providing in the body of her essay vivid examples of each category. While her audience may be cat lovers, the essay's playfulness, its superb organization, and its effective use of examples to illustrate each class make Cannon's essay worth our reading. Here is her opening paragraph:

> According to the *Funk & Wagnalls Standard Dictionary, International Edition* (1978), a cat is "a domesticated carnivorous mammal with retractable claws: it kills mice and rats and is of worldwide distribution in various breeds." However, a cat evokes more

of a mental picture than the definition elicits. Usually the image is defined better by the demeanor of the animal than by the simple anatomy of the creature. The demeanor of cats can vary as much as the behavior of people. However, I have noticed that the behavior of most cats falls into categories. Although most cats show characteristics of more than one behavior type, they display one type prominently. As a cat owner, I have found that domestic felines can be divided into three groups according to their behavior: royal cats, lover cats, and weird cats.

Students are often encouraged not to rely upon dictionaries to begin their essays. However, Cannon makes particularly effective use of *Funk & Wagnalls* as she points out that the standard definition of *cat* fails to capture the essence of this animal. Along with this, her objection to the accepted definition represents her attempts to engage her reader's interest and introduces her topic; as well, it leads to her establishing the basis of her own classification: the demeanor or behavior of cats. Her thesis, the last sentence of this first paragraph, is very specific and tells the reader that the body will consist of three parts, each one focusing upon a different feline personality. Finally, in her opening paragraph, Cannon also establishes the tone of playfulness that she maintains throughout the essay.

Now let's look at a body paragraph from the same essay. Notice that Cannon uses the first or topic sentence of the following paragraph to introduce the classification; she uses the second sentence to touch upon characteristics that distinguish this type of cat from the others. Then, becoming even more specific, she moves on to two examples.

Royal cats, the first group, believe they own the castle and treat their owners like attendants. Royal cats allow their attendants to pet them occasionally, require gourmet dinners, rest in the most comfortable place in the house, and play very little. Princess exemplified a royal cat. She endured petting. When one of her attendants (owners) would pet her, she would sigh deeply and look into the distance to prove her inattentiveness. If she tired, she would stand, glare at the offender, and move out of reach. There she would settle herself in a regal manner. When mealtime arrived she sauntered to the kitchen and sat on the exact same tile on which she expected her bowl placed. Never lowering herself to cry for food, she would wait in erect posture for her dinner. She accepted only moist, foil-packaged cat food since she believed that peasants ate dry, bagged food and slobs ate wet, canned food. Thomas also illustrated a royal cat. He slept only on a pillow on his attendants' bed. If his attendants moved the pillow, he would make known his displeasure by rearranging the covers. He never played games. Very rarely, the play of his attendants would entertain him, as long as he thought no one knew. Royal cats do not make the best companions; however, they make excellent showcase pets.

The examples are noteworthy for their use of specific and concrete details that allow the reader to "see" these two royal cats: Princess and Thomas. Also effective are words suggesting the royal cats' conceit: owners are referred to as "attendants"; Princess "endured petting"; she practices "inattentiveness"; she is said to "glare at offenders"; and she "sauntered" rather than merely walked to the kitchen. The word choice here not only gives the reader a clear picture of the royal cat; it also maintains the writer's humorous tone.

Now let us move on to Cannon's conclusion:

> When a proud new cat owner first takes possession of that playful bundle of fur, the owner has no idea how the personality of the kitten will develop. One morning, the owner pours the cat's dry food as usual. What's this? The cat balks! One day, the playful kitten refuses to play. This kitten has developed into a royal cat. Or perhaps the kitten soon learns to jump into the bed. Each morning, the owner awakens to the loving purr of the kitten. The kitten becomes the owner's constant companion. The owner has acquired a lover cat. In yet another scene, the kitten matures physically but continues to behave like a kitten. One morning, the owner finds his cat hiding under a pile of newspaper. The owner has acquired, by questionable fortune, a weird cat. In all these instances, the sweet little kitten has become a cat and, in the meantime, a relationship has developed. Whether royal, lover, or weird, that cat is loved.

In this conclusion, Cannon uses example and concrete detail not only to review the three kinds of cats but to suggest that the behaviors, or demeanors, are interchangeable. Any cat is likely, at one time or another, to exhibit all three behaviors.

PARADIGM

Teresa Cannon's "The Cat's Meow" provides a clear example of how to write a classification essay. The paradigm that she has followed in putting together her essay is one that the student needs to keep in mind. Obviously, students should remember that they are not necessarily limited to a five-paragraph essay.

Introduction
    1. Engage the reader's attention.
    2. Introduce topic.
    3. Establish tone.
    4. Present thesis.

First Body Paragraph
1. Use topic sentence to introduce class.
2. Give distinguishing characteristics.
3. Support with examples and/or concrete details.

Second Body Paragraph
1. Use topic sentence to introduce class.
2. Give distinguishing characteristics.
3. Support with examples and/or concrete details.

Third Body Paragraph
1. Use topic sentence to introduce class.
2. Give distinguishing characteristics.
3. Support with examples and/or concrete details.

Conclusion (options)
1. Summarize main points and restate thesis.
2. Offer a final image, message, or judgment.
3. Take a broader view.
4. End with quotation.
5. End with striking statistic.
6. Challenge the reader.
7. Something else.

APPLICATION—DIVISION

The division essay may seem a little more demanding that the classification essay simply because division requires us to go into more specific detail as we break our topic into its component parts. Yet, almost any subject lends itself to division: the human body, specific organs in the body, a restaurant, a hotel, a ship, a leaf, a game, a city council, a baseball team, birth, death, ad infinitum. Further, we should have been exposed in our reading or in other classes to the use of division. Sigmund Freud, the father of psychoanalysis, employed division when he theorized that the human mind has three parts: Id, Ego, and Superego. Again, Thomas Harris, in his bestseller *I'm OK—You're OK*, uses division when he breaks the human personality into three distinct yet related parts:

> Continual observation has supported the assumption that these three states [parent, adult, and child] exist in all people. It is as if in each person there is the same little person he was when he was three years old.

There are also within him his own parents. These are recordings in the brain of actual experiences of internal and external events, the most significant of which happened during the first five years of life. There is a third state, different from these two. The first two are called parent and child, and the third, adult.

This paragraph, coming as it does in the introduction to Harris's second chapter entitled "Parent, Adult, and Child," serves as the thesis for the entire chapter. Harris then goes on to discuss each component of the human personality in specific detail, even occasionally giving examples to ensure that the reader has a clear idea of what he's discussing.

Now let's look at a student example. In her essay "Me," Cheryl Alberto breaks one thing—herself—into its various components: wife, mother, friend, student, and so on. While Alberto gives us a fairly good essay, one weakness is that she does not make much of an effort to engage her reader's attention in the opening paragraph and implicitly convince the reader that this is an essay that needs to be read. What could she have done to capture the reader's interest more effectively?

Here is an excerpt from her essay:

Sometimes I feel that I am becoming like Sybil and separating into my different selves. Wife, mother, friend, student, housekeeper, and just I myself all have a different story to tell. At times it is hard to believe that they, who seem so very different from one another, are all me.

The side of myself that is a wife I consider to be one of the most important. She expects to be married to the same man long after the children are grown and gone, and so she works hard at keeping her marriage happy. Giving her husband encouragement in his decisions and emotional support when needed, sharing in the everyday problems, and even offering advice when he has problems in his job are some of the issues she deals with.

The part of me that is a mother is always trying to be perfect. She reads her children stories at bedtime, listens to her children when they want to speak, drives them to school and picks them up, and attends all the school functions. Mothering to her is always being concerned with the emotional and mental well-being of her children. When the mother in me has to take a backseat to another part of myself and can't be as perfect as she wants to be, she becomes terribly frustrated.

Frustration is common also to the part of myself that is a friend to others. The friend in me wishes she could wave a magic wand and make all the troubles of her friends vanish in a puff of smoke. Since she realizes that she can't accomplish that feat, she usually takes on more of others' problems than she can handle. When friends call and say that they need her, this part of me will surface immediately and drop just about everything to rush to their aid.

While Alberto's essay may seem bit general in places—she could have used specific and briefly developed examples in her body paragraphs—it does illustrate what a division essay is supposed to do: break one thing into component parts with the intention of showing how these parts function in relation to the whole.

In her conclusion, instead of simply summarizing the essay's main points, Alberto challenges the readers to see the many facets of their own personalities that make them unique:

> It is the different selves in each of us that make us unique. Some people have more sides to their personality, and some people have fewer, but no one has the same sides in the same priority as someone else. I for one am very thankful for this as the thought of being unique appeals to "all my selves."

Consciously or unconsciously, we regularly employ division. For instance, when we sit down at the breakfast table in the morning and decide how we are going to partition our day, we are using division. When we discuss why a certain TV commercial is so effective, we have to break the commercial into component parts—product, actors, implied story line or situation, background images and sounds, etc. The aim would be to come to an understanding of how all of these elements work together to promote the sales of such and such a product.

PARADIGM

Like the other expository essays we have discussed, division can be visually understood in terms of a paradigm. Keep in mind that the paradigm is only a guide and that introductions may consist of more than one paragraph just as each component part of the topic to be divided may require more than one body paragraph.

Introduction
  1. **Engage the reader's attention.**
  2. **Introduce topic.**
  3. **Establish tone.**
  4. **Present thesis.**

First Body Paragraph
  1. **Use topic sentence to name first component.**
  2. **Explain/describe this component in detail.**

Second Body Paragraph
1. Use topic sentence to name second component.
2. Explain/describe this component in detail.

Third Body Paragraph
1. Use topic sentence to name third component.
2. Explain/describe this component in detail.

Conclusion (options)
1. Summarize main points and restate thesis.
2. Offer a final image, message, or judgment.
3. Take a broader view.
4. End with quotation.
5. End with striking statistic.
6. Challenge the reader.
7. Something else.

SUMMARY

Classification always breaks up groups of things into various classes or categories. We classify doctors perhaps on the way in which they relate to us, we classify friends on the basis of their trustworthiness, and we classify books according to their subject matter. (See local library.) Division, on the other hand, breaks one thing into its component parts. We might have to mentally break a computer into its component parts to figure out what's wrong with it; when we schedule our day, we break it into component parts; and when we discuss an essay, we do so by breaking it into its component parts of introduction, body, and conclusion. A knowledge of how to organize reality by using these two methods can only make us better thinkers.

HERE A BURGER, THERE A BURGER

BY BONAR TUCKER (student)

It's a fact of life. After most soccer, football, or basketball games, spectators can be found munching on a hamburger at one of our many fast-food restaurants. Lunches are served there daily to millions of open-campus teenagers, stressed-out businessmen, and famished construction workers who all need food in a hurry due to limited lunch breaks and fast-approaching deadlines. Busy mothers, caught between children's appointments, household duties, and perhaps a job of their own, will race into one of several drive-thrus to pick up dinners-to-go many times a month. The golden arches, "Where's the Beef?" and the Whopper are all a part of nearly everyone's vocabulary. However, we must pay a high price for patronizing these convenient locations: burgers we so frequently indulge in are loaded with sodium, heavy in fat, and pumped full of hormones and antibiotics before reaching the grills of America.

The connection between high sodium intake and poor health has been known for several years. The sodium in fast-food hamburgers is outrageously high. Meanwhile, the potassium needed to balance or flush out all that extra salt is dangerously low. If this sodium onslaught keeps up, as it does in our fast-paced society, the kidneys are forced to work overtime and high blood pressure may be the result. Most of us believe that blood pressure naturally rises with age. But that's a misconception born of the fact that ours is a hamburger-eating, high-salt-consuming society. In places where salt consumption is low (for instance, New Guinea) the blood pressure of older people isn't any higher than that of the younger ones. Is it any wonder our country ranks high in coronary problems when so much of our diet consists of fast hamburgers? The meat itself is high in sodium. Then, while cooking, the chef adds a shake of meat seasoner, which is also sodium rich. And, finally, so many of us add a dash of salt to the patty before eating it.

There is also an estimated 37% fat content in the average hamburger served where you "have it your way." This amount is a solid explanation for our bulging cancer and heart disease statistics. In America alone, beef consumption has jumped from 50 pounds per person per year in 1948 to a whopping 95 pounds in 1980. Medical studies report that too much beef can increase chances of developing cancer of the colon and rectum. And the assumption is well published that our constant taste for the almighty hamburger has made colo-rectal cancer the most common form of cancer in the United States and has made America a main territory for the ubiquitous heart and circulatory disabilities. The feedlot-grown, fatty beef that modern man eats every day during his hurry-scurry schedule is a far cry from the lean, wild meat that our ancestors ate, if and when they could catch it. The wild deer and antelope were certainly not a risk factor for heart disease because there was simply no fat in their meat to clog man's arteries and build up around his heart.

Perhaps the most distressing news which must be considered if we are among the burger-oriented of our day is the shocking number of tranquilizers, hormones, antibiotics and any of 2,500 FDA-approved drugs the cattle are fed before birth and long after their deaths. The 100% beef hamburger we are promised may well have 100% of drugs lingering within its buns. A female hormone (DES) is shot into the animal's ears to make the animal grow faster on less feed. Another hormone (MGA) eliminates the sex drive of cattle so they do not lose valuable pounds by engaging in sexual activity. Cows are fed tranquilizers through their feed to calm them in their crowded conditions. Antibiotics are introduced as their bodies rebel with abscessed livers from being forced to eat such huge amounts of rich grains. Again, before being ground into what becomes our recent staple food, the now dead meat is dipped into antibiotic solutions and chemical preservatives to increase shelf life.

When we hear the jingle "You deserve a break today" implying that no day or event is complete without sinking your teeth into a convenient, luscious burger, perhaps we should consider just what kind of break we really do deserve. Indeed, the label of "fast food" is correct. But is it worth paying for the convenience of these fast foods with fast illnesses and quickly deteriorating health? We need to take a hard look at the facts and choose for our own wellbeing and not merely for our convenience. We must think not so much in terms of making our lives a little easier today but in terms of still having a healthy body to enjoy life with tomorrow.

STUDY QUESTIONS for "Here a Burger, There a Burger"

COMPREHENSION

1. Is this essay an example of classification or division? Explain your answer.
2. What is the thesis to this essay? Where in this essay does the author state her thesis?
3. According to the essay, what are the consequences of patronizing fast-food hamburger restaurants? For instance, how are our bodies endangered by high sodium intake? By high fat intake? And what is the danger of pumping a "shocking number of tranquilizers, hormones, antibiotics, and any of 2,500 FDA approved drugs" into cattle that provide the beef for the hamburgers that we eat?
4. What is the central purpose of this essay? That is, why was it written?

DEVELOPMENT AND ORGANIZATION

1. How does the use of statistics in the third and fourth paragraphs of this essay strengthen it?
2. What other techniques does Tucker use to develop her essay? Where, for instance, does she make use of example(s)? And how might this essay also be said to illustrate cause-and-effect analysis?
3. Reread paragraph two. Identify as many transitions as you can. What is gained by using transitions between sentences?
4. What kinds of "linking" devices—transitions, pronouns, repeated nouns and phrases, etc.—does Tucker use to connect her paragraphs?
5. How does she link each body paragraph clearly back to her thesis?

STYLE AND TECHNIQUE

1. What is the tone of this essay? Is it clearly established in the opening paragraph?
2. What is the concluding paragraph for an expository essay supposed to do? Does Tucker's concluding paragraph do these things?

TEN-MINUTE TOPICS

1. Write a division analysis in which you break one of your favorite meals into its component parts.
2. Write a division analysis of a typical fast-food restaurant. Try to focus on a particular store or chain. What are its component parts? Make sure to describe each with specific details.

FOOTSTEPS

BY LAGENA MAKARON (student)

In the darkest hour of the sultry summer night, a low blood-curdling moan escaped from the cracked lips of the man bathed in his own sweat. They were back. The demons had haunted him now for many long nights. He had tried everything he could think of to push them from his tortured mind. He had all kinds of tricks to ward off the night devils, from thinking pleasant thoughts before falling asleep to holding his wife very tightly to his body during the night, trying to absorb some of her goodness and sweetness. He had even tried to pray to her God, but it was like talking to the wind, for all the comfort he got.

Somehow, he had to stop the black void that was trying to engulf him. He was never really sure what the void held, but the bitter taste of fear and terrifying sense of horror and dread told him that he didn't want to find out. As he wrestled with the unspeakable thing inside his mind, his breathing became faster and faster. His eye movements became erratic, darting up, down, back and forth. He could feel it coming. This time he could not awaken from the nightmare. He was caught in the viselike grip of the fury of the thing, and this time there would be no escape. His heart began to beat so rapidly, he could almost feel it jump out of his chest. He was choking! Somehow he could not get enough air into his burning lungs. His hands twisted and crushed the sweat-soaked tangle of sheets as he plunged over the edge into the endless black void.

The first demon to enter was Fear. It spread throughout his body with such tangible force that his heart almost stopped. Once again he was a child, and his father, long since dead, stood over the bed in a drunken rage. The wide leather belt was gripped tightly in his father's trembling hand, the gleam of anticipation shining in the bloodshot eyes. This time as always before he didn't know the cause of punishment, but the result would be the same. Once again his young tender flesh would be left bruised and in bloody tatters, before his father stumbled to his own bed to lie for hours in a drunken stupor.

The next two demons, Rage and Revenge, came together. As he turned to his side he threw out his arm to ward them off, but just as before they would not be stopped. Again he was overpowered by the black unspeakable Rage that began to boil within his fifteen-year-old body. This latest and most vicious of the beatings would be the last. He accepted this thought, when he accepted the icy calm of Revenge. This time after his father staggered off to bed, he followed. The knife gleamed in the light as Revenge had his way. Revenge felt wonderful as the sheets became saturated with thick crimson blood.

Suddenly, Fear was back. He worked frantically to cover what Rage had done. He could smell the heavy scent of burning wood and flesh as the fire consumed the evidence of the murder. Everyone just said he was a very lucky young man to have gotten out of the tinderbox before the roof collapsed and forever buried his crime.

It was a long time before the demon Guilt began to visit. In fact he was happily married and had a son of his own before Guilt began to spread decay and rot. Good God, why didn't they leave him alone? Hadn't he suffered enough? He deserved his happiness.

He loved his wife and child! He wanted to forget the past! Why couldn't they leave instead of visiting him night after night, making him cry out in his sleep?

The last demon to visit was Footsteps. He didn't want Footsteps, but there was no choice. He was here uninvited and unwanted but nonetheless must be accepted.

As the man awakened from the horrible grip of the nightmare, a slow icy calm invaded. He no longer had a mind or a will of his own as he stumbled to the closet. The wide leather belt beckoned to him and he hated himself as he answered the call. By the time he reached his son's peaceful sleeping form, his bloodshot eyes were gleaming in joyous anticipation.

STUDY QUESTIONS for "Footsteps"

COMPREHENSION

1. On the basis of what you have read in the essay, what causes the fear? The rage? The need for revenge? The guilt?
2. What are the Footsteps?
3. Do you find the subject matter of this essay objectionable? How might such an essay serve a constructive purpose?

DEVELOPMENT AND ORGANIZATION

1. Discuss this essay as an example of division. What is it that the writer breaks into the component parts of Fear, Rage, Revenge, Guilt, and Footsteps?
2. How do these different parts—Fear, Rage, Revenge, Guilt, and Footsteps—work together in this essay?
3. Why does the writer refer to these parts of the nightmare as "demons"?
4. How might this essay also be considered a narrative? Consider the following questions:
    a. What is the setting for the narrative? In what paragraph does the author establish the setting?
    b. What do we learn about the main character? How would you describe him? Is he able to distinguish fantasy/nightmare from reality?
    c. What conflict(s) does he face? Does he overcome his conflicts?
    d. Where is the climax of this narrative, the point at which the conflicts are resolved for or against the main character?
    e. What is the full significance of the conclusion?
5. Comment upon the writer's use of concrete/descriptive detail in this essay. How does the use of such detail contribute to the effectiveness of this narrative?

STYLE AND TECHNIQUE

1. The writer uses *personification* to bring the emotions to life. What is personification? Why did the author choose to use it here? How effective is it as a method of presenting the main character's emotions to us?
2. Count the sentences in which the author uses description. In how many does he use subjective description? Objective? Which does he use more? (You may count sentences twice if he uses both kinds or multiple examples in a single sentence.)

TEN-MINUTE TOPICS

1. Using a narrative structure, break an activity, ritual, habit, or obsession into component parts.
2. Write a division analysis of one specific emotion, either one mentioned here or another of your choice. You may use personification to add detail to your analysis.

THE PLOT AGAINST PEOPLE

BY RUSSELL BAKER

Inanimate objects are classified scientifically into three major categories—those that break down, those that get lost, and those that don't work.

The goal of all inanimate objects is to resist man and ultimately to defeat him, and the three major classifications are based on the method each object uses to achieve its purpose. As a general rule, any object capable of breaking down at the moment when it is most needed will do so. The automobile is typical of the category.

With the cunning peculiar to its breed, the automobile never breaks down while entering a filling station which has a large staff of idle mechanics. It waits until it reaches a downtown intersection in the middle of the rush hour, or until it is fully loaded with family and luggage on the Ohio Turnpike. Thus it creates maximum inconvenience, frustration, and irritability, thereby reducing its owner's lifespan.

Washing machines, garbage disposals, lawn mowers, furnaces, TV sets, tape recorders, slide projectors—all are in league with the automobile to take their turn at breaking down whenever life threatens to flow smoothly for their enemies.

Many inanimate objects, of course, find it extremely difficult to break down. Pliers, for example, and gloves and keys are almost totally incapable of breaking down. Therefore, they have had to evolve a different technique for resisting man.

They get lost. Science has still not solved the mystery of how they do it, and no man has ever caught one of them in the act. The most plausible theory is that they have developed a secret method of locomotion which they are able to conceal from human eyes.

It is not uncommon for a pair of pliers to climb all the way from the cellar to the attic in its single-minded determination to raise its owner's blood pressure. Keys have been known to burrow three feet under mattresses. Women's purses, despite their great weight, frequently travel through six or seven rooms to find hiding space under a couch.

Scientists have been struck by the fact that things that break down virtually never get lost, while things that get lost hardly ever break down. A furnace, for example, will invariably break down at the depth of the first winter cold wave, but it will never get lost. A woman's purse hardly ever breaks down; it almost invariably chooses to get lost.

Some persons believe this constitutes evidence that inanimate objects are not entirely hostile to man. After all, they point out, a furnace could infuriate a man even more thoroughly by getting lost than by breaking down, just as a glove could upset him far more by breaking down than by getting lost.

Not everyone agrees, however, that this indicates a conciliatory attitude. Many say it merely proves that furnaces, gloves and pliers are incredibly stupid.

The third class of objects—those that don't work—is the most curious of all. These include such objects as barometers, car clocks, cigarette lighters, flashlights and toy-train locomotives. It is inaccurate, of course, to say that they *never* work. They work once, usually for the first few hours after being brought home, and then quit. Thereafter, they never work again.

In fact, it is widely assumed that they are built for the purpose of not working. Some people have reached advanced ages without ever seeing some of these objects—barometers, for example—in working order.

Science is utterly baffled by the entire category. There are many theories about it. The most interesting holds that the things that don't work have attained the highest state possible for an inanimate object, the state to which things that break down and things that get lost can still only aspire.

They have truly defeated man by conditioning him never to expect anything of them. When his cigarette lighter won't light or his flashlight fails to illuminate, it does not raise his blood pressure. Objects that don't work have given man the only peace he receives from inanimate society.

STUDY QUESTIONS for "The Plot against People"

COMPREHENSION

1. What is the central idea expressed in the essay? Does Baker express this idea in a clearly stated thesis, or does he imply it? If the former, write out the thesis as it appears in the text, and identify by number the paragraph in which it appears; if the latter, summarize the central idea in fifteen words.
2. What audience does Baker have in mind as he writes? Does Baker assume that they are familiar with the objects he names? What attitude does he assume that the audience holds toward these objects?
3. What is Baker's purpose for writing this essay?

DEVELOPMENT AND ORGANIZATION

1. What are the categories into which Baker classifies objects? Do you agree or disagree with his classifications? Why or why not? What other categories may exist?
2. Which objects does Baker use to exemplify his categories? Are they common objects?
3. How closely does Baker's essay follow the methods of organization set forth in the paradigms for the classification and division essays? Does he use any other plan for organizing his categories in conjunction with (or instead of) the paradigms?

STYLE AND TECHNIQUE

1. Count the number of words in this essay. Count the number of sentences. Now come up with a ratio of words per sentence. Count the number of words and sentences in one of your own essays and find the same ratio. How close is your ratio to Baker's?

2. What tone does Baker take in this essay: formal, informal, humorous, serious? What words and phrases lead you to your conclusion? From the tone, can you tell what attitude the writer has towards the objects he describes?

TEN-MINUTE TOPICS

1. Classify the appliances/gadgets/furnishings in one of the rooms of your apartment or house. Be sure to explain why you create the categories you use.
2. Using Baker's essay as a model, classify jobs according to how they frustrate humankind. Be sure to include examples for the categories you create.

A SEARCH FOR UNDERSTANDING THE ESSAY

BY MANDY KALISH

I recently went to a job interview for a position at a local retail store. Much to my surprise, the manager asked me to write a short essay about why I wanted to work at that particular store. It was pretty tense, sitting there trying to guess how to write a good essay, and trying to guess why in the world it would be important in the retail setting. I started off writing about my grandmother, who used to design and sew her own clothes, and then talked about how great capitalism is, because we can buy whatever we want as long as we have the money. Then, I guess I got sidetracked, because I spent the last few sentences talking about my favorite candy: Milky Bites. Well, needless to say, I did not get the job. After the interview, I challenged myself to look into how to write an effective essay.

Let's think of an essay as two legs that like to run. When we write an essay, we enter our legs into a race. There are two kinds of races: ones that have a starting line at the beginning and a finish line somewhere far away, and ones that take place on a track, so that the starting line also ends up being the finish line. If essays are races, they are the kinds of races that take place on a track, so that wherever you start, you end up finishing in a very similar, if not the same, place. Introductions are important to essays, not just because they grab the reader's attention (which they should), but also because they set the terms for how the piece will end as well. Following an effective introduction should be like following a map. Effective introductions tell the reader and the writer exactly what topics will be discussed in the paper, how and/or why those topics will be discussed, and what the writer's thoughts are on these topics.

Looking back on my job interview essay attempt, I see that by the end of my short essay, I made no reference to the beginning. If I mentioned my grandmother in the beginning, why did I end up talking about Milky Bites? Probably because I was hungry and nervous, but that's beside the point. The point is that I should have worked my grandmother back in there somehow, even if it meant using Milky Bites as a linking device. A linking device is really a complex way of saying ideas have to clearly relate to each other in an effective essay. I could have made Milky Bites belong more in my essay by linking them to my grandmother, perhaps saying something like "as I mentioned earlier, my grandmother loved to design and sew clothes, and I also inherited another of her great traits: an obsessive love for Milky Bites."

In my attempt to search for good essay rules, I also discovered that linking devices have more to do than just link the introduction and the conclusion of a piece of writing. Linking devices help join together paragraphs. Paragraphs are like friends, or members of the same team. As with most groups of friends, you want to be sure that everyone knows everyone else. You don't want to be reading a paragraph that seems to have no idea there are other paragraphs all around it. Try and link your paragraphs by referring to the ideas that have already been explored or will be explored later in the essay. No party or team works when everyone acts as if they are the only ones in the room. By referring to the end of the previous paragraph when starting a new one, it's like acknowledging when someone introduces you to a new person by thanking the person who introduced you and *then* going on to talk to the new person. In truth, the coolest person at the party is the one who seems to know everybody and has the ability to include everybody in conversation. It's the same with essays. The coolest essay is the one that seems to know everything it contains, referring to itself as it goes and therefore including main ideas all along.

Looking back, I think another reason I didn't get the job was that my essay seemed pretty weak. I kept saying things like "I don't know, but," and "sort of good experience," and "this seems like a good job." No one wants to hang around with a flimsy whiner. Strengthen up! Make sure your opinions, ideas or thoughts come out as strongly as possible. Even if you're not 100% sure about your topic, pretend. Strengthen statements from "seems like a good job" to "I have no doubt this is the best job available." Strengthen statements like "I'm not sure, but," to "I believe without a doubt." Who wants to be on a ship captained by a weak, insecure leader? Same thing with an essay: we want our captain/author to have authority. Look at the word *authority* and notice its root is the word *author*. Having authority means writing like you strongly believe everything you're saying. Otherwise, the reader will tear you to shreds.

Speaking of shreds (notice the linking device!), I went back to that clothing store a few weeks later, after they had hired someone to fill the vacant position, and asked the manager how my essay could have been better. She said she really enjoys writing that is simple, clear and descriptive. She said I never mentioned any physical or sensory details. In other words, she wanted to know what style of clothes my grandmother made, what material she used, where she lived. She wanted to know what my own personal tastes were, and I could have told her easily by describing the colors and styles I'm drawn to as a consumer. In essays, we should always be looking for places to add physical or sensory details. For example, the retail store where I had applied and then returned to speak to the manager had the smell of a hospital cafeteria and the lighting of a nightclub. The manager was in her fifties and looked at me like I had crawled out of the sewer with a snake on my forehead. Just by your adding a few details, the reader can have more fun and construct a better mental picture of the actions or ideas being described.

On my way out of the store, I decided to do some window-shopping in the mall. I noticed a new store that had a FOR HIRE sign in the display window. The doors were wide open, so I went in and spoke to the man in charge. He asked me to fill out an application and write a short essay describing why I wanted to work for their store. Then he told me the reason they have people write a short essay when applying was that communication skills are essential in dealing with customers on a regular basis. Well, I wrote the best essay ever and got the job! This just goes to show that knowing how to write effectively is a skill that will help in expected and unexpected ways all throughout our lives. Take it from me, learning the tricks to writing a good essay will not only improve your grades, it will improve your entire life. If you have any questions, come on down to the mall; I'll be the girl behind the big display window, trying to sell you some socks.

STUDY QUESTIONS for "A Search for Understanding the Essay"

COMPREHENSION

1. What is the thesis of this essay? If it is explicit, write it out word for word and give the number of the paragraph in which it appears. If it is implicit, summarize it in about twenty-five words.
2. What problems did this writer identify in the first application essay she wrote? What could she have done better?
3. What reason was she given for her being asked to write an application essay? Do you agree with the explanation given? Why or why not?

DEVELOPMENT AND ORGANIZATION

1. Is this a division essay or a classification essay? How do you know? What are the categories into which she puts the parts of an essay?
2. Kalish also uses an analogy to compare the essay to something else. To what does she make the comparison? Why do you think she made the analogy? Do you think the analogy is valid? Why?
3. Kalish uses several transitions (she calls them "linking devices") throughout the essay. What are they? What kind are they (look again at the types of transitions mentioned in the organization section of chapter one)?

STYLE AND TECHNIQUE

1. Kalish begins and ends her essay by telling us that she had to write an essay for two separate job applications. Why do you think she does this? What effect does it have on the essay? If you were to write a different conclusion, what would you write?
2. Kalish talks about the importance of using strong language in the essay. When do you see her being the most forceful with her own? When do you see her needing to be more forceful, perhaps? Give examples.
3. Take another look at the fourth paragraph. How many sentences are there? How many of them begin directly with the subject noun phrase? How many of them begin with a prepositional phrase? A subordinate clause? Some other structure? What percentage of the total number of sentences begins with the subject noun phrase?

TEN-MINUTE TOPICS

1. Were you ever asked to write an essay for an application (job, scholarship, etc.)? What were you asked to write about? Did your essay get you the position? If you were to write that essay again, now, what changes would you make?
2. Imagine that you've been asked to write a 200-word essay in order to win a contest for the car of your dreams. In the essay, you have to explain why you like the car, why you want the car, and why you should win. What would you say?

3. Write a humorous series of suggestions about how to write a college essay for a friend who will be taking this class next semester. What should this person do? What should this person not do? What do you see as being the most important parts of a good essay?

CHAPTER NINE

DEFINITION

DEFINITION

The goal of this essay is to develop an extended definition of a term, concept, trend, or even a place with which our audience may not be familiar. Thus, if we are interested in history or political science, we may take as our topic something like imperialism, socialism, or communism. If we are interested in philosophy or religion, we may wish to define existentialism or Christianity. Since these topics may be too broad for a 500- to 700-word essay, we may wish to focus upon something more specific—by narrowing Christianity, for example, down to sin or grace. However, we cannot simply provide a dictionary definition of the word or concept that we have chosen as a subject. Whatever topic we choose, we must develop our essay by using one or more of the methods that we have studied elsewhere in this book: narration, description, example, comparison and contrast, analogy, process, and so on.

APPLICATION

In the two body paragraphs excerpted from his essay "Success," student Eric Dandurand relies upon examples to define a word that, as he says in his introductory paragraph, "can be given virtually any definition that one cares to give it." The essay seems primarily directed to culturally aware readers who either share his cynicism or at least acknowledge and appreciate it:

> To the Perrier-drinking resident of Beverly Hills named Buffy, success means having the best of everything, or at least, having better than everyone else. To the saints of our planet, success means going to bed after having helped one's fellow human beings. To the Hitlers of the world, ultimate success is achieved by having power over the people. Since World War II, the idea of success for many Americans has been measured against the Joneses. Two-car garages, color TV, and a kitchen full of appliances was the formula for happiness that seemed to light the way to success. However, after the materialistic boom of the fifties, the United States underwent the most dramatic upheaval of its young history short of the Civil War: the social revolution of the sixties and seventies. Obviously, the pressure to keep up with the Joneses did not stimulate the feelings of happiness in the generation that had all the trappings of success. It led to the complete restructuring of our society from within; our society, like the phoenix, burned itself and regenerated from those ashes, attempting to be more successful than the generation before it.

Reinforcing his cynical tone, Dandurand uses his examples to support his conviction that, currently, there seems to be no definition of success beyond the merely subjective.

Now let's look at parts of another definition essay. In her essay "The Generations of Yesteryear and Today," student Vicki Constantin combines contrast, example, and narration to define the current generation:

> What the younger people want, at all costs, is not to find themselves in "false situations." Life is full of false situations, especially American life today. The most frequent and glaring of them is incompetence in high places. Yesterday's generation saw a great deal of this in government, in the armed forces, in culture, and in education. They exercised their wit upon it, but were still vaguely respectful of rank and office and status. This generation is not impressed by any vested authority whatever. And their freedom to judge authority is accompanied by their unwillingness to be judged. Their caution reposes upon their unwillingness to exercise any authority or responsibility for which they do not feel themselves to be solidly prepared and adequate.
>
> For instance, in 1981, a teenage girl in northern California was raped and murdered by a high school classmate. For two days, the murderer took his buddies out to the gully where the dead girl lay until someone finally told. Neal Jimenez, a screenwriting student then, has used that incident as a bare bones starting point for a movie that, while fictional, even surreal, also seems as shatteringly true as the toughest documentary. Jimenez, who was born in 1960, has said that the film is a record of his generation's despair, about kids who "have to make up their own moral codes. They're not getting it from teachers, parents, or society; or society is saying one thing and doing another. Where do they learn what to do?"

The film that Constantin has in mind is *The River's Edge*. What is remarkable about these paragraphs as well as the entire essay, written in the late eighties, is that it is applicable to the early twenty-first century and therefore demonstrates just how important good writing is in enabling us to make sense of the often confusing and violent world around us.

In her writing, Constantin uses at least three methods of development to support her definition of the younger generation. Beyond briefly *contrasting* the generation of yesteryear with the generation of today, Constantin uses *narration* as she tells a story— the murder in northern California—and the story as well provides an *example*. Too, we can see *cause and effect* implicitly at work here: current despair among the younger generation is caused at least in part by incompetence in high places, apathy verging upon numbing self-interestedness, and the breakdown of traditional moral codes. As she explains in the following paragraph, the current generation often responds to this despair by making up and following its own code:

In *The River's Edge*, the young people try to figure out from one another what to do, what loyalty and friendship and honor might mean. (The only adult they trust is a fugitive killer played by Dennis Hopper, who lives in seclusion with a life-size sex doll.) They're not so much growing up as groping up, through a world hazy with pot smoke, only occasionally hearing the voice of a parent. "Is that you, Clarissa?" a mother calls sleepily, when the girl comes home in the middle of the night. "Yes," Clarissa says, rummaging in the closet for a sleeping bag, which she and Matt will take down to the park. In the careful language all of us enlightened educators and parents use today, these kids are "sexually active."

Constantin's tone is one of cynicism verging on the incredulous. Her allusion to the absence of the traditional concepts of "loyalty and friendship and honor" is balanced against her cynical reference to the one adult figure that the young people in the movie apparently respect. And her use of direct quotations to help us visualize the scene involving Clarissa and her mother also emphasizes perhaps the central point of this essay: the spiritual and moral bankruptcy of a generation so adrift that it no longer recognizes its own despair. Vicki Constantin has written a definition essay that is both startling and challenging; implicitly, she forces the reader into a self-examination that, she hopes, will point to the need for the entire culture to establish a code that is understood by all.

PARADIGM

Keep in mind that when we write the definition essay, we are not obligated to make use of all the methods of developing an essay. We can and should be selective. The method, or methods, that we use will depend upon our topic. For instance, if we focus upon bravery, we can develop our definition with examples and narration. In other words, we can tell a story that illustrates the characteristic that we are attempting to define. If we choose a sport, say soccer, we can use a combination of process and division, first providing an explanation of how the game is played and then splitting the eleven players upon a team into their positions and describing how each position is to be played. And if we define something like lying, we could use classification, breaking lies into various categories and providing examples for each.

Introduction
1. **Engage the reader's attention.**
2. **Introduce topic.**
3. **Establish tone.**
4. **Present thesis/suggest direction.**

First Body Paragraph
   1. Topic sentence.
   2. Supporting details using one or more of the techniques
      you have studied.

Second Body Paragraph
   1. Topic sentence.
   2. Supporting details using one or more of the techniques
      you have studied.

Third Body Paragraph
   1. Topic sentence.
   2. Supporting details using one or more of the techniques
      you have studied.

Conclusion (options)
   1. Summarize main points and restate thesis.
   2. Offer a final image, message, or judgment.
   3. Take a broader view.
   4. End with quotation.
   5. End with striking statistic.
   6. Challenge the reader.
   7. Something else.

SUMMARY

Clearly, then, when we are writing our definition essay, our method of organization depends upon our topic. For instance, Dandurand's very topic of success requires examples to illustrate that most definitions of this concept are extremely subjective. And Constantin, defining the younger generation, writes a remarkably thought-provoking essay using the methods of example, contrast, and narration.

THE EQUALITY RACKET

BY PATRICK J. BUCHANAN

Our mainstream media have discovered a new issue: inequality in America. The gap between the wealthiest 1 percent and the rest of the nation is wide and growing wider.

This, we are told, is intolerable. This is a deformation of American democracy that must be corrected through remedial government action.

What action? The rich must pay their fair share. Though the top 1 percent pay 40 percent of federal income taxes and the bottom 50 percent have, in some years, paid nothing, the rich must be made to pay more.

That's an appealing argument to many, but one that would have horrified our founding fathers. For from the beginning, America was never about equality, except of God-given and constitutional rights.

Our revolution was about liberty; it was about freedom.

The word *equality* was not even mentioned in the Constitution, the Bill of Rights or the Federalist Papers. The word *equal* does not make an appearance until the 14th Amendment's equal protection of the laws after the Civil War. The feminists' Equal Rights Amendment was abandoned and left to die in 1982 after ten years of national debate.

When Thomas Jefferson wrote that memorable line—All men are created equal—he was not talking about an equality of rewards, but of rights with which men are endowed by their Creator. He was talking about an ideal.

For as he wrote John Adams in 1813, Jefferson believed nature had blessed society with a precious gift, a natural aristocracy of virtue and talents to govern it. In his autobiography, a half decade before his death in 1826, he restated this idea of the aristocracy of virtue and talent which nature has wisely provided for the direction of the interests of society.

Equality, *egalité*, was what the French Revolution, the Bolshevik Revolution, Mao's Revolution of 1949, Castro's Revolution of 1959 and Pol Pot's revolution of 1975 claimed to be about.

This was the Big Lie, for all those revolutions that triumphed in the name of equality were marked by mass murders of the old ruling class, the rise of a new ruling class more brutal and tyrannical, and the immiseration of the people in whose name the revolution was supposedly fought.

Invariably, Power to the people! winds up as power to the party and the dictator, who then act in the name of the people. The most egalitarian society of the twentieth century was Mao's China. And that regime murdered more of its own than Lenin and Stalin managed to do.

Inequality is the natural concomitant of freedom.

For just as God-given talents are unequally distributed, and the home environments of children are unequal, and individuals differ in the drive to succeed, free societies, where rewards of fame and fortune accrue to the best and brightest, must invariably become unequal societies.

In the nineteenth and twentieth centuries, no nation achieved greater prosperity for working men and women than the United States, where all were born free, but equal only in constitutional rights.

Yet, though inequalities of income and wealth have endured through the history of this republic, each generation lived better and longer than the one that came before.

That was the America we grew up in. As long as life for the working and middle classes was improving, who cared if the rich were getting richer?

Today's new inequality is due to several factors.

One is a shift from manufacturing as the principal source of wealth to banking and finance. A second is the movement of US production abroad.

This has eliminated millions of high-paying jobs while enriching the executives and shareholders of the companies that cut the cost of production by relocating overseas.

With globalization, the interests of corporations—maximizing profit—and the interests of the country—maintaining economic independence—diverged. And the politicians who depend on contributions from executives and investors stuck with the folks that paid their room, board and tuition.

Yet, behind the latest crusade against inequality lie motives other than any love of the poor. They are resentment, envy and greed for what the wealthy have, and an insatiable lust for power.

For the only way to equalize riches and rewards in a free society is to capture the power of government, so as to take from those who have, to give to those who have not.

And here is the unvarying argument of the left since Karl Marx: If you give us power, we will take from the rich who have so much and give it to you who have so little. But before we can do that, you must give us power.

This is the equality racket. As Alexis de Tocqueville wrote:

> The sole condition which is required in order to succeed in centralizing the supreme power in a democratic community, is to love equality, or to get men to believe you love it. Thus the science of despotism, which was once so complex, is simplified, and reduced . . . to a single principle.

When they come preaching equality, what they want is power.

STUDY QUESTIONS for "The Equality Racket"

COMPREHENSION

1. What does Buchanan mean by the phrase "Equality Racket"? How does he define *equality*?
2. According to the essay, what countries have been involved in the "Equality Racket"?

3. Do you agree that the search for freedom excludes the search for equality? Are the two ever the same?
4. The essay is a defense of a society divided by class and money. What would motivate someone to write such a defense?
5. How do you think someone associated with the "mainstream media"—or the president of the United States, for that matter—would respond to Buchanan's essay?

DEVELOPMENT AND ORGANIZATION

1. How effectively does he prove his argument? Explain your answer.
2. Many arguments are a combination of inductive and deductive reasoning (see explanations for these terms in the chapter on argument). From an inductive standpoint, the writer must provide proofs to support what otherwise become a series of "hasty generalizations." How many hasty generalizations can you find in the Buchanan essay?
3. How relevant to the purpose of this essay are the paragraphs in which Buchanan explains what Jefferson really meant when he wrote "All men are created equal"? (One source that Buchanan quotes from, the Declaration of Independence, appears elsewhere in this book.)
4. Buchanan's essay is built around an assumption that provides the basis for this deductive syllogism:
   a. Major Premise: Political groups that call for equality are really seeking power for themselves.
   b. Minor Premise: The mainstream media (and related political groups) are calling for equality.
   c. Conclusion: These people are really seeking power.
   Are the premises true? Explain.
5. Any essay that you write should be unified, coherent, logically organized, and fully developed. Does Buchanan's essay meet these four criteria? For instance, do all of his paragraphs support the thesis? Are the connections between ideas clearly established? What points in his essay need further development?

STYLE AND TECHNIQUE

1. Buchanan relies on short, often choppy paragraphs. Do you consider this a strength or weakness of this essay? Explain.
2. What tone does Buchanan adopt in this essay? Is it humble, condescending—what? Support your answer with details from the essay.
3. You may have noted that Buchanan makes no mention of those members of the mainstream media or of the US Congress. What is the effect of omitting these names?

TEN-MINUTE TOPICS

1. What does equality mean to you? Elaborate in some detail.
2. What does freedom mean?
3. When is revolution ever necessary?

A TRAFFIC LIGHT IS A BRAINLESS MACHINE

BY DAVID SCHOENBRUN

The "intellectualism" of the French is found at every level of society. The café waiter, the taxicab driver, the restaurateur, the so-called "little people" of France are the most stimulating, if frequently exasperating, conversationalists in the world. Of them all, the most anarchistic and voluble is the taxicab driver. I deliberately provoke arguments with them—an easy thing to do—to see what they will say next. Of the hundreds of discussions in cabs one remains in my memory as uniquely, superbly French. It could not have occurred in any other country, except possibly in Brooklyn, where there exists a species of man akin in spirit if not in actual form to the French.

It was midnight in Paris and we were rolling along the Quai d'Orsay toward the Avenue Bosquet, where I live, on the left bank of the river Seine. As we came to the Pont Alexandre III, the cab slowed down, for the traffic light was red against us, and then, without stopping, we sailed through the red light in a sudden burst of speed. The same performance was repeated at the Alma Bridge. As I paid the driver, I asked him why he had driven through two red lights.

"You ought to be ashamed of yourself, a veteran like you, breaking the law and endangering your life that way," I protested.

He looked at me, astonished. "Ashamed of myself? Why, I'm proud of myself. I am a law-abiding citizen and have no desire to get killed either." He cut me off before I could protest.

"No, just listen to me before you complain. What did I do? Went through a red light. Well, did you ever stop to consider what a red light is, what it means?"

"Certainly," I replied. "It's a stop signal and means that traffic is rolling in the opposite direction."

"Half-right," said the driver, "but incomplete. It is only an automatic stop signal. And it does not mean that there is cross traffic. Did you see any cross traffic during our trip? Of course not. I slowed down at the light, looked carefully to the right and to the left. Not another car on the streets at this hour. Well, then! What would you have me do? Should I stop like a dumb animal because an automatic, brainless machine turns red every forty seconds? No, monsieur," he thundered, hitting the doorjamb with a huge fist. "I am a man, not a machine. I have eyes and a brain and judgment, given me by God. I would only be ashamed of myself if I let those blinking lamps do my thinking for me. Good night, monsieur."

Is this bad, is this good? Frankly I no longer am sure. The intellectual originality of the French is a corrupting influence if you are subjected to it for long. I never doubted that it was wrong to drive through a red light. After more than a decade of life in Paris, however, I find my old Anglo-Saxon standards somewhat shaken. I still think it is wrong to drive through a stop signal, except possibly very late at night, after having carefully checked to make sure there is no cross traffic. After all, I am a man, not a machine.

STUDY QUESTIONS for "A Traffic Light Is a Brainless Machine"

COMPREHENSION

1. What is Schoenbrun defining in this essay: intellectualism, the French, or the intellectualism of the French?
2. What does the author mean by the "intellectualism of the French"? On the basis of this essay, try to explain what Schoenbrun means by this phrase in your own words.
3. What is so "uniquely and superbly French" about the author's conversation with the French cab driver?
4. Is there anything really exasperating about the author's conversation with the cab driver? (See paragraph one.)
5. What point concerning the traffic light is the cab driver trying to make to the author? How does this conversation illustrate the "intellectualism" of the French?

DEVELOPMENT AND ORGANIZATION

1. What sort of examples does the author employ in this piece of writing?
2. Trace the progression of thought in the opening paragraph. Does the writer move from the specific to the general or from the general to the specific?
3. Answer the following questions concerning the final paragraph:
   a. Why does the author ask the question "Is this bad, is this good?"
   b. How can the "intellectual originality" of the French be a "corrupting influence"?
   c. What Anglo-Saxon standards do you imagine that the author is talking about in this paragraph? Are these standards evident in the body of the essay? Where?
   d. What is the effect of the final sentence?

STYLE AND TECHNIQUE

1. What does dialogue contribute to this essay?
2. What tone does the writer take in this essay? What words contribute to the tone he has created? What words does he use that imply a judgment?

TEN-MINUTE TOPICS

1. Using examples, define the character of a particular city, state, or country.
2. Write about a conversation you have had that has given you a different perspective about an everyday object or process. With whom were you speaking? What was the object you spoke of? What did you learn?

GOAT ROPERS

BY HEIDI WARREN (student)

They are commonly called rednecks, but if they're from Texas I prefer to call them goat ropers. Although there are many variations, from rancher or farmer to factory worker, they have one basic characteristic in common. All goat ropers were born and raised in the South. Although they're a rare breed, goat ropers are seldom seen in public alone. This tendency makes them easy to spot and almost scary to confront after dark. But I have grown accustomed to this breed of man. After dating a goat roper for almost five years now, I have mastered the art of dealing with the entire species. Although I can deal with these men, however, I still have difficulty understanding them.

My difficulty in understanding goat ropers began five years ago and continues every day. I keep assuring myself that the day will come when I understand these creatures, but to my dismay I only seem to grow more and more confused as time passes. One thing that has come to haunt me is the goat roper's deep hatred of "Yankees." Since I was born in Wisconsin, this hatred truly frightened me. And my living in Texas for twelve years wasn't enough to make me a Texan! According to my goat roper boyfriend there is no naturalization process. You are either a Yankee or a Southerner. But wasn't the Civil War fought long ago? Not to a true goat roper. It's not baseball, hot dogs, and apple pie to a goat roper, but rather a pickup truck, Red Man, and the Confederate States of America! This point is stressed by the popular bumper sticker that reads, WELCOME TO TEXAS—NOW GO HOME!

Living with the label "Yankee" never truly bothered me (I found myself saying, "At least we won the war!"). But the way a goat roper wanted to live really confused me, especially since it was with this particular goat roper that I was going to spend my life! Although most goat ropers live on farms or ranches, some don't. And this is their parents' fault. A true goal of a city-dwelling goat roper is to get out of the city. This I never quite understood. I've seen many a goat roper have lots of fun in the city, but he would never admit it. He'd rather be poor and urinate in the woods than have a good-paying nine-to-five job in the city! Being rather enamored of money and city life, I can't understand this at all.

The most disturbing and confusing aspect of a goat roper is his consistent, annoying jealousy. Not only are goat ropers jealous of old boyfriends, but they are also jealous of boys who are just friends, cousins, passersby, and all males who even look the way of their "women." Goat ropers will do anything to break up friendships or seize control of situations they deem out of hand. The targets of their hostility can range from the boy next door that the girl grew up with to the dentist that she has trusted since her first filling. While goat ropers won't admit their insane jealousies, they also won't tolerate jealousy on the part of the girl. They will plainly state that they'll be friends with whomever they please. End of discussion.

For five years now I have lived with every quirk goat ropers have to offer. I have debated and analyzed every confusion they've had to offer me. These goat ropers are a difficult species, and I've come to realize I will never truly understand them.

STUDY QUESTIONS for "Goat Ropers"

COMPREHENSION

1. What is the central idea expressed in the essay? Does Warren express this idea in a clearly stated thesis, or does she imply it? If the former, write out the thesis as it appears in the text, and identify by number the paragraph in which it appears; if the latter, summarize the central idea in fifteen words.
2. What audience does Warren seem to have in mind as she writes? What would that audience's view on goat ropers be?
3. What is Warren's purpose for writing this essay?
4. Why do you think she uses the term *goat roper*? Does this term take an objective or a subjective stance toward goat ropers? What exactly is her stance?

DEVELOPMENT AND ORGANIZATION

1. What method of organization does Warren use for this essay? Does this method effectively aid her in communicating her central idea?
2. How many examples does Warren use to illustrate her definition? What sort of details does she use in her examples? Which ones are best at helping her to define her term?

STYLE AND TECHNIQUE

1. What tone does Warren take in this essay, formal, informal, humorous, serious? What words and phrases lead you to your conclusion?
2. Count the total number of words in the essay. Now count the number of coordinating conjunctions and the number of subordinating conjunctions. Find a ratio of coordinating conjunctions to the total number of words and a ratio for subordinating conjunctions to the total number of words. Find the ratio of coordinating conjunctions to subordinating conjunctions. Find the same ratios for one of your own pieces of writing. What do you learn in comparing the ratios?

TEN-MINUTE TOPICS

1. Write about an abstract concept like independence, desire, concern, arrogance, or delight. Come up with several concrete examples that explain the concept in a manner that your audience will be able to visualize in concrete terms. Make sure that you describe any people, places, and objects involved with strong sensory details.

2. Using Warren's essay as a model, create your own unusual term for someone whom you are close to. Come up with some concrete details to allow your audience to understand why that term fits that person.

TO EVERYTHING THERE IS A SEASON
BY JEANIE FRENCH

Nature's first green is gold
Her hardest hue to hold.
Her early leaf's a flower;
But only so an hour.
Then leaf subsides to leaf.
So Eden sank to grief,
So dawn goes down to day.
Nothing gold can stay.

—Robert Frost

As summer's golden sunshine gives way to autumn hues, soon to be followed by winter's monochromatic shades, I'm reminded of Frost's poem. The oaks and aspens near my home have darkened from shades of gold and orange to a sere brown. Leaves have begun to fall, lying in drifts on the forest floor. Many of the songbirds which inhabit this high desert country east of California's northern Sierra Nevada have migrated out before the coming of winter. These are the times when I wish I too could sprout wings and fly south to brighter and warmer climes.

In the summer, when the sun comes up at four-thirty in the morning and the sky is completely light by five, I wake at first light to birdsong—loud and vivid calls of jays and flycatchers, robins and chickadees. I am filled with energy, ready to leap up and start my day with writing, gardening, or whatever household chore is on the agenda. I have energy to burn, and it propels me through a sixteen-hour, activity-filled day with ease. It is a different story in the fall.

In September, the sun rises later in the morning—at about 6:30. My abundance of energy begins to wane. As the days shorten, I find it difficult to rise in the dark at six a.m. and prepare to teach my eight o'clock class. I am slow to wake—the alarm jerks me from sleep with pounding heart and a rush of startle-induced adrenaline, but my eyes are heavy and my body drags; my mind is less alert than it should be when facing a class full of college freshmen resistant to learning anything about writing. By twelve o'clock, my body insists on a nap so that I can face my evening classes, which begin at six o'clock—after dark has fallen—and end at nine. By eight, nap or no, I am dragging once more, struggling to make it through to the end of class. And this sluggishness only becomes more pronounced as autumn wears into winter. What has happened to the body which breezed through a sixteen-hour summer day?

The problem, when severe, is called Seasonal Affective Disorder (SAD). The symptoms are depression, loss of energy, increased need for sleep and difficulty getting up in the morning, difficulty doing tasks that are normally easy, increased appetite and carbohydrate cravings often accompanied by weight gain, a desire to avoid people, irritability and crying spells, decreased sex drive, suicidal thoughts or feelings.

This disorder has been around a long time—people used to call it "winter blues." Researchers believe that the areas in our brains which control our moods and biological rhythms are affected by the amount of light that enters our eyes. One theory is that the reduced light levels of winter cause the brain to produce lower levels of serotonin, a neurotransmitter which carries signals from nerve ending to nerve ending inside the brain. Reduced serotonin levels can result in depression, and depression can cause folks to have difficulty performing accustomed tasks. It seems clear that there is a connection between lower natural light levels and the symptoms of Seasonal Affective Disorder. The longer, darker, and colder the winter, the more severe the symptoms may become. Like every other problem in life, stress aggravates the condition. SAD may affect as many as 11 million people in the US, and more than twice as many others may suffer from a milder form of the "winter blues." Four times more women than men are affected by SAD.

It was this last fact that made me begin to question the label. It occurred to me that the "disorder" is not actually a disorder at all, but a kind of order that makes perfect sense when looked at from a natural perspective. Many mammals experience a reduction in metabolism in the wintertime called "hibernation" or "winter sleep." During the darkest, coldest months of the year, these mammals—bears come immediately to mind—drowse away periods of severe weather, living on their fat layers. Food would be impossible to find during these periods, and animals would waste energy looking for it. Winter sleep is a natural, healthy, protective reaction of the animal body to a reduction of stimuli, primarily light and warmth. I began to think about how we have created a "disorder" out of a natural, biological process.

The "disordering" of SAD occurs because modern life requires us to punch a time clock at eight o'clock in the morning, regardless of when *daytime* actually begins. We force our bodies into artificial patterns in wintertime, using artificial lights to extend our "days" on both ends, when the natural pattern for many mammals is a reduction of activity in extended periods of colder, shorter days. Our modern lifestyles have us working contrary to our internal, biological clocks.

Our present custom of switching back and forth from Standard to Daylight Savings Time exacerbates the problem. Some relief occurs in October when Daylight Standard Time allows us to rise an hour later. But while Daylight Standard Time gives us daylight an hour "earlier" in the winter, midday occurs at about 10:30 a.m., with full dark falling at five o'clock in the afternoon. Rather than ending our day at dark, as the natural pattern would indicate, most of us are still up at eleven o'clock at night, watching the evening news, even though we will be rising in the dark for work the next "day"—and most likely this will be before *day* actually begins. In the spring, when we switch to Savings Time, 6 a.m. is actually 5 a.m., and once again we are rising in the dark for several months until the sun moves farther north of the equator and daylight hours begin to increase.

Why do more women than men suffer from Seasonal Affective Disorder? The answer is actually very simple, I think. Because of their reproductive systems, women are often more aware of their bodies than men are. They have to be. Women must track and understand their cycles of menstruation, fertility, pregnancy, lactation, and menopause. It is vital for a woman's health that she be in tune with her body's cycles. Because of this, women are more prone to SAD than are men, because they are more aware of their bodies' responses to natural cycles and stimuli, or in this case, the lack of light stimuli.

What are those of us who suffer from the symptoms of SAD to do? Obviously, those who experience severe depression or suicidal thoughts should seek the help of a professional therapist. But for those of us who simply find it difficult to function in the wintertime and don't have the luxury of hibernating the season away, there are some self-help solutions. Some of these tips were gleaned from *The Medical Advisor: The Complete Guide to Alternative and Conventional Treatments* published by Time-Life Books; others were compiled from various Internet sources.

- Exercise to keep your body's metabolism high and reduce winter slow-down.
- Get out into natural light at midday once a day, if possible. Take a walk on your lunch break when the sun is highest in the sky and natural light is strongest. One study of SAD showed that walking for an hour outside, even in winter sunlight, was as effective as more than twice as much time spent under strong, artificial lights.
- Install stronger lights in your home; at least 2500 lux (five times brighter than the average office) is needed according to some sources, and brighter is supposed to be better. Some people have reported good results with plant lights which simulate full-spectrum daylight. One sufferer recommends putting plant lights in the bathroom, where you can get the benefit of light that mimics natural daylight while you're getting ready for work in the morning. (Remember, however, that plant lights do emit ultraviolet light rays.)
- Consider installing a lamp in your bedroom with a dimmer switch on a timer, so that the light comes on automatically and gradually brightens with the "dawn effect." Dawn simulation has been reported to be effective even at low light levels. (An added benefit might be that you'll be able to get rid of your noisy, heart-stopping alarm because you will wake up naturally and gradually as the light increases.)
- Increase natural light in your home by pruning trees and bushes away from your windows. When you're home, open the drapes to natural light. You can install sheers if you have nosy neighbors.
- Do whatever is possible to reflect the light that enters your home. Paint the walls light colors in glossy or semi-gloss paint, which reflects rather than absorbs light. Decorate with mirrors and other reflective materials to magnify the effects of natural light.
- Stay warm. Warmth gives the illusion of light.
- Concentrate on pleasurable activities and avoid stress as much as possible. Learn to say "no" when necessary to reduce stress.
- Balance carbohydrates and proteins in your diet if you want to avoid putting on that extra layer of winter fat.
- Take winter vacations in warm, sunny climates, and if you are suffering severe symptoms, consider moving south!

One other piece of advice from a fellow sufferer. Stop looking at the problem as a disorder, and start seeing it as part of a natural process that has gone just a bit awry. There is no need to compound the problem with the guilt and shame that so many of us feel when faced with something that has been labeled as a disorder. Being aware of our bodies is a good thing, and ultimately, it is the thing that will allow us to cope with the "winter blues."

STUDY QUESTIONS for "To Everything There Is a Season"

COMPREHENSION

1. What is Seasonal Affective Disorder (SAD)? Be specific.
2. Is it a natural process of life or is it a physical and mental disorder? Be specific.

DEVELOPMENT AND ORGANIZATION

1. What rhetorical techniques already studied in this text does French use to define SAD? Where, for instance, does she make use of examples? What is gained through the use of examples? Discuss other modes used in the essay.
2. Does the essay make clear her view of SAD? Explain.
3. Where does she make use of concrete and sensory details? How do these details engage the reader's interest and understanding in the issue?

STYLE AND TECHNIQUE

1. What is the tone of the essay? Does it read like a medical dictionary definition of a disease or does it read like a human understanding of a disorder?
2. Name the solutions offered by the writer. Does providing a list of solutions serve as an adequate conclusion to this essay? How does it stand in contrast to the narrative which she uses to open the essay?
3. Who is the essay's intended audience? Can this essay inform someone who does not suffer from SAD?

TEN-MINUTE TOPICS

1. Define and illustrate a disorder that receives insufficient attention by the media.
2. Describe a series of steps or practices to overcome a mental or physical disorder.
3. Describe how you change—both mentally and physically—with the seasons.

CHAPTER TEN
ANALOGY

DEFINITION

A comparison between two things not in the same category, analogy is frequently used to familiarize the reader—or listener, as the case may be—with something with which he or she is not very familiar. For instance, to discuss the working of the brain, we could develop an analogy comparing the brain to the computer. We could thus elaborate upon the point that both the computer and the brain assimilate, store, and process information. Too, we could develop an analogy comparing the mind to a tree, using the trunk, branches, and leaves to refer to the conscious mind and the complex root system to refer to the subconscious mind.

APPLICATION

As a means of knowing reality, analogy may have fallen into disfavor recently simply because it is not empirical or inductive. While the examples, process, classification, and division essays are generally rooted in the premise that truth is that which can be perceived through the senses, analogy relies upon association and generally cannot be subjected to the same criteria. Yet analogy is worth studying precisely because it is a distinct way of perceiving and interpreting reality, one that relies upon enabling the reader to see likeness connecting two objects not in the same category.

For instance, Jesus makes use of analogy to enable his audience to grasp difficult truths: "The kingdom of heaven is like to a grain of mustard seed, which a man took and sewed into his field: Which indeed is the least of all seeds, but when it is grown, it is the greatest among herbs, and becometh a tree, so that the birds of the air come and lodge in the branches thereof" (Matthew 13:31-32). Jesus wants his listeners to see that the "kingdom of heaven" is like a mustard seed: small at first, it grows to an immense size.

While complete courses of study were devoted to it in the Middle Ages, analogy is a device that today we most frequently associate with literature, specifically with poetry. In the following poem, "A Noiseless Patient Spider," nineteenth-century American poet Walt Whitman uses analogy to descriptively characterize the poet's role in a new and still emerging American society:

> A noiseless patient spider,
> I mark'd where on a little promontory it stood isolated,
> Mark'd how to explore the vacant vast surrounding,
> It launch'd forth filament, filament, filament, out of itself,
> Ever unreeling them, ever tirelessly speeding them.

And you O my soul where you stand,
Surrounded, detached, in measureless oceans of space,
Ceaselessly musing, venturing, throwing, seeking the spheres to connect them,
Till the bridge you will need be form'd, till the ductile anchor hold,
Till the gossamer thread you fling catch somewhere, O my soul.

As Whitman uses the word, *soul* is not to be understood in the traditional Judeo-Christian sense; rather, it is the innate creative capacity that enables the poet to make order of the surrounding world. To enable the reader to grasp this truth, Whitman asks us to visualize the creative and unifying force of the soul in terms of something we can understand, a spider spinning its web.

Often writers like Whitman employ the reader's senses to establish a connection between the analogy's concrete element to its intangible or less familiar counterpart—Whitman's "soul" and "patient spider." Similarly, Chad Lietz in his essay "We're All in the Wrong Song" laments that the essay has "lost its mojo." In an attempt to remedy this problem, he equates the act of composing an essay to that of composing music. He beckons writers to see the value in their craft—to find their unique voice and rhythms. For example, Lietz suggests that

> Fundamentally, measured progression and a sense of time (all musical terms, mind you) afford the work its "go." Once a rhythmic foundation is laid, the piece assumes a kinesis. Both music and the written word express this flow in lines, phrases, and ideatic variations. Music begins after the first note ends, a melody after the second; the same holds true for sentences and paragraphs. Short, terse statements speed ahead, while lugubrious lines linger, each affecting the mood and overall response to the piece. Attend to the resonance and duration of each sentence, in relation to tone, purpose, and to those around it.
>
> Too little attention is paid to the ring of lingual things. Description and consonance, alliteration and image become an ensemble of players in the crafting of a captivating account. Essay writing, like any art, seeks to affect some cathartic response from its audience toward the intent of the work—be it persuasion, sympathy, or understanding. Music composers use aural images and impressions to create an emotional atmosphere; authors the same through a symphony of words. Listen to each line independently; find the rhythm of sentences singing together.

As the above examples have demonstrated, analogy can be used to enable the reader to visualize or understand that which is unfamiliar or beyond conception. Beyond this, analogy can be used to support a theme, if we are writing a narrative, or a thesis, if we are writing an expository essay. For instance, the preacher in Langston Hughes's "Salvation" employs a brief analogy when he compares the children, or young "sinners," to young lambs, thereby intensifying the internal conflict that Hughes as a young boy was experiencing and ultimately reinforcing the theme that social pressures often force us to take actions that may prove disillusioning. The eighteenth-century American Puritan preacher Jonathan Edwards, in his famous "Sinners in the Hands of an Angry God," uses several striking analogies to depict the relationship of the "unrepentant sinner" to his God and reinforce the thesis that this "sinner" is destined for the "flames" of hell:

> The wrath of God is like great waters that are dammed for the present; they increase more and more, and rise higher and higher, till an outlet is given; and the longer the stream is stopped, the more rapid and mighty is its course, when once it is let loose. It is true, that judgment against your evil works has not been executed hitherto; the floods of God's vengeance have been withheld; but your guilt in the meantime is constantly increasing, and you are every day treasuring up more wrath; the waters are constantly rising, and waxing more and more mightily; and there is nothing but the mere pleasure of God, that holds the waters back, that are unwilling to be stopped, and press hard to go forward. . . .
>
> The God that holds you over the pit of hell, much as one holds a spider, or some loathsome insect over the fire, abhors you, and is dreadfully provoked: his wrath towards you burns like fire; he looks upon you as worthy of nothing else, but to be cast into the fire. . . .

In these two passages, the terms of the analogy should be very clear: in the first, the wrath of God is compared to rising waters that are temporarily dammed but that are threatening to overwhelm the unrepentant sinner; in the second, the sinner is compared to a spider held over a fire, waiting to be consumed by the flames of hell.

PARADIGM

As the following essays demonstrate, there is no rigid model for setting up the analogy essay. In "God, the Universe, and My Aquarium," Philip Yancey has written an essay that is descriptive. John Donne's piece is a meditation, composed when he thought that he had contracted the plague and was soon to die. Henry David Thoreau's "The Battle of the Ants" reads partly like a press release from a war correspondent and partly like a scientific lab report. The point is that all these essays contain an analogy that is either identifiable with the central purpose and main idea of the essay or that is supportive of a larger point the writer is trying to make.

The model below simply suggests where certain tasks should be performed:

> **Introduction: Engage audience interest, and offer analogy of person, place, object idea, etc., that serves as the issue of the essay.**

Body: Extend the original analogy or offer a series of analogies of the main idea. (The analogy or analogies may be organized around a best-for-last principle.)

Conclusion: Bring essay to a close by summarizing dominant impression or by offering lasting image, judgment, or message.

SUMMARY

In our writing, we may use analogy to develop part of an essay—or the analogy may constitute the entire essay. If we are writing an essay developed by the use of analogy, we must be sure that our thesis, or main idea, is clearly stated or implied and that the basis of our analogy—the similarity linking the two compared objects—is clearly established.

GOD, THE UNIVERSE, AND MY AQUARIUM

BY PHILIP YANCEY

When I look out my window, I see a twelve-story apartment building, all concrete and glass, with bicycles, Weber grills and lawn chairs propped up at random on its balconies. And also twisted metal aerials protruding from a video store, the pebble-gray roof of Winchell's Donut House, the aluminum vent from an Italian restaurant, and a web of black wires to bring electricity to all these monuments of civilization. We didn't choose this place for the view.

But if I turn my head to the left, as I often do, I can watch a thriving tropical paradise. A corner of the Caribbean has reproduced itself in my study. A glass rectangle contains five seashells coated with velvety algae, stalks of coral planted like shrubbery in the gravel bottom, and seven creatures as exotic as any that exist on God's earth.

Salt-water fish have pure, lustrous colors, so rich that it seems the fish themselves are creating and radiating the hues, rather than merely reflecting light waves to produce them. The most brightly colored fish in my aquarium is split in half, with a glowing yellow tail portion and a shocking magenta head portion, as if he had stuck his head in a paint bucket.

My marine tastes tend toward the bizarre, and in addition to the beautiful fish, I have two that are startling but hardly beautiful. A long-horned cowfish, who gets his name from horns extending from his head and tail, propels his boxy body around the tank with impossibly small side fins. If a bumblebee defies aerodynamics, the cowfish defies aquatics. Another, a lionfish, is all fins and spikes and menacing protuberances, resembling one of the gaudy paper creatures that dances across the stage in a Chinese opera.

I keep the aquarium as a reminder. When writer's loneliness sets in, or personal suffering hits too close, or the gray of Chicago sky and buildings invades to color my mind and moods, I turn and gaze. There are no Rockies out my window, and the nearest grizzly bear or blue whale is half a continent away. But I do have this rectangle that reminds me of the larger world outside. Half a million species of beetles, ten thousand wild butterfly designs, a billion fish just like mine poking around in coral reefs—a lot of beauty is going on out there, often unobserved by human eyes.

Yet even here in the beauty of my artificial universe, suffering thrives as well. Nature, said Chesterton, is our sister, not our mother; it too is fallen. The spikes and fins on my lionfish are appropriately menacing; an adult's can contain enough toxin to kill a person. And when one fish shows a sign of weakness, the others will turn on it, tormenting without mercy. Just last week the other six fish were brutally attacking the infected eye of the cowfish. In aquariums, pacifists die young.

I spend much time and energy trying to counteract the parasites, bacteria, and fungi that invade the tank. I run a portable chemical laboratory to test the specific gravity, nitrate and nitrite levels, and ammonia content. I pump in vitamins and antibiotics and sulfa drugs, and enough enzymes to make a rock grow. I filter the water through glass fibers and charcoal and expose it to an ultraviolet light. Even so, the fish don't last long. Fish are dubious pets, I tell my friends; their only "tricks" are eating, getting sick, and dying.

The arduous demands of aquarium management have taught me a deep appreciation for what is involved in running a universe based on dependable physical laws.

To my fish I am a deity, and one who does not hesitate to intervene. I balance the salts and trace elements in their water. No food enters their tank unless I retrieve it from my freezer and drop it in. They would not live a day without the electrical gadget that brings oxygen to the water. You would think, in view of all this energy expended on their behalf, that my fish would at least be grateful. Not so. Every time my shadow appears above the tank, they dive for cover into the nearest shell. Three times a day I open the lid and drop in food, yet they respond to each opening as a sure sign of my designs to torture them. Fish are not affirming pets.

Whenever I must treat an infection, I face an agonizing choice. Ideally, I should move the infected fish to a quarantine tank to keep the others from pestering it, and also to protect them from contagion. But such violent intervention in the tank, the mere act of chasing the sick fish with the net, could do more damage than the infection. The treatment itself may cause death because of the stress it produces.

I often long for a way to communicate with those small-brained water dwellers. In ignorance, they perceive me as a constant threat. I cannot convince them of my true concern. I am too large for them, my actions too incomprehensible. My acts of mercy they see as cruelty; my attempts at healing they view as destruction. To change their perceptions would require a form of incarnation.

I bought my aquarium to brighten a dull room, but ended up learning a few lessons about running a universe. Maintaining one requires constant effort and precarious balancing of physical laws. Often the most gracious acts go unnoticed or even cause resentment. As for direct intervention, that is never simple, in universe large or small.

STUDY QUESTIONS for "God, the Universe, and My Aquarium"

COMPREHENSION

1. Of what value is the aquarium to the writer?
2. What does the writer mean when he comments that "nature . . . too is fallen"?
3. In what sense is the aquarium an "artificial universe"?
4. How is Yancey like a "deity" to the inhabitants of the aquarium?
5. Why do Yancey's actions of mercy seem to the creatures of the aquarium like acts of cruelty?
6. What is the central purpose of this essay?
7. Define the following words: *random* (1); *algae* (2); *lustrous, hues, magenta* (3); *aerodynamics, aquatics, gaudy* (4); *toxin, pacifists* (5); *fungi, nitrate, enzymes, dubious* (6); *arduous* (7); *deity* (8); *contagion* (9); *incarnation* (10).

DEVELOPMENT AND ORGANIZATION

1. What is the thesis of the essay? Is it implied or directly stated? If the former, summarize it in about fifteen words. If the latter, write is out as it appears in the reading and note the paragraph number where it is located.
2. What is the central analogy of the essay? Where does Yancey establish the points of his analogy?
3. How valid is this analogy? How, for instance, are the writer like God, the aquarium like creation, and the fish like people?
4. Where does the writer use the following methods to support or lead up to his analogy: description, examples, comparison and contrast?

STYLE AND TECHNIQUE

1. What is the effect of using the personal pronoun "I" throughout the essay? Does the use of the pronoun strengthen or weaken the essay?
2. What is the full significance of the final sentence as it relates to the central purpose of the essay?

TEN-MINUTE TOPICS

1. Use analogy to describe how America relates to another country.
2. Use analogy to describe your view of God's relationship to humans, or humans' relationship to God or to each other.
3. Observe a single microcosm of plant or animal or human life and describe it. Focus on the interaction between members of this unit.

MEDITATION XVII

BY JOHN DONNE

Perchance he for whom this bell tolls may be so ill as that he knows not it tolls for him; and perchance I may think myself so much better than I am as that they who are about me and see my state may have caused it to toll for me, and I know not that. The church is catholic, universal, so are all her actions; all that she does belongs to all. When she baptizes a child, that action concerns me; for that child is thereby connected to that body which is my head too and ingrafted into that body whereof I am a member. And when she buries a man, that action concerns me. All mankind is of one author, and is one volume; when one man dies, one chapter is not torn out of the book, but translated into a better language; and every chapter must be so translated.

God employs several translators; some pieces are translated by age, some by sickness, some by war, some by justice; but God's hand is in every translation, and his hand shall bind up all our scattered leaves again for that library where every book shall lie open to one another. As therefore the bell that rings to a sermon calls not upon the preacher only but upon the congregation to come, so this bell calls us all; but how much more me who am brought so near the door by this sickness! There was a contention as far as a suit—in which piety and dignity, religion and estimation, were mingled—which of the religious orders should ring to prayers first in the morning; and it was determined that they should ring first that rose earliest. If we understand aright the dignity of this bell that tolls for our evening prayer, we would be glad to make it ours by rising early, in that application, that it might be ours as well as his, whose indeed it is.

The bell doth toll for him that thinks it doth; and though it intermit again, yet from that minute that that occasion wrought upon him he is united to God. Who casts not up his eye to the sun when it rises? but who takes off his eye from a comet when that breaks out? Who bends not his ear to any bell which upon any occasion rings? but who can remove it from that bell which is passing a piece of himself out of this world? No man is an island entire of itself; every man is a piece of the continent, a part of the main. If a clod be washed away by the sea, Europe is the less, as well as if a promontory were, as well as if a manor of thy friend's or of thine own were. Any man's death diminishes me, because I am involved in mankind, and therefore never send to know for whom the bell tolls; it tolls for thee.

Neither can we call this a begging of misery or a borrowing of misery, as though we were not miserable enough of ourselves but must fetch in more from the next house, in taking upon us the misery of our neighbors. Truly it were an excusable covetousness if we did, for affliction is a treasure, and scarce any man hath enough of it. No man hath affliction enough that is not matured and ripened by it and made fit for God by that affliction. If a man carry treasure in bullion or in a wedge of gold and have none coined into current money, his treasure will not defray him as he travels. Tribulation is treasure in the nature of it, but it is not current money in the use of it, except we get nearer and nearer our home, heaven, by it.

Another man may be sick too, and sick to death, and this affliction may lie in his bowels as gold in a mine and be of no use to him; but this bell that tells me of his affliction digs out and applies that gold to me, if by this consideration of another's danger I take mine own into contemplation and so secure myself by making my recourse to my God, who is our only security.

STUDY QUESTIONS for "Meditation XVII"

COMPREHENSION

1. What is the subject of this composition—that is, what is it that Donne is meditating upon?
2. According to this brief meditation, what is Donne's world view? What does he believe in? What is important to him?
3. Why does the baptism of a child—or the burial of a man—concern Donne as an individual? What is Donne implying about the relationship between individuals within the "catholic, universal" church?
4. Who or what are the "translators" about whom Donne writes? What is the "library"?
5. What does Donne mean when he writes, "Any man's death diminishes me"?
6. Donne comments that "affliction is a treasure." What does Donne mean when he writes this? How, according to Donne, are we "made fit for God by that affliction"?
7. Interpret Donne's final sentence, "Another man may be sick too, and sick to death. . . ."
8. What is the central idea that unifies this meditation? What is the central point?

DEVELOPMENT AND ORGANIZATION

1. What analogies does Donne employ in this essay? What is gained by using them?
2. At one point, Donne writes, "All mankind is of one author, and is one volume; when one man dies, one chapter is not torn out of the book, but translated into a better language." In your own words, explain what message Donne is conveying through this analogy.
3. The most significant analogy of the meditation is expressed in the passage beginning, "No man is an island entire of itself." Discuss what Donne means as he develops this analogy and explain the relationship of this analogy to the rest of the essay.

STYLE AND TECHNIQUE

1. What are some of the things that the tolling of the bell symbolizes for Donne?
2. What is the tone in which this meditation is written? In other words, what attitude does Donne display toward his subject? Toward his audience?

TEN-MINUTE TOPICS

1. Use analogy to define God, love, hatred, jealousy, greed, success, or failure.
2. Use analogy to define birth, death, or sickness.
3. Describe your own meditation process.

THE BATTLE OF THE ANTS

BY HENRY DAVID THOREAU

One day when I went out to my wood-pile, or rather my pile of stumps, I observed two large ants, the one red, the other much larger, nearly half an inch long, and black, fiercely contending with one another. Having once got hold they never let go, but struggled and wrestled and rolled on the chips incessantly. Looking farther, I was surprised to find that the chips were covered with such combatants, that it was not a *duellum,* but a *bellum,*[1] a war between two races of ants, the red always pitted against the black, and frequently two red ones to one black. The legions of these Myrmidons covered all the hills and vales in my woodyard, and the ground was already strewn with the dead and dying, both red and black. It was the only battle which I have ever witnessed, the only battle-field I ever trod while the battle was raging; internecine war; the red republicans on the one hand, and the black imperialists on the other. On every side they were engaged in deadly combat, yet without any noise that I could hear, and human soldiers never fought so resolutely. I watched a couple that were fast locked in each other's embraces, in a little sunny valley amid the chips, now at noonday prepared to fight till the sun went down, or life went out. The smaller red champion had fastened himself like a vise to his adversary's front, and through all the tumblings on that field never for an instant ceased to gnaw at one of his feelers near the root, having already caused the other to go by the board; while the stronger black one dashed him from side to side, and, as I saw on looking nearer, had already divested him of several of his members. They fought with more pertinacity than bulldogs. Neither manifested the least disposition to retreat. It was evident that their battle-cry was "Conquer or die." In the meanwhile there came along a single red ant on the hillside of this valley, evidently full of excitement, who either had dispatched his foe, or had not yet taken part in the battle; probably the latter, for he had lost none of his limbs; whose mother had charged him to return with his shield or upon it. Or perchance he was some Achilles, who had nourished his wrath apart, and had now come to avenge or rescue his Patroclus.[2] He saw this unequal combat from afar,—for the blacks were nearly twice the size of the red,—he drew near with rapid pace till he stood on his guard within half an inch of the combatants; then, watching his opportunity, he sprang upon the black warrior, and commenced his operations near the root of his right fore leg, leaving the foe to select among his own members; and so there were three united for life, as if a new kind of attraction had been invented which put all other locks and cements to shame. I should not have wondered by this time to find that they had their respective musical bands stationed on some eminent chip, and playing their national airs the while, to excite the slow and cheer the dying combatants. I was myself excited somewhat even as if they had been men. The more you think of it, the less the difference. And certainly there is not the fight recorded in Concord history, at least, if in the history of America, that will bear a moment's

---

[1] *Duellum* (Latin) is a combat of two persons and *bellum* is a war.
[2] In the *Iliad*, Achilles fights to avenge the death of his second-in-command, Patroclus.

comparison with this, whether for the numbers engaged in it, or for the patriotism and heroism displayed. For numbers and for carnage it was an Austerlitz or Dresden.[3] Concord fight! Two killed on the patriots' side, and Luther Blanchard wounded! Why here every ant was a Buttrick,—"Fire, for God's sake fire!"—and thousands shared the fate of Davis and Hosmer[4]. There was not one hireling there. I have no doubt that it was a principle they fought for, as much as our ancestors, and not to avoid a three-penny tax on their tea; and the results of this battle will be as important and memorable to those whom it concerns as those of the battle of Bunker Hill, at least.

I took up the chip on which the three I have particularly described were struggling, carried it into my house, and placed it under a tumbler on my window-sill, in order to see the issue. Holding a microscope to the first-mentioned red ant, I saw that, though he was assiduously gnawing at the near fore leg of his enemy, having severed his remaining feeler, his own breast was all torn away, exposing what vitals he had there to the jaws of the black warrior, whose breastplate was apparently too thick for him to pierce; and the dark carbuncles of the sufferer's eyes shone with ferocity such as war only could excite. They struggled half an hour longer under the tumbler, and when I looked again the black soldier had severed the heads of his foes from their bodies, and the still living heads were hanging on either side of him like ghastly trophies at his saddle-bow, still apparently as firmly fastened as ever, and he was endeavoring with feeble struggles, being without feelers and with only the remnant of a leg, and I know not how many other wounds, to divest himself of them; which at length, after half an hour more, he accomplished. I raised the glass, and he went off over the window-sill in that crippled state. Whether he finally survived that combat, and spent the remainder of his days in some Hôtel des Invalides, I do not know; but I thought that his industry would not be worth much thereafter. I never learned which party was victorious, nor the cause of the war, but I felt for the rest of that day as if I had my feelings excited and harrowed by witnessing the struggle, the ferocity and carnage, of a human battle before my door.

Kirby and Spence tell us that the battles of ants have long been celebrated and the date of them recorded, though they say that Huber[5] is the only modern author who appears to have witnessed them. "Aeneas Sylvius," say they, "after giving a very circumstantial account of one contested with great obstinacy by a great and small species on the trunk of a pear tree," adds that "'this action was fought in the pontificate of Eugenius the Fourth, in the presence of Nicholas Pistoriensis, an eminent lawyer, who related the whole history of the battle with the greatest fidelity.' A similar engagement between great and small ants is recorded by Olaus Magnus, in which the small ones, being victorious, are said to have buried the bodies of their own soldiers, but left those of their giant enemies a prey to the birds. This event happened previous to the expulsion of the tyrant Christiern [sic] the Second from Sweden." The battle which I witnessed took

---

[3] Battles fought during the time of Napoleon Bonaparte (early 1800s).

[4] Major John Buttrick led the American militia in the first battle of the Revolutionary War, which took place at Concord Bridge. Davis and Hosmer died, and Blanchard was wounded in the fighting.

[5] Kirby, Spence, and Huber were entomologists.

place in the presidency of Polk, five years before the passage of Webster's Fugitive-Slave Bill.

STUDY QUESTIONS for "The Battle of the Ants"

COMPREHENSION

1. What is the central idea expressed in the passage? Does Thoreau express this idea in a clearly stated thesis, or does he imply it? If the former, write out the thesis as it appears in the text, and identify by number the paragraph in which it appears; if the latter, summarize the central idea in fifteen words.
2. Who are the Myrmidons? Look them up in a dictionary or an encyclopedia and see if you can find a version of the myth that explains their creation. Why does Thoreau allude to them in this passage? What other allusions to battle and warfare appear in the essay?
3. Does Thoreau seem to take the side of the red ants or the black ants? What words and phrases lead you to your conclusion?
4. What audience does Thoreau seem to have in mind as he writes? What would that audience's view on warfare be? What view does Thoreau seem to take on warfare?
5. In the last paragraph, Thoreau states that other writers have described battles between ants. Why is this so, do you think? Are these other writers drawing analogies similar to that drawn by Thoreau?
6. What is Thoreau's purpose for writing this passage?

DEVELOPMENT AND ORGANIZATION

1. In his description of the battle, Thoreau uses subjective (imbued with his own feelings) and objective (devoid of emotion) description. Quote an example of each as they appear in the passage.
2. What general plan of organization does Thoreau's passage follow? Does he follow the paradigm for the analogy essay? Or does he seem to follow the paradigm for the comparison and contrast essay? The narrative? The description? Or does he use a different plan? Which one?

STYLE AND TECHNIQUE

1. Look closely at the second full paragraph of the passage. Count the number of words and count the number of sentences. Find the ratio of words per sentence. Now look at the start of each sentence. Does Thoreau begin the sentences with the grammatical subject, or does he begin them with some other word group? Categorize and count the methods he uses to open his sentences.
2. Does Thoreau use personification in this essay? Where? Write down each instance and describe the effect they have on the passage.

TEN-MINUTE TOPICS

1. Write an analogy in which an animal or a group of animals seems to engage in a human activity. What makes you think of the human activity? What do you learn about human beings by watching these animals so engaged? Make sure that the common element is clearly presented and elaborated on with examples.
2. Is there another way in which ants are similar to humans? Write an analogy that presents the similarity and provides examples of it.

CHAPTER ELEVEN
REPORTING

DEFINITION

Much of the reading we do exposes us to the writing style known as *reporting*. Magazines and newspapers in particular use reporting to tell us about current events, the latest styles and trends, the best and worst movies and shows and CDs, and the opinions of experts and the people in the streets. While not in the same mode as expository writing, reporting is a task that you may be called upon to perform during your college studies and during your career.

The most general function of reporting is to gather facts and observations and shape them into a coherent whole. The facts and observations can come from many sources, most of which originate outside the writer. The writer may be a passive observer, simply setting down newsworthy events, or an active interpreter, putting a personal or editorial spin on the material.

A glance at a good daily newspaper, however, reveals that reporting can involve many different kinds of writing with many different purposes. The front page reports on trials, murders, disasters, wars and other events around the world. The lifestyle page may offer gossip about famous people, movie reviews, recipes, and advice columns. The sports page recounts games, offers analyses of player performance, and predicts the outcomes of upcoming contests. The opinion page gives us letters from concerned citizens and editorials from professional commentators. Weekly magazines such as *Time* and *Newsweek* perform many of the same tasks.

You will see as you begin your own reporting that many of the modes we have discussed to this point in the textbook—description, narration, process, etc.—will come into play. Reporters cannot give us a picture of a war without describing a battle zone, or recounting a country's history, or narrating the life story of one of the fighters involved, or showing us step-by-step how an enemy city was captured. Reviewers like Roger Ebert cannot judge a movie without describing one of its key scenes, giving us a glance at an actor's background, or telling us how the writing, the directing, the costuming, and so on, were carried out.

At all times, however, the writer of the report must remember the audience. The main purpose of reporting is to present the facts and observations clearly to readers. The readers, in their turn, can thereby become more informed and capable of making their own judgments about current events, world leaders, sports, entertainment, and other interests.

APPLICATION

Several different processes make up the task of reporting. While by no means complete, the list provided for you below should help you to understand the task both as a reader and as a writer. Keep in mind as you go through the list that these different processes

222

are not mutually exclusive. A good reporter may engage in more than one at the same time to produce a newspaper or magazine article. The writing assignments you are given in your classes will likely require that you engage in more than one process also. If the journalistic style of writing intrigues you, consult your institution's course offerings in the field.

Eyewitnessing

The basis of many of the facts and observations reported in an article comes from *eyewitnessing*. The reporter goes into the field to gain a first-hand look at the battle, the disaster, the movie premier, the World Series game, that will be the subject of the article. The reporter relies upon his or her own impressions to record the events, the facts, and the significant details. To aid the reporter, a photographer or camera operator may also be present to provide pictures or film coverage. Together, the images and the text give the reader a sense of what it was like to be there with the reporter.

Sometimes a reporter will create an article by gathering information eyewitnessed by others. You may sometimes see in a magazine article credit given to a writer but also to correspondents. Those correspondents are working in the field and sending back their reports to the writer, who then puts them together for the article.

Interviewing

At the same time that a reporter witnesses a newsworthy event, he or she may also *interview* someone who is closely associated with what is transpiring. After a battle, for example, the reporter might talk to one of the soldiers who was in combat, one of the natives whose houses were captured, or one of the government leaders running the campaign. These interviews give readers more insight into the events and put a human face upon them. Hearing about the tsunami that killed tens of thousands of people in Japan may cause us concern, but seeing the grief-wracked face of a mother who saw her daughter washed away by the killer waves will make us understand that these globe-shattering events are happening to people like ourselves. Our sympathy (as well as our knowledge) is much greater as a result.

Research and Interpretation

When a reporter has time to do an article that gives us a broader view of an issue, he or she will commonly follow an investigative process. An investigative reporter will interview experts, but just as importantly, do some *research* and then *interpret* the data that come to light. The reporter may therefore turn to books, journals, magazine and newspaper articles, biographies, records of prior interviews, and other sources to discover and to substantiate the facts that relate to the issue. This portion of the process involves a good set of library skills. You will read more about the research process in another chapter.

The process of interpretation is trickier than simply reporting the facts. Often a series of facts comes to light, and the reporter must make a connection between them so that they will make sense. For example, if a reporter is writing about a new highway project in her hometown, but if she finds records from three different companies that show financial links between the county transportation board and the contractor that was awarded the job, then she will likely interpret those findings as a possible conflict of interest.

Be aware, however, that a good reporter will make an interpretation that fits the facts. The reporter should not arrange or alter the facts to support a preconceived or faulty opinion. For example, if a reporter learns that a baseball player was teammates with three other men accused of using steroids, the reporter should not paint the player as a user by exaggerating his association with the other players. In this sense, a good reporter is like a good scientist who is willing to change a bad hypothesis once more facts come to light.

Critical Commentary

Much of what we read in a newspaper or a magazine comes from a professional commentator or critic. These specialists are considered knowledgeable in their fields because they have researched and reported on it for many years or because they have special training or work experience in the field itself. Roger Ebert, for example, has won a Pulitzer Prize for his film criticism and written several books about movies, but he also wrote the screenplay for the cult classic *Beyond the Valley of the Dolls*. Professional commentators therefore often have insights, facts, or opinions worth listening to—even if you disagree with them—because of their expertise. These commentators will also have a higher level of credibility because of their experience. When watching a baseball game, for example, we trust the commentary of Joe Morgan because he is a Hall of Fame second baseman and hence knowledgeable of strategy and player skill.

The specialist is likely to draw upon the other three processes outlined above. You are likely to see, therefore, an interview, or a statistic gleaned from a book, or even first-hand experience depending on the subject and the audience's needs. Some specialists, for example, will not only try to inform the reader about an issue but also offer guidance to readers who are interested in the same field. Tom and Ray Magliozzi (Click and Clack, the Tappet Brothers), who host *Car Talk* on public radio and write a newspaper column about cars, answer listener and reader concerns about car troubles and advise them about repairs, scams, and recalls. Over the years, we have read and enjoyed the writing of specialists such as Erma Bombeck, Ann Landers, Julia Child, William Safire, Russell Baker, and others.

The specialist may also attempt to put forth a reasoned opinion about an event that affects his or her area of expertise. You will note, for example, in the following readings that Roger Ebert and Vince Mancini have opposing views about the hugely popular film *Avatar*. Ebert praises the film after comparing it favorably to other science fiction and fantasy movies and examining the complexity of the story and the movie's use of special effects. Vince Mancini, on the other hand, disparages the film's use of clichéd action and characters.

A main source of critical commentary is the editorial page of the newspaper or magazine. These writers will often present an opinion about current events or about an important back-burner issue that relates to his or her areas of expertise. The chapter nine reading "The Equality Racket" by Patrick J. Buchanan, for example, appeared in several op-ed pages around the country, and deals with an area he discusses frequently, Constitutional law. George Will, a well-known columnist, offers comments and research about issues of the day—everything from Nevada's resistance to the nuclear depository to baseball to President Obama's health care plan.

Editorial Vision and Bias

One other element to be aware of as you read and write in this mode is *editorial vision and bias*. This is a behind-the-scenes influence that can shape an article presented in a magazine or newspaper. Editorial vision can be positive. For example, you will note that certain magazines print articles that have to do with a certain field such as dining, home improvement, or sports. These articles represent the vision of the magazine and its editors. This vision can be narrowed further by examining the types of articles written about the chosen subject. For example, *Gourmet* magazine focuses its attention on fine dining and on recipes gathered from around the world. *Vegetarian Times*, on the other hand, focuses on recipes that vegetarian eaters can enjoy.

Editorial bias, on the other hand, can be a positive or a negative influence. You will often note that a magazine or a newspaper has a slant toward a particular political, religious, or socio-economic viewpoint. A quick way to determine the bias of a publication is to look at its editorial section and read how its feature articles have been written. What is said, by whom it is said, and how it is said will give you a feel for the publication's viewpoint. On the positive side, all groups—from gays, to African Americans, to big businesses, to militia members—can express an opinion. On the negative side, these groups may try to confuse an issue, attack opponents, or spread propaganda by bending or reshaping facts to suit their viewpoints. For example, a conservative publication may print an article attacking pro-abortionists as killers, conveniently hiding the fact that anti-abortion activists have bombed doctors' offices and killed surgeons. A left-leaning publication may print an article attacking a conservative senate candidate for an extramarital affair while ignoring the fact that his liberal opponent is under suspicion of embezzling campaign funds.

A good reporter will balance the positive and negative influences so that an article will appear unbiased and fair. While opinion has its place in reporting, deliberately misleading the reader on the basis of that opinion pushes the writing out of the realm of reporting. Sticking to the facts, whatever their form or content, is always a good strategy for a reporter.

PARADIGM

Because a report can take the form of a news article, an editorial, a review, a commentary, an advice column, a feature, or one of many other shapes, setting forth a single paradigm for this mode is not possible. At best, we can offer you some general advice about where certain information is likely to fall:

> **Introduction: Relate Key Event—Who/What/When/Where/ How or Why.**

> **Body: Give relevant facts, events, interviews, statistics, opinions, judgments.**

> **Conclusion: Close report by offering lasting image, judgment, fact, or quote.**

SUMMARY

Reporting is based upon facts and observations. Different types of reporting—feature writing, reviews, editorials—will have different purposes and needs and will therefore determine how you present those facts and observations. At all times, you should appear unbiased when reporting facts or thoughtful when presenting opinions. You should also remember that your chief purpose is to inform your audience, presenting them with enough information so that they can form their own opinions.

A LIGHT SHOW AND A MYSTERY

BY STEVE CHAWKINS

Is solstice illumination of altar an accident? Researcher says no.

On the darkest day of the year, a hushed crowd in a dim church awaited a few minutes of sheer brilliance.

It was just after dawn Wednesday, the day of the winter solstice. Outside the two-hundred-year-old mission at the heart of tiny San Juan Bautista, Native American drummers sang, urging the sun to rise. Inside, dozens of parishioners rubbed the sleep from their eyes. A woman stood up and sang in cadences haunting and solemn—phrases in no known tongue, she said, but "the language of the heart."

They were gathered for what has come to be known as an "illumination," a brief, breathtaking interval when a sunbeam penetrates the church's front window to bathe the altar and the sacred objects around it in a blazing patch of light. The mission perched at the edge of the San Andreas Fault sees it but once a year.

As roosters crowed, a luminous rectangle appeared on the wall just to the left of the altar. Turning gold and then fiery, it slowly moved over the altar. At that moment, someone threw open the church's great double doors and a river of light shot down the 188-foot-long main aisle. One by one, parishioners were led to the altar for their moment in the sun.

It was a spectacular moment—but what it means is an open question. Some researchers say the illuminations at San Juan Bautista and other missions are nothing more than great special effects.

But for Ruben Mendoza, an archaeologist who teaches at Cal State Monterey Bay, they're more significant. According to Mendoza, Franciscan architects carefully engineered the luminous event for the sun-worshiping local Indians they sought to convert.

"For many Native American groups," he said, "the solstice was the most dreaded day of the year. They believed the sun was dying and only its rebirth could ensure their survival."

Mendoza has been researching illuminations for years. He saw his first one eleven years ago, and it moved him deeply. At the time, he was both a worshiper at San Juan Bautista and a researcher supervising an archaeological dig on the mission's grounds.

In 1997, the mission's priest spotted an illumination while opening the church for a small group of post-dawn pilgrims. After that, he held a number of solstice observances, hoping the Central Coast's morning fog wouldn't seal out the sun.

Both as a Catholic and as a scientist, Mendoza was eager to see it.

The son of a Spanish-language radio announcer, he grew up in Fresno but fell in love with history on a fourth-grade field trip to San Juan Bautista. As a student and then as head of his university's Institute of Archaeology, he poured himself into Aztec cosmology, archaeoastronomy and, most recently, the solar geometry of California's missions.

On that morning in 2000, Mendoza saw the light.

"As I approached the altar-borne tabernacle with camera at the ready, I was smitten by the most unusual sensation that I was soon to share two centuries of a most esoteric and spiritual experience," he later wrote in the mission's newsletter. "I couldn't help but feel what many describe when in the course of a near-death experience—they see the light of the great beyond."

Since then, he has toted his cameras, compasses and computers throughout the West, chasing sunbeams into California's twenty-one missions, as well as dozens of other churches built by early Spanish friars throughout the Southwest and Mexico.

So far, he says, he has found "solstice, equinox and feast day solar illuminations of main altar tabernacles" at sixty sites.

In California, Old World diseases devastated the Native Americans who lived and toiled at the missions. Native languages and cultures died as well. But Junipero Serra's Franciscan monks were so intent on winning new souls that, according to Mendoza, they precisely oriented at least thirteen missions and an old Spanish chapel to capture illuminations—some on days that would have been sacred in Native American faiths.

The buildings functioned as "ecclesiastical computers," he said—much like cathedrals built in Europe centuries before the missions. Those great, vaulted, dark spaces also served as observatories, with astronomers focusing sunbeams through strategically carved openings to make a variety of calculations—from the date of Easter Sunday to the diameter of the sun.

At San Juan Bautista, the science was focused on the solstice, according to Mendoza. With ancient building techniques and the kind of instruments mariners had been using for centuries, the friars, he said, created the kind of solar spectacle that wouldn't have been out of place at Stonehenge or in ancient Rome.

Over the last decade, Mendoza has seen other such moments. At Mission San Carlos Borromeo in Carmel, it's on the summer solstice. At Mission San Miguel, statues of saints are illuminated on a series of their feast days in October. In San Jose, the illumination occurs at sunset on the spring and fall equinoxes.

"They manifest themselves in ways that require an incredible amount of planning," Mendoza says. In San Juan Bautista, builders seeking the perfect alignment for the solstice show even set their church slightly off kilter—about three degrees from the rest of the mission quadrangle.

"It can't be coincidence," he says. "It's too perfect."

That's just the problem, according to Mendoza's critics.

Andrew Galvan, curator of San Francisco's Mission Dolores, said he doubts that Franciscan friars of the late eighteenth century would have been so accommodating to native faiths. The illumination of the tabernacle—the receptacle for consecrated bread and wine—would have been an empty display because Indians weren't allowed to receive Communion until 1808, after most of the missions had been designed.

"This would be considered pagan, not Christian," he said. "Junipero Serra would have boarded over the windows if he were aware of it."

Galvan, himself a descendant of the region's Ohlone Indians, said he believes the illuminations are nothing more than ornament.

"It's a fluke of nature, a curiosity, a 'Wowee!' kind of thing," he said. "Every single church that has a main window facing east or west will get a light show on some day during the year."

Others believe the illuminations were far more calculated.

In Santa Barbara, Chumash Indians were accustomed to the magic of their solstice caves, where penetrating sunlight would shine upon painted images. It would have been natural, some scholars say, for the Franciscans to win over sun worshipers with sunbeams.

"Instead of replacing a religion, you're fulfilling it," said Tina Foss, director of the museum at Mission Santa Barbara. "It's a synthesis instead of a conquest."

According to Mendoza, Mission Santa Barbara's orientation is "virtually identical" to that of San Juan Bautista. A solstice illumination would have been particularly dazzling in Santa Barbara, he said, where the altar was inlaid with mother of pearl from local abalone shells.

Foss believes he's right. She and other mission officials are raising funds to remove a wall and renovate an organ that since the 1920s have blocked the window through which sunlight would have poured.

"People lost touch with why the church was built the way it was," she said. "It's like inheriting an old house: Your grandma knew who planted the trees out front, but after two or three generations people aren't necessarily aware of it."

STUDY QUESTIONS for "A Light Show and a Mystery"

COMPREHENSION

1. What is an illumination? How many illuminations has Mendoza found? Where else do similar "solar spectacles" occur?
2. What is the connection between the illuminations and the Native American cultures surrounding the missions? Why did the Spanish allegedly attempt to exploit that connection?
3. What are the objections to the theories proposed by Mendoza? What are the arguments that supporters have raised?

DEVELOPMENT AND ORGANIZATION

1. Chawkins relies heavily on interviews to write this article. How many people does he interview? What are their credentials? Does he interview people whose expertise is suitable for the topic?
2. Chawkins reported this article from San Juan Bautista, California, on December 22, 2011. Why would it be important for him to report from that place and at that time? Pictures of the illumination also appeared with the article (they may still be available online). How would those pictures help the reader understand the article?

3. How does Chawkins introduce the arguments for and against Mendoza's theories? In what order does he present them? Does his presentation of them give balance to the article?
4. Where does Chawkins use definitions? Why are the definitions important?

STYLE AND TECHNIQUE

1. A description of a service on the winter solstice begins the article. Why did Chawkins choose to begin with this description? What mood does it set for the rest of the article?
2. Look closely at how the illumination is described. What words in the description stand out? What images do they conjure? Are they subjective or objective? What tone do they give to the passage and to the idea of the illumination itself?
3. Some of the paragraphs in the article are only a single sentence long. When do they occur? What is Chawkins saying at those times? Why do you think he chose to use such paragraphs when he did?

TEN-MINUTE TOPICS

1. Write about a strange phenomenon that occurs where you live. What is it? When and how is it encountered? How do people react to it?
2. Write about a historical building that you have visited or that exists where you live. Describe it. What does it look like? How old is it? What happened there that makes the building famous? In what condition is it, well maintained or falling apart? Is it still in use?
3. Take an ordinary event, one that you have experienced frequently, and write about it, to a person who has not seen it happen, as if it were a strange, eerie, or once-in-a-lifetime occurrence. Describe the event in some detail, but in a way that makes it sound unusual or unique.

BEAUTIFUL BRAINS

BY DAVID DOBBS

Moody. Impulsive. Maddening. Why do teenagers act the way they do? Viewed through the eyes of evolution, their most exasperating traits may be the key to success as adults.

Although you know your teenager takes some chances, it can be a shock to hear about them.

One fine May morning not long ago my oldest son, seventeen at the time, phoned to tell me that he had just spent a couple hours at the state police barracks. Apparently he had been driving "a little fast." What, I asked, was "a little fast"? Turns out this product of my genes and loving care, the boy-man I had swaddled, coddled, cooed at, and then pushed and pulled to the brink of manhood, had been flying down the highway at 113 miles an hour.

"That's more than a little fast," I said.

He agreed. In fact, he sounded somber and contrite. He did not object when I told him he'd have to pay the fines and probably for a lawyer. He did not argue when I pointed out that if anything happens at that speed—a dog in the road, a blown tire, a sneeze—he dies. He was in fact almost irritatingly reasonable. He even proffered that the cop did the right thing in stopping him, for, as he put it, "We can't all go around doing 113."

He did, however, object to one thing. He didn't like it that one of the several citations he received was for reckless driving.

"Well," I huffed, sensing an opportunity to finally yell at him, "what would you call it?"

"It's just not accurate," he said calmly. "'Reckless' sounds like you're not paying attention. But I was. I made a deliberate point of doing this on an empty stretch of dry interstate, in broad daylight, with good sight lines and no traffic. I mean, I wasn't just gunning the thing. I was driving.

"I guess that's what I want you to know. If it makes you feel any better, I was really focused."

Actually, it did make me feel better. That bothered me, for I didn't understand why. Now I do.

My son's high-speed adventure raised the question long asked by people who have pondered the class of humans we call teenagers: What on Earth was he doing? Parents often phrase this question more colorfully. Scientists put it more coolly. They ask, What can explain this behavior? But even that is just another way of wondering, What is wrong with these kids? Why do they act this way? The question passes judgment even as it inquires.

Through the ages, most answers have cited dark forces that uniquely affect the teen. Aristotle concluded more than 2,300 years ago that "the young are heated by Nature as drunken men by wine." A shepherd in William Shakespeare's *The Winter's Tale* wishes "there were no age between ten and three-and-twenty, or that youth would sleep out the rest; for there is nothing in the between but getting wenches with child, wronging the ancientry, stealing, fighting." His lament colors most modern scientific inquiries as well. G. Stanley Hall, who formalized adolescent studies with his 1904 *Adolescence: Its Psychology and Its Relations to Physiology, Anthropology, Sociology, Sex, Crime, Religion and Education*, believed this period of "storm and stress" replicated earlier, less civilized stages of human development. Freud saw adolescence as an expression of torturous psychosexual conflict; Erik Erikson, as the most tumultuous of life's several identity crises. Adolescence: always a problem.

Such thinking carried into the late twentieth century, when researchers developed brain-imaging technology that enabled them to see the teen brain in enough detail to track both its physical development and its patterns of activity. These imaging tools offered a new way to ask the same question—What's wrong with these kids?—and revealed an answer that surprised almost everyone. Our brains, it turned out, take much longer to develop than we had thought. This revelation suggested both a simplistic, unflattering explanation for teens' maddening behavior—and a more complex, affirmative explanation as well.

The first full series of scans of the developing adolescent brain—a National Institutes of Health (NIH) project that studied over a hundred young people as they grew up during the 1990s—showed that our brains undergo a massive reorganization between our twelfth and twenty-fifth years. The brain doesn't actually grow very much during this period. It has already reached ninety percent of its full size by the time a person is six, and a thickening skull accounts for most head growth afterward. But as we move through adolescence, the brain undergoes extensive remodeling, resembling a network and wiring upgrade.

For starters, the brain's axons—the long nerve fibers that neurons use to send signals to other neurons—become gradually more insulated with a fatty substance called myelin (the brain's white matter), eventually boosting the axons' transmission speed up to a hundred times. Meanwhile, dendrites, the branchlike extensions that neurons use to receive signals from nearby axons, grow twiggier, and the most heavily used synapses—the little chemical junctures across which axons and dendrites pass notes—grow richer and stronger. At the same time, synapses that see little use begin to wither. This synaptic pruning, as it is called, causes the brain's cortex—the outer layer of gray matter where we do much of our conscious and complicated thinking—to become thinner but more efficient. Taken together, these changes make the entire brain a much faster and more sophisticated organ.

This process of maturation, once thought to be largely finished by elementary school, continues throughout adolescence. Imaging work done since the 1990s shows that these physical changes move in a slow wave from the brain's rear to its front, from areas close to the brain stem that look after older and more behaviorally basic functions, such as vision, movement, and fundamental processing, to the evolutionarily newer and more complicated thinking areas up front. The corpus callosum, which connects the brain's left and right hemispheres and carries traffic essential to many advanced brain functions, steadily thickens. Stronger links also develop between the hippocampus, a sort of memory directory, and frontal areas that set goals and weigh different agendas; as a result, we get better at integrating memory and experience into our decisions. At the same time, the frontal areas develop greater speed and richer connections, allowing us to generate and weigh far more variables and agendas than before.

When this development proceeds normally, we get better at balancing impulse, desire, goals, self-interest, rules, ethics, and even altruism, generating behavior that is more complex and, sometimes at least, more sensible. But at times, and especially at first, the brain does this work clumsily. It's hard to get all those new cogs to mesh.

Beatriz Luna, a University of Pittsburgh professor of psychiatry who uses neuroimaging to study the teen brain, used a simple test that illustrates this learning curve. Luna scanned the brains of children, teens, and twentysomethings while they performed an antisaccade task, a sort of eyes-only video game where you have to stop yourself from looking at a suddenly appearing light. You view a screen on which the red crosshairs at the center occasionally disappear just as a light flickers elsewhere on the screen. Your instructions are to not look at the light and instead to look in the opposite direction. A sensor detects any eye movement. It's a tough assignment, since flickering lights naturally draw our attention. To succeed, you must override both a normal impulse to attend to new information and curiosity about something forbidden. Brain geeks call this response inhibition.

Ten-year-olds stink at it, failing about forty-five percent of the time. Teens do much better. In fact, by age fifteen they can score as well as adults if they're motivated, resisting temptation about seventy to eighty percent of the time. What Luna found most interesting, however, was not those scores. It was the brain scans she took while people took the test. Compared with adults, teens tended to make less use of brain regions that monitor performance, spot errors, plan, and stay focused—areas the adults seemed to bring online automatically. This let the adults use a variety of brain resources and better resist temptation, while the teens used those areas less often and more readily gave in to the impulse to look at the flickering light—just as they're more likely to look away from the road to read a text message.

If offered an extra reward, however, teens showed they could push those executive regions to work harder, improving their scores. And by age twenty, their brains respond to this task much as the adults' do. Luna suspects the improvement comes as richer networks and faster connections make the executive region more effective.

These studies help explain why teens behave with such vexing inconsistency: beguiling at breakfast, disgusting at dinner; masterful on Monday, sleepwalking on Saturday. Along with lacking experience generally, they're still learning to use their brain's new networks. Stress, fatigue, or challenges can cause a misfire. Abigail Baird, a Vassar psychologist who studies teens, calls this neural gawkiness—an equivalent to the physical awkwardness teens sometimes display while mastering their growing bodies.

The slow and uneven developmental arc revealed by these imaging studies offers an alluringly pithy explanation for why teens may do stupid things like drive at 113 miles an hour, aggrieve their ancientry, and get people (or get gotten) with child: They act that way because their brains aren't done! You can see it right there in the scans!

This view, as titles from the explosion of scientific papers and popular articles about the "teen brain" put it, presents adolescents as "works in progress" whose "immature brains" lead some to question whether they are in a state "akin to mental retardation."

The story you're reading right now, however, tells a different scientific tale about the teen brain. Over the past five years or so, even as the work-in-progress story spread into our culture, the discipline of adolescent brain studies learned to do some more-complex thinking of its own. A few researchers began to view recent brain and genetic findings in a brighter, more flattering light, one distinctly colored by evolutionary theory. The resulting account of the adolescent brain—call it the adaptive-adolescent story—casts the teen less as a rough draft than as an exquisitely sensitive, highly adaptable creature wired almost perfectly for the job of moving from the safety of home into the complicated world outside.

This view will likely sit better with teens. More important, it sits better with biology's most fundamental principle, that of natural selection. Selection is hell on dysfunctional traits. If adolescence is essentially a collection of them—angst, idiocy, and haste; impulsiveness, selfishness, and reckless bumbling—then how did those traits survive selection? They couldn't—not if they were the period's most fundamental or consequential features.

The answer is that those troublesome traits don't really characterize adolescence; they're just what we notice most because they annoy us or put our children in danger. As B. J. Casey, a neuroscientist at Weill Cornell Medical College who has spent nearly a decade applying brain and genetic studies to our understanding of adolescence, puts it, "We're so used to seeing adolescence as a problem. But the more we learn about what really makes this period unique, the more adolescence starts to seem like a highly functional, even adaptive period. It's exactly what you'd need to do the things you have to do then."

To see past the distracting, dopey teenager and glimpse the adaptive adolescent within, we should look not at specific, sometimes startling, behaviors, such as skateboarding down stairways or dating fast company, but at the broader traits that underlie those acts.

Let's start with the teen's love of the thrill. We all like new and exciting things, but we never value them more highly than we do during adolescence. Here we hit a high in what behavioral scientists call sensation seeking: the hunt for the neural buzz, the jolt of the unusual or unexpected.

Seeking sensation isn't necessarily impulsive. You might plan a sensation-seeking experience—a skydive or a fast drive—quite deliberately, as my son did. Impulsivity generally drops throughout life, starting at about age ten, but this love of the thrill peaks at around age fifteen. And although sensation seeking can lead to dangerous behaviors, it can also generate positive ones: The urge to meet more people, for instance, can create a wider circle of friends, which generally makes us healthier, happier, safer, and more successful.

This upside probably explains why an openness to the new, though it can sometimes kill the cat, remains a highlight of adolescent development. A love of novelty leads directly to useful experience. More broadly, the hunt for sensation provides the inspiration needed to "get you out of the house" and into new terrain, as Jay Giedd, a pioneering researcher in teen brain development at NIH, puts it.

Also peaking during adolescence (and perhaps aggrieving the ancientry the most) is risk-taking. We court risk more avidly as teens than at any other time. This shows reliably in the lab, where teens take more chances in controlled experiments involving everything from card games to simulated driving. And it shows in real life, where the period from roughly fifteen to twenty-five brings peaks in all sorts of risky ventures and ugly outcomes. This age group dies of accidents of almost every sort (other than work accidents) at high rates. Most long-term drug or alcohol abuse starts during adolescence, and even people who later drink responsibly often drink too much as teens. Especially in cultures where teenage driving is common, this takes a gory toll: In the US, one in three teen deaths is from car crashes, many involving alcohol.

Are these kids just being stupid? That's the conventional explanation: They're not thinking, or by the work-in-progress model, their puny developing brains fail them.

Yet these explanations don't hold up. As Laurence Steinberg, a developmental psychologist specializing in adolescence at Temple University, points out, even fourteen- to seventeen-year-olds—the biggest risk takers—use the same basic cognitive strategies that adults do, and they usually reason their way through problems just as well as adults. Contrary to popular belief, they also fully recognize they're mortal. And, like adults, says Steinberg, "teens actually overestimate risk."

So if teens think as well as adults do and recognize risk just as well, why do they take more chances? Here, as elsewhere, the problem lies less in what teens lack compared with adults than in what they have more of. Teens take more risks not because they don't understand the dangers but because they weigh risk versus reward differently: In situations where risk can get them something they want, they value the reward more heavily than adults do.

A video game Steinberg uses draws this out nicely. In the game, you try to drive across town in as little time as possible. Along the way you encounter several traffic lights. As in real life, the traffic lights sometimes turn from green to yellow as you approach them, forcing a quick go-or-stop decision. You save time—and score more points—if you drive through before the light turns red. But if you try to drive through the red and don't beat it, you lose even more time than you would have if you had stopped for it. Thus the game rewards you for taking a certain amount of risk but punishes you for taking too much.

When teens drive the course alone, in what Steinberg calls the emotionally "cool" situation of an empty room, they take risks at about the same rates that adults do. Add stakes that the teen cares about, however, and the situation changes. In this case Steinberg added friends: When he brought a teen's friends into the room to watch, the teen would take twice as many risks, trying to gun it through lights he'd stopped for before. The adults, meanwhile, drove no differently with a friend watching.

To Steinberg, this shows clearly that risk-taking rises not from puny thinking but from a higher regard for reward.

"They didn't take more chances because they suddenly downgraded the risk," says Steinberg. "They did so because they gave more weight to the payoff."

Researchers such as Steinberg and Casey believe this risk-friendly weighing of cost versus reward has been selected for because, over the course of human evolution, the willingness to take risks during this period of life has granted an adaptive edge. Succeeding often requires moving out of the home and into less secure situations. "The more you seek novelty and take risks," says Baird, "the better you do." This responsiveness to reward thus works like the desire for new sensation: It gets you out of the house and into new turf.

As Steinberg's driving game suggests, teens respond strongly to social rewards. Physiology and evolutionary theory alike offer explanations for this tendency. Physiologically, adolescence brings a peak in the brain's sensitivity to dopamine, a neurotransmitter that appears to prime and fire reward circuits and aids in learning patterns and making decisions. This helps explain the teen's quickness of learning and extraordinary receptivity to reward—and his keen, sometimes melodramatic reaction to success as well as defeat.

The teen brain is similarly attuned to oxytocin, another neural hormone, which (among other things) makes social connections in particular more rewarding. The neural networks and dynamics associated with general reward and social interactions overlap heavily. Engage one, and you often engage the other. Engage them during adolescence, and you light a fire.

This helps explain another trait that marks adolescence: Teens prefer the company of those their own age more than ever before or after. At one level, this passion for same-age peers merely expresses in the social realm the teen's general attraction to novelty: Teens offer teens far more novelty than familiar old family does.

Yet teens gravitate toward peers for another, more powerful reason: to invest in the future rather than the past. We enter a world made by our parents. But we will live most of our lives, and prosper (or not) in a world run and remade by our peers. Knowing, understanding, and building relationships with them bears critically on success. Socially savvy rats or monkeys, for instance, generally get the best nesting areas or territories, the most food and water, more allies, and more sex with better and fitter mates. And no species is more intricately and deeply social than humans are.

This supremely human characteristic makes peer relations not a sideshow but the main show. Some brain-scan studies, in fact, suggest that our brains react to peer exclusion much as they respond to threats to physical health or food supply. At a neural level, in other words, we perceive social rejection as a threat to existence. Knowing this might make it easier to abide the hysteria of a thirteen-year-old deceived by a friend or the gloom of a fifteen-year-old not invited to a party. These people! we lament. They react to social ups and downs as if their fates depended upon them! They're right. They do.

Excitement, novelty, risk, the company of peers. These traits may seem to add up to nothing more than doing foolish new stuff with friends. Look deeper, however, and you see that these traits that define adolescence make us more adaptive, both as individuals and as a species. That's doubtless why these traits, broadly defined, seem to show themselves in virtually all human cultures, modern or tribal. They may concentrate and express themselves more starkly in modern Western cultures, in which teens spend so much time with each other. But anthropologists have found that virtually all the world's cultures recognize adolescence as a distinct period in which adolescents prefer novelty, excitement, and peers. This near-universal recognition sinks the notion that it's a cultural construct.

Culture clearly shapes adolescence. It influences its expression and possibly its length. It can magnify its manifestations. Yet culture does not create adolescence. The period's uniqueness rises from genes and developmental processes that have been selected for over thousands of generations because they play an amplified role during this key transitional period: producing a creature optimally primed to leave a safe home and move into unfamiliar territory.

The move outward from home is the most difficult thing that humans do, as well as the most critical—not just for individuals but for a species that has shown an unmatched ability to master challenging new environments. In scientific terms, teenagers can be a pain in the ass. But they are quite possibly the most fully, crucially adaptive human beings around. Without them, humanity might not have so readily spread across the globe.

This adaptive-adolescence view, however accurate, can be tricky to come to terms with—the more so for parents dealing with teens in their most trying, contrary, or flat-out scary moments. It's reassuring to recast worrisome aspects as signs of an organism learning how to negotiate its surroundings. But natural selection swings a sharp edge, and the teen's sloppier moments can bring unbearable consequences. We may not run the risk of being killed in ritualistic battles or being eaten by leopards, but drugs, drinking, driving, and crime take a mighty toll. My son lives, and thrives, sans car, at college. Some of his high school friends, however, died during their driving experiments. Our children wield their adaptive plasticity amid small but horrific risks.

We parents, of course, often stumble too, as we try to walk the blurry line between helping and hindering our kids as they adapt to adulthood. The United States spends about a billion dollars a year on programs to counsel adolescents on violence, gangs, suicide, sex, substance abuse, and other potential pitfalls. Few of them work.

Yet we can and do help. We can ward off some of the world's worst hazards and nudge adolescents toward appropriate responses to the rest. Studies show that when parents engage and guide their teens with a light but steady hand, staying connected but allowing independence, their kids generally do much better in life. Adolescents want to learn primarily, but not entirely, from their friends. At some level and at some times (and it's the parent's job to spot when), the teen recognizes that the parent can offer certain kernels of wisdom—knowledge valued not because it comes from parental authority but because it comes from the parent's own struggles to learn how the world turns. The teen rightly perceives that she must understand not just her parents' world but also the one she is entering. Yet if allowed to, she can appreciate that her parents once faced the same problems and may remember a few things worth knowing.

Meanwhile, in times of doubt, take inspiration in one last distinction of the teen brain—a final key to both its clumsiness and its remarkable adaptability. This is the prolonged plasticity of those late-developing frontal areas as they slowly mature. As noted earlier, these areas are the last to lay down the fatty myelin insulation—the brain's white matter—that speeds transmission. And at first glance this seems like bad news: If we need these areas for the complex task of entering the world, why aren't they running at full speed when the challenges are most daunting?

The answer is that speed comes at the price of flexibility. While a myelin coating greatly accelerates an axon's bandwidth, it also inhibits the growth of new branches from the axon. According to Douglas Fields, an NIH neuroscientist who has spent years studying myelin, "This makes the period when a brain area lays down myelin a sort of crucial period of learning—the wiring is getting upgraded, but once that's done, it's harder to change."

The window in which experience can best rewire those connections is highly specific to each brain area. Thus the brain's language centers acquire their insulation most heavily in the first thirteen years, when a child is learning language. The completed insulation consolidates those gains—but makes further gains, such as second languages, far harder to come by.

So it is with the forebrain's myelination during the late teens and early twenties. This delayed completion—a withholding of readiness—heightens flexibility just as we confront and enter the world that we will face as adults.

This long, slow, back-to-front developmental wave, completed only in the mid-twenties, appears to be a uniquely human adaptation. It may be one of our most consequential. It can seem a bit crazy that we humans don't wise up a bit earlier in life. But if we smartened up sooner, we'd end up dumber.

STUDY QUESTIONS for "Beautiful Brains"

COMPREHENSION

1. What behaviors is a teen most prone to? What behaviors are not yet fully developed? What "key transitional" need is met by the teen brain's developmental process?
2. What is the most important neurological factor behind the development of the teen brain?
3. In what important ways is a teenager different from an adult? From a child?

DEVELOPMENT AND ORGANIZATION

1. What sort of reporting does Dobbs rely on most heavily: eyewitnessing, interviewing, or research and investigation? Make a list of the sources Dobbs uses and categorize them under these three headings.
2. Reread the section on organization in chapter one. What transition strategies does the author use to link his paragraphs? What transitions does he use within paragraphs to link ideas together?
3. Look also at the overall organizational plans set forth in chapter one (for description, narration, etc.). Which model most closely resembles the plan Dobbs uses for this article?

STYLE AND TECHNIQUE

1. Dobbs opens the article with a personal experience, the phone call he receives from his son. Why do you think he opens with this call? How effectively does it lead into the rest of the article?

2. Despite the formal tone of the article, Dobbs occasionally uses slang and swear words. What words? When does he use them? Why do you think he uses them when he does? What is their effect on the passages around them? On you as the reader?

3. Why does Dobbs use the quote from Shakespeare? How does it fit into the issue of teen behavior? Why do you think it comes in front of the more scientific sources he cites in the article?

TEN-MINUTE TOPICS

1. Write about one of the riskiest things you did (or have done) as a teenager. What did you do? What caused you to do it? What reward were you expecting to come of it? Looking back now, do you think the reward was worth the possible risk?

2. Write about leaving home. If you have done so already, write about the circumstances: how old you were, why you left, what you first encountered, what the end result was. If you have not yet left home, write about the reasons you foresee as being important in a decision to do so. Why would you leave? What do you hope will happen? What risks will you face?

3. Write a letter to a younger sibling, or to one of your children, in which you tell your audience about the significance of the teenage years. Focus on one event from your own experience that has shaped your view of life, and try to explain what lesson your audience can learn from it.

4. Create your own news article about teens and teen behavior by interviewing friends or relatives who are still teenagers. Ask them about things they have done, risks they have taken, rewards (or dangers) they have experienced as a result. Try to come up with your own conclusions for why teens act as they do, but try to present an unbiased view of teen behavior.

BLACK AND WHITE AND BLUE ALL OVER

BY LISA G. LEITZ

Not everyone learns about their legendary mistakes while standing in line at the grocery store, but if a piano is going to land on a community newspaper publisher, that's exactly where it will happen.

"Can you believe they put that photo in there?"

The guy in front of me slapped a copy of my newspaper against the checkstand. It was fairly early in the morning; after delivering all my newsstand, I'd just dropped the kids off at school—and I'd come back to the grocery store to pick up a couple of gallons of milk.

"Oh, I know," the checker said, her hands busy swiping the guy's beef jerky over her scanner. "Nobody can believe it."

I didn't recognize the guy. The checker fussed over bagging his half-case of Bud Light and potato chips. *Probably a hunter*, I thought.

"What's wrong with the photo?" I asked the guy, quickly, before the checker noticed me and could tell him who I was. I tried not to wince as he angrily jammed the copy of my newspaper back onto the checkstand. He left the paper hanging, cockeyed, over the edge of the counter.

"I mean, there's just common decency, isn't there?" he muttered. "Who else but a newspaper would put a picture of a dismembered hand on the friggin' front page?"

Who else but a newspaper, indeed? By the time the infamous hand photo was printed, I *was* the newspaper. Equal parts honest and nosy, I sported such an abysmal level of self-esteem that I was convinced that working eighty hours a week—*every* week—was exactly what I deserved. I was also just stupid enough to believe that I had a shot at redemption every week, too—which shackled me so firmly to my black-and-white mistress that the two of us became indistinguishable.

The schizophrenic ability of a good journalist to remain invisible in public but fearless in print might have served me well on an anonymous big-city beat, but in a small town . . . well, people cannot be blamed for thinking that I was completely crazy.

Those people showed up to holler at me on my front porch, since the newspaper office was in our house. I knew all of them. I knew the tearful ones who showed up clutching notebook-paper obituaries. I knew the city councilmember who sent me drunken emails every Saturday night—he'd cruelly point out all the mistakes I'd made in the paper that week before hinting that he wanted to sleep with me.

"I've never seen anyone with such an easily-triggered sense of justice, Goldilocks," he sneered in one email.

Since the business was continually strapped for cash, I had to take accident pictures. (A front-page wreck photo in a small town is a guaranteed sellout.) I became a wizard at finding access to blocked scenes—plowing my old Taurus through the weeds on canal roads if necessary. It wasn't uncommon for me to beat the ambulance.

But the hand photo was taken at a double fatality that featured easy parking. The victims had ended up in the parking lot of an ag chemical company just east of Royal City, and I felt like I was cheating when I pulled up—it was almost too easy, like going to the mall.

I remember shooting a little mangled red and white Coleman cooler that was lying next to the car as the blanket-covered bodies of the two women were loaded.

The women's lunch—tinfoil-wrapped tamales—had spilled out of the cooler and onto the gravel of the parking lot. Everything was splattered with blood. I couldn't stop thinking about how they'd probably grabbed a few things from the fridge right before they'd left for work—in a hurry, laughing maybe—never knowing it would be one of the last things they ever did.

Although I was used to cops making inappropriate jokes at fatalities, when a trooper rolled his eyes about the "whole famdamily" (while nodding toward the silent relatives of the dead women), I barely managed a polite smile.

Over a dozen people stood and watched the bloody sedan—not wailing, not crying, just staring. They rimmed the edge of the WSP-required fifty-foot fatality buffer like a guardrail. The EMTs had half-heartedly flung disposable blue sheeting over the back door of the mangled sedan for privacy as they had worked to remove the bodies of the two women. I noticed they'd even left their discarded nitrile gloves lying around: a sign of frustration they'd lost both the victims.

I came home, still thinking about the tamales on the bloodstained gravel, and threw up in the utility sink in my laundry room. Then I Photoshopped the pictures of the crushed car, sharpening the focus, and—as advised by our press—I changed the photos into black and white so they would "dot up" better.

And that was how a bright blue nitrile glove thrown on the shattered back window of a Honda became a dismembered hand.

The newspaper went under last year, after the Recession choked off the last of our dying ad revenue. All I have is a stack of silent morgue books now, big, awkward library-bound things stacked in my downstairs pantry along with cans of kidney beans and extra paper towels. I used to pay the bindery in Walla Walla every year to make us a tidy book of our back issues, and I always wondered what the binders thought as they lined up a whole year of our news to sew together. Not that it matters now.

It doesn't seem like those silent morgue books should be able to contain my raucous eight years of being a newspaper. But isn't the past always muffled by the ash of history as it sifts down on all of us? Sifting and sifting, until even someone who had to know everything can forget, until even the most high-contrast black and white memories start to gray and blur, until even a rubber glove in the back of a wrecked car can look like it's waving goodbye.

STUDY QUESTIONS for "Black and White and Blue All Over"

COMPREHENSION

1. What is the image that raises such a furor in the community where the author lives? What was the truth behind that image?
2. In what significant way is the job of a small-town reporter different from that of a reporter in a big city?
3. What were the circumstances at the accident scene surrounding the taking of the photograph? What was the effect of that scene on the author?

DEVELOPMENT AND ORGANIZATION

1. Leitz divides the article into four large sections. What is the main point raised by each of the four sections? Why do you think the section breaks occur where they do?
2. Leitz relies heavily on eyewitnessing in this account. Where do you see her reporting as an eyewitness? Does she use any of the other modes (description, narrative, etc.)? Which ones? How?
3. Leitz also relies on interpretation. Where are the passages when she uses this technique? What do they add to the article?

STYLE AND TECHNIQUE

1. How does Leitz open the article? What does she do to grab your attention? Explain whether her strategy for doing so is effective or not.
2. The image of a hand returns at the very end of the article. What meaning does it have at this point? How is that meaning different from that which it had when it first appeared in the article?
3. In a few passages, Leitz uses dashes (—) to set off parts of a sentence. What sort of words and phrases is she setting off? What is the effect on the rest of the sentence?

TEN-MINUTE TOPICS

1. Write about a time you were (as victim or spectator) in an accident. What happened? How were you involved? What were the effects, on you, on others involved, on your community? In what ways did that accident change your life view?
2. Take a look at a newspaper or a magazine at a checkout stand. What stories are they promoting? How are they being promoted? Are these stories in good taste or bad? What do you think determines whether the stories are in good or bad taste?
3. Create your own newspaper. What stories would you include in it and why? What sort of art or photography would you include and why? To whom would you market it? How would you do so?

AVATAR: CAMERON RETAINS HIS CROWN

BY ROGER EBERT

Watching *Avatar*, I felt sort of the same as when I saw *Star Wars* in 1977. That was another movie I walked into with uncertain expectations. James Cameron's film has been the subject of relentlessly dubious advance buzz, just as his *Titanic* was. Once again, he has silenced the doubters by simply delivering an extraordinary film. There is still at least one man in Hollywood who knows how to spend $250 million, or was it $300 million, wisely.

Avatar is not simply a sensational entertainment, although it is that. It's a technical breakthrough. It has a flat-out Green and anti-war message. It is predestined to launch a cult. It contains such visual detailing that it would reward repeating viewings. It invents a new language, Na'vi, as *Lord of the Rings* did, although mercifully I doubt this one can be spoken by humans, even teenage humans. It creates new movie stars. It is an Event, one of those films you feel you must see to keep up with the conversation.

The story, set in the year 2154, involves a mission by US Armed Forces to an earth-sized moon in orbit around a massive star. This new world, Pandora, is a rich source of a mineral Earth desperately needs. Pandora represents not even a remote threat to Earth, but we nevertheless send in ex-military mercenaries to attack and conquer it. Gung-ho warriors employ machine guns and pilot armored hover ships on bombing runs. You are free to find this an allegory about contemporary politics. Cameron obviously does.

Pandora harbors a planetary forest inhabited peacefully by the Na'vi, a blue-skinned, golden-eyed race of slender giants, each one perhaps twelve feet tall. The atmosphere is not breathable by humans, and the landscape makes us pygmies. To venture out of our landing craft, we use avatars—Na'vi lookalikes grown organically and mind-controlled by humans who remain wired up in a trancelike state on the ship. While acting as avatars, they see, fear, taste and feel like Na'vi, and have all the same physical adeptness.

This last quality is liberating for the hero, Jake Sully (Sam Worthington), who is a paraplegic. He's been recruited because he's a genetic match for a dead identical twin, who an expensive avatar was created for. In avatar state he can walk again, and as his payment for this duty he will be given a very expensive operation to restore movement to his legs. In theory he's in no danger, because if his avatar is destroyed, his human form remains untouched. In theory.

On Pandora, Jake begins as a good soldier and then goes native after his life is saved by the lithe and brave Neytiri (Zoe Saldana). He finds it is indeed true, as the aggressive Col. Miles Quaritch (Stephen Lang) briefed them, that nearly every species of life here wants him for lunch. (Avatars are not made of Na'vi flesh, but try explaining that to a charging thirty-ton rhino with a snout like a hammerhead shark).

The Na'vi survive on this planet by knowing it well, living in harmony with nature, and being wise about the creatures they share with. In this and countless other ways they resemble Native Americans. Like them, they tame another species to carry them around—not horses, but graceful flying dragonlike creatures. The scene involving Jake capturing and taming one of these great beasts is one of the film's great sequences.

Like *Star Wars* and *LOTR*, *Avatar* employs a new generation of special effects. Cameron said it would, and many doubted him. It does. Pandora is very largely CGI. The Na'vi are embodied through motion capture techniques, convincingly. They look like specific, persuasive individuals, yet sidestep the eerie Uncanny Valley effect. And Cameron and his artists succeed at the difficult challenge of making Neytiri a blue-skinned giantess with golden eyes and a long, supple tail, and yet—I'll be damned. Sexy.

At 163 minutes, the film doesn't feel too long. It contains so much. The human stories. The Na'vi stories, for the Na'vi are also developed as individuals. The complexity of the planet, which harbors a global secret. The ultimate warfare, with Jake joining the resistance against his former comrades. Small graceful details like a floating creature that looks like a cross between a blowing dandelion seed and a drifting jellyfish, and embodies goodness. Or astonishing floating cloud-islands.

I've complained that many recent films abandon storytelling in their third acts and go for wall-to-wall action. Cameron essentially does that here, but has invested well in establishing his characters so that it matters what they do in battle and how they do it. There are issues at stake greater than simply which side wins.

Cameron promised he'd unveil the next generation of 3-D in *Avatar*. I'm a notorious skeptic about this process, a needless distraction from the perfect realism of movies in 2-D. Cameron's iteration is the best I've seen—and more importantly, one of the most carefully employed. The film never uses 3-D simply because it has it, and doesn't promiscuously violate the fourth wall. He also seems quite aware of 3-D's weakness for dimming the picture, and even with a film set largely in interiors and a rain forest, there's sufficient light. I saw the film in 3-D on a good screen at the AMC River East and was impressed. It might be awesome in True IMAX. Good luck in getting a ticket before February.

It takes a hell of a lot of nerve for a man to stand up at the Oscarcast and proclaim himself King of the World. James Cameron just got re-elected.

STUDY QUESTIONS for "*Avatar*: Cameron Retains His Crown"

COMPREHENSION

1. What is Ebert's opinion of the movie? Where does he state this opinion?
2. What is the who/what/when/where/how/why presented in this review, and where does Ebert present it?
3. What relationship forms between Jake and Pandora, the world where he meets the Na'vi?

DEVELOPMENT AND ORGANIZATION

1. Which of the reporting processes does Ebert rely on most heavily? Compare your answer here to the one you wrote down for the Chawkins, the Dobbs, or the Leitz article. What is different about the processes used? What is the same?
2. What elements of the movie does Ebert focus on when making his review? Are they important elements? If you have seen the movie, do you agree with his assessment of those elements?
3. Ebert draws comparisons between *Avatar* and other films. What are the comparisons? Why does he draw the comparisons? In what ways are the comparisons effective? Do they help us understand *Avatar* and its characters?

STYLE AND TECHNIQUE

1. Ebert closes his review by talking about Cameron's behavior at the Oscarcast after this movie came out. Why does he end the review on this note? Is it an effective ending? Why or why not?
2. Take a look at the first three paragraphs of this review. How many prepositional phrases appear in them? How many words are there in all the prepositional phrases? What percentage of the total number of words is bound in the prepositional phrases?

TEN-MINUTE TOPICS

1. Write a review of the last movie you have seen. What was your opinion of it? What elements of the movie (plot, acting, special effects, etc.) made the movie enjoyable? What elements detracted from the movie?
2. If you were to create a movie about your own life, what story would you want told? Who would you want to portray you onscreen? Who would you want to direct the movie? Would the movie have a happy or sad ending?
3. Write your own review of *Avatar* or of another film that has a science-fiction backdrop.
4. Write about movie reviewers in general. Do you find that they accurately rate the movies? Do they have any credibility with you? Do their opinions vary greatly from your own? On which movie have you and the reviewers agreed most closely? On which have you had the most differing opinion?

AVATAR IS THE FINEST PIECE OF TRASH SINCE *TITANIC*

BY VINCE MANCINI

It's hard to review a James Cameron movie, because whether you like it is sort of irrelevant. It becomes part of pop culture, like a song. People will talk about it, children will think of it nostalgically in ten years, and you'll probably find yourself humming it on the subway, even if you hate it. Call *Avatar* brilliant trash. It's a lot like *Titanic*—grandiose and impressive on an epic scale, and riddled with clichés throughout. But James Cameron is a smart guy. You figure he knows a cliché when he's writing one. He likes them and he doesn't care what you think, much the way your mom likes bikers.

Sam Worthington, who's a pretty solid leading man even if he can't get rid of his Aussie accent, plays Jake Sully, a paraplegic marine (they have the technology to fix his spine, but he can't afford it). When Sully's identical twin brother, a scientist on Pandora, gets murdered, they need Sully to take his brother's place on a research expedition. Since he shares his brother's DNA, he's the only one who can operate his avatar, a cloned being made from the DNA of his brother mixed with that of the twelve-foot, blue cat-monkeys that live there. Sigourney Weaver, who runs the research expedition on a grant from the corporation mining Pandora, isn't happy that she has to take on a Marine with no science training. Meanwhile, corporate guy Giovanni Ribisi, who wants the scientists to figure out how to get the Na'vi to move out of the giant tree they live in so he can mine for the "unobtanium" underneath (yes, they call it that unironically; it's retarded), hopes Sully will be the non-tree-hugging pussy he needs for intel on the ground. Ditto Stephen Lang, a scarred Marine leading the force of ex-military mercenaries providing security on Pandora. Michelle Rodriguez is there too, and she's a hardcore Latina.

You can pretty much predict what's going to happen from there, and the only reason you don't totally expect everything that happens is that you're thinking, "Wait, no, he couldn't possibly have made it this simplistic . . . could he?" He did. But the story is really just a skeleton for the visuals, which are pretty mind blowing. I'm not ready to say that it wouldn't have been just as good in 2-D, but the 3-D here is easily the best that's been done. It doesn't hurt your eyes or make the picture dim like in *Up*. It's still a gimmick, but Cameron uses it better than anyone has before. A few of the scenes of climbing and pterodactyl riding in the beginning actually had my ass puckering because the threat of falling seemed so real.

Right, the story. It's so cheesy in so many ways that you'll find yourself actually rooting against it at times. We know Jake's going to fall for one of the native broads, fine—you can't blame him, lanky topless chicks with sensual tails and ears that move like a cat? Hawt.—but then all you're thinking is "Oh God, just don't let his girl be the Chief's daughter." Sorry. Not only is she the chief's daughter, the chief is that guy who played Geronimo.

I'm not into the whole assuming-every-character-and-plot-point-is-a-philosophical-metaphor-and-reflection-of-political-ideology thing, and I kind of despise anyone who is, but the Na'vi couldn't fit the description of the "noble savage" more perfectly. In fact, considering he called the mineral "unobtanium," it's a wonder he didn't just call them Noble Savages. The Na'vi are perfectly good and the corporate guys are perfectly evil. The Na'vi are basically American Indians and the plot is basically *Dances with Wolves*. While I'm sure there've been plenty of times in US history when the white man was perfectly evil and killed a bunch of innocent Indians for no better reason than because they were squatting on some gold, anyone who went to school between the '70s and the present gets a little sick of hearing that story. At some point you wonder what the purpose of retelling it is, especially as simplistically as it's delivered here, other than trying to make us feel like crap. I get it, I suck because of my soulless lifestyle and technology. Is there an iPhone app for white guilt?

In this case, the purpose of retelling that story is mainly to take us to a vivid new world and show off some technological toys. Which *Avatar* does incredibly well. Exploring a new world is always welcome. But that's no excuse for making such a bonehead parable. And I'd love to enjoy it completely on its own merits without considering the political parallels, but when you call the mercenaries' plan to blow up the Na'vi's Tree of Memories (. . . don't ask) "a shock and awe campaign," and the natives fight back with suicide missions while ululating, you sort of force us to. You have to cut the references to contemporary political realities if you don't want us to see it as a parable. And if it is meant as a parable, it's a pretty bad one, one which largely boils down to "Your way of life is wrong. Grow dreadlocks, strip off your clothes, and live in the f-cking forest."

The good guys fight the bad guys. The hero leads his army and gets the girl. Someone dies and gets revived (because of love, and miracles!). The main bad guy dies last, and he gets the best death, courtesy of the main good guy. I could've done without any or all of these things (come on, at least one???), but like I said, it's well-done trash. Well done because despite the faithfulness to a tried-and-true narrative, James Cameron takes the time to make you believe it. It's not like in *Terminator: Salvation* when Christian Bale jumps out the back of a cargo plane into an ocean heaving with thirty-foot swells and then just shows up looking wet on the bridge of a submarine with no explanation as to how he got there. James Cameron is a nerd. You know he'd have thought of an explanation for that. It might not be a great or totally plausible explanation, but it'd be more than just "uh, because jump cut?"

Is it a great movie? No. But it's an incredibly watchable bad one.

STUDY QUESTIONS for "*Avatar* Is the Finest Piece of Trash since Titanic"

COMPREHENSION

1. What is Mancini's opinion of the movie? Where does he state this opinion?
2. Mancini objects that the movie sets up an overused conflict between good and evil. Who are the good guys, and who are the bad? In what way does he explain how the conflict is overused?

3. What is Mancini's opinion of the name "unobtanium"? Where does the word actually come from?

DEVELOPMENT AND ORGANIZATION

1. Which of the reporting processes does Mancini rely on most heavily? Compare your answer here to the one you wrote down for the Ebert article. What is different about the processes used? What is the same?
2. What elements of the movie does Mancini focus on when making his review? Are they important elements? If you have seen the movie, do you agree with his assessment of those elements?
3. Mancini, like Ebert, refers to the 3-D process used in the movie. What is his opinion of the 3-D? What effect does he say the 3-D has on his viewing of the film?
4. Mancini, like Ebert, draws comparisons between *Avatar* and other films. What are the films he mentions? Why does he draw the comparisons? In what ways are the comparisons effective?

STYLE AND TECHNIQUE

1. Mancini uses a style of writing laden with fragments, interjections, exaggerations, and commentary that is at turns humorous, ironic, or sarcastic. When do these elements appear in the review? How do they affect the tone of the review?
2. The name of the filmmaker, James Cameron, is repeated frequently in the review. Why does Mancini do so? When does he refer to Cameron in a negative way? When in a positive? What is the net effect of these references?
3. Mancini's last paragraph is built from three very short sentences. Why does he do that? What effect do they have on the article?

TEN-MINUTE TOPICS

1. If you have ever been in battle, answer the following questions. How accurately does *Avatar* portray the battle scenes? When is it most realistic? When does it stray?
2. Write about a time you traveled to a foreign country. What conflicts or problems arose during your travels? When did you get along best with the natives there? How did their customs differ from your own?
3. Write about a time you were unable to perform a basic action such as walking or eating. What prevented you? In what ways did you get around the difficulty?

CHAPTER TWELVE

ARGUMENT

DEFINITION

Every essay that you have written up to this point has helped prepare you for the argumentative essay. When you write an argumentative essay, you generally take a stand on one side or the other of a controversial issue, one for which two sides—pro and con—exist, and try to move your readers, through the process of logical argumentation, to accept your thesis, or central proposition.

The process of logical argumentation involves using reasons or claims and proofs to support your thesis. For the sake of illustration, let's say that you have selected as your topic rock music, a topic that has sparked controversy since its beginnings. Since you can't stand this kind of music, your thesis is that rock music should be outlawed in your county. If you want your audience even to consider your position, admittedly an outrageous one, you must support your thesis with reasons, claims, and proofs. Thus, your first reason for wanting rock music banned might be that it is harmful to one's physical health since, as far as you can understand, rock music played at a high decibel level can damage the listener's hearing. As proof, you could cite a magazine article that you may have read within the past year in which the writer's findings support your contention. From this point, you could go on to present your second reason that rock music should be outlawed: in your opinion, it can damage its listeners morally, even spiritually. To try to prove your point, you could state that much rock music endorses drugs, promiscuous sex, and, in some instances, worship of the occult. Before you can expect your audience to accept your statement, you must offer supporting proofs: not only must you refer to specific rock songs that endorse these things; you should also provide as proof examples of people whose values have actually been twisted by rock music as well as summaries or paraphrases of studies that have been conducted upon the subject. (For more information on how to incorporate and document information taken from primary and secondary sources, read chapter thirteen.)

Of course, we have been treating this topic hypothetically. It's certainly questionable whether your audience will completely accept your argument even if you do provide reasons and supporting proofs. As you can see, however, written argument involves a thesis, or central proposition, which must be supported by specific reasons and proofs. Now let's see how a written argument should be organized.

APPLICATION

We organize the argumentative essay much as we do an expository essay. The introduction, therefore, catches the reader's attention, introduces the issue, and generally states or implies the thesis. Additionally, the introduction should refer to the situation causing the controversy around which your argument is based. The following introductory paragraph from student Kathy Ford's essay fulfills these requirements:

> Capital punishment has been debated since the founding of this country by small, informal groups, as well as in the Congress of the United States. During such debates, emotions tend to run high, making logical and meaningful debate most difficult. Those in favor of capital punishment often cite particularly terrible crimes such as mass murders, torture killings, and similar atrocities as justification for capital punishment. Those opposed often base their opposition on the smell of burning flesh as a charge of electricity surges through the condemned's body, his gasp for air in the cyanide-gas chamber, or the sound of rifles cocked while aim is taken on his heart. Although some may consider capital punishment cruel or unusual or a violation of civil rights, it is provided for by law in America's democratic society, and when the requirements of that law are met, it is the will of the people and thus appropriate.

The writer manages to capture the reader's interest with her reference to "particularly terrible crimes such as mass murders, torture killings, and similar atrocities." Too, as she catches our attention, she introduces the issue in the opening sentences: capital punishment. And as she states her thesis—that capital punishment is the "will of the people and thus appropriate"—she establishes her argumentative stance: she is in favor of capital punishment. Finally, she summarizes the situation—the long-running debate concerning capital punishment—that provides the basis for the controversy. After we develop an introduction, we must go on to develop our thesis with reasons, claims, and proofs. And as we develop our thesis, we should at some point in the essay acknowledge and refute the opposition's arguments. In the following paragraph, a continuation of the capital punishment essay, the writer summarizes the opposition's view:

> Those opposed to capital punishment clearly have a rational case which appeals emotionally as well. According to the United States Magistrate Philip M. Pro, society should be better than the individuals who make it up; therefore, although individuals want retribution and revenge, society should reject these urges to retaliate and fashion a more humane punishment. Federal public defender Dan Markoff cites the inability to reverse a carried-out death penalty should new evidence be found clearing an executed individual. Another interesting proposition is that merely passing the law makes execution right, good, and proper, when in reality it is killing every bit as much as the homicide which precipitated it. The basic law on this point from our Judeo-Christian heritage from which much of Western society has evolved makes no exceptions; it simply states, "Thou shalt not kill."

The student strengthens her paper by summarizing her opposition's arguments. She shows, or indicates, that she has considered both sides to this controversy before she reached her own position. Thus, she gives the reader the impression that she is not narrow-minded but rather open to both sides of the debate. Her paper is also strengthened because now she has a foundation for presenting her own arguments: every reason she presents in favor of capital punishment is a rebuttal of her opponents' viewpoint.

She thus develops three claims in support of capital punishment: it is legal in certain "narrowly defined circumstances," it is economical, and it reflects the will of the people. Further, she uses facts and statistics to develop her reasons. Consider, for instance, the following paragraph:

> In addition to citing its legality, advocates of capital punishment cite the monetary cost to society in keeping a truly dangerous individual away from the population indefinitely. The cost of caring for a criminal serving a life sentence is much more expensive to society than terminating his life following a legal trial and sentence. This is a position taken by Las Vegas FBI Special Agent in Charge Joseph Yablonsky: "It is cheaper to send a student to Stanford for a year than it is to keep a con in nearby San Quentin ($10,000 vs. $20,000)." As of January 24, 1983, there were 1,137 people on death row in the United States. Assuming an average cost of $20,000 per inmate per year, American taxpayers spend $22,740,000 per year to keep these individuals and receive no benefits from them, except the elimination of these people from the streets for that period of time. An injection, a bullet, an electrical charge, or a cyanide capsule is a one-time expense and much less expensive than even one year on death row.

Note that to develop this paragraph, the writer has used facts and statistics to strengthen her argument: it costs more to keep someone in San Quentin for a year than it does to go to Stanford for a year; further, the people on death row cost the taxpayers around $22,740,000 per year.

After we develop the body of our essay, setting forth the claims supporting the thesis, our final step is to write the conclusion. In the following conclusion, the student summarizes the main points of her essay favoring capital punishment:

> Capital punishment for premeditated, knowing, and willful homicide is justified when the requirements set down by the Supreme Court listed above are met. Society must protect itself and each of its members from individuals who have clearly demonstrated an inability to function without senseless killing of fellow citizens by eliminating them from the face of the earth. Society should not be required to keep these individuals permanently when they make no contribution to society and, in fact, often live better than some law-abiding citizens.

(Many American citizens live on less than $20,000 per year.) It would be tragic, indeed, to see the law taken into the hands of the individuals because society wants justice done regardless of judges' decrees. The arguments against capital punishment are far outweighed by the reasons for imposition of the penalty in the narrowly defined circumstances discussed above, and when the requirements of the law have been met.

Here, the student restates in different words her thesis that capital punishment is justified, expresses the will of the people, and is appropriate.

Induction

Generally speaking, there are two processes by which we can develop an argumentative essay. The first is *induction*, according to which we arrive at a general conclusion, or hypothesis, on the basis of specific proofs. The second process is *deduction*, in which we apply a general premise to a specific person or thing.

Let's begin with induction. Thomas Henry Huxley, in his essay "The Method of Scientific Investigation," gives a clear explanation of the inductive method:

> Suppose you go into a fruiterer's shop, wanting an apple. You take up one, and on biting it you find it is sour; you look at it and see that it is hard and green. You take up another one, and that too is hard, green, and sour. The shopman offers you a third; but before biting it you examine it and find that it is hard and green, and you immediately say that you will not have it, as it must be sour like those that you have already tried.
>
> Nothing can be more simple than that, you think; but if you will take the trouble to analyze and trace out into its logical elements what has been done by the mind, you will be greatly surprised. In the first place you have performed the operation of induction. You have found that in two experiences hardness and greenness in apples went together with sourness. It was so in the first case, and it was confirmed by the second. True, it is a very small basis, but still it is enough to make an induction from; you generalize the facts, and you expect to find sourness in apples where you get hardness and greenness. You found upon that a general law that all hard and green apples are sour; and that, as far as it goes, is a perfect induction.

Huxley is saying that we naturally use the process of induction on a regular basis. For instance, we can conclude, using the inductive process of reasoning, that Clint Eastwood, at least early in his movie career, almost always played the hard-boiled tough guy who carried a big gun and finally triumphed in the end. We can arrive at this conclusion after having seen his westerns such as *The Good, the Bad, and the Ugly, A*

Fistful of Dollars, and *For a Few Dollars More* as well as his Dirty Harry Callahan movies. Similarly, we may have inductively reached the conclusion that jogging is good for us if, after jogging several times, we experienced a general feeling of wellbeing.

Deduction

Whereas induction proceeds from specific proofs to a general conclusion, deduction involves applying a general conclusion to a specific person or thing. Again, Huxley's discourse on green apples should prove very helpful in explaining deduction:

> Well, having got your natural law in this way [that all hard green apples are sour], when you are offered another apple which you find is hard and green, you say, "All hard and green apples are sour; this apple is hard and green; therefore this apple is sour." That train of reasoning is what logicians call a syllogism, and has all its various parts and terms—its major premise, its minor premise, and its conclusion. And, by the help of further reasoning, which, if drawn out, would have to be exhibited in two or three other syllogisms, you arrive at your final determination, "I will not have that apple." So that, you see, you have, in the first place, established a law by induction, and upon that you have founded a deduction, and reasoned out the special particular case.

Deduction, moving from a general conclusion to a specific instance, is a process that, as Huxley indicates, can be reduced to a syllogism:

> Major premise: All hard green apples are sour.
> Minor premise: This apple is hard and green.
> Conclusion: This apple must be sour.

Further, deduction is a thought pattern that is common to us all. For instance, through repeated experiences, we learned as children that a hot stove can burn fingers; having grasped this fundamental truth, expressed in the following syllogism, we now avoid touching the heated elements on our stoves:

> Major premise: One can burn his finger by touching the heated element
> of a stove.
> Minor premise: This is a heated element of my stove.
> Conclusion: If I touch it, I shall burn my fingers.

As a further example, doctors rely upon deductive reasoning when diagnosing and treating illness. From past experience, they can assume that patients experiencing chills, muscular aches, lethargy, loss of appetite, nausea, and weakness probably have the flu. Thus, when you visit the doctor and announce that you are suffering from most of the above symptoms, he can deduce that you probably have the flu. The syllogism would look something like this:

> Major premise: Patients experiencing chills, muscular aches, lethargy,
>   loss of appetite, nausea, and weakness generally have the flu.
> Minor premise: Professor Jabbowitz is experiencing these symptoms.
> Conclusion: Professor Jabbowitz probably has the flu.

Syllogisms follow an almost formulaic pattern. The major premise generally ascribes certain traits (B) to a group of things (A).
Example:

	A		B
All	men	are	mortal.

The minor premise usually states that someone or something (C) is a part of that group (A).
Example:

C			A
Socrates	is	a	man.

The logical conclusion therefore asserts that the someone or something possesses traits common to the group.
Example:

C			B
Socrates	is	therefore	mortal.

PARADIGM

There are many paradigms that you can use as you write your argumentative essay. The one which we have set out below is the most standard. The inductive and deductive arguments are variations of this one.

Introduction
  1. **Engage reader's interest as you summarize situation creating controversy.**
  2. **Introduce central issue.**
  3. **Establish tone.**
  4. **Present position/central argument/assertion to be proved.**

First Body Paragraph
   1. State first reason to support central argument.
   2. Provide proofs in form of facts, statistics, narrative, etc.

Second Body Paragraph
   1. State second reason to support central argument.
   2. Provide proofs in form of facts, statistics, narrative, etc.

Third Body Paragraph
   1. State third reason to support central argument.
   2. Provide proofs in form of facts, statistics, narrative, etc.

Fourth Body Paragraph
   1. State fourth reason to support central argument.
   2. Provide proofs in form of facts, statistics, narrative, etc.

Fifth Body Paragraph: acknowledge and refute opposition with proofs.

Conclusion (options)
   1. Summarize main points and restate central argument.
   2. Offer a final image, message, or judgment.
   3. Take a broader view.
   4. End with quotation.
   5. End with striking statistic.
   6. Challenge the reader.
   7. Something else.

When using this form of the argumentative essay to draft an inductive argument, you simply follow the statement of your central point, which generally includes your reason for taking this particular stand, with well-developed proofs. Thus, if you are arguing that professional hockey, because it has become too violent in the past few years, needs far stricter controls than ever before, you will need to devote a number of paragraphs to providing specific proofs to back up your central claim. Each paragraph may be devoted to a separate proof. For instance, you may devote three or four paragraphs to describing particularly violent incidents that have occurred on the ice in the past three years; and you could follow that with a study, done by a creditable sports analyst, that would verify your claim and suggest the need for stricter controls. The very rough outline to such an essay would look like this:

> Thesis/assertion (included in introduction): Because it has become too violent, professional hockey needs more rules ensuring stricter discipline.
>
> I. First body paragraph: offer first proof, say an account of a particularly violent incident that occurred during a particular game.
> II. Second body paragraph: provide a second proof, detailing another specific incident.
> III. Third body paragraph: provide third proof.
> IV. Summarize, in specific detail, finding of study by sports analyst.

Of course, at some point in this tentative essay, you would need to acknowledge and refute your opposition, who may argue that hockey has always involved contact and injury and that bringing in more rules would irrevocably change the game. And you would also need to devote a paragraph or two to specific rule changes. But this essay would depend upon your ability to develop an effective inductive argument: your proofs would have to be known, sufficient, and representative.

To set up a deductive argument, you need to remember and use the form of the syllogism. Thomas Jefferson's Declaration of Independence is an excellent example of a deductive argument:

> Major premise (expressed in introductory paragraph): Any government that denies its citizens their basic rights must be overthrown.
> Minor premise (expressed in body paragraphs): The present British government has repeatedly violated the rights of the citizens of this country. (Jefferson follows this statement with numerous "proofs")
> Conclusion (expressed in final paragraph): Therefore, this government should be overthrown.

In the introduction to a deductive argument, you'll present as your central point the premise upon which the entire argument is based. Thus, your argument might be built around the following syllogism:

> Major premise: Any candidate with a proven history of lying and corruption should not be trusted to hold a public office.
> Minor premise: Citizen X, currently running for office, has a history of lying and corruption.
> Conclusion: Therefore, Citizen X should not be allowed to hold public office.

If we follow Jefferson's model, the resulting outline for this tentative argumentative essay might look like this:

> Central argument, expressed in introduction: Because he has a history of
>   lying and corruption, Citizen X should not be elected.
> Body of paper: Present documented proofs to substantiate the claim that
>   this candidate has lied and is corrupt.
> Conclusion: Restate central argument in different words.

Notice that in the introduction to this tentative essay, the central argument has combined the major premise and the conclusion, much as Jefferson's document does. The body paragraphs will be devoted to proving the minor premise, that so-and-so has indeed lied.

SUMMARY

When we write our argumentative essays, we use the format similar to the one that we followed when writing our expository compositions. Yet the argumentative essay has a set of requirements that distinguish it from other essays: our topic must be a debatable one; our thesis or proposition must state what side of the debate we are choosing; employing induction or deduction, we must use the body to elaborate upon the reasons, claims, or specific proofs that support our thesis; and we must be sure at one point or another to acknowledge and refute the arguments of the opposition.

NURSES

BY LEWIS THOMAS

When my mother became a registered nurse at Roosevelt Hospital, in 1903, there was no question in anyone's mind about what nurses did as professionals. They did what the doctors ordered. The attending physician would arrive for his ward rounds in the early morning, and when he arrived at the ward office the head nurse would be waiting for him, ready to take his hat and coat, and his cane, and she would stand while he had his cup of tea before starting. Entering the ward, she would hold the door for him to go first, then his entourage of interns and medical students, then she followed. At each bedside, after he had conducted his examination and reviewed the patient's progress, he would tell the nurse what needed doing that day, and she would write it down on the part of the chart reserved for nursing notes. An hour or two later he would be gone from the ward, and the work of the rest of the day and the night to follow was the nurse's frenetic occupation. In addition to the stipulated orders, she had an endless list of routine things to do, all learned in her two years of nursing school: the beds had to be changed and made up with fresh sheets by an exact geometric design of folding and tucking impossible for anyone but a trained nurse; the patients had to be washed head to foot; bedpans had to be brought, used, emptied, and washed; temperatures had to be taken every four hours and meticulously recorded on the chart; enemas were to be given; urine and stool samples collected, labeled, and sent off to the laboratory; throughout the day and night, medications of all sorts, usually pills and various vegetable extracts and tinctures, had to be carried on trays from bed to bed. At most times of the year about half of the forty or so patients on the ward had typhoid fever, which meant that the nurse couldn't simply move from bed to bed in the performance of her duties; each typhoid case was screened from the other patients, and the nurse was required to put on a new gown and wash her hands in disinfectant before approaching the bedside. Patients with high fevers were sponged with cold alcohol at frequent intervals. The late-evening back rub was the rite of passage into sleep.

In addition to the routine, workaday schedule, the nurse was responsible for responding to all calls from the patients, and it was expected that she would do so on the run. Her rounds, scheduled as methodical progressions around the ward, were continually interrupted by these calls. It was up to her to evaluate each situation differently: a sudden abdominal pain in a typhoid patient might signify intestinal perforation; the abrupt onset of weakness, thirst, and pallor meant intestinal hemorrhage; the coughing up of gross blood by a tuberculous patient was an emergency. Some of the calls came from neighboring patients on the way to recovery; patients on open wards always kept a close eye on each other: the man in the next bed might slip into coma or seem to be dying, or be indeed dead. For such emergencies the nurse had to get word immediately to the doctor on call, usually the intern assigned to the ward, who might be off in the outpatient department or working in the diagnostic laboratory (interns of that day did all the laboratory work themselves; technicians had not yet been invented) or in his room.

Nurses were not allowed to give injections or to do such emergency procedures as spinal punctures or chest taps, but they were expected to know when such maneuvers were indicated and to be ready with appropriate trays of instruments when the intern arrived on the ward.

It was an exhausting business, but by my mother's accounts it was the most satisfying and rewarding kind of work. As a nurse she was a low person in the professional hierarchy, always running from place to place on orders from the doctors, subject as well to strict discipline from her own administrative superiors on the nursing staff, but none of this came through in her recollections. What she remembered was her usefulness.

Whenever my father talked to me about nurses and their work, he spoke with high regard for them as professionals. Although it was clear in his view that the task of the nurses was to do what the doctor told them to, it was also clear that he admired them for being able to do a lot of things he couldn't possibly do, had never been trained to do. On his own rounds later on, when he became an attending physician himself, he consulted the ward nurse for her opinion about problem cases and paid careful attention to her observations and chart notes. In his own days of intern training (perhaps partly under my mother's strong influence, I don't know) he developed a deep and lasting respect for the whole nursing profession.

I have spent all of my professional career in close association with, and close dependency on, nurses, and like many of my faculty colleagues, I've done a lot of worrying about the relationship between medicine and nursing. During most of this century the nursing profession has been having a hard time of it. It has been, although not entirely, an occupation for women, and sensitive issues of professional status, complicated by the special issue of the changing role of women in modern society, have led to a standoffish, often adversarial relationship between nurses and doctors. Already swamped by an increasing load of routine duties, nurses have been obliged to take on more and more purely administrative tasks: keeping the records in order; making sure the supplies are on hand for every sort of ward emergency; supervising the activities of the new paraprofessional group called LPNs (licensed practical nurses), who now perform much of the bedside work once done by RNs (registered nurses); overseeing ward maids, porters, and cleaners; seeing to it that patients scheduled for X-rays are on their way to the X-ray department on time. Therefore, they have to spend more of their time at desks in the ward office and less time at the bedsides. Too late the nurses have begun to realize that they are gradually being excluded from the one duty which had previously been their most important reward but which had been so taken for granted that nobody mentioned it in listing the duties of a nurse: close personal contact with patients. Along with everything else nurses did in the long day's work, making up for all the tough and sometimes demeaning jobs assigned to them, they had the matchless opportunity to be useful friends to great numbers of human beings in trouble. They listened to their patients all day long and through the night, they gave comfort and reassurance to the patients and their families, they got to know them as friends, they were depended on. To contemplate the loss of this part of their work has been the deepest worry for nurses at large, and for the faculties responsible for the curricula of the nation's new and expanding nursing schools. The issue lies at the center of the running argument between medical school and nursing school administrators, but it is never clearly stated. Nursing education has been upgraded in recent years. Almost all the former hospital schools, which took in high school graduates and provided an RN certificate after two or three years, have been replaced by schools attached to colleges and universities, with a four-year curriculum leading simultaneously to a bachelor's degree and an RN certificate.

The doctors worry that nurses are trying to move away from their historical responsibilities to medicine (meaning, really, to the doctor's orders). The nurses assert that they are their own profession, responsible for their own standards, coequal colleagues with physicians, and they do not wish to become mere ward administrators or technicians (although some, carrying the new and prestigious title of "nurse practitioner," are being trained within nursing schools to perform some of the most complex technological responsibilities in hospital emergency rooms and intensive care units). The doctors claim that what the nurses really want is to become substitute psychiatrists. The nurses reply that they have unavoidable responsibilities for the mental health and wellbeing of their patients, and that these are different from the doctors' tasks. Eventually the arguments will work themselves out, and some sort of agreement will be reached, but if it is to be settled intelligently, some way will have to be found to preserve and strengthen the traditional and highly personal nurse-patient relationship.

I have had a fair amount of firsthand experience with the issue, having been an apprehensive patient myself off and on over a three-year period in the wards of the hospital for which I work. I am one up on most of my physician friends because of this experience. I know some things they do not know about what nurses do.

One thing the nurses do is to hold the place together. It is an astonishment, which every patient feels from time to time, observing the affairs of a large, complex hospital from the vantage point of his bed, that the whole institution doesn't fly to pieces. A hospital operates by the constant interplay of powerful forces pulling away at each other in different directions, each force essential for getting necessary things done, but always at odds with each other. The intern staff is an almost irresistible force in itself, learning medicine by doing medicine, assuming all the responsibility within reach, pushing against an immovable attending and administrative staff, and frequently at odds with the nurses. The attending physicians are individual entrepreneurs trying to run small cottage industries at each bedside. The diagnostic laboratories are feudal fiefdoms, prospering from the insatiable demands for their services from the interns and residents. The medical students are all over the place, learning as best they can and complaining that they are not, as they believe they should be, at the epicenter of everyone's concern. Each individual worker in the place, from the chiefs of surgery to the dieticians to the ward maids, porters, and elevator operators, lives and works in the conviction that the whole apparatus would come to a standstill without his or her individual contribution, and in one sense or another each of them is right.

My discovery, as a patient first on the medical service and later in surgery, is that the institution is held together, *glued* together, enabled to function as an organism, by the nurses and by nobody else. The nurses, the good ones anyway (and all the ones on my floor were good), make it their business to know everything that is going on. They spot errors before errors can be launched. They know everything written on the chart. Most important of all, they know their patients as unique human beings, and they soon get to know the close relatives and friends. Because of this knowledge, they are quick to sense apprehensions and act on them. The average sick person in a large hospital feels at risk of getting lost, with no identity left beyond a name and a string of numbers on a plastic wristband, in danger always of being whisked off on a litter to the wrong place to have the wrong procedure done, or worse still, *not* being whisked off at the right time. The attending physician or the house officer, on rounds and usually in a hurry, can murmur a few reassuring words on his way out the door, but it takes a confident, competent, and cheerful nurse, there all day long and in and out of the room on one chore or another through the night, to bolster one's confidence that the situation is indeed manageable and not about to get out of hand.

Knowing what I know, I am all for the nurses. If they are to continue their professional feud with the doctors, if they want their professional status enhanced and their pay increased, if they infuriate the doctors by their claims to be equal professionals, if they ask for the moon, I am on their side.

STUDY QUESTIONS for "Nurses"

COMPREHENSION

1. What is the central argument—or thesis—for Thomas's essay? Where does he first state his thesis?
2. At what point—or points—does Thomas refer to the occasion or controversy that led to his decision to write this essay?
3. Who is Thomas's intended audience for this essay? How do you know?
4. According to Thomas, what do nurses contribute to the running of a hospital?

DEVELOPMENT AND ORGANIZATION

1. What proofs—or examples—does he present to support his position concerning nurses? How many proofs does he use? Are the proofs relevant to his argument, sufficient, and representative? In other words, does Thomas's essay provide an example of valid induction?
2. What is the effect of using his mother's and father's experiences and perceptions regarding the importance of nurses as proof? Do these particular proofs, drawn from family members, strengthen or weaken Thomas's argument? Explain.
3. Where does Thomas make use of division? Of process? Does the use of these methods of organization interfere with the effectiveness of Thomas's argument? Why or why not?
4. Where does Thomas acknowledge and refute his opposition's arguments concerning the importance of nurses? Does Thomas effectively refute his opposition? Explain your answer in some detail.

STYLE AND TECHNIQUE

1. What, if anything, is gained by Thomas's not stating his thesis—or central argument—at the beginning of the essay?
2. What is the tone of this essay? Is Thomas's tone consistent throughout the essay?
3. Reread and comment upon the effectiveness of the final paragraph. Does this paragraph provide a strong ending to Thomas's argument? Why or why not?

TEN-MINUTE TOPICS

1. Argue that some frequently overlooked profession—one that does not seem to receive the credit it is due—has great value. As you defend the usefulness or value of this profession, be sure to provide reasons (and proofs in the form of examples, facts, statistics, etc.) to support your position. Be sure to acknowledge and answer your opposition.
2. Take a position contrary to the one presented by Thomas, making claims or general statements supporting the view that nurses should not have the same status as doctors.
3. Discuss the similarities and differences between the job climate of today to that of past decades. What jobs warrant the most need and interest? What does their "popularity" reveal about our society?

THE WORKPLACE AS THE PLATFORM OF GENDER STRATIFICATION

BY GUILLERMO VIVAS (student)

It has been noted by social scientists that individuals create countless erroneous conceptions when they perceive or distinguish each other. These erroneous conceptions stratify and classify a person by race, class, and gender. Stereotypes center on these three factors and are intended to reduce an individual's humanity, oppress them, and lessen their opportunities. Racial labels torment minorities, class domination minimizes opportunities, and gender-role stereotypes build stratification within our community. Gender stratification as a result of stereotypes is found at home and in public but particularly in workplace environments. The most pervasive form of gender stratification is that in which many companies perpetuate the wage gap between men and women.

The Equal Pay Act of 1963 provided women the chance to balance the wage disparity that was present at the time. This legislation forces employers to give equal pay to all employees, regardless of gender, who are in the same job classification, are equally proficient, and hold the same degrees. However, that effort was not enough to bring a significant change. Before the law was passed, women were earning very little compared to men, about 58 cents for every dollar ("Wage"). In 1979, according to the Bureau of Labor Statistics, women earned 62 cents for every dollar men earned (55). In 2006, The National Women's Law Center found that women's wages grew to 77 cents for every dollar men earned, which is roughly a half of penny per year ("Wage"). During those years, employers paid women less than men because of a socially constructed concept that women only worked to earn money in addition to their husbands'. This concept, known as "needle money," classified women as low class workers—individuals who could only work with a needle. Although some women were employed in the same areas as men, they still earned very little because of the label that was given to them.

There are other erroneous stereotypes that oblige women to earn less. Men and women are biologically different but their gender roles are socially developed as they grow. Men are most often classified as individuals that can hold high-level management positions in a company just because they have traditional manliness. Women, however, are classified and viewed by society as individuals who cannot hold a management position because its demands are suitable only for a man. So in other words, men obtain jobs that are typically male jobs and women obtain jobs that are typically female jobs. However, this notion has a hidden wage disparity that many people do not see. The jobs that men obtain, which are only seen suitable for males, give the highest pay. On the other hand, the jobs that women obtain pay less than the jobs men have because they are viewed as female jobs and as less demanding.

There are many factors that set hurdles for women. According to sociologists, women are most likely to be strained by balancing the demands of a job and the demands of home and family. Therefore, some women prefer to be employed in less demanding jobs so that they will not fail at home. Further, it is because of these family responsibilities that women traditionally obtain jobs categorized as female. Jobs like child care, teaching, nursing, and cleaning are predominantly filled by females and the positions fail to pay as well as the jobs in fields such as engineering, management, political science, and global media, which are predominately obtained by males. A clear and current example of this is a study commissioned by the International Women's Media Foundation, which found that 73 percent of high-level positions in global media are held by men and that only 27 percent are held by women (Kerr). This number is alarming and many are troubled by the results. Liza Gross, the executive director of the foundation, stated, "While there have been some gains since the mid-'90s, women still have a long way to go to gain parity as workers in the news industry globally. In many regions of the world, just representation of women in the newsroom as journalists is an issue" (Kerr). The evidence suggests that the wage disparity in many job fields greatly affects women with the exception of a few who are among the top earners. Women have striven to be recognized as leaders in the workplace, but the barrier reflecting their possibilities downward is too extreme for most women. Therefore, the wage disparity remains.

Another factor that determines the disparity is employment discontinuation as women go on "time out" to recover from childbirth. Their long-term detachment from work because of maternity leave sometimes gives the wrong impression to employers and coworkers. Companies are stressed to replace and refill the positions pregnant women leave vacant and are sometimes discontent with the amount of work they have to cover for. But it is obvious that women need maternity leave after giving birth to a child because of the lengthy amount of time needed to fully recover. That is the reason why Congress passed the Family Medical Leave Act. This act assures individuals that they can take advantage of this benefit to take an urgency leave without worrying about losing their jobs. Despite the fact that the law supports women who take leave after childbirth, the wage disparity remains. The reason why taking a medical leave is such a huge disadvantage for women is that they do not earn money when they are away from work.

A further reason why such a startling disproportion is taking place is that women, to take care of their children and elderly, prefer jobs that are part-time and less intrusive in their lives. This means that women have less probability of obtaining jobs which demand traveling often—jobs that pay a substantial amount of money. Unfortunately, studies from various authors show that most women who have children and are employed full-time will eventually have to either demote their status to part-time or to a lower rank, or resign from the job. These obligations fall more heavily on women and most employers do not tolerate their needs. Some women take some time off to be with their children because they cannot find a daycare to provide for them. Some who do not have the money to cover such expenses prefer jobs that start at a different time than their spouse's job. In most cases, they are stuck with graveyard shifts. As mentioned above, the class-conscious belief is affecting women because society has not yet established an adjustment to allow women to control their demanding personal lives and their strenuous work at the same time.

Paula Rothenberg, the editor of the integrated study called *Race, Class, and Gender in the United States*, states, "Men and women have been portrayed as polar opposites with innately different abilities and capacities" (7). This merely means that society perceives both genders as different in ability, and it is because of this perception that society sees women as incapable of obtaining jobs that are categorized as male gendered. Sadly, the jobs that have the higher pay are male categorized jobs, which makes women struggle to rise to the top. However, Stephen J. Rose, an economist at Marco International, Inc., and Heidi I. Hartmann, president of the Institute for Women's Policy Research in Washington, have found that women can actually obtain high-paying jobs that are male categorized by society if they "behave like traditional men" (Bernstein 371). According to these authorities, if women overlook their family responsibilities and focus on success in their careers, equality will eventually be achieved (Bernstein 371). These observations could be correct since society perceives men as individuals who have the proper skills to lead large companies. If women were to disguise themselves with the absolute comportment that men are perceived to have, they would most likely succeed at being employed in high-paying jobs.

The world is full of disparities. Gender inequality is not the only predicament that humanity has encountered. There are other dimensions like race and class which cause oppression, discrimination, categorization and many afflictions that most individuals regard as undesirable. The stereotypes are countless and therefore unmanageable. Individuals who are victims of oversimplified conceptions and erroneous categorizations of gender, class, and race have few opportunities to gain wealth or live free of stress and domination. It is because of these erroneous conceptions that many disparities have evolved over time and have impacted society greatly, leaving many disadvantaged.

At heart, all of the racial slurs and gender inequity concepts are erroneous because they overlook the actual quality of a person. As individuals, it is important to know that everyone is equally worthy of approval, despite the gender he or she might be, the race he or she is associated with, or the socioeconomic status that individual holds. Of course, there is immense diversity in the United States, but unfairness resulting from gender labels should not be used by any of the social institutions that are present today.

With the evidence that scientists have provided, it is expected that women will eventually close the gap with men. More and more women are graduating from college and obtaining exceptional degrees. The numbers that calculate the disparity are decreasing gradually over the years and hopefully the socially constructed differences will perish. That means gender inequality in the workplace may come to an end and equal pay will come to women who work the same jobs as men.

Works Cited

Bernstein, Aaron. "Women's Pay: Why the Gap Remains a Chasm." Rothenberg 370-72.

Kerr, Jennifer. "Study: Men Hold Top Jobs in Global Media." *Cnsnews.com*. Cybercast News Service. 23 Mar. 2011. Web. 14 Apr. 2011.

Rothenberg, Paula, ed. *Race, Class, and Gender in the United States*. New York: Worth, 2007. Print.

United States. Dept. of Labor. Bureau of Labor Statistics. *Highlights of Women's Earnings in 2008*. July 2009. Web. 20 Apr. 2011.

"The Wage Gap." *Infoplease*. Pearson Education, 2007. Web. 22 Apr. 2011.

STUDY QUESTIONS for "The Workplace as the Platform of Gender Stratification"

COMPREHENSION

1. What is gender stratification? Where is it found?
2. What was the purpose of the Equal Pay Act of 1963?
3. What is "needle money"? How does it diminish women in the workplace?
4. What is the purpose of the Family Medical Leave Act?
5. According to Rose and Hartman, how can women obtain high-paying jobs?

DEVELOPMENT AND ORGANIZATION

1. What is Vivas's claim?
2. What factors does Vivas claim "set hurdles for women"?
3. Pretend this is your essay and revise paragraph three by adding concrete examples of the jobs described in it.
4. What expert knowledge or statistical data could be added to paragraph six to support its controlling idea?

STYLE AND TECHNIQUE

1. Which patterns of development (cause and effect, comparison and contrast, etc.) does Vivas employ in the essay? Which ones work best to validate his claim?
2. List the transitions used in this essay.
3. Vivas relies heavily on interpreting his sources to validate his claim. What other techniques could he have employed?

TEN-MINUTE TOPICS

1. Discuss your own workplace environment. Does it function with or without gender stratification? If so, how? If not, why not?
2. Is gender equality a realistic goal?
3. Discuss any individual who has worked to eliminate gender stratification.

THE DECLARATION OF INDEPENDENCE
BY THOMAS JEFFERSON

When in the course of human events, it becomes necessary for one people to dissolve the political bands which have connected them with another, and to assume among the powers of the earth, the separate and equal station to which the Laws of Nature and of Nature's God entitle them, a decent respect to the opinions of mankind requires that they should declare the causes which impel them to the separation.

We hold these truths to be self-evident, that all men are created equal, that they are endowed by their Creator with certain unalienable Rights, that among these are Life, Liberty and the pursuit of Happiness. That to secure these rights, Governments are instituted among Men, deriving their just powers from the consent of the governed. That whenever any Form of Government becomes destructive of these ends, it is the Right of the People to alter or to abolish it, and to institute new Government, laying its foundation on such principles and organizing its powers in such form, as to them shall seem most likely to affect their Safety and Happiness. Prudence, indeed, will dictate that Governments long established should not be changed for light and transient causes; and accordingly all experience hath shown that mankind are more disposed to suffer, while evils are sufferable, than to right themselves by abolishing the forms to which they are accustomed. But when a long train of abuses and usurpations pursuing invariably the same Object evinces a design to reduce them under absolute Despotism, it is their right, it is their duty, to throw off such government, and to provide new Guards for their future security. Such has been the patient sufferance of these Colonies; and such is now the necessity which constrains them to alter their former Systems of Government. The history of the present King of Great Britain is a history of repeated injuries and usurpations, all having in direct object the establishment of an absolute Tyranny over these States. To prove this, let Facts be submitted to a candid world.

He has refused his Assent to Laws, the most wholesome and necessary for the public good.

He has forbidden his Governors to pass Laws of immediate and pressing importance, unless suspended in their operation till his Assent should be obtained; and when so suspended, he has utterly neglected to attend to them.

He has refused to pass other Laws for the accommodation of large districts of people, unless those people would relinquish the right of Representation in the Legislature, a right inestimable to them and formidable to tyrants only.

He has called together legislative bodies at places unusual, uncomfortable, and distant from the depository of their Public Records, for the sole purpose of fatiguing them into compliance with his measures.

He has dissolved Representative Houses repeatedly, for opposing with manly firmness his invasions on the rights of the people.

He has refused for a long time, after such dissolutions, to cause others to be elected; whereby the Legislative Powers, incapable of Annihilation, have returned to the People at large for their exercise; the State remaining in the mean time exposed to all the dangers of invasion from without, and convulsions within.

He has endeavored to prevent the population of these States; for that purpose obstructing the Laws of Naturalization of Foreigners; refusing to pass others to encourage their migration hither, and raising the conditions of new Appropriations of Lands.

He has obstructed the Administration of Justice, by refusing his Assent to Laws for Establishing Judiciary Powers.

He has made Judges dependent on his Will alone, for the tenure of their offices, and the amount and payment of their salaries.

He has erected a multitude of New Offices, and sent hither swarms of Officers to harass our People, and eat out their substance.

He has kept among us, in time of peace, Standing Armies without the Consent of our legislatures.

He has affected to render the Military independent of and superior to the Civil Power.

He has combined with others to subject us to a jurisdiction foreign to our constitution, and unacknowledged by our laws; giving his Assent to the Acts of pretended Legislation:

For quartering large bodies of armed troops among us:

For protecting them, by a mock Trial, from punishment for any Murders which they should commit on the Inhabitants of these States:

For cutting off our Trade with all parts of the world:

For imposing Taxes on us without our Consent:

For depriving us in many cases, of the benefits of Trial by Jury:

For Transporting us beyond Seas to be tried for pretended offenses:

For abolishing the free System of English Laws in a Neighboring Province, establishing therein an Arbitrary government, and enlarging its Boundaries so as to render it at once an example and fit instrument for introducing the same absolute rule into these Colonies:

For taking away our Charters, abolishing our most valuable Laws and altering fundamentally the Forms of our Governments:

For suspending our own Legislatures, and declaring themselves invested with Power to legislate for us in all cases whatsoever.

He has abdicated Government here, by declaring us out of his Protection and waging War against us:

He has plundered our seas, ravaged our Coasts, burnt our towns and destroyed the lives of our people.

He is at this time transporting large Armies of foreign Mercenaries to complete the works of death, desolation and tyranny, already begun with circumstances of Cruelty & Perfidy scarcely paralleled in the most barbarous ages, and totally unworthy the Head of a civilized nation.

He has constrained our fellow Citizens taken Captive on the high Seas to bear Arms against their Country, to become the executioners of their friends and Brethren, or to fall themselves by their Hands.

He has excited domestic insurrections amongst us, and has endeavored to bring on the inhabitants of our frontiers, the merciless Indian Savages, whose known rule of warfare, is an undistinguished destruction of all ages, sexes, and conditions.

In every stage of these Oppressions We have Petitioned for Redress in the most humble terms: Our repeated petitions have been answered only by repeated injury. A Prince whose character is thus marked by every act which may define a Tyrant is unfit to be the ruler of a free people.

Nor have We been wanting in attention to our British brethren. We have warned them from time to time of attempts by their legislature to extend an unwarrantable jurisdiction over us. We have reminded them of the circumstances of our emigration and settlement here. We have appealed to their native justice and magnanimity, and we have conjured them by the ties of our common kindred to disavow these usurpations, which would inevitably interrupt our connections and correspondence. They too have been deaf to the voice of justice and of consanguinity. We must, therefore, acquiesce in the necessity, which denounces our Separation, and hold them, as we hold the rest of mankind, Enemies in War, in Peace, Friends.

We, THEREFORE, the Representatives of the UNITED STATES OF AMERICA, in General Congress Assembled, appealing to the Supreme Judge of the world for the rectitude of our intentions, do, in the Name, and by Authority of the good People of these Colonies, solemnly publish and declare, That these United Colonies are, and of Right ought to be FREE AND INDEPENDENT STATES; that they are Absolved from all Allegiance to the British Crown, and that all political connection between them and the State of Great Britain, is and ought to be totally dissolved; and that as Free and Independent States, they have full Power to levy War, conclude Peace, contract Alliances, establish Commerce, and to do all other Acts and Things which Independent States may of right do. And for the support of this Declaration, with a firm reliance on the protection of Divine Providence, we mutually pledge to each other our lives, our Fortunes, and our sacred Honor.

STUDY QUESTIONS for The Declaration of Independence

COMPREHENSION

1. What is the central proposition of the Declaration? (You might try to answer the first question in the Development and Organization section below before responding.)
2. Who was the intended audience for the Declaration? What was that audience's response to it?
3. What is Jefferson's purpose for writing the Declaration? Do you think he achieved it?

DEVELOPMENT AND ORGANIZATION

1. Jefferson's Declaration is a good example of deductive logic, for his entire argument is framed by a syllogism.
   a. What is the major premise upon which this argument is based?
   b. What is the minor premise?
   c. What is the conclusion?
2. Where does Jefferson make use of inductive reasoning in the Declaration? How many inductive proofs does it contain?
3. What is the relationship between the deductive and inductive sections of the Declaration?
4. Is Jefferson's inductive reasoning valid? That is, are his proofs known, sufficient, and representative?
5. Is his deductive logic valid as well? Are his premises true, his terms unambiguous, and his form correct?

STYLE AND TECHNIQUE

1. Where in the Declaration does Jefferson make use of parallel sentence structure? What is gained by making use of parallelism in the Declaration?
2. In what style is the Declaration written: formal, conversational, or informal? Explain your answer.

TEN-MINUTE TOPICS

1. Write an argument supporting or opposing what you perceive to be a rather restrictive code.
2. Write an argument supporting or opposing a change being made at your place of work.
3. Discuss a particular group of people's fight for independence and/or solidarity.

FOR THE CHILDREN

BY PAT WALLS

All laws are useless, for good men do not need them, and bad men are made no better by them.
—Demonax, quoted in Plutarch's *Apothegms*

Today, the United States faces one of the greatest challenges of our history: how to raise our children. American babies deserve the best, and current methods of childcare are woefully insufficient and potentially dangerous. Daycare centers are not an ideal solution because putting babies and small children there exposes them to the lustful diaper-changing attentions of potential child molesters; nor are grandparents ideal caregivers because they often do not have the physical stamina necessary to chase toddlers all day. Boyfriends may shake crying babies or strike them until they forget how to cry. The teenaged babysitter, who eats everything in the refrigerator while talking to her boyfriend on the telephone, leaves the baby wearing a heavily loaded diaper that the mother will have to change when she arrives home at midnight. These failed childcare solutions are no longer good enough, and parents who entrust their children to those who are not reliable or responsible for their actions must be stopped. The alternative to personal irresponsibility is always legislation.

In order to correct this situation, the President's Council on Raising Them Right, in concert with the Institute of Post-Modern Neonate Physiology and Potty Training, proposes the No Baby Left Behind in the Back Seat Act, HR 123. This act requires that every newborn baby and child under the age of three years must be tethered to a parent for twenty-four hours a day. According to Dr. Ludwig von Smartypants, one of this bill's strengths is that it is totally democratic; the childcare burden falls equally on every parental shoulder regardless of a couple's race, creed, ethnicity, gender, or political party affiliation. No one is exempt from the opportunity to raise the best of children. In order to assist new parents in the challenges that they will face as caregivers, the federal government will send the new family home from the hospital with a box that contains the Harmonious Ephemera for Lassitude Prevention. The HELP box will contain two sets of soft gel-filled cuffs that are connected by a coiled vinyl cord that will allow the parent to remain within three feet of the baby at all times. One cuff embraces the parent's wrist and leads to a smaller cuff that encircles the baby's wrist. A list of rules for using the cuffs is also included. The new parents must understand that if the cuffs are removed for more than five minutes, the cuff will emit a silent signal that will bring the Baby Police to their doorstep immediately. Names will be taken and the episode will appear on the parents' permanent record. The box also contains two deluxe sets of industrial strength earplugs guaranteed to prevent hearing loss, and a 1-800 phone number, which, when used in an emergency by the parents of colicky, teething babies, will summon an expert team of baby soothers. A collection of books that will answer questions about the approved method of childcare that parents should use is also contained in the HELP box. Included are the following titles: *The Seven Habits of Highly Effective Tyrants*; *Ear Infections:*

What to Do When the Medicine Fails; Colic Is Not for Cowards; First Aid for Roof-Jumpers and Amateur Bomb-Makers, and, most importantly, the first ten volumes of *Common Sense for Dummies*. These books, selected by a panel of experts led by the distinguished Ivy League Professor Hee Shr Knowsitall, will help parents to find the answers to every childcare question. By using the books and the other equipment in the HELP box, parents will become skilled and discover for themselves the benefits of this national childcare system. An important benefit is getting to know your baby, and parents and babies who spend all their time together form strong bonds as the parents hold, stroke, feed, and lovingly bathe the baby. Babies will be happier because they will be fed and changed immediately, and parents will notice when the baby has a runny nose or is running a fever and will treat the problem before it gets worse. Parents will be encouraged to read aloud to their baby as the baby sits in the parent's lap. As they listen to the parent's voice, the babies learn about language and develop verbal skills while bonding emotionally. These bonds will be so strong that when these children become teenagers, they will not dare to dye their hair an outrageous color and think that their parents will approve.

Not only will parents grow close to their babies, they will also become more physically fit. Carrying babies all day will build a parent's upper body strength over a period of months. By the time the baby is old enough to talk, cries of "Hold me! Mommy, hold me!" will become commonplace, and Mommy will sport a set of muscles that rival those of a Venice Beach bodybuilder. Dads will also build bulk in their legs from chasing toddlers in hopes of preventing them from jumping off of the roof of the house. (This is the day when the first-aid book will come in handy.) Finding themselves in constant motion while caring for their babies, parents will be more physically fit.

While parents and babies will benefit from this program, so will society. Parents who are bound to the baby will not have any privacy, and the birthrate will go down. Once this program is used all over the country, only those who are willing and dedicated to raising a child will have a baby. According to the eminent Dr. Snip E. Happi, after the passage of HR 123, the number of couples choosing to undergo tubal ligation or vasectomy operations should skyrocket. Also, when one parent from each family stays home to raise the baby, there will be fewer members of the workforce, wages will rise, and the economy will improve. Raising babies will be good for Wall Street, and what is good for Wall Street is good for all Americans, whether they like it or not. Another boon to society from the passage of this bill will be the improvement of adult behavior. Incidences of public drunkenness will be reduced because babies will not be allowed entrance into bars and nightclubs. Establishments that serve adult beverages will be required to post signs that state: ADULTS ONLY. NO BABIES ALLOWED. Professional baby bouncers will guard the door and prevent determined babies and toddler children from going inside. Additionally, babies must have out-of-state license plates on their cars in order to check into a motel. This regulation will cut down on all sorts of hanky-panky, and occurrences of adultery will be sharply reduced, thereby strengthening and protecting the family. Adult behavior will also improve because adults who are moored to a baby will be prohibited from purchasing and using tobacco products. According to Dr. U. Cant Haveit, the head of the prestigious Foundation for the Prohibition of the Utilization of Nicotine Containment Cylinders, babies and toddler children actually inhale much more smoke from a lit cigarette than the smoker does. Researchers have found indisputable evidence that molecules of tar in tobacco smoke collect inside a baby's tender pink lungs, turning them inky black in a heartbeat. Therefore, allowing small children to be close to smokers is detrimental to young children's health and should be stopped immediately before millions of American babies choke on billows of noxious fumes. Dr. Haveit and his partner, Dr. Iman Oral Vice, believe that including the ban on parental smoking in HR 123 is the only way to protect the lungs of America's children. The decision to live smoke-free lives is one that all parents should make.

Although parents will be required to comply with smoking restrictions in the No Baby Left Behind in the Back Seat Act, there are other passages of the bill that provide incentives to parents. The Department of Motor Vehicles and grocery stores will be required to provide express lanes for the sole use of parents with small children. There will also be parking places by the handicapped slots for those with young children. When mothers and fathers can run their errands more quickly, the young children will be less likely to throw fits. The most valuable incentive will be the generous tax rebate given to parents for the first three years of the baby's life. The tax rebate returns to the parents one hundred percent of the federal income tax that the couple has paid, plus a monthly stipend large enough to cover the baby's entire expenses. By offering these incentives, the federal government encourages parents to have children and to raise them in the best possible circumstances. When the government changes the way that people live, American industry will respond with new innovative goods and services. Babysitters and daycare workers will lose their jobs, but they will find new jobs in service industries that cater to the needs of families. More pool and lawn care workers will be needed to do the work that cannot be done by a parent holding a small child. Teenaged babysitters will become housemaids or personal shoppers. Beauticians and dog groomers will make home visits to serve their clients, and special bookmobiles with shelves that are filled with picture books and best-selling paperback novels will deliver a family's weekly reading needs. American industry quickly responds to the needs of those with money to spend. One of the more interesting new services that will be available if HR 123 passes is that of the baby psychic. With a great demand for this service, dog and animal psychics will be retrained at government expense to listen to and interpret the screams of babies. These brave souls will arrive at the child's bedside and tell the parents exactly what that baby needs. The baby may want to be held, rocked, fed, or driven to Kalamazoo in the middle of the night. The parents, who are so battered from hearing their precious child's shrill wails that they would do almost anything to silence the noise, will gratefully carry out whatever action the psychic says must be done. The use of baby psychics will save the sanity of millions of parents across the country and allow parents to survive their child's babyhood.

Babyhood officially comes to an end when the child has his or her third birthday. On that day, a government representative will remove the cuffs forever at a ceremony that will be witnessed by the child's extended family. The government representative will present the parents with a coupon good for one year of free therapy at the mental health clinic of their choice, and the happy family will enter the future together. The guiding premise of the No Baby Left Behind in the Back Seat Act, HR 123, is to prepare the United States for the best and most productive future possible. The promise of the future depends on the actions that you, as an adult citizen, take today. Talk to your neighbors about this important piece of legislation. Speak to PTA meetings and church groups; visit your congressman and senator, and make sure that they are aware of your support for this bill. All children must be protected and trained in the most equitable and American way. Do it for the babies, for the children, for their future. There can be no more important function of government than to assist parents in raising the best citizens, not only of America, but also of the world.

STUDY QUESTIONS for "For the Children"

COMPREHENSION

1. What is the catalyst of No Baby Left Behind in the Back Seat Act, HR 123? Be specific.
2. What is the purpose of the HELP box?
3. What marks the official end of babyhood? How is it celebrated?

DEVELOPMENT AND ORGANIZATION

1. What rhetorical techniques already studied in this text does Walls use to persuade her reader of the importance of this groundbreaking legislation? Where, for instance, does she make use of examples? Of cause and effect? Of analogy? Discuss other modes used in the essay.
2. List some of the names of the agencies and their respective directors mentioned in the essay. What is the purpose of such naming?
3. What known—real-life—events and individuals is the writer alluding to? What is the purpose of taking a known event (or person) and exaggerating it (or him/her)?
4. What does the writer suggest through her examples has happened to parenting?

STYLE AND TECHNIQUE

1. What is the tone of the essay? That is, what is the writer's attitude towards her subject matter?
2. What is the call to action made in the concluding paragraph? How effective is it?
3. How effective is the essay's satire at revealing the truths that plague our society?

TEN-MINUTE TOPICS

1. Take one of the many parenting-centered issues in the essay and write your own thoughts about them. The first time you write be serious; the next time, use satire.
2. Discuss society's inability to think for itself. Why is there such a reliance on government intervention?
3. Discuss the death of common sense.
4. Discuss the content of one of your favorite comic's standup routines. Does the content reflect our society's real problems?

A MODEST PROPOSAL

BY JONATHAN SWIFT

For Preventing the Children of Poor People in Ireland from Being a Burden to Their Parents or Country, and for Making Them Beneficial to the Public

It is a melancholy object to those who walk through this great town or travel in the country, when they see the streets, the roads, and cabin-doors crowded with beggars of the female sex, followed by three, four, or six children, all in rags and importuning every passenger for an alms. These mothers, instead of being able to work for their honest livelihood, are forced to employ all their time in strolling to beg sustenance for their helpless infants, who, as they grow up, either turn thieves for want of work, or leave their dear native county to fight for the Pretender in Spain, or sell themselves to the Barbadoes.

I think it is agreed by all parties that this prodigious number of children in the arms, or on the backs, or at the heels of their mothers, and frequently of their fathers, is in the present deplorable state of the kingdom a very great additional grievance; and therefore whoever could find out a fair, cheap, and easy method of making these children sound and useful members of the commonwealth would deserve so well of the public as to have his statue set up for a preserver of the nation.

But my intention is very far from being confined to provide only for the children of professed beggars; it is of a much greater extent, and shall take in the whole number of infants at a certain age who are born of parents in effect as little able to support them as those who demand our charity in the streets.

As to my own part, having turned my thoughts for many years upon this important subject, and maturely weighed the several schemes of other projectors, I have always found them grossly mistaken in their computation. It is true a child just dropped from its dam may be supported by her milk for a solar year with little other nourishment, at most not above the value of two shillings, which the mother may certainly get, or the value in scraps, by her lawful occupation of begging; and it is exactly at one year old that I propose to provide for them, in such a manner as instead of being a charge upon their parents or the parish, or wanting food and raiment for the rest of their lives, they shall, on the contrary, contribute to the feeding and partly to the clothing of many thousands.

There is likewise another great advantage in my scheme, that it will prevent those voluntary abortions, and that horrid practice of women murdering their bastard children, alas! too frequent among us, sacrificing the poor innocent babes, I doubt, more to avoid the expense than the shame, which would move tears and pity in the most savage and inhuman breast.

The number of souls in Ireland being usually reckoned one million and a half, of these I calculate there may be about two hundred thousand couples whose wives are breeders; from which number I subtract thirty thousand couples who are able to maintain their own children, although I apprehend there cannot be so many under the present distresses of the kingdom; but this being granted, there will remain an hundred and seventy thousand breeders. I again subtract fifty thousand for those women who miscarry, or whose children die by accident or disease within the year. There only remain an hundred and twenty thousand children of poor parents annually born. The question therefore is, how this number shall be reared and provided for, which, as I have already said, under the present situation of affairs is utterly impossible by all the methods hitherto proposed. For we can neither employ them in handicraft or agriculture; we neither build houses (I mean in the country) nor cultivate land: they can very seldom pick up a livelihood by stealing till they arrive at six years old, except where they are of towardly parts; although I confess they learn the rudiments much earlier, during which time they can, however, be properly looked upon only as probationers, as I have been informed by a principal gentleman in the County of Cavan, who protested to me that he never knew above one or two instances under the age of six, even in a part of the kingdom so renowned for the quickest proficiency in that art.

I am assured by our merchants that a boy or a girl before twelve years old is no saleable commodity; and even when they come to this age they will not yield above three pounds or three pounds and half-a-crown at most on the Exchange; which cannot turn to account either to the parents or the kingdom, the charge of nutriment and rags having been at least four times that value.

I shall now therefore humbly propose my own thoughts, which I hope will not be liable to the least objection.

I have been assured by a very knowing American of my acquaintance in London that a young healthy child well nursed is at a year old a most delicious, nourishing, and wholesome food, whether stewed, roasted, baked, or boiled; and I make no doubt that it will equally serve in a fricassee or a ragout.

I do therefore humbly offer it to public consideration that of the hundred and twenty thousand children already computed, twenty thousand may be reserved for breed, whereof only one-fourth part to be males, which is more than we allow to sheep, black cattle, or swine; and my reason is that these children are seldom the fruits of marriage, a circumstance not much regarded by our savages; therefore one male will be sufficient to serve four females. That the remaining hundred thousand may at a year old be offered in sale to the persons of quality and fortune through the kingdom, always advising the mother to let them suck plentifully in the last month, so as to render them plump and fat for a good table. A child will make two dishes at an entertainment for friends; and when the family dines alone, the fore or hind quarter will make a reasonable dish, and seasoned with a little pepper or salt will be very good boiled on the fourth day, especially in winter.

I have reckoned upon a medium that a child just born will weigh twelve pounds, and in a solar year if tolerably nursed increaseth to twenty-eight pounds.

I grant this food will be somewhat dear, and therefore very proper for landlords, who, as they have already devoured most of the parents, seem to have the best title to the children.

Infants' flesh will be in season throughout the year, but more plentiful in March, and a little before and after; for we are told by a grave author, an eminent French physician, that fish being a prolific diet, there are more children born in Roman Catholic countries about nine months after Lent than at any other season; therefore reckoning a year after Lent, the markets will be more glutted than usual, because the number of Popish infants is at least three to one in this kingdom; and therefore it will have one other collateral advantage, by lessening the number of Papists among us.

I have already computed the charge of nursing a beggar's child (in which list I reckon all cottagers, labourers, and four-fifths of the farmers) to be about two shillings *per annum*, rags included, and I believe no gentleman would repine to give ten shillings for the carcass of a good fat child, which, as I have said, will make four dishes of excellent nutritive meat, when he hath only some particular friend of his own family to dine with him. Thus the Squire will learn to be a good landlord and grow popular among his tenants, the mother will have eight shillings net profit, and be fit for work until she produces another child.

Those who are more thrifty (as I must confess the times require) may flay the carcass; the skin of which artificially dressed will make admirable gloves for ladies, and summer boots for fine gentlemen.

As to our city of Dublin, shambles may be appointed for this purpose in the most convenient parts of it, and butchers we may be assured will not be wanting; although I rather recommend buying the children alive, and dressing them hot from the knife, as we do roasting pigs.

A very worthy person, a true lover of his country, and whose virtues I highly esteem, was lately pleased, in discoursing on this matter to offer a refinement upon my scheme. He said that many gentlemen of this kingdom, having of late destroyed their deer, he conceived that the want of venison might be well supplied by the bodies of young lads and maidens, not exceeding fourteen years of age nor under twelve, so great a number of both sexes in every country being now ready to starve for want of work and service: and these to be disposed of by their parents, if alive, or otherwise by their nearest relations. But with due deference to so excellent a friend and so deserving a patriot, I cannot be altogether in his sentiments. For as to the males, my American acquaintance assured me from frequent experience that their flesh was generally tough and lean, like that of our schoolboys, by continual exercise, and their taste disagreeable; and to fatten them would not answer the charge. Then as to the females, it would, I think, with humble submission, be a loss to the public, because they soon would become breeders themselves: and besides, it is not improbable that some scrupulous people might be apt to censure such a practice (although indeed very unjustly) as a little bordering upon cruelty; which I confess, hath always been with me the strongest objection against any project, how well soever intended.

But in order to justify my friend, he confessed that this expedient was put into his head by the famous Psalmanazar, a native of the island Formosa, who came from thence to London above twenty years ago, and in conversation told my friend that in his country when any young person happened to be put to death, the executioner sold the carcass to persons of quality, as a prime dainty, and that in his time the body of a plump girl of fifteen, who was crucified for an attempt to poison the emperor, was sold to his Imperial Majesty's Prime Minister of State, and other great Mandarins of the Court, in joints from the gibbet, at four hundred crowns. Neither indeed can I deny that if the same use were made of several plump young girls in this town, who, without one single groat to their fortunes, cannot stir abroad without a chair, and appear at the playhouse and assemblies in foreign fineries, which they never will pay for, the kingdom would not be the worse.

Some persons of a desponding spirit are in great concern about that vast number of poor people, who are aged, diseased, or maimed, and I have been desired to employ my thoughts what course may be taken to ease the nation of so grievous an encumbrance. But I am not in the least pain upon that matter, because it is very well known that they are every day dying and rotting, by cold and famine, and filth and vermin, as fast as can be reasonably expected. And as to the younger labourers, they are now in almost as hopeful a condition. They cannot get work, and consequently pine away from want of nourishment, to a degree that if at any time they are accidentally hired to common labour, they have not strength to perform it; and thus the country and themselves are in a fair way of being soon delivered from the evils to come.

I have too long digressed, and therefore shall return to my subject. I think the advantages by the proposal which I have made are obvious and many, as well as of the highest importance.

For first, as I have already observed, it would greatly lessen the number of Papists, with whom we are yearly overrun, being the principal breeders of the nation as well as our most dangerous enemies; and who stay at home on purpose with a design to deliver the kingdom to the Pretender, hoping to take their advantage by the absence of so many good Protestants, who have chosen rather to leave their country than stay at home and pay tithes against their conscience to an idolatrous Episcopal curate.

Secondly, the poorer tenants will have something valuable of their own, which by law may be made liable to distress, and help to pay their landlord's rent; their corn and cattle being already seized, and money a thing unknown.

Thirdly, whereas the maintenance of an hundred thousand children, from two years old and upwards, cannot be computed at less than ten shillings a piece *per annum*, the nation's stock will be thereby increased fifty thousand pounds *per annum*, besides the profit of a new dish introduced to the tables of all gentlemen of fortune in the kingdom who have any refinement in taste. And the money will circulate among ourselves, the goods being entirely of our own growth and manufacture.

Fourthly, the constant breeders, besides the gain of eight shillings sterling *per annum* by the sale of their children, will be rid of the charge of maintaining them after the first year.

Fifthly, this food would likewise bring great custom to taverns, where the vintners will certainly be so prudent as to procure the best receipts for dressing it to perfection, and consequently have their houses frequented by all the fine gentlemen, who justly value themselves upon their knowledge in good eating; and a skilful cook, who understands how to oblige his guests, will contrive to make it as expensive as they please.

Sixthly, this would be a great inducement to marriage, which all wise nations have either encouraged by rewards or enforced by laws and penalties. It would increase the care and tenderness of mothers towards their children, when they were sure of a settlement for life to the poor babes, provided in some sort by the public to their annual profit instead of expense. We should soon see an honest emulation among the married women, which of them could bring the fattest child to the market. Men would become as fond of their wives during the time of their pregnancy as they are now of their mares in foal, their cows in calf, or sows when they are ready to farrow; nor offer to beat or kick them (as it is too frequent a practice) for fear of a miscarriage.

Many other advantages might be enumerated. For instance, the addition of some thousand carcasses in our exportation of barreled beef, the propagation of swine's flesh, and improvement in the art of making good bacon, so much wanted among us by the great destruction of pigs, too frequent at our tables, and are no way comparable in taste or magnificence to a well-grown, fat yearling child, which roasted whole will make a considerable figure at a lord mayor's feast, or any other public entertainment. But this and many others I omit, being studious of brevity.

Supposing that one thousand families in this city would be constant customers for infants' flesh, besides others who might have it at merry meetings, particularly weddings and christenings, I compute that Dublin would take off annually about twenty thousand carcasses, and the rest of the kingdom (where probably they will be sold somewhat cheaper) the remaining eighty thousand.

I can think of no one objection that will possibly be raised against this proposal, unless it should be urged that the number of people will be thereby much lessened in the kingdom. This I freely own, and it was indeed one principal design in offering it to the world. I desire the reader will observe that I calculate my remedy for this one individual Kingdom of Ireland, and for no other that ever was, is, or, I think, ever can be upon earth. Therefore let no man talk to me of other expedients: Of taxing our absentees at five shillings a pound: Of using neither clothes nor household furniture except what is of our own growth and manufacture: Of utterly rejecting the materials and instruments that promote foreign luxury: Of curing the expensiveness of pride, vanity, idleness, and gaming in our women: Of introducing a vein of parsimony, prudence, and temperance: Of learning to love our country, wherein we differ even from Laplanders and the inhabitants of Topinamboo: Of quitting our animosities and factions, nor acting any longer like the Jews, who were murdering one another at the very moment their city was taken: Of being a little cautious not to sell our country and consciences for nothing: Of teaching landlords to have at least one degree of mercy towards their tenants; Lastly, of putting a spirit of honesty, industry, and skill into our shopkeepers, who, if a resolution could now be taken to buy only our native goods, would immediately unite to cheat and exact upon us in the price, the measure, and the goodness, nor could ever yet be brought to make one fair proposal of just dealing, though often and earnestly invited to it.

Therefore I repeat, let no man talk to me of these and the like expedients, till he hath at least a glimpse of hope that there will ever be some hearty and sincere attempt to put them in practice.

But as to myself, having been wearied out for many years with offering vain, idle, visionary thoughts, and at length utterly despairing of success, I fortunately fell upon this proposal, which, as it is wholly new, so it hath something solid and real, of no expense and little trouble, full in our own power, and whereby we can incur no danger in disobliging England. For this kind of commodity will not bear exportation, the flesh being of too tender a consistence to admit a long continuance in salt, although perhaps I could name a country which would be glad to eat up our whole nation without it.

After all, I am not so violently bent upon my own opinion as to reject any offer proposed by wise men, which shall be found equally innocent, cheap, easy, and effectual. But before something of that kind shall be advanced in contradiction to my scheme, and offering a better, I desire the author or authors will be pleased maturely to consider two points. First, as things now stand, how they will be able to find food and raiment for an hundred thousand useless mouths and backs? And secondly, there being a round million of creatures in human figure throughout this kingdom, whose whole subsistence put into a common stock would leave them in debt two millions of pounds sterling, adding those who are beggars by profession, to the bulk of farmers, cottagers, and labourers, with their wives and children, who are beggars in effect; I desire those politicians who dislike my overture, and may perhaps be so bold to attempt an answer, that they will first ask the parents of these mortals whether they would not at this day think it a great happiness to have been sold for food at a year old in the manner I prescribe, and thereby have avoided such a perpetual scene of misfortunes as they have since gone through by the oppression of landlords, the impossibility of paying rent without money or trade, the want of common sustenance, with neither house nor clothes to cover them from the inclemencies of weather, and the most inevitable prospect of entailing the like or greater miseries upon their breed for ever.

I profess in the sincerity of my heart that I have not the least personal interest in endeavoring to promote this necessary work, having no other motive than the public good of my country, by advancing our trade, providing for infants, relieving the poor, and giving some pleasure to the rich. I have no children by which I can propose to get a single penny; the youngest being nine years old, and my wife past child-bearing.

STUDY QUESTIONS for "A Modest Proposal"

COMPREHENSION

1. What is the central proposal of this essay? That is, what does Swift's persona propose as a means for eradicating Ireland's social ills? (You might answer the first question in the Style and Technique section below before responding.)
2. Reread the opening paragraph. What seems to be the persona's attitude towards his subject matter? What words and/or phrases reveal this attitude?
3. In the same paragraph where objections are mentioned (see question 4 in the Development and Organization section below), a long list of other measures is mentioned, introduced by the clause, "Therefore let no man talk to me of other expedients." What do you think was Swift's (not the persona's) attitude toward these other measures?

4. Do you think it is possible that the real purpose of "A Modest Proposal" is to get people to study these other measures, and that the proposal itself served merely to shock readers into the awareness that *something* needs to be done? What was Swift trying to accomplish? Be sure to study paragraph twenty-nine carefully before answering this.

5. The Irish people considered Swift a hero. Would they have felt this way about him if they had thought he was serious about the proposal his persona makes in this essay?

6. Who or what is the intended audience for this essay? To whom is Swift, through his persona, most immediately directing his proposal? What does the nature of the proposal reveal about the immediate audience?

7. Answer the following questions concerning the final paragraph:
   a. Is the persona being sincere? Does he write anything that is not altogether sincere?
   b. Does the persona seem to have a personal interest in making this proposal?
   c. What does the final sentence contribute to this essay and reveal about the persona?

DEVELOPMENT AND ORGANIZATION

1. Where does the persona first present his proposal? Why does he take so long to present his proposal? Why doesn't he make his ghastly proposal in the first or second paragraph?

2. What reasons or claims does Swift's persona cite to support his proposal? Where in the rather lengthy introduction does the persona present reasons in support of the proposal-to-come? Where in the body of the essay does the persona list reasons?

3. Where does the persona make use of examples, facts, and statistics to support his reasons?

4. Where does the persona address the objections that his opponents are likely to bring against his proposal? Does the persona effectively refute these objections?

STYLE AND TECHNIQUE

1. Swift creates a persona to present his argument. In other words, the point of view adopted in this essay is not Swift's own. What are some of the persona's distinguishing characteristics?

2. Swift's essay uses irony and hyperbole (exaggeration) to get its points across. In what sense may the entire essay be regarded as ironic? What is the effect upon the intended audience of the hyperbole? Find examples of both irony and hyperbole and comment on their effectiveness.

3. Does the persona maintain a consistent tone throughout the essay? What passages can you refer to to support your answer?

4. Consider the choice of words Swift, through his persona, makes use of in this essay. What is the effect of referring to wives as "breeders" (see paragraph six), of suggesting that a young, healthy child be served "in a fricassee or a ragout," of referring to a supporter of his proposal as "a very worthy person, a true lover of his country" (see paragraph seventeen)?

TEN-MINUTE TOPICS

1. Write a "modest proposal" of your own, suggesting an outrageous solution to an urgent problem of our day, such as environmental pollution, the national debt, violent crime, governmental waste and fraud, or any other serious, longstanding problem that government has not been able to deal with effectively. If you can, include somewhere in your proposal other measures you consider less outrageous and more workable, dismissing them ironically as impossible, unworkable, or even insane.
2. In imitation of Swift, write a highly ironic argument in which, appearing to defend an extremely popular or unpopular position, you actually take the opposite position.
3. Discuss an issue that you've changed your beliefs about.

THE EFFECTIVENESS OF HARSHER PUNISHMENT ON JUVENILE OFFENDERS

BY RAHNI WALDEN (student)

Historically, America's attitude toward juvenile justice has shifted from reformative to punitive and has coincided with a rise in the number and severity of juvenile crimes. This leads to speculation about the effectiveness of current policies and to questions regarding what it means to implement truly progressive reform. The search for answers has stretched over a century; however, lawmakers (and some constituents) have yet to realize solutions. Although many legislators and parents continue to believe harsher sentences will lead to a decrease in juvenile crime, they seem to ignore or simply do not realize that the bulk of research reveals numerous failings with such an approach.

The question arises as to how juvenile crime became such a serious social issue. Peter Katel offers an insightful look into the lives of urban dwellers during the startling growth of early US cities. In the early nineteenth century, populations in many US states rose sharply with the influx of immigrants. Katel points out that, generally speaking, most immigrants arrived with little financial backing. With the adults working multiple jobs and long hours at low wages, children were often left unsupervised. In increasingly urban neighborhoods children often roamed the streets and, due to the somewhat perilous and desperate nature of their lives, often got into trouble (922). In 1824 the New York House of Refuge was founded by a group of prominent and concerned citizens. This was closely followed by the establishment of the Society for the Reformation of Juvenile Delinquents (922). Through the efforts of this group, legislation was passed which established facilities that would house "boys under a certain age who become subject to the notice of our police, either as vagrants, or homeless, or charged with petty crimes" (922). At the same time, the children would receive a basic education and were "subjected to a course of treatment that [would] afford a prompt and energetic corrective of their vicious propensities" (922). A number of additional cities, including Baltimore, Boston, and Philadelphia, followed suit in establishing similar institutions; however, refuge houses founded in these and other cities proved unable to cope with the increasing number of poor or homeless youth, and the capacities of these institutions were soon overwhelmed (922).

The majority of youths found themselves in trouble only for petty crimes, such as stealing, but as Thomas Billitteri notes in his article "Youth Violence," there was no separate system for dealing with juvenile offenders, and thus many children found themselves in adult prisons for much less severe crimes. Many civic reformers believed it was the responsibility of the state to protect children from the corrupting influence of adult prisoners, which could lead the child down a path of more serious crimes. As a result of this line of thinking, in 1899 America's first juvenile court was founded in Chicago (Billitteri 201; Katel 922). For a while, however, the same rights afforded to adults by the Constitution were absent in the sentencing of juveniles. The fate and sentencing of the child were left exclusively up to the judge present at the trial. This standard practice was overthrown in the 1966 *Kent v. United States,* which laid the groundwork for extending constitutionally guaranteed rights to minors, and upheld in the following year by the ruling for *In re Gault,* which "laid down specific requirements for juvenile court. . . . In such cases, courts had to grant adequate notice of specific charges, notice of right to a lawyer, the right to confront witnesses and the right against self-incrimination" (Katel 924). In 1974 Congress passed the Juvenile Justice and Delinquency Prevention Act, which established the Office of Juvenile Justice and Delinquency Prevention. The act also aimed to reduce the number of juvenile offenders by ordering states to distinguish between two types of juvenile crime: a status offense (that depends on age to determine legality), and delinquent offense (in which it is illegal, no matter what the age of the offender). With new laws in place in later years, types and lengths of sentences which can be applied to juvenile offenders have been toughened, but contemporary critics ask whether these harsher consequences are effective or not, and what sort of impact a more punitive—or punishment based—system of justice has on convicted minors and youth crime as a whole.

In the 1990s, for example, juvenile boot camps were formed as a response to the rise in juvenile crimes. However, critics of boot camps say there is too much potential for abuse. According to "Alternative Ways of Dealing with Juvenile Crime," they cite incidents in which "the combination of insubordinate juveniles and aggressive instructors has led to physical abuse, resulting in some states abandoning their boot camp programs." There have also been instances in which minors have died as a result of overexertion. Further, the recidivism rates for those who went through a boot camp were about the same as for those who had completed standard juvenile-correction programs. Also pointed out is the fact that despite the popularity of boot camp programs, there is a lack of evidence showing they prevent repeat offenses any better than simple incarceration. Critics cite a recidivism rate that is no better than the one for youths who attend adult prisons (between fifty and seventy percent).

The data contends that rehabilitative programs offer better rates of integration into society, and lower rates of repeat offenders. Even some who support boot camps say that they are more effective when juveniles are given some sort of assistance after leaving. "All the national research has shown that it takes more than a kick in the pants and someone telling you to march, march, march to really change your thinking and change your behavior," says Pamela Ward of the Texas Youth Commission, which oversees serious youth offenders ("Alternative"). However, it seems legislation is heading in the opposite direction, instituting laws which make incarceration more of an incentive to state and county legislatures and prison officials than lowering the number of inmates ("Alternative").

Perhaps one of the strongest supportive arguments for harsher sentencing is deterrence. A number of supporters cite data which draws a correlation between harsher sentencing (including capital punishment) and a decrease in the number of crimes committed. According to David Muhlhausen, for every execution three to eighteen murders are prevented. In fact, a majority of the American public (sixty-seven percent) supports capital punishment and believes it does indeed serve as a deterrent:

"Supporters . . . say that punishment should be based not on a perpetrator's age, but on the severity of the crime. An 'adult' crime requires an adult punishment, they argue," ("Juvenile"). Most young people understand that crimes such as murder are wrong. The threat of more severe punishments, or possibly even death for certain crimes, acts as a strong deterrent for prospective offenders.

However, critics note that the system doles out punishments too harsh for the crime, sending juveniles to adult prisons from which—through sexual, physical, and emotional abuse—they emerge much worse than they went in. According to the US Department of Justice Bureau of Justice Statistics, in 2005 and 2006, "21% and 13% . . . of the victims of inmate-on-inmate sexual violence in jails were youth under the age of 18—a surprisingly high percentage of victims considering that only 1% of all jail inmates are juveniles" ("Juveniles"). Courts intend to act efficiently to churn out answers in the quickest manner, but in doing so the result will often lean toward the most cursory, not the most effective, and conclude with solutions which serve no practical purpose other than calming the public on a purely temporary basis, and which may do more harm than good.

Even though courts and policies have toughened standards for punishment of juvenile offenders, there has been a rise in the number of alternative programs being offered, and—it seems—the alternatives are offering promising results. New York City's Juvenile Justice Initiative was launched in early 2007. A year later, statistics released showed a recidivism rate of less than thirty-five percent for the 275 youths who had been through the program (Kaufman). This drop in repeat offenses was a direct result of implementing a different approach to dealing with youth offenders. Unlike their adult counterparts, youths will be more receptive to behavioral influences and emotional support and counseling. These approaches come much closer to addressing the initial problem which resulted in delinquent behavior than do others.

Supporters of rehabilitative procedures cite a number of statistics in another recent study which defend their position. According to "Alternative Ways of Dealing with Juvenile Crime," the Annie E. Casey Foundation, a charity that works with disadvantaged children, published a report which found that "while the average rate of repeat offenses (recidivism rate) in juvenile justice institutions was 50% to 70%, the recidivism rate for four of the fifteen workforce development programs examined was below 20%." Not only does this support rehabilitative procedures for juvenile offenders, but it comes as a blow against simply using punishment as a means of dealing with the issue. With a failure rate so significant, those who deal with juvenile crime should examine the root causes for offenses more deeply and be open to alternative forms of treatment.

What needs to be examined are the circumstances surrounding each situation, taking into account history, home life, severity, and mental and emotional health. Today, while overall occurrences have decreased since their peak in 1993, youth violence has become much more severe in nature and also more widespread. While youth crimes are more prevalent among minorities and generally centered in certain neighborhoods, the factors stretch far beyond race—to socioeconomic conditions and inequality in regard to education and adult supervision.

Sadly, the only thing being considered is the length of time of incarceration—punishment already being a given. While this is due in some cases, more widely spread is the practice of ignoring solutions where causes are taken into account. It is about time legislators and the citizenry start holding themselves accountable for the problems born out of more deeply rooted social issues that result in the neglect and lack of realistic guidance and creative and productive outlets its youth receives. Is it any real question why their frustrations boil over in such a volatile manner? There are far more things needing fixing than many people are willing to admit. David Brown, executive director of the National Youth Employment Coalition, a youth training group, states, "If young people have a little money in their pockets and are productively occupied in employment activities, they're less likely to commit delinquent acts and more likely to be productive members of society" ("Alternative"). If more opportunities were afforded to at-risk youth, especially those who come from poor or underprivileged families and neighborhoods, there would be fewer reasons to commit petty crimes like stealing, which make up the majority of juvenile offenses.

The solutions being implemented have increasingly served only to address the issue once it has become a problem serious enough for there to be legal consequences; dealing only with the effect of any given issue once it has already become a problem does nothing to address the root causes and, in effect, does nothing to confront the issue at hand. To prevent juvenile crime from continuing or from becoming more severe, federal and state legislatures need to pass and enforce measures which thoroughly examine the social structures currently in place. These measures must also work to prevent children from falling into a life of crime and be geared toward the rehabilitation of those children who prove to be receptive to such. Without such measures, parents, cities, states, and social and political systems will bear both the brunt of criticism and the effects of a deteriorating social model.

Works Cited

"Alternative Ways of Dealing with Juvenile Crime." *Issues & Controversies On File* 22 Nov. 2002: n. pag. *Issues and Controversies*. Web. 16 Apr. 2011.

Billitteri, Thomas J. "Youth Violence." *CQ Researcher* 20.9 (2010): 193-216. *CQ Researcher Online*. Web. 20 Apr. 2011.

"Juvenile Death Penalty." *Issues & Controversies On File* 25 May 2003: n. pag. *Issues and Controversies*. Web. 20 Apr. 2011.

"Juveniles Should Not Be Placed in Adult Prisons." *Opposing Viewpoints: America's Prisons*. Ed. Noah Berlatsky. Detroit: Greenhaven Press, 2010. *Opposing Viewpoints Resource Center*. Web. 20 Apr. 2011.

Katel, Peter. "Juvenile Justice." *CQ Researcher* 18.39 (2008): 913-36. *CQ Researcher Online*. Web. 23 Apr. 2011.

Kaufman, Leslie. "A Home Remedy for Juvenile Offenders. *New York Times*. New York Times, 20 Feb. 2008. Web. 24 Apr. 2011.

Muhlhausen, David B. "The Death Penalty Deters Crime." *Opposing Viewpoints: Crime and Criminals*. Ed. James D. Torr. San Diego: Greenhaven Press, 2010. N. pag. *Opposing Viewpoints Resource Center*. Web. 24 Apr. 2011.

STUDY QUESTIONS for "The Effectiveness of Harsher Punishment on Juvenile Offenders"

COMPREHENSION

1. When was the New York House of Refuge founded? In response to what societal problem was it created?
2. Where was America's first juvenile court founded?
3. What motivated the creation of boot camps for juveniles?

DEVELOPMENT AND ORGANIZATION

1. What claim is at the basis of Walden's argument? Copy out the sentence in which it appears.
2. Identify the best statistics Walden uses to support her argument in favor of rehabilitative programs for juvenile offenders.
3. Identify the causal chain regarding juvenile delinquency reform from 1824 to 2007 as presented in this essay.
4. Where is comparison and contrast used in this essay? Why is it a necessary pattern for presenting this particular evidence?
5. In the sixth paragraph, Walden makes a claim that appears to be a logical fallacy: "In fact, a majority of the American public (sixty-seven percent) supports capital punishment and believes it does indeed serve as a deterrent." The fallacy is *argument by consensus*, which rests on the assumption that a statement is true because a majority of people believe it. What claim should Walden have made here instead? What evidence would have been a more effective way of supporting her point about deterrence?
6. If this were your essay, what additional types of development and support would you use to enrich the body paragraphs? What additional points would you make?

STYLE AND TECHNIQUE

1. The essay's conclusion contains a call to action. Write a new conclusion using a different technique.
2. Why doesn't the essay's first parenthetical citation (in paragraph two) contain the author's last name or the article's title?
3. Examine the essay's title. Does it adequately reflect the essay's content? Why or why not?

TEN-MINUTE TOPICS

1. In a sentence, write out your own claim regarding juvenile offenders. Then discuss how your position relates to your community. Who do you think should correct this problem, and how should it be solved?
2. What kind of offenders did you see in a school you have previously attended? How were the offenders handled? Do you think they were handled effectively? Why or why not?

CHAPTER THIRTEEN

WRITING WITH RESEARCH: HOW TO INTEGRATE OTHER WRITERS' IDEAS AND INFORMATION WITH YOUR OWN

DEFINITION

You are about to embark on a new composition task: writing a researched essay[1]. Until now, your experiences, observations, and knowledge alone have made your writing engaging, informative, and significant. Until now, you have used your expertise and insight to present your topics with authority and aplomb. What happens, though, when a college or career writing task challenges you to write out of your depth, beyond what you already know? When you need to learn more about your topic, you must turn to research, defined by Robert Dees of Orange Coast College as "*learning* in its most fundamental form: the acquisition and interpretation of information" (2). Soon enough, you may appreciate research for the surprising ideas you discover and the unusual perspectives that reshape your understanding of the world. Research is curiosity's toolbox, and its versatile investigative techniques support any purpose you pursue in writing: creativity, reflection, exposition, or argumentation.

As with any effective writing to these purposes, good researched writing need not be dull and lifeless. Try telling horror-fiction maestro Stephen King that his 1996 novel *Desperation*, which he researched with travel and personal interviews conducted in Ely and other mining towns of rural Nevada, should not have been written as a thrilling page-turner. Many authors writing in more popular narrative genres—historical romance, murder mystery, and science fiction, to name a few—routinely investigate their subjects so that they can create the detailed characters and settings, realistic crime-solving techniques and intriguing plot twists, and fantastic future technologies and intergalactic societies that grip our imaginations as we read their works.

Anne Cushman, writing for *Tricycle* magazine, similarly recognizes the value of bringing an intimate, engaging voice to her expository essay, "Clearing Clutter." Reflecting on a life-long "scatterbrained inability" to organize her home and work spaces, Cushman uses narrative and description from personal life to illustrate the embarrassment and havoc her uncontrolled messiness has caused (43). After relating how in first grade she learned she was different from other children whose school supplies were always neatly arranged in their desks, Cushman surveys her adult surroundings while "sitting on the floor of [her] home office, paying bills":

---

[1] The terms "researched essay" and "researched writing" are preferred in this chapter to the familiar "research paper" in order to emphasize research's usefulness to different genres and writing situations. "Research paper" specifies its own genre, an expository document written strictly to report its author's investigations of a topic to readers who expect to be informed rather than entertained or persuaded by the writing.

My desk is so littered with papers—unpaid bills, unanswered letters, outdated check registers, notes written on napkins and ripped envelopes, a phone number scrawled in eyeliner on an empty paper towel roll—that I never work there. Instead, I spread out paperwork on the carpet and write on my laptop on the sofa, surrounded by books, folders, and pillows. (43)

Her essay's tone blends honesty and humor: "I used to be able to live with this disability, even laugh it off as an eccentricity intimately linked to my creativity. But now, as a working single mom, I can't afford to spend twenty minutes looking for my car keys or a pair of matching socks" (43). Cushman brings research to her writing as she explains how she looked for her problem's solution. For example, here are her brief summaries of two books she read to learn how to organize her clutter:

The first one, *Organizing from the Inside Out*, tells me that the basic model for organization is the kindergarten classroom: a home for every object, all organized according to activity, and everything labeled. The second one, *Simply Organized!*, warns me sternly that if I have two of anything—anything!—I should get rid of one of them immediately. Hmmm, I think, nonplussed. I set both books down, intending to choose between them. A few days later, it takes me twenty minutes to find them. (43)

Cushman persists with her research until she finds the answers she needs both to get organized and to complete her article. Along the way, she realizes she has been engaged in a journey of self-discovery, so she writes:

Bringing order to clutter . . . is not just about putting my spices in alphabetical order. On a deeper level, it's about balancing the twin poles of spiritual life: cherishing life and holding it sacred, while knowing that it will pass away. It's about learning to care for the things and people that are precious to me—and, when it's time, freely letting them go. (47)

Composing her essay for *Tricycle*'s Western Buddhist audience, Cushman knows that presenting her research with a personable style best suits her purpose of inspiring readers by her example. Are you becoming inspired to see that researched writing can offer more than dry reports of facts and figures and more than carbon copies of other people's ideas and opinions?

Even when adopting a formal tone, as Celestine Bidaure does in "The Price of Perfection," good researched writing not only reflects its author's interests and questions but also stimulates its readers' involvement with the topic. Writing this argumentative essay for her composition class, Bidaure parlays personal curiosity about the television series *Toddlers and Tiaras* into an academic opportunity to examine psychological and sociological effects of child beauty pageants' growing popularity. Addressing a scholarly rhetorical situation, Bidaure's narrative voice confidently uses technical terms like "socialization agents" (1) and "correlation" (3) even as emotional words like "abhorrent" (3) express concern for child beauty pageants' "unhealthy obsession with society's idealized standard of femininity and beauty" (3). Incorporating anecdotes from *Toddlers and Tiaras* that peel away the pageants' "façade of being harmless" (2) to expose parents consumed with their daughters' "flawlessness and perfection" (3) and little girls "transformed into looking like miniature adults" (3), Bidaure sets her topic's social-science issues into a context familiar to readers: the parent-child relationship. Readers not only learn from Bidaure's research how "detrimental" (1) are society's ideals of female "beauty and perfection" (6), but we may also feel encouraged to rethink the costs girls and women pay to live limiting, harmful gender norms and to question our participation in reinforcing such ideals.

As the Cushman and Bidaure examples illustrate, researched writing is not so different from other compositions you have already completed without using information sources outside your perspective, memory, knowledge, and insight. For instance, your researched essay still conveys your thesis and key ideas about your topic; your writing still reflects your patterns of thinking as you develop, organize, and present the relevant reasoning, examples, facts, statistics, and expert opinions that support your assertions, even when other writers furnish that support. You still define your audience and purpose just as you still craft your writing's original voice, even though other writers' voices may be heard in your borrowed quotations. In short, when you prepare a researched essay, you alone remain responsible for any writing that appears on its pages, whether that text originates from you or another. The key difference is only that a researched essay shows where and how you have used other people's learning and experience to enlarge and enlighten your understanding of your topic.

APPLICATION

In one form or another, you have been doing research all your life if only because experience involves curiosity, discovery, and learning. If you are already adept at finding the resources and new information you need every day, then academic research may feel like a natural extension of your investigative abilities. Still, even though research may be "something writers naturally do whenever they have questions they can't answer on their own" (Ballenger 440), the informal methods of inquiry you use to find, for example, "your dentist's phone number," "what movies are showing on television," or "the current price of Raleigh mountain bikes" can differ significantly from the formal methods used in college when writers consult library, Internet, and other scholarly sources (Veit 1; Veit and Gould 57). Granted, you may devote to your everyday searches the same attitude of "careful, serious, and systematic investigation" as you give to your pursuit of academic questions (Roth 1), but your audiences' expectations markedly differ. After all, the friends who want you to recommend a dentist, watch a movie, or take a bicycle tour probably will never ask you to cite the telephone book, program guide, or sales catalog you consulted. The audiences for your academic writing will expect you to summarize, paraphrase, or quote and then cite your sources correctly following established source citation rules. Your ability to respond to these divergent reader expectations depends on your flexibility to adopt the research methods appropriate to your rhetorical situation.

Whether informal or formal, research always proceeds by trial and error: you predict where certain types or details of information may be found, you test these ideas by looking for your sources, and the success or failure of your predictions shapes your next steps along your inquiry path. Informal, everyday research may seem easier to do than formal, academic research for any number of reasons. If the prospect of taking on an academic research project causes you anxiety or unhappiness, you can help yourself by identifying and reflecting on these feelings and your reasons for them. You may discover that a lack of formal research confidence comes from having not yet learned the social expectations, strategies, techniques, and habits of mind associated with college inquiry. Given your success at learning informal research practices, you should feel assured that with study and practice you can master formal research methods, too.

Writing a researched essay, then, immerses you in two types of learning: topical knowledge and procedural mastery. Whereas research results enlarge *what you know* about reality, doing research develops and strengthens *how you learn*: your abilities not just to gather facts and opinions but also to question, analyze, test, evaluate, interpret, and synthesize your sources' information with your own experiences and ideas. Research makes you the authority who can write with meaning, confidence, and credibility in any situation, from college to career.

Planning a Research Project

Writing with research, like writing without it, begins with your decisions upon all aspects of your writing task. Your familiar invention and planning process changes as you address the implications of writing with research. Think, for a moment, about the first step: defining a topic. Writing a researched essay requires a topic about which you do not already know everything; you must need new information that research can fill, and, if your professor specifies the kind(s) of sources to consult, this new information should be available in such sources. Within these limits, almost anything that engages your curiosity could be a good topic for research. If a topic has shared significance to you and your community, so much the better: narrow and develop your topic to appeal to people whose lives are touched by it.

You already know that "narrowing a topic" means focusing on your strongest interest or specific concern about a general subject. Another factor in your treatment of a research topic is your assessment of the formality or informality of your writing's rhetorical situation. Consider Celestine Bidaure's curiosity about the socialization of girls and women in our culture: this general subject encompasses every aspect of human female growth and maturation in which these individuals' ideas about their gender—what it means to be a "girl" or "woman"—are formed, reinforced, or corrected by their interactions with others. Knowing this subject to be too large for the scope of her assignment and engaged by the popularity of television's *Toddlers and Tiaras*, Bidaure focuses on discovering and evaluating the effects of toddler girls' participation in child beauty pageants on their future development to adulthood. Her project's rhetorical situation as a composition class assignment in argumentative writing dictates that her research produce sources of authoritative support acceptable to scholarly standards. Alternately, had Bidaure written commentary for a blog on the effects of child beauty pageants, she could have based her opinion on anecdotal research provided by the television show alone. While planning any writing project requires writers to balance their interests with their readers', planning researched writing presents the more complicated challenge of developing a topic with sources of new information and expert opinion that an intended audience will accept as valid, even persuasive.

Assistance for narrowing a research topic effectively may be found by opening a Johari Window[2]. The heuristic's basic design looks like this (see fig. 1).

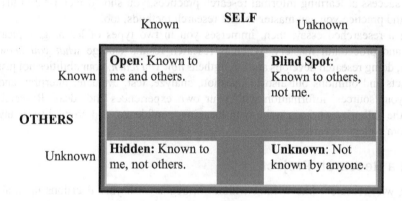

Fig. 1. A Johari Window for "self-awareness, personal development, group development and understanding relationships" (Chapman; Chimaera).

In this basic form, the diagram illustrates for psychologists, personnel managers, team trainers, and others involved with improving interpersonal dynamics and communication how information about an individual or group (the "Self") is shared by, allocated to, and hidden from "me" and "others." With minor modifications, the Window can graphically organize your thinking about a topic and the research questions that will focus and guide your inquiry and learning (see fig. 2).

---

[2] Psychologists Joseph Luft and Harrington Ingham first published the Johari Window in 1955 as a model of personal interaction dedicated to "illustrating and improving selfawareness, and mutual understanding between individuals within a group" (Chapman).

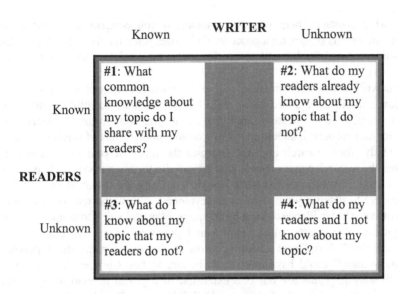

Fig. 2. A Johari Window for topic development and research planning.

Planning to write, you answer this question: "What new information and insight about my topic can I give my readers?" The Johari Window for topic development and research planning helps you organize what you know and do not know about a topic in a framework that compares your experience with that of your intended readers. You can then form ideas about the topical issues that would be most useful for your writing: ideas that are not already common knowledge (#1) or part of your readers' expertise (#2) but rather ideas that provide new information and insight (#4). As you plan to write with research, the Window becomes even more helpful: it exposes facets of your topic where you would be required or advised to do research. To write convincingly to an audience more knowledgeable of the topic than you (#2), you need research to make your understanding match your readers'. To discover new information and contribute provocative ideas to the ongoing communal discussion of your topic, you may use research to probe the topic's unknown dimensions. Once you have mapped the topical boundaries for your research, you may begin brainstorming questions that will guide your explorations of your topic's *terra incognita*.

Forming research questions—questions to answer with primary and/or secondary sources of information—is an essential component of planning a research project. Working with a personally meaningful topic, you may experience no difficulty creating relevant and engaging questions to pursue. Whenever you might struggle to ask probing questions, seek help in familiar invention and organization techniques. For example, try brainstorming or freewriting for five or ten minutes all the *what, who, when, where, why,* and *how* questions you can imagine; record every idea, and worry about editing your list later. Play "What if?" to explore using different modes of development and support in your writing: what questions help you, for instance, if you compare and contrast or analyze causes and effects or explain a process? Only after you have listed many possible questions should you read the list and select the one(s) most relevant to your interests, audience, and purpose.

When you write a research paper, one question should stand out as *the research question*: Bidaure might have asked, "Are child beauty pageants harmful to girls who participate in them?" Your question identifies what you most want to learn and communicate to your readers; it should motivate you to commit hours of precious time to research and study. Your research question narrows the focus of your topic, and your answer becomes the research paper's thesis. When you write for any purpose with research, your questions should identify gaps in your knowledge or argument that, if left unfilled, would lead readers to dismiss your ideas as undeveloped or unsupported. For example, Bidaure's use of statistical evidence linking beauty pageant participation to women's eating disorders originates in a question like "How can I prove my claim that child beauty pageants are harmful?" A different question, "How do beauty pageants shape people's attitudes about women?" could have motivated Bidaure to find Christine Yano's expert opinion that "Beauty pageants are but one extension of a global network of gendered images proliferating through media, fashion, and celebrity culture" (qtd. in Bidaure 1). As Bidaure's essay shows, researched writing may require using several related questions about your topic.

Locating and Evaluating Sources

With questions in hand, your next step is to plan how and where to seek their answers. Maybe some questions point toward primary research methods or primary materials found in Internet and library searches; other questions may lead to secondary sources. How do you know what to do and where to go? The "primary" and "secondary" classifications for research define the researcher's proximity to the information: let us imagine a gift wrapped in one or two boxes. Primary research methods like field observations, interviews and surveys, and scientific experiments gather new data (gift); the reports of this data (gift-wrapped box) prepared by those who gathered it are primary sources. Primary materials also include autobiographies, diaries and letters, literary works, travelogues, etc.—any writing or other media originating in the creator's personal experience, whether by "direct participation or observation" (University Libraries). Secondary sources (shipping box) represent their authors' work with other people's primary or secondary materials[3]. Thus, your researched writing becomes a secondary

---

[3] Has your professor warned you not to use encyclopedia information in your paper? Encyclopedias are one type of tertiary sources (a truck full of shipping boxes) that abstract, condense, digest, or summarize content from other, primary and secondary, sources. While the general subject overviews and common knowledge presented in tertiary sources may be helpful at the earliest, topic exploration stage of research project planning, their distance from original information—the gift—makes them unsuitable development and support for academic writing.

source for its readers, just as other authors' reports, analyses, interpretations, commentaries, and arguments on information they did not create all serve as secondary sources for you. As useful as this classification system is, it is complicated in that any given text may combine primary and secondary content. For instance, a famous historical person you are profiling may have written a diary (primary) in which she reviews (secondary) a play she saw performed. Similarly, your researched writing may combine support from interviews you conducted and commentaries you read. "The Price of Perfection" blends Bidaure's observations (primary) of pageant mothers' behavior with their contestant daughters gathered through the medium of a reality television show with her reading (secondary) of other researchers' studies of women's attitudes toward beauty and body image. How much and what kinds of primary and secondary material you bring into your researched writing depends on your perceptions and your readers' expectations of the authority and credibility of each type of source.

Finding authoritative and credible information on the Internet can be difficult. Anyone with an opinion, including people who know next to nothing factual or true about their topics, can create a Web site or post commentary to a blog or user forum. The old adage "Don't believe everything you read" remains excellent advice for navigating online media. You risk your work's credibility and your authority if you use trash sources as your support. To conduct Internet research successfully, you must not only verify the information you find but also investigate the commercial or political bias of the sponsor who published it. You can find source evaluation assistance from many sources—your professor, a reference librarian, writer's handbooks—but the UC Berkeley Library's online tutorial, "Evaluating Web Pages," offers excellent instruction you may consult anytime. With study and practice, you will learn to use Internet domain classifications, webpage design, rhetorical stance, and other clues to determine the academic suitability of Web sites you encounter.

Finding authoritative and credible sources in college and community libraries is far easier. Reference librarians are trained professionals who will happily guide you through the library's maze of paper, audio, video, and electronic holdings: just ask! Putting your hands on a library's books, magazines and newspapers, academic journals, and audio/visual recordings requires you to understand the cataloguing system it uses. Graduating from grade school libraries' Dewey decimal organization to college libraries' Library of Congress (LOC) system can seem daunting, but LOC's combination of letters, numbers, and dates offers the most efficient way to manage publications numbering into the millions, as in big university and government libraries. In order to read her book source, Christine Yano's *Crowning the Nice Girl: Gender, Ethnicity, and Culture in Hawai'i's Cherry Blossom Festival*, Bidaure first had to find it on the library shelf. The

LOC's unique call number for this book[4], HQ1220.U5 Y36 2006, communicates the following information about it:

- The H in HQ classifies the book as *Social Science*.
- HQ refers to the *Family. Marriage. Women* subclass of social sciences.
- 1220 falls within the numerical range 1101-2030.7 designating *Women. Feminism* topics. (Library of Congress).
- U5 is a cutter number identifying a subtopic of *Women. Feminism*.
- Y36 is a cutter number designating the author, Yano.
- 2006 is the copyright year of Yano's book. (ANMH Research Library)

To acquire this book, Bidaure found the library shelves where HQ books are placed; then she scanned their spines to find those numbered 1220; within the 1220s, she looked for the .U# books; within that group, she discovered the Y36 book by Yano. You can read any LOC call number and find the book or other resource it describes if you proceed step by step, following Bidaure's example.

Bidaure also consulted her library's databases of electronic sources to locate popular magazine and academic journal articles. Electronic databases collect not only periodical article abstracts with bibliographic citations for locating physical sources in the library but also, in many cases, the articles' complete text online. Additionally, a library's online holdings may include e-books, streaming audio and video, and art image collections, all accessible from an Internet-connected computer. Electronic database subscriptions give libraries a cost-effective means to maximize the information they offer their patrons: a student searching the *EBSCO Complete* metadatabase provided by her community college has access to the same information as the students whose Ivy League college library also subscribes to *EBSCO Complete* (Sawyer). Using electronic databases offers many conveniences that save time, improve learning, and increase enjoyment of the research process.

With no need to drive across town to the library or wander through its stacks to find your sources, you have time to begin your online library search by skimming the titles and brief descriptions of the databases available. Interdisciplinary databases like *Academic Search Premier* (an EBSCO product specializing in academic disciplines), *EBSCO Complete*, and *ProQuest* include abstracts and full-text articles from thousands of periodicals: newspapers, popular magazines, scholarly journals, and trade publications. While a basic keyword search of these databases is guaranteed to return results, often a longer list of titles than you could skim in a lifetime, advanced search commands can quickly identify the potentially most relevant items, even a specific article. For example, to search *EBSCO Complete* for the Anderson and Wallace source Bidaure used, you would find the advanced search form to follow these search steps (figures 3-4) (*EBSCO*

---

[4] A book's LOC call number is the same regardless of the library in which the book is housed. This feature of the LOC system is especially helpful for researchers who rely on interlibrary loans to acquire materials not available at their local libraries.

Complete).

Searching: All Databases, Show all | Choose Databases by Subject »
Anderson
in AU Author
Search
AND
Glamour Girls
in TI Title
AND
Los Angeles Magazine
in SO Source
Add Row

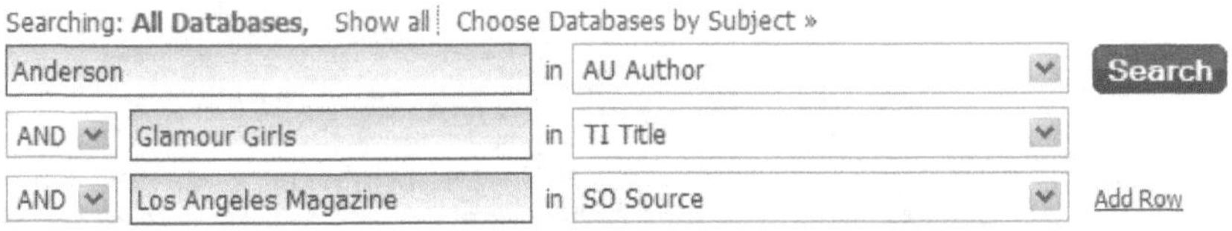

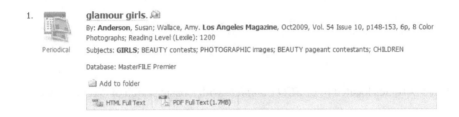

Fig. 3. Type source details in the left column and select the detail type in the right column. Click SEARCH.

1.
glamour girls.
By: Anderson, Susan; Wallace, Amy. Los Angeles Magazine, Oct2009, Vol. 54 Issue 10, p148-153, 6p, 8 Color Photographs; Reading Level (Lexile): 1200
Periodical
Subjects: GIRLS; BEAUTY contests; PHOTOGRAPHIC images; BEAUTY pageant contestants; CHILDREN
Database: MasterFILE Premier
Add to folder
HTML Full Text
PDF Full Text (1.7MB)

Fig. 4. Enjoy your search success! Choose the full-text file you want to read.

In any basic or advanced search, you may also limit your results to full-text articles, sources published during a specified time period, articles published by a specified periodical, or peer-reviewed articles from scholarly journals, among other options.

Your library might also subscribe to specialized databases like *JSTOR*, *Congressional Quarterly Researcher*, *Opposing Viewpoints in Context*, and *Issues and Controversies on File*. *JSTOR*, a gold-standard information source for academic writing, archives only full-text articles from scholarly journals representing a wide range of disciplines. *CQ Researcher* publishes weekly briefing papers on current news topics; these reports, prepared by "seasoned journalist[s]," provide comprehensive coverage including historical and social context, opposing viewpoints from subject-matter experts, illustrative graphics, and bibliographies ("About *CQ*"). *Opposing Viewpoints* supports its pro and con arguments on timely social controversies with academic journal articles, primary sources, and other media while *Issues and Controversies* includes research and instruction tools for students and teachers with its analyses of competing perspectives in society's debates of contemporary issues. These databases are easy to use: they offer topics lists for browsing along with basic and advanced searches. Like all subscription databases, they vet their articles and resources so that users can be assured of accessing only authoritative, credible information.

Databases often list your search results in order of relevance to your search keywords so that articles listed first are likely to be more useful than those listed last. Article descriptions can be scanned quickly to determine whether, given your research question(s), the complete source could be worth studying. Consider, for example, that a search of

EBSCO Complete using the keywords "child beauty pageants" returned these two items (figure 5).

Periodical

Toddlers & Tiaras TOO MUCH TOO SOON? 🔍

(cover story) By: Triggs, Charlotte; West, Kay; Aradillas, Elaine. *People*, 9/26/2011, Vol. 76 Issue 12, p160-168, 9p, 11 Color Photographs; Reading Level (Lexile): 1310

Subjects: UNITED States; TODDLERS & Tiaras (TV program); **BEAUTY** contests -- Moral & ethical aspects; BODY image in **children**; **CHILD** development; **BEAUTY pageant** contestants -- Abuse of; **CHILDREN** & sex; REALITY television programs -- Moral & ethical aspects; SOUTHERN States -- Social life & customs; SOUTHERN States

Database: MasterFILE Premier

Academic Journal

Nymphet Fantasies **CHILD BEAUTY PAGEANTS** AND THE POLITICS OF INNOCENCE. 🔍

By: Giroux, Henry A.. *Social Text*, Winter1998, Vol. 16 Issue 4, p31, 23p

Subjects: INNOCENCE (Psychology); **CHILDREN**; SOCIAL sciences; **CHILD** labor -- Law & legislation; UNITED States; Research and Development in the Social Sciences and Humanities

Database: Academic Search Premier

Fig. 5. Articles located in *EBSCO Complete* with a basic search of "child beauty pageants."

What do we learn about these sources from their database descriptions? A large captioned icon designates each article's source type. Each index entry's first line states the article's title and, beneath, its print publication data. Each description's SUBJECTS section lists keywords for the article's contents. Now, if our research question is "How do child beauty pageants affect their participants' thoughts and feelings about their bodies?" which of these two articles seems more useful? Though the academic journal source promises more authoritative research and opinion, the popular magazine story's subject "body image in children" better fits our research interests.

The next step is to save and/or print the full text of the selected article. Databases allow you to create an online account and save your articles in a folder on their server; you may also save full-text files to your computer. Your professor may recommend printing article-length materials since working with paper copies facilitates writing while you read. Beyond coloring pages with highlighting, good note-taking answers your research questions, explains these answers, and grows your understanding of your topic's other facets. Fill the margins of your printouts as well as your researcher's notebook with your reactions, ideas, questions, connections to other sources, and associations with your experience. Writing more notes during your active reading makes creating your researched essay's first draft easier because you will have greater comprehension of your subject matter and a map of the information treasures in each source.

Taking Notes and Integrating Sources in Your Writing

You record notes while reading and thinking about your sources in order to form insights about your topic and research questions. Writing aids memory, but writing to restate source information in your own words can be difficult and time consuming. Lacking confidence and feeling pressure, students sometimes resort to copying source content as their notes. One could rationalize this habit, saying that copying provides a wealth of direct quotes to use in the researched essay, but excessive quotation creates problems of voice and coherence. Researched writing is not assembling a jigsaw puzzle of quotes from authors whose word choices and sentence rhythms do not sound like you. Observe from the sources you read that writing with research is controlled by one strong original viewpoint and that quotations from others, used sparingly, fit neatly into the writing's logical flow. Your note taking should help you master source material. You progress toward this goal by relying more on summarizing and paraphrasing than on copying when you select source content for your notes.

Summary and paraphrase as active reading techniques in your research process are somewhat different activities than the summarizing and paraphrasing grade-school teachers asked of you so they could assess your reading comprehension. As an adult researcher, you are not learning to read but reading to learn; summary and paraphrase are now your tools, not your instructors'. The familiar activity of summarizing a source's main idea and key points helps you represent accurately and fairly the author's position or purpose. But summarizing in research notes also means distilling complex analysis, explanation, or argument to its essential point so that you borrow from your source only what is most relevant to your writing. Consider, for example, Bidaure's statement, "Beauty pageants have been around since 1921, but child beauty pageants made their debut in 1960 in Miami, Florida, with Little Miss Universe" (2). Here, Bidaure condenses four decades of beauty pageant history, presented in the multipage "Pageant History" section of the *Pageant Center* Web site, to a single sentence putting child beauty pageants in historical context. Although many fascinating developments shaped the beauty pageant business in the forty years dividing its first pageant for adult women from its first for little girls, Bidaure realized that this part of pageant history offered nothing to her argument. "The Price of Perfection" uses source information selectively in ways that reinforce Bidaure's control over her topic.

Paraphrasing in researched writing shares this selectivity with summarizing but differs in allowing you to capture important source details. Bidaure's example of five-year-old Alexis suffering an eyebrow waxing is persuasive because paraphrasing relates key events from a telling episode of *Toddlers and Tiaras* (2). We can examine another illustration of paraphrasing in Bidaure's essay when we compare one of her sources, the peer-reviewed article "Childhood Beauty Pageant Contestants: Associations with Adult Disordered Eating and Mental Health," with her writing. Within this article, on a page Bidaure cites, readers find a table of statistics and the authors' interpretation of this data:

> These results indicate a significant association between childhood beauty pageant participation and increased body dissatisfaction, difficulty trusting interpersonal relationships, and greater impulsive behaviors, and indicate a trend toward increased feelings of ineffectiveness.
>
> . . . Despite being matched on BMI, females who had participated in beauty pageants perceived their current figure as larger, and

preferred their figure to be smaller than females who had not participated in beauty pageants. Furthermore, the calculations of their ideal BMI also were smaller. However, none of these results were statistically significant. (Wonderlich et al. 296)

Compare the authors' results with Bidaure's paraphrase:

As Anna Wonderlich and her team explain in their study of the correlation between childhood beauty pageants and adult eating disorders, women who competed in childhood beauty pageants are more likely to be dissatisfied with their bodies than women who have never competed. (3)

Has Bidaure accurately conveyed the information discovered in the authors' research? The data are qualified by the statement, "none of these results were statistically significant," because the authors write for a scientific audience of health professionals who differentiate levels of sturdiness in the evidence that supports hypotheses. The authors' results may not be strong enough to prove a causal relationship as fact, but they are sufficiently suggestive for the authors to report "a significant association" of factors. Bidaure's paraphrase is, therefore, accurate.

Should Bidaure have placed quotation marks around "childhood beauty pageants" in her paraphrase? She seems to have copied this phrase from the authors, and copying word for word without quotation marks is a form of plagiarism. Bidaure's usage is appropriate here, though; "childhood beauty pageant" is a common name for the event, not unique to the authors' writing. In contrast, let us say that Bidaure had written, "Women who competed in childhood beauty pageants are more likely to display increased body dissatisfaction than women who have never competed (Wonderlich et al. 296)." Should Bidaure have quoted "increased body dissatisfaction"? Yes, this phrase is the authors', it conveys their judgment, and that judgment is their intellectual property. Bidaure's use of that phrase without quotation marks would be plagiarism even though the paraphrase ends with a parenthetical source citation.

Bidaure provides a real example of blending direct quotation with paraphrase when she introduces information from Susan Anderson and Amy Wallace's "Glamour Girls": "child beauty pageants are an embodiment of how society places valued emphasis on 'beauty, success, and glamour'" (5). Bidaure quotes "beauty, success, and glamour" because Anderson and Wallace list these attributes in this exact order: "'Our own values of beauty, success, and glamour are reflected in the dreams of thousands of young girls'" (Anderson and Wallace 153). The blending of single and double quotation marks displayed in this paragraph's two examples may appear unusual but is also correct as it signifies nested quotation, the quoting of content already quoted in Anderson and Wallace's article.

Incorporating quotations into your writing is not always as complicated as our latest illustrations prove. Still, quoting effectively requires your closest attention to the mechanics (punctuation and grammar) of weaving a source's words into your sentences. As you study more and more examples of researched writing, you may observe distinct patterns of sentence structure that writers use to integrate direct quotes and paraphrases. The familiar "my source says" formula follows basic rules for using a comma, quotation marks, capitalization, and a period or other end mark to show where the borrowed author's voice begins and ends. Bidaure seems to prefer a related source integration template, in which an introductory adverb clause refers to her source's author and the main clause delivers the quotation: for example, from her first paragraph, "As Christine Yano describes in her book *Crowning the Nice Girl*, 'Beauty pageants are but one extension of a global network of gendered images proliferating through media, fashion, and celebrity culture' (18)" (1). The adverb clause's verb "describes" has been chosen to relay precisely Yano's stance in her writing. The original context of borrowed source content is an important part of representing your sources accurately and fairly; choose the wrong signal verb from the hundreds English offers to define the varieties and nuances of human communication, and you risk misstating your source's attitude and intent, harming your credibility in the process. If you remember how much you dislike being misquoted by family and friends, you may better understand how published authors feel when their words are mischaracterized or taken out of context.

As patterns for source integration deviate further from the basic formula, you have more stylistic freedom and greater need for mastering the conventions of English mechanics. The general rule is to fit your writing and your source's writing together seamlessly, producing a composite sentence with structural integrity, logical coherence, and grammatical correctness. Sometimes, this practice means using a piece of a source's complete sentence, rather than a whole, as Bidaure demonstrates: "One popular show is *Toddlers and Tiaras* on The Learning Channel, documenting 'little girls . . . [parading] around wearing makeup, false eyelashes, spray tans, and fake hair to be judged on their beauty, personality, and costumes' ("About")" (2). Here, Bidaure's main clause comments on her TV-show source, ending with a participial phrase in which the "little girls" quotation fills the phrase's noun slot[5]. Bidaure's example also illustrates two techniques you may use to adapt a source quotation to your writing's syntax: ellipsis and bracketing.

To understand how Bidaure has modified her source, let us examine the original: "On any given weekend, on stages across the country, little girls and boys parade around wearing makeup, false eyelashes, spray tans and fake hair to be judged on their beauty, personality and costumes" ("About"). Bidaure selected this sentence's main clause, omitting the introductory prepositional phrases describing the prevalence of child beauty pageants in America. What else did Bidaure omit from this source statement? Her ellipsis after "little girls" sits where "and boys" appears in the original, a phrase dropped because it diverts attention from her paper's focus. The brackets around "parading" in Bidaure's text signify an alteration of the original, which we see is "parade," a verb conjugated for the

---

[5] If you expected to see a comma follow "documenting" because you believe commas always precede quotations, please note that omitting the comma here is correct because participial phrases never use commas to separate the participle from its noun object.

main clause about "little girls and boys." Having written her own main clause, Bidaure does not need to borrow that syntax from her source; she needs to change the structure of what she borrows so that it completes her sentence. Transforming the conjugated verb into a present participle achieves this purpose, and using brackets alerts readers to this structural change. Permissible minor adaptations of sources with brackets include providing names or nouns for clarification of the original's pronouns, changing singular nouns or pronouns to plural (and vice versa) to agree with antecedents, and shifting verb tense for accurate chronology. At no time are you permitted to remove words with ellipses or add words with brackets in order to make your source say something it really did not. Sadly, our society is rife with examples from advertising to politics of this unethical usage. As a member of researched writing's community, you are expected to hold yourself and your work to the higher moral standard that protects scholarship's search for truth. Using your sources accurately and fairly ensures your contributions to the communal quest for knowledge and understanding will always be welcome.

Citing Your Sources

To cite sources is not only to name them as you integrate their words and ideas into your writing but also to provide complete publication information about them as proof they exist and you read them. You help yourself achieve the second purpose when you develop the habit of taking bibliography notes before you begin recording content and reaction notes during active reading. Articles saved or printed from electronic databases come with all their publication details; some databases even offer a citation link that provides already prepared bibliographic citations you may copy and paste wherever you need them. Add to this technological assistance the convenience of software and Web sites that create citations for you from forms you complete with your sources' publication data, and you might wonder what there is to learn about source citation beyond instructions for using these tools. Source citation is, in effect, a collection of languages within the culture of scholarship, each discipline or field of study choosing one of these languages as part of its professional identification. A researcher in the health sciences, for example, is often expected by her peers to follow American Psychological Association (APA) citation conventions because they all perceive themselves as "health professionals." Scholars of the world's languages and literatures work adhere to the citation standards established by the Modern Language Association (MLA) to cement their professional identity, too. Many other citation standards exist, creating a Tower of Babel of methods, and as a college student you will very likely need to learn and use more than one. You will more effectively use the citation tools modern technology offers once you understand the general principles of any citation system.

MLA citation starts with the premise that source references in the body of a paper should not break the flow of reading. Readers do not enjoy stopping to look at footnotes or endnotes to learn source information. A complete MLA citation of any source, therefore, uses parenthetical references, as many as required, in the paper's text and a single bibliographic citation in the closing works cited list to inform readers without distracting them. You have seen many examples of parenthetical citation while reading this chapter, instances where after a source was named and/or used the sentence ended with parentheses containing either a name or a number or both. Hopefully, seeing these notations did not obstruct your reading; they were placed so that if you were curious to learn where your author found a specific source, you could mark the page and turn later to the works cited list at the end of this chapter to find all the publication information needed to acquire your own copy. To use parenthetical references correctly, remember that they work in concert with source information already included in your sentence's wording. For instance, when you name the author in your lead-in to a direct quotation, the parenthetical reference at the end should include only the page number where you found the quote in its source document. If you have quoted an online source without page numbers, that sentence needs no parenthetical reference at all if you have named the author in your sentence. Quoting an anonymous online source without first introducing its title leads to ending that sentence with parentheses containing that title (or a shortened version of long titles). As a general rule, parenthetical references are kept clean by not using abbreviations or words for *page* or commas between the author's name and page number. Exceptions and special situations do exist, however, and consulting a writers' handbook, especially the most recent edition of the *MLA Handbook for Writers of Research Papers*[6], will help you address them.

Parenthetical references cannot work alone, so if you have *not* prepared a works cited list naming every source that appears in your text, your citation work is not done. The converse is also true: every source listed on your works cited *must* be referenced in your text and linked to a summary, paraphrase, or direct quotation. While you may refer to one source many times as you develop and support your topic, your works cited list will contain one bibliographic citation for it. If this source has page numbers, any parenthetical reference will identify only the one or more pages associated with the source content you summarized, paraphrased, or quoted at that point in your writing; your works cited citation will report the complete range of page numbers where the source was printed. As your researched writing becomes more complex, synthesizing ideas and information from an extensive array of sources, it becomes more necessary for you to take special care in matching your works cited list to your in-text references. Correctness of source usage and citation may take precedence, for some readers, over other aspects of your researched writing in determining the credibility and value of your work. While every complexity of correct citation lies beyond the scope of this chapter, examining a few sample citations of the most common sources students encounter may help you grasp some key principles of the MLA system.

---

[6] As of 2009, the *MLA Handbook* is in a 7th edition featuring significant changes to citation practices over earlier editions. Whenever you write with research, follow the most up-to-date guidelines for your citation system.

Principle #1: Citation format changes with the type of source being cited.

Let us imagine a scenario in which you are writing about Jonathan Swift's "A Modest Proposal," a satirical essay originally published in 1729. If you read the copy of this essay located in your *Red Rock Reader*, you would use the MLA citation template for "works in anthologies" (MLA 158). If, however, you read an e-text version of Swift's piece online, your citation should follow the MLA template for Web publications "also appear[ing] in print" (MLA 187-88). Please compare and contrast these two citations.

```
Swift, Jonathan. "A Modest Proposal." Red Rock Reader. 4th

      ed. Ed. Richard Logsdon, Todd Moffett, and Tina

      Eliopulos. Boston: Pearson Custom, 2012. 276-81.

      Print.

Swift, Jonathan. A Modest Proposal. 1729. Project Gutenberg.

      27 July 2008. Web. 26 Feb. 2012.
```

Both citations start with your source author's name and his work's title. Their similarities stop there. The *Red Rock Reader* citation lists Swift's essay as a shorter work collected with others and italicizes the book's title to signify its status as a longer, independent publication. The *Project Gutenberg* citation reflects the e-book publisher's decision to present Swift's work as an e-book and to furnish its first printing date. In the anthology citation, this publication information follows the book's title: the book's edition number and editors; its city of publication, publisher's imprint and company name, and copyright date; and the page numbers locating Swift's essay inside. The word *Print* reports the anthology's medium of publication. In the Web publication citation, the Web site title is italicized and followed by the date on which Swift's work was added to its database; the word *Web* identifies the medium of publication and the closing date reports when a reader first accessed this online source. For each bibliographic citation you prepare, you must first classify your source correctly so that you can choose its proper template in the MLA system.

Principle #2: Editors of an anthology are not authors of its collected works.

Source citation requires writers to know some basic facts about publishing. For example, you must be able to differentiate *author* from *editor* when working with anthologies like *Red Rock Reader*. When an anthology's producers write original material, such as the instructional content at the front of this book's modes chapters, they are deemed its authors, and you may cite them as authors only if you have summarized, paraphrased, or quoted from that content. The anthology producers' relationship to anthologized articles, essays, and stories is that of editors because they did not create these works but selected and arranged them to make the anthology.

When citing more than one work collected in an anthology, you may establish a network of cross-references in your works cited list. One citation must provide the complete publication data for the anthology itself. Then, citations for selected works may use an abbreviated reference to that complete anthology citation and avoid repeating most of the publishing information. The examples here demonstrate cross-references to *Red Rock Reader*.

Chopin, Kate. "The Story of an Hour." Logsdon, Moffett, and

Eliopulos 343-44.

Logsdon, Richard, Todd Moffett, and Tina Eliopulos, eds. *Red*

Rock Reader. 4th ed. Boston: Pearson Custom, 2012.

Print.

Nelson, Jennifer Schwenk. "Writing with Research: How to

Integrate Other Writers' Ideas and Information with

Your Own." Logsdon, Moffett, and Eliopulos 290-310.

Swift, Jonathan. "A Modest Proposal." Logsdon, Moffett, and

Eliopulos 276-81.

Principle #3: Articles in Internet magazines and articles in library databases are two different sources and use different citation templates.

As magazine publishers wrestle with paper publishing's uncertain future, they continue to experiment with different business models, looking for ways to make information distribution profitable. Time, Inc. offers an illuminating example that illustrates how changes in the publishing industry cause repercussions for researchers and writers. The company's weekly paper publication, *Time*, has a companion Web site offering subscribers-only online access to electronic texts of the magazine's articles as well as supplementary, online-only content. However, Time, Inc. also maintains a free-access Web site featuring continuously updated news stories and sensationalism, a different constellation of content than that offered subscribers. If you do not subscribe to *Time*, do not purchase copies at your local bookstore or newsstand, and cannot visit your local library to read its paper copies, how can you acquire full-text articles from this publication? Visiting Time, Inc.'s free Web site cannot help you, but *EBSCO Complete* can. As you study the two sample citations below, can you identify the source type of each?

Chua-Eoan, Howard. "The Murder of JonBenet Ramsey, 1996."

    Time Specials: Crimes of the Century. Time, Inc., 1

    Mar. 2007. Web. 27 Feb. 2012.

Gleick, Elizabeth, et al. "Playing at Pageants." *Time* 20

    Jan. 1997: 48. *Academic Search Premier*. Web. 27 Feb.

    2012.

Principle #4: People who study source citation can correct errors discovered in citations packaged with database articles or prepared by Web sites.

Mistakes happen; everyone makes them. These admissions of human frailty are not rationalizations for assuming that no one should care whether citations already prepared for your full-text database resources are 100% correct. Quite the contrary, we writers cannot escape our obligation to improve our knowledge and understanding of citation rules so that we can ensure the accuracy and completeness of our source documentation.

Here is an example of an improperly crafted citation for *CQ Researcher*'s 2009 report on human rights.

Jost, Kenneth. "Human Rights Issues." *CQ Researcher*. CQ

    Press, 30 Oct. 2009. Web. 27 Feb. 2012.

What is wrong with it? Answering this question begins with close examination of the source itself to determine its classification in the MLA citation system. Being included in an electronic database yet existing as a print periodical, Kenneth Jost's report is "a periodical publication in an online database" (MLA 192). Citations for this kind of source need the following information: the author's name, the article's title, the periodical's title with volume and issue numbers, the year of publication, and the page numbers for the print edition; then, the database name, the publication medium, and the date of researcher's access. The citation we have follows the template for "a nonperiodical publication on the Web" (MLA 184); thus, this citation misinforms readers about the source's real characteristics. The corrected citation looks like this.

Jost, Kenneth. "Human Rights Issues." *CQ Researcher* 19.38

    (2009): 909-32. *CQ Researcher Online*. Web. 27 Feb.

    2012.

Once you have prepared bibliographic citations for all your sources, you arrange them in alphabetical order to create your works cited list. This list is not numbered!

Hanging indentation—that is, authors' names and anonymous sources' titles touching the left margin with space underneath—facilitates ease of reading. With your citations carefully completed, punctuated, formatted, and arranged at the end of your well-developed, insightful essay, you can take pride in a research job well done.

PARADIGM

Regardless of rhetorical situation or writing purpose, or the array of modes you first select to guide your research and then combine to develop and support your topic, the key point to remember about writing with research is this: you control your paper. In practice, this control looks like paragraphs that begin with your original topic sentences, all associated with your paper's thesis and not a source. This control also appears in your understanding of each source's different relative value to your development and support of that thesis, as in your ability to draw out hidden connections among pairs and groups of sources. This control always manifests in your careful revising and editing, your proofreading and polishing, your crafting of an artful style and sincere voice. You will have achieved success with researched writing if your readers see that you, not your sources, have shaped an insightful and engaging presentation of your topic.

SUMMARY

When approached with an open mind, research can be an engaging, even wonderful learning experience. Your curiosity may bloom and your imagination may grow with the fertile ideas and rich information you discover in the intellectual property of other writers. Granted, academic research is a demanding process; it requires both attention to detail and a soaring vision of your topic's significance to your readers. Pursuing answers to your research questions need not be a lonely or frustrating process. You inhabit a learning community where professors, librarians, tutors, and classmates are ready and willing to help you surmount any obstacle. These individuals may not be the sources you cite in your paper, but their conversations and shared experiences can inspire you to persevere until you have reached your project's finish line, the winner of new learning, authority, and confidence in your topic, your writing skill, and yourself.

Works Cited

"About *CQ Researcher Online* and Related Resources." *CQ Researcher*. CQ Press/Sage Publications, 2012. Web. 25 Feb. 2012.

"About *Toddlers and Tiaras*." *TLC*. Discovery Communications, 2012. Web. 26 Feb. 2012.

Anderson, Susan, and Amy Wallace. "Glamour Girls." *Los Angeles Magazine* 1 Oct. 2009: 148-53. *MasterFILE Premier*. Web. 21 Apr. 2011.

Ballenger, Bruce. *The Curious Writer*. New York: Pearson-Longman, 2005. Print.

Barker, Joe, and John Kupersmith, eds. "Evaluating Web Pages: Techniques to Apply & Questions to Ask." *Finding Information on the Internet: A Tutorial*. UC Berkeley Lib., 20 Sept. 2011. Web. 25 Feb. 2012.

Bidaure, Celestine. "The Price of Perfection." *Red Rock Reader*. 4th edition. Ed. Richard Logsdon, Todd Moffett, and Tina Eliopulos. Boston: Pearson Custom, 2012. 311-17. Print.

Chapman, Alan. "Johari Window." *BusinessBalls*. Alan Chapman, 2010. Web. 16 Feb. 2012.

Chimaera Consulting. "Johari Window." *Famous Models*. Chimaera Consulting Limited, 1999. Web. 24 Feb. 2012.

Cushman, Anne. "Clearing Clutter." *Tricycle: The Buddhist Review* 14.3 (2005): 42-7. Print.

Dees, Robert. *Writing the Modern Research Paper*. 4th ed. New York: Pearson-Longman, 2003. Print.

EBSCO Complete. EBSCO Industries, 2012. Web. 25 Feb. 2012.

Hekman Library. *KnightCite*. Calvin College, n.d. Web. 26 Feb. 2012.

Library of Congress. "Class H-Social Sciences." *Library of Congress Classification Outline*. LOC.gov, n.d. Web. 24 Feb. 2012.

"Library of Congress Call Numbers." *American Museum of Natural History Research Library*. American Museum of Natural History, 2012. Web. 24 Feb. 2012.

MLA. *MLA Handbook for Writers of Research Papers*. 7th ed. New York: MLA, 2009. Print.

Roth, Audrey J. *The Research Paper: Process, Form, and Content*. 6th ed. Belmont: Wadsworth, 1989. Print.

Sawyer, John. "Introduction to Library Research." English 100, College of Southern Nevada. 21 Feb. 2012. Lecture.

University Libraries. "Primary, Secondary, and Tertiary Sources." *Introduction to Library Research. Virginia Tech: Inventing the Future*. Virginia Polytechnic Institute and State University, 2012. Web. 23 Feb. 2012.

Veit, Richard. *The Student's Guide to Writing Research Papers*. 4th ed. New York: Pearson-Longman, 2004. Print.

Veit, Richard, and Christopher Gould. *Writing, Reading, and Research*. 6th ed. New York: Pearson-Longman, 2004. Print.

Wonderlich, Anna, et al. "Childhood Beauty Pageant Contestants: Associations with Adult Disordered Eating and Mental Health." *Eating Disorders* 13.3 (2005): 291-301. *Academic Search Premier*. Web. 21 Apr. 2011

This chapter was written by Jennifer Schwenk Nelson

Celestine Bidaure

Professor Eliopulos

English 102-002

2 May 2011

The Price of Perfection

From the time an individual is born to the time he or she reaches adulthood, he or she is exposed to various social learning experiences, learning how to interact with peers and within society. In general, boys are taught what it means to be masculine, and girls are taught what it means to be feminine. In order to be feminine, girls are usually taught to be docile, pleasant, and beautiful. Through various socialization devices, young girls are taught at a vulnerable age how society expects them to behave and carry themselves as they grow older. For toys, young girls are given Barbie dolls to play with, as Barbie epitomizes perfection and womanhood. Furthermore, as child beauty pageants have become increasingly popular within the United States, they are also becoming socialization agents for young girls. As Christine Yano describes in her book *Crowning the Nice Girl*, "Beauty pageants are but one extension of a global network of gendered images proliferating through media, fashion, and celebrity culture" (18). Beauty pageants, similar to various socialization agents, define the ways in which women should look, dress, and behave. However, this yearning for perfection, this socialized need to have young girls grow up into real-life Barbie dolls has taken its toll on today's girls. Although parents may feel there is no harm in showcasing their daughters in a child beauty pageant, in actuality, stressing the societal importance of beauty and perfection at such a young age can result in detrimental long-lasting effects.

Beauty pageants have been around since 1921, but child beauty pageants made their debut in 1960 in Miami, Florida, with Little Miss Universe ("Pageant History"). When six-year-old JonBenét Ramsey died in 1996, the United States was given a glimpse into the world of child beauty pageants; ever since then, child beauty pageants have grown tremendously popular. Various television shows allow curious spectators to further delve into the realm of child beauty pageants. One popular show is *Toddlers and Tiaras* on The Learning Channel, documenting "little girls . . . [parading] around wearing makeup, false eyelashes, spray tans, and fake hair to be judged on their beauty, personality, and costumes" ("About"). As the show demonstrates, child beauty pageants consist of three judging categories: talent, beauty, and a swimsuit competition. The pageants are also divided into age groups: babies, toddlers, and teens. Although the toddlers category varies from pageant to pageant, *Toddlers and Tiaras* focuses more on the toddler age group, ranging from two to six. Some of the girls documented have been participating in child beauty pageants since before their first birthdays; the parents of two-year-old Ava admit to signing her up for her first pageant when she was only eight months old. Another mother exclaimed her joy when she discovered she was pregnant with a daughter, admitting to being excited to being able to place her daughter in child beauty pageants.

One episode of *Toddlers and Tiaras* follows a five-year-old girl named Alexis. In preparation for her beauty contest, her mother Nicole decides to take her to a salon to get her eyebrows waxed. Because of a previous traumatic experience with eyebrow waxing, Alexis begs and pleads to not get her eyebrows waxed; however, despite her daughter's kicking and screaming, the mother holds down Alexis's head while the aesthetician waxes away. As this particular episode of *Toddlers and Tiaras* exhibits, although the glamorous world of child beauty pageants may maintain the façade of being harmless to children, parents are willing to subject their daughters to any means necessary in order to satisfy their obsession with flawlessness and perfection. Furthermore, many pageant parents admit to hiring professional makeup and hair artists for their girls. Once these toddlers have been made over by their makeup and hair artists, they are instantly transformed into looking like miniature adults; their facial features resemble older, more mature women while their bodies are still those of toddlers.

Pageant parents may argue that placing their daughters into child beauty pageants has its rewards. Excluding the monetary rewards that pageant winners receive, child beauty pageants teach young girls how to behave in a poised manner. Additionally, winning a child beauty pageant can give young girls a sense of accomplishment and pride, boosting their morale and self-esteem. However, underneath the veil of etiquette and emotional gratification also lie destructive behaviors and attitudes that may eventually reveal themselves as young girls grow into young women. There is an old saying that pain is beauty, but to what extent must the idealized standard of beauty consist of painful repercussions? As seemingly beautiful as beauty pageants are, they are abhorrent in the sense that they perpetuate an unhealthy obsession with society's idealized standard of femininity and beauty.

As depicted on *Toddlers and Tiaras*, pageant parents justify placing their daughters into child beauty pageants to boost their self-confidence and self-esteem; consequently, as various studies have shown, these young girls may develop negative body images when they grow older. As Anna Wonderlich and her team explain in their study of the correlation between childhood beauty pageants and adult eating disorders, women who competed in childhood beauty pageants are more likely to be dissatisfied with their bodies than women who have never competed (296). Society tends to prefer skinnier, slenderer bodies over curvier, larger bodies, and the inclusion of a swimsuit competition in a child beauty pageant reiterates this preference for slimness;

furthermore, judging young girls on their beauty stresses the social importance of perfection. Because beauty pageants are competitive in nature, young girls begin to acknowledge this constant striving for perfection; therefore, they develop negative body images and self-loathing and begin to constantly seek various methods to attain and maintain society's ideal image, to do whatever it takes to be beautiful and win life's beauty contest.

In accordance with the development of negative body images, Wonderlich and her team describe how childhood beauty pageants correlate with adult eating disorders. As shown in their study, women who participated in childhood beauty pageants are also more likely to develop an eating disorder than those who never competed (295). According to another study referenced by Wonderlich and her team, out of 131 women who participated in beauty pageants, nearly half of them were believed to have eating disorders (292). This development of eating disorders is associated with beauty pageants' apparent gravitation towards thinner contestants; there has yet to be a winner of a teen or adult beauty pageant that possesses an average-sized body. Girls who have been subjected to beauty pageants since they were younger have been socialized to praise thinness; therefore, they would be more likely to engage in disordered eating behaviors in order to remain slim and slender—unhealthy dieting, bulimia, and anorexia. The commonality of disordered eating behaviors with the appraisal of thinness equates to the ends justifying the means: young girls who participate in child beauty pageants will grow to believe it is okay to take harmful risks as long as they shed pounds.

If young girls involved in child beauty pageants eventually develop negative body images and disordered eating behaviors, then the justifications made by pageant parents are no longer credible. Pageant parents believe that having their daughters participate in child beauty pageants will give them a strong sense of confidence and high self-esteem; however, as the Wonderlich team's study shows, women who participated in child beauty pageants are more likely to have low self-esteem issues and develop depression (296). While participating in child beauty pageants may naively give a young girl a sense of accomplishment and a boost of morale, especially if a girl has won her share of pageants, the immediate emotional gratification will eventually fade as a girl grows older. Between the ages of two and six, young girls are incapable of understanding the complexities of intense competition; however, this changes as they reach adolescence and adulthood. Young girls' comprehension of competitions is the realization that only one girl per age group can walk away with the crown and scepter; once they grow older, they become aware of the various methods they can engage in to enhance their likelihood of winning.

In addition to the negative body images, disordered eating behaviors, and lack of self-esteem that girls can later develop in life, participation in child beauty pageants reaffirms the traditional perceptions of gender roles and femininity, socializing young girls to believe their self-worth is dependent on beauty and public approval. As *Toddlers and Tiaras* illustrates, girls participating in glitzy child beauty pageants wear plenty of makeup, are dressed in glamorous attire, and often opt to wear hair extensions and false eyelashes to enhance their looks; after becoming completely made over and transformed into miniature adults, they are judged on their beauty, with categories such as Most Photogenic and Prettiest Face. As Susan Anderson and Amy Wallace describe in their article "Glamour Girls," child beauty pageants are an embodiment of how society places valued emphasis on "beauty, success, and glamour." Out of the three judicial categories of child beauty pageants, the talent aspect is the only one that does not judge young girls on the basis of appearance; however, this one-dimensional category often relies on a child's playful and imaginative nature. Other than the talent aspect of child beauty pageants, these impressionable young girls are forced to believe that only their beauty will take them far in life. Child beauty pageants build a weak foundation for girls to improve their intellect, overemphasizing one's physical appearance.

Society wants its women to be creatures of beauty and perfection, and unfortunately this adult realization is being socialized at a young age with child beauty pageants being a highly influential force. As Jeannie Ralston argues in her article "The High Cost of Beauty," child beauty pageants teach young girls that "looks [are not] everything—[they are] the only thing." Older women are constantly being sold cosmetic products to conceal any signs of aging, stressing the importance of looking young despite a woman's biological age; at the same time, young girls participating in child beauty pageants are plastered with makeup and dressed glamorously, giving the impression that natural youth should be concealed with the appearance of premature adolescence. The ideal standard of beauty is not only harmful to adolescent and adult women; it is also spilling into the vulnerable minds of young girls. Child beauty pageants are all fun and games until young girls grow into older women that have developed negative body images, disordered eating behaviors, and low self-esteem.

Bidaure 7

Works Cited

"About *Toddlers and Tiaras*." *TLC*. Discovery Communications, 2011. Web. 21 Apr. 2011.

Anderson, Susan, and Amy Wallace. "Glamour Girls." *Los Angeles Magazine* 1 Oct. 2009: 148-

    53. *MasterFILE Premier*. Web. 21 Apr. 2011.

"Pageant History." *Pageant Center*. Pageant Center, 1998. Web. 28 Apr. 2011.

Ralston, Jeannie. "The High Cost of Beauty." *Parenting* Nov. 2001: 132-8. *EBSCOhost*. Web. 21

    Apr. 2011.

Wonderlich, Anna, et al. "Childhood Beauty Pageant Contestants: Associations with Adult

    Disordered Eating and Mental Health." *Eating Disorders* 13.3 (2005): 291-301.

    Academic Search Premier. Web. 21 Apr. 2011.

Yano, Christine. *Crowning the Nice Girl: Gender, Ethnicity, and Culture in Hawai'i's Cherry

    Blossom Festival*. Honolulu: U of Hawai'i P, 2006. Print.

CHAPTER FOURTEEN

LITERARY ANALYSIS

One task you may perform in your English class is a literary analysis. For this task, you will read (or view) a work such as a play, poem, novel, movie, or short story; then you will write an essay in which you discuss how that work was put together. Ideally, this task will give you a better appreciation of the work. Practically, the task will prepare you for times in your career when you might provide an analysis of a report, or a proposal, or the costs and benefits of adopting a certain course of action. Below you will find the points a literary analysis may cover and directions for how to create an essay.

THE BASIC TOOLS OF STORYTELLING

If you are experiencing a work that is telling a story, such as a play, novel, movie, or short story, then you will need to look for the six following elements: *setting*, *character*, *plot*, *point of view*, *symbolism*, and *theme*.

Setting

The setting is the time and place during which a story occurs. Few authors will tell you this information directly. You will have to look closely at how places and people are described to pick up the clues you will need. For example, if a group of people is sitting in a cave around a fire, wearing animal skins, and using tools of stone and bone, then the story might be set in prehistoric times. If a group of people is escaping in a spaceship from hostile aliens firing at them with laser cannons, then the story might be set in the future or in an alternate universe.

Setting is important because it limits how characters can act and thus creates expectations in the reader. If in the opening pages of a story a man is riding a horse and wearing a ten-gallon hat, a gingham shirt, leather chaps, and a gun belt circled by bullets, then the reader will expect the story to be a Western, or at the least a story set in the American West. The reader will also expect this man to act and think the way people acted and thought during that time.

In a fantastical setting like that of *Lord of the Rings* or *Star Wars*, looking at the details will be even more important. As viewers, we will not know the rules for how these worlds work until we see how the characters interact with their settings.

Character

A character is any agent that exhibits a distinct personality and affects the outcome of the story. A character can be human, animal, machine, or some other imaginative form. Again, as readers (and viewers), we must pay attention to how characters are described so that we can determine how they fit into the story, how they may act, and how we should respond to them (Is this person likeable? Should I be sympathetic?).

318

The most important character in a story is the *hero* or *protagonist*. This is the character that the story seems to be about, the one who has the most effect on the outcome. Other characters can be ranked as *major* or *minor* based on how much influence they have. The protagonist's love interests, allies, or rivals (the main rival being the story's *antagonist*) are usually major characters. Other characters met in passing during the course of the story are usually minor characters.

Two aspects of the major characters to consider are their *motivations* and *goals*. A motivation is the cause of a character's action; a goal is a character's desired outcome. Sometimes these two are the same, but sometimes they are not. If all we know about a character is that she hopes to run her own bakery someday, then motivation and goal are the same. But if we know that the character wants to run the bakery because her mother once owned one, then motivation and goal are different. Something in her past provides motivation for something she wants in the future.

It's important to know the characters' motivations and goals because they often shape the action and the outcome of a story. For instance, if two rival characters hope to find a buried treasure, we immediately sense a conflict between them. We must weigh the reasons each has for finding the treasure to determine whom we should root for, and we should have a sense of what would happen if our chosen character should fail. The moment when our character is closest to achieving or losing his goal is typically the moment of highest tension in the story. Our enjoyment of the story may well hinge on his success or failure and on the circumstances surrounding this outcome.

Plot

The basics of plot have already been laid out for you in chapter one (in the discussion of the best-for-last organizational strategy) and in chapter three (in the analysis of Wade Cruse's "The Vegetable Patch"). But because of the plot's importance in storytelling and analysis, we have provided more information here.

Plot and story are not the same. A story is a series of events that involves a set number of characters. A plot is the structure behind those events. The author chooses which event opens a story, which event closes it, and which events make up its contents. The author also chooses the order in which the events occur: sometimes in chronological order, but sometimes not. A *loop plot*, for example, will pose a mystery or problem in the opening and then lead us into the past to solve the puzzle for us. Such a plot shapes movies like *Titanic* or *Inception*. *Flashbacks*, like loops, return us to the past, but only for a moment or for a scene before the plot resumes its normal flow of time. A story with *subplots*—storylines featuring characters other than the protagonist—may have many events occurring at the same time.

To analyze a story's plot, you must look at the events of the story. An *event* is an action that changes the course of a character's life. If a woman decides to leave her betrothed at the altar, for example, or if she learns her husband has been unfaithful, or if her bakery suddenly goes bankrupt, then we have an action important to her life—and, in turn, to the direction of the story. These examples, by the way, illustrate three of the most important actions to look for: *decision, discovery,* and *reversal*. Sometimes, however, an action is simply a random happening that the universe may interpose at a crucial moment. If, for example, two characters need to climb to the top of a mountain and it suddenly begins to snow, the universe has stepped in to throw an obstacle in their path. Here, too, we have an action becoming an event.

A plot begins with an event that knocks the hero's life, or the universe around him, out of its usual path. This event may be called the *inducer* (in the Aristotelian plot, the initial conflict). Any action that precedes the inducer is the *exposition*, often describing the setting and the hero's circumstances. The story may form a loop, or use flashbacks, to show us the events that led to the inducer or to take us back to the inducer itself. Aside from it being near the start, there is no set moment when the inducer occurs. In *Titanic*, the inducer—the moment when the older Rose Calvert sees the news story about the ship on television—happens after Brock Lovett and his team discover the safe in the wreckage; they are still in the present time of the story. In contrast, in *Inception*, the inducer—the moment when businessman Saito offers Dom Cobb the job of planting the inception into rival Robert Fischer—takes place well after the story has entered the loop.

Another kind of inducer arises when at the story's outset the universe of the hero is already off track and the hero has not yet been affected. Alternately, the hero may be in a state of paralysis created by his universe's disorder, unable to act. (In many legends, the hero has yet to be born.) The inducer occurs either when the disorder touches the hero's life or when the hero breaks out of his paralysis (as at his birth). Again, the story may take the form of a loop, or use flashbacks, to show the events that led to the inducer or to take us back to the moment when the inducer occurred. The inducer in *Inception* is actually of this kind: Saito's job offer will allow Cobb to break out of the legal paralysis that has prevented him from returning to America and seeing his children.

The hero has three responses to the inducer. First, the hero can react immediately. Second, the hero can delay reaction, the delay occurring for a number of reasons. For example, the inducer may occur at some time or place away from the hero and the hero may not learn of it until later. Or the hero may be prevented from immediate action. Or the hero is not ready to act. And third, the hero may resist reaction or deny the inducer has occurred; in this case, a second event will occur that forces the hero to react. Rose reacts immediately, calling Lovett to ask him if he has found the Heart of the Ocean, the necklace he is seeking. Dom also reacts immediately, accepting Saito's offer and moving forward to assemble his team.

A plot ends when one of three events occurs. First, the hero restores order to his life or to the universe. Second, the hero assimilates to the new conditions brought by the inducer. Or third, the hero is overcome by the new conditions brought on by the inducer. This event is a permanent change that no further action by the characters or the universe can affect (though in a sequel . . .). Rose makes peace with her life and a final avowal of her love for Jack Dawson by dropping the necklace into the deep. Dom, too, finds a measure of peace by successfully completing his job and returning to his children—though the final image of the spinning top creates a final tease of doubt.

Point of View

Point of view is the perspective through which the story is told. Of course, the author is ultimately the person who wrote the story. However, another persona, the *narrator*, may actually give the story its voice. Thus, you may see the I-pronoun used, but you must never assume that it's the author behind the I.

We label the narrator by his or her distance from the story and by the pronouns used to identify him or her. A *first-person narrator* is one who frequently appears as a character in the story and refers to him- or herself with the I-pronouns. The first-person narrator can be *central* or *peripheral*. If central, the narrator is also the story's protagonist. If peripheral, the narrator is either a character associated with the protagonist or else someone telling the story to a waiting audience. In the latter case, the action of the story is often already complete, and the narrator is telling it in retrospect.

A *second-person narrator* stands somewhat outside the story and addresses all of the characters as *you*. The effect of this narration is to create a story that reads like an extended one-sided dialogue or else a series of challenges to the characters.

A *third-person narrator* stands completely outside the story and addresses all characters as *he* or *she*. The third-person narrator is further categorized by the control s/he has over the characters and their environment. An *omniscient* narrator can enter the thoughts of any of the characters, offer judgment on them and their actions, move the story backwards and forwards through time, or transport the setting to any place in the universe. A *limited omniscient* narrator allows the reader access to the thoughts of only one character (who thus becomes our point-of-view character) and narrows our perceptions of the universe to those of that character. This narrator offers no judgment. Time and place change only if the character changes position. An *objective* narrator stays completely out of the thoughts of the characters and simply records the surface details of their appearances and actions. In this mode, the narrator is like a camera that follows the characters around.

Symbolism

Symbolism is the use of symbols, and *symbols* in turn are objects or actions that have a meaning beyond themselves. For example, on a first date, a man gives a woman a bird he has folded out of paper. The bird is just that to an outside observer—a bird. However, for the man it might symbolize the effort he is willing to make to please the woman. For the woman, the bird might represent that first date and the beginning of their relationship. If, later in the story, the woman encases the bird in glass, or throws it into a fire, then her action becomes symbolic: an acknowledgment or a rejection of the man's efforts, or her feelings about the relationship itself.

Symbols grow out of the meanings that the characters, the narrator, and we as readers attach to those objects and actions. They may create a web that lies under the surface of the story. When that web is discovered, it may help our understanding of the characters' motivations and goals, of the shape of the plot, and of the theme of the story.

Theme

A theme is a broad conclusion that the work as a whole draws about the characters and their actions. Typically, a theme involves an idea such as love, time, fate, or some other cultural or universal concept. Thus, if in a story a man and a woman grow to love each other but must endure separations, temptations, struggles, and other obstacles before they can unite happily at the end, one theme of the story might be that love is worth the difficulties one might face.

Because of its scope, a theme depends upon the other elements described above. Setting, character, plot, and the rest will all have something to contribute to the building of a theme, so you will have to pay close attention to them. Rarely will a modern storyteller simply lay out a theme in the introduction or in the conclusion the way a fable might, or the way we present a controlling idea when writing expository essays.

Since stories are individual creations with their own settings, characters, plots, and so on, they will each have a unique vision in their themes even if they tackle the same ideas. The movies *Titanic* and *Inception* both treat the idea of love—they even feature the same lead actor—but the theme they each develop is quite different. In the first, when Rose takes Jack's last name after her rescue and, much later, sends the necklace to his grave, the theme is that love (not precious jewelry) is worth keeping. In the second, when Dom finds his life increasingly troubled by his memories of his dead wife, Mal—at the end, she tries to prevent his return from the realm of dreams to the real world—the theme is that when love becomes obsessive and dangerous, it must be let go.

It's also possible that a well-crafted story has more than one theme. If two or more ideas are in play in the characters' actions, then the story will say something about each. *Titanic* has something to say about human arrogance: the moment when humanity thinks itself invulnerable is the moment when the universe will put an iceberg in its path. *Inception* warns us that perhaps the suggestive power of dreams should not be manipulated toward selfish ends.

THE BASIC TOOLS OF POETRY

When you experience a poem, you will need to use all of the elements described above when creating your analysis. However, you will also have four others to consider.

Narrative or Lyric

All poems can be broadly categorized as *narrative* or *lyric*. A narrative poem is one that tells a story. It can be long or short, but it will have a clearly defined plot following the model described above. To understand the narrative poem, then, you must closely follow the events of the plot. Certain types of poems, like the epic or the ballad, will almost always be narratives. Thus, poems such as Homer's *Iliad* and *Odyssey* (both epics) and Samuel Coleridge's "The Rime of the Ancient Mariner" (a ballad) fall into this category.

A lyric poem is one that surrounds a central image or series of images. An *image* is a picture, though in poetry (and in storytelling) images must be created using words rather than paint or clay or film. Typically, the lyric poem is short, no more than a page or two, though some can run longer. The image at the heart of the poem will likely have a symbolic meaning that will be central to its theme; identifying the image, then, is paramount to understanding the poem.

Closed Form or Open Form

In form, all poems distinguish themselves from prose by the use of line breaks and stanzas. A *line break* is the poet's conscious ending of a line before the end of the page. Prose forms such as the short story, novel, or essay let the lines run as wide as the page, breaking only at the ends of paragraphs. Poems, on the other hand, have internal rules, determined by the poet or by the poem itself, as to when lines end. The result is that a poem looks quite different from a short story or a novel when printed.

A *stanza* is a series of lines set together as a unit. It is the rough equivalent of the paragraph in prose writing. Usually, stanzas are separated from one another by an extra blank line, though there are other methods. Stanzas, too, have internal rules governed by the poet or by the type of poem; thus, a poem could be written as a series of one- or two-line stanzas, or it could have stanzas of different lengths, or it could have no stanzas at all, just one continuous stream of lines.

Beyond these similarities, though, all poems can further be categorized as *closed form* or *open form*. A closed-form poem has strict rules for the length of lines and stanzas, the use of rhymes and repetition, and the pattern of stressed and unstressed syllables (called a *foot*). A sonnet, for example, has fourteen lines of ten syllables each, the syllables generally in an unstressed-stressed pattern. It also has two rhyme schemes that affect the organization of the poem. A ballad usually relies on four-line stanzas following an 8-6-8-6 or 4-4-6, 4-4-6 syllable count and an alternating rhyme scheme. Villanelles, pantoums, and sestinas have a set pattern of repeated lines (or words) and stanza lengths. The poet, however, may create her own closed form by following an original pattern of rhymes, syllables, and stanza lengths.

An open-form poem follows no strict patterns of rhyme, syllable count, repetition, or stanza length. Hence, most open-form poems are called *free verse*. Open-form poems, however, aren't simply poems without rules, and they aren't prose passages forced into a poetic form with arbitrary line breaks. The poet's use of stanzas and line breaks still follows a conscious design, and we as readers must determine the nature of that design. Further, the poet uses other resources of language to distinguish his work as a poem. Some of those resources are described below.

Concrete versus Abstract

As you learned earlier, description is the most basic mode of essay writing. However, all writers, no matter what they are writing, must use details to make an effective impression upon the reader. Essays use details to support a thesis or tell a narrative. Fiction uses details to bring settings, characters, and symbols to life. But poetry, in particular lyric poetry, is largely defined by the skill with which writers create and use details that appeal to the senses.

Sensory details must be *concrete* rather than *abstract*. We have touched upon this difference, and the importance of concreteness, before, but this concept bears repeating. A concrete detail such as *red 1966 Mustang convertible* makes a far bigger impression than does the abstract *vehicle*. Not only will a reader be able to visualize the car, but all readers will be able to visualize the same car, a necessary step in creating images. Poems that repeat vague terms like *love, sorrow, death,* or *joy,* will never make the experience of these concepts personal to the reader.

Some poets, like John Keats in his "Ode to a Nightingale," will try to overwhelm the reader with sensory details not to cause confusion but to break open the shell of our conscious and lift us to a greater level of physical, moral, or spiritual awareness. Done correctly, the poem will forevermore change how we view the world around us. Hence, Keats, by taking such great pains to describe the nightingale's music, and the setting in which the narrator listens to it, has changed the experience of birdsong from mere enjoyment to high transcendence.

Compression

All writers may use *figures of speech* to make their language musical, meaningful, or memorable. Speechwriters use these figures so that listeners will retain the key themes of the speech. Fiction writers use figures to subtly underscore dramatic moments in a story. But again, however, poets go a step further. Poetry might be described as the art of using concentrated figures to squeeze the greatest amount of meaning into the fewest number of words. This art is also known as *compression*.

The fundamental figures are widely known: *simile, metaphor, metonymy, synecdoche.* These can be classified as figures of comparison. There are also figures of opposition such as *litotes, paradox,* and *antithesis.* Others, such as *parallelism, anaphora,* and *epistrophe,* create pleasing forms of repetition. *Elision* drops unneeded words so that sentences are more compact. *Function shift* lets poets turn nouns into verbs, or verbs into adjectives, and so on, to create colorful descriptions that arrest the eyes. The *rule of three* can create harmonies of sound, sense, and structure that reinforce the connection between a poem's form and its content.

PARADIGM

When writing a literary analysis, start by stating the name of the author (if known) and the title of the work. In the same sentence and into the next, set forth the work's *premise*—that is, a very brief summary of what happens or what major ideas are in play.

You can usually assume that the reader of your essay is familiar with the work you are analyzing, so your premise should have just enough detail to show that you've read and understood the work. The next two sentences should present the element you will be analyzing in your paper (setting, plot, theme, compression, etc.) and your thesis. Much like the argument paper, a literary analysis requires that you take a stand. Your thesis must clearly state how your chosen element appears in your work, how it affects that work, or what greater meaning it may hold.

The body of the literary analysis then supports the stance you take in your thesis. The structure of the body paragraphs should follow the five-step model set forth in chapter one: topic sentence, narrow down, quotation, explanation, and conclusion. Each body paragraph should start with a topic sentence that, piece by piece, restates your stance. The rest of the paragraph then develops and explains your stance. The main source of support is the work itself. You must be able to show where in the work your chosen element appears and why you believe it functions as it does. For example, if you are analyzing the plot of a story, you must be able to name the events you believe are the inducer, the hero's reaction, and the climax (or alternately, the initial conflict, gradual rise in tension, and climax) and explain how those events fulfill the definitions supplied above.

To point out where your element appears in the work, you must use and cite quotations, much like you did in your researched essay. Quotations can be direct (word for word from the text and enclosed in quotation marks) or indirect (rewritten in your own words and not enclosed). To cite your sources, you must use MLA format, again as you did for your researched essay. Typically, for works of prose (novel, short story), you will cite by author's last name and the page number on which the quoted passage appears in your printed source. Poems are cited by author's last name and line number. Plays, if they are divided into act, scene, and line numbers (as Shakespeare's are), should be cited by those numbers; if not, then by page number.

However, the literary analysis is not simply an exercise in stringing quotes together. Never assume your reader sees the same meanings in the passages that you do. You will have to take the time to introduce your quotations to your reader (much like you would handle introductions at a party) and then, perhaps most importantly, take the time to explain how and why the passages support your stance.

The final paragraph of your essay should clearly signal that you have finished your analysis. As with the other essay types, you can simply restate your thesis and summarize your main points. However, depending on your instructor's guidelines, you also have the option of judging the effectiveness of your chosen element or relating your essay topic to a broader concept. You may also, if allowed, raise and refute an alternative interpretation of your element.

Following is a general paradigm for organizing your literary analysis:

Introduction
   1. **State name of author and title of work.**
   2. **State the premise of the work.**
   3. **Introduce the element(s) you will be focusing on (character, plot, etc.).**
   4. **Set forth your thesis.**

First Body Paragraph
1. Topic sentence (What aspect of your thesis will you develop in this paragraph?).
2. Narrow down: introduce quote (Who speaks? What is being said?)
3. Quotation (direct or indirect) and citation.
4. Explanation of the key terms of your quotation in light of your topic sentence.
5. Conclusion: round out the explanation to prepare reader for next paragraph.

Second Body Paragraph
1. Topic sentence (What aspect of your thesis will you develop in this paragraph?).
2. Narrow down: introduce quote (Who speaks? What is being said?)
3. Quotation (direct or indirect) and citation.
4. Explanation of the key terms of your quotation in light of your topic sentence.
5. Conclusion: round out the explanation to prepare reader for next paragraph.

Third Body Paragraph, etc.
1. Topic sentence (What aspect of your thesis will you develop in this paragraph?).
2. Narrow down: introduce quote (Who speaks? What is being said?)
3. Quotation (direct or indirect) and citation.
4. Explanation of the key terms of your quotation in light of your topic sentence.
5. Conclusion: round out the explanation to prepare reader for next paragraph.

Conclusion (options)
1. Restate thesis and summarize main points.
2. Judge whether or not the element as used helps or hinders the work.
3. Discuss how literary element analyzed in essay reflects the human community.
4. Refute an alternative interpretation of the element you have chosen.

Based on this paradigm, an introduction and body paragraph of a literary analysis might look like this:

> While reading William Shakespeare's play *The Tragedy of Othello*, we are saddened by the deaths of Othello and Desdemona, and we are appalled by Iago's treachery. Often, an audience will ask itself, Why did Iago do it? This question, though simple, is important to our understanding of the play because Iago's actions move the play forward. Iago is motivated by his jealousy of Othello and by his ambition to rise through the ranks of the Venetian army.
>
> The first of Iago's motivations is jealousy for Othello. He first expresses this jealousy when he relates a rumor concerning his wife, Emilia, and Othello: "It is thought abroad that 'twixt my sheets / H'as done my office" (1.3.360-1). The "office" he refers to is the duty of a husband to maintain sexual relations with his wife, so he is stating his belief that Othello has slept with Emilia. This belief, denied later by Emilia herself, is nevertheless a major reason why Iago seeks revenge against Othello.

Here is another example:

> In the short story "The Chrysanthemums," John Steinbeck describes how a woman longs to see the world beyond her farm. When a drifting repairman appears at her flower garden, she sees a chance to escape her limitations. Steinbeck uses the fence surrounding the garden and Elisa's clothing to symbolize the many boundaries she has imposed upon her life. Little does Elisa realize, however, that those boundaries might serve to protect her from those who would take advantage of her dreams.
>
> The attention given to the characters' movements around the wire fence emphasizes Elisa's need for protection from intruders. For example, Steinbeck draws his readers' attention to the Drifter's movements as he works his way from one side of the fence to the other: "He drew a big finger down the chicken wire and made it sing" (Steinbeck 348); then "He leaned confidentially over the fence" (349); and finally "The man leaned farther over the fence" (349). The fence, a boundary designed to keep out barnyard animals and others who might trample and uproot the flowers, is not strong enough to shield Elisa from the Drifter's insidious encroachment. As he physically moves near the garden, he distracts Elisa with garden chatter. Steinbeck describes how Elisa's initial "irritation and resistance" for the Drifter has

"melted" once the Drifter engages her in a conversation about the flowers (349). The Drifter's physical proximity to the flowers equals his emotional link to Elisa. Once the Drifter has overcome Elisa's boundary, he can then pursue his goal and leave.

Here is a breakdown of the steps used in the sample analysis of Shakespeare:

Introductory Paragraph

<u>Author-Title + Premise</u>: While reading William Shakespeare's play *The Tragedy of Othello*, we are saddened by the deaths of Othello and Desdemona, and we are appalled by Iago's treachery.

<u>Introduction of Literary Element</u>: Often, an audience will ask itself, Why did Iago do it? This question, though simple, is important to our understanding of the play because Iago's actions move the play forward.

<u>Thesis</u>: Iago is motivated by his jealousy of Othello and by his ambition to rise through the ranks of the Venetian army.

Body Paragraph

<u>Topic sentence</u>: The first of Iago's motivations is jealousy for Othello.

<u>Narrow down</u>: He first expresses this jealousy when he relates a rumor concerning his wife, Emilia, and Othello:

<u>Quotation</u>: "It is thought abroad that 'twixt my sheets / H'as done my office" (1.3.360-1).

<u>Explanation of Key Term</u>: The "office" he refers to is the duty of a husband to maintain sexual relations with his wife, so he is stating his belief that Othello has slept with Emilia.

<u>Conclusion</u>: This belief, denied later by Emilia herself, is nevertheless a major reason why Iago seeks revenge against Othello.

Here is a breakdown of the steps used in the sample analysis of Steinbeck:

Introductory Paragraph

<u>Author-Title + Premise</u>: In the short story "The Chrysanthemums," John Steinbeck describes how a woman longs to see the world beyond her farm. When a drifting repairman appears at her flower garden, she sees a chance to escape her limitations.

<u>Introduction of Literary Element</u>: Steinbeck uses the fence surrounding the garden and Elisa's clothing to symbolize the many boundaries she has imposed upon her life.

<u>Thesis</u>: Little does Elisa realize, however, that those boundaries might serve to protect her from those who would take advantage of her dreams.

Body Paragraph

<u>Topic sentence</u>: The attention given to the characters' movements around the wire fence emphasizes Elisa's need for protection from intruders.

<u>Narrow down</u>: For example, Steinbeck draws his readers' attention to the Drifter's movements as he works his way from one side of the fence to the other:

<u>Quotation</u>: "He drew a big finger down the chicken wire and made it sing" (Steinbeck 348); then "He leaned confidentially over the fence" (349); and finally "The man leaned farther over the fence" (349).

<u>Explanation of Key Term</u>: The fence, a boundary designed to keep out barnyard animals and others who might trample and uproot the flowers, is not strong enough to shield Elisa from the Drifter's insidious encroachment.

<u>Narrow down</u>: As he physically moves near the garden, he distracts Elisa with garden chatter.

<u>Quotation</u>: Steinbeck describes how Elisa's initial "irritation and resistance" for the Drifter has "melted" once the Drifter engages her in a conversation about the flowers (349).

Explanation of Key Term: The Drifter's physical proximity to the flowers equals his emotional link to Elisa.

Conclusion: Once the Drifter has overcome Elisa's boundary, he can then pursue his goal and leave.

The body paragraph in the Steinbeck analysis is more complex, repeating steps two, three, and four to extend the analysis of the symbolism behind the image of the fence. Note, however, that all quotations used are carefully introduced, cited, and explained so that the author has clearly located and documented his sources.

SUMMARY

The literary analysis examines the elements which make up plays, poems, novels, movies, and short stories. As noted earlier in this book, the analysis works like a division essay, breaking an object (in this case a story or a poem) into its parts, but it usually focuses on the use of just one or two of the parts. The analysis is also like an argument paper, in which you take a stance by presenting your interpretation of how the element is used. The analysis is also like the researched essay in that you must use and cite quotations in support of your stance. Much of what you learned about the narrative essay—conflict, problem, irony, crisis, climax, etc.—applies to literary works as well. If you enjoy learning how things work and have ever taken apart a toy or a gadget to see what it looks like inside, then the literary analysis should appeal to your sense of discovery.

THE CASK OF AMONTILLADO

BY EDGAR ALLAN POE

The thousand injuries of Fortunato I had borne as I best could, but when he ventured upon insult, I vowed revenge. You, who so well know the nature of my soul, will not suppose, however, that I gave utterance to a threat. *At length* I would be avenged; this was a point definitely settled—but the very definitiveness with which it was resolved precluded the idea of risk. I must not only punish, but punish with impunity. A wrong is unredressed when retribution overtakes its redresser. It is equally unredressed when the avenger fails to make himself felt as such to him who has done the wrong.

It must be understood that neither by word nor deed had I given Fortunato cause to doubt my good will. I continued, as was my wont, to smile in his face, and he did not perceive that my smile *now* was at the thought of his immolation.

He had a weak point—this Fortunato—although in other regards he was a man to be respected and even feared. He prided himself on his connoisseurship in wine. Few Italians have the true virtuoso spirit. For the most part their enthusiasm is adopted to suit the time and opportunity to practice imposture upon the British and Austrian *millionaires.* In painting and gemmary Fortunato, like his countrymen, was a quack, but in the matter of old wines he was sincere. In this respect I did not differ from him materially: I was skillful in the Italian vintages myself, and bought largely whenever I could.

It was about dusk, one evening during the supreme madness of the carnival season, that I encountered my friend. He accosted me with excessive warmth, for he had been drinking much. The man wore motley. He had on a tight-fitting parti-striped dress, and his head was surmounted by the conical cap and bells. I was so pleased to see him, that I thought I should never have done wringing his hand.

I said to him—"My dear Fortunato, you are luckily met. How remarkably well you are looking to-day! But I have received a pipe of what passes for Amontillado, and I have my doubts."

"How?" said he. "Amontillado? A pipe? Impossible! And in the middle of the carnival?"

"I have my doubts," I replied; "and I was silly enough to pay the full Amontillado price without consulting you in the matter. You were not to be found, and I was fearful of losing a bargain."

"Amontillado!"

"I have my doubts."

"Amontillado!"

"And I must satisfy them."

"Amontillado!"

"As you are engaged, I am on my way to Luchesi. If anyone has a critical turn, it is he. He will tell me—"

"Luchesi cannot tell Amontillado from Sherry."

"And yet some fools will have it that his taste is a match for your own."

"Come, let us go."

"Whither?"

"To your vaults."

"My friend, no; I will not impose upon your good nature. I perceive you have an engagement. Luchesi—"

"I have no engagement; come."

"My friend, no. It is not the engagement, but the severe cold with which I perceive you are afflicted. The vaults are insufferably damp. They are encrusted with niter."

"Let us go, nevertheless. The cold is merely nothing. Amontillado! You have been imposed upon; and as for Luchesi, he cannot distinguish Sherry from Amontillado."

Thus speaking, Fortunato possessed himself of my arm. Putting on a mask of black silk, and drawing a *roquelaure* closely about my person, I suffered him to hurry me to my palazzo.

There were no attendants at home; they had absconded to make merry in honor of the time. I had told them that I should not return until the morning, and had given them explicit orders not to stir from the house. These orders were sufficient, I well knew, to insure their immediate disappearance, one and all, as soon as my back was turned.

I took from their sources two flambeaux, and giving one to Fortunato, bowed him through several suites of rooms to the archway that led into the vaults. I passed down a long and winding staircase, requesting him to be cautious as he followed. We came at length to the foot of the descent, and stood together on the damp ground of the catacombs of the Montresors.

The gait of my friend was unsteady, and the bells upon his cap jingled as he strode.

"The pipe," said he.

"It is farther on," said I; "but observe the white web-work which gleams from these cavern walls."

He turned towards me, and looked into my eyes with two filmy orbs that distilled the rheum of intoxication.

"Niter?" he asked, at length.

"Niter," I replied. "How long have you had that cough?"

"Ugh! ugh! ugh!—ugh! ugh! ugh!—ugh! ugh! ugh!—ugh! ugh! ugh!—ugh! ugh! ugh!"

My poor friend found it impossible to reply for many moments.

"It is nothing," he said, at last.

"Come," I said, with decision, "we will go back; your health is precious. You are rich, respected, admired, beloved; you are happy, as once I was. You are a man to be missed. For me it is no matter. We will go back; you will be ill, and I cannot be responsible. Besides, there is Luchesi—"

"Enough," he said; "the cough is a mere nothing; it will not kill me. I shall not die of a cough."

"True—true," I replied; "and, indeed, I had no intention of alarming you unnecessarily—but you should use all proper caution. A draught of this Medoc will defend us from the damps."

Here I knocked off the neck of a bottle which I drew from a long row of its fellows that lay upon the mould.

"Drink," I said, presenting him the wine.

He raised it to his lips with a leer. He paused and nodded to me familiarly, while his bells jingled.

"I drink," he said, "to the buried that repose around us."

"And I to your long life."

He again took my arm, and we proceeded.

"These vaults," he said, "are extensive."

"The Montresors," I replied, "were a great and numerous family."

"I forget your arms."

"A huge human foot *d'or*, in a field azure; the foot crushes a serpent rampant whose fangs are imbedded in the heel."

"And the motto?"

"*Nemo me impune lacessit.*"

"Good!" he said.

The wine sparkled in his eyes and the bells jingled. My own fancy grew warm with the Medoc. We had passed through walls of piled bones, with casks and puncheons intermingling, into the inmost recesses of the catacombs. I paused again, and this time I made bold to seize Fortunato by an arm above the elbow.

"The niter!" I said; "see, it increases. It hangs like moss upon the vaults. We are below the river's bed. The drops of moisture trickle among the bones. Come, we will go back ere it is too late. Your cough—"

"It is nothing," he said; "let us go on. But first, another draught of the Medoc."

I broke and reached him a flagon of De Grave. He emptied it at a breath. His eyes flashed with a fierce light. He laughed and threw the bottle upwards with a gesticulation I did not understand.

I looked at him in surprise. He repeated the movement—a grotesque one.

"You do not comprehend?" he said.

"Not I," I replied.

"Then you are not of the brotherhood."

"How?"

"You are not of the masons."

"Yes, yes," I said, "yes, yes."

"You? Impossible! A mason?"

"A mason," I replied.

"A sign," he said.

"It is this," I answered, producing a trowel from beneath the folds of my *roquelaure*.

"You jest," he exclaimed, recoiling a few paces. "But let us proceed to the Amontillado."

"Be it so," I said, replacing the tool beneath the cloak, and again offering him my arm. He leaned upon it heavily. We continued our route in search of the Amontillado. We passed through a range of low arches, descended, passed on, and descending again, arrived at a deep crypt, in which the foulness of the air caused our flambeaux rather to glow than flame.

At the most remote end of the crypt there appeared another less spacious. Its walls had been lined with human remains, piled to the vault overhead, in the fashion of the great catacombs of Paris. Three sides of this interior crypt were still ornamented in this manner. From the fourth the bones had been thrown down, and lay promiscuously upon the earth, forming at one point a mound of some size. Within the wall thus exposed by the displacing of the bones, we perceived a still interior recess, in depth about four feet, in width three, in height six or seven. It seemed to have been constructed for no especial use within itself, but formed merely the interval between two of the colossal supports of the roof of the catacombs, and was backed by one of their circumscribing walls of solid granite.

It was in vain that Fortunato, uplifting his dull torch, endeavored to pry into the depths of the recess. Its termination the feeble light did not enable us to see.

"Proceed," I said; "herein is the Amontillado. As for Luchesi—"

"He is an ignoramus," interrupted my friend, as he stepped unsteadily forward, while I followed immediately at his heels. In an instant he had reached the extremity of the niche, and finding his progress arrested by the rock, stood stupidly bewildered. A moment more and I had fettered him to the granite. In its surface were two iron staples, distant from each other about two feet, horizontally. From one of these depended a short chain, from the other a padlock. Throwing the links about his waist, it was but the work of a few seconds to secure it. He was too much astounded to resist. Withdrawing the key I stepped back from the recess.

"Pass your hand," I said, "over the wall; you cannot help feeling the niter. Indeed it is *very* damp. Once more let me *implore* you to return. No? Then I must positively leave you. But I must first render you all the little attentions in my power."

"The Amontillado!" ejaculated my friend, not yet recovered from his astonishment.

"True," I replied; "the Amontillado."

As I said these words I busied myself among the pile of bones of which I have before spoken. Throwing them aside, I soon uncovered a quantity of building stone and mortar. With these materials and with the aid of my trowel, I began vigorously to wall up the entrance of the niche.

I had scarcely laid the first tier of masonry when I discovered that the intoxication of Fortunato had in a great measure worn off. The earliest indication I had of this was a low moaning cry from the depth of the recess. It was *not* the cry of a drunken man. There was then a long and obstinate silence. I laid the second tier, and the third, and the fourth; and then I heard the furious vibrations of the chain. The noise lasted for several minutes, during which, that I might hearken to it with the more satisfaction, I ceased my labors and sat down upon the bones. When at last the clanking subsided, I resumed the trowel, and finished without interruption the fifth, the sixth, and the seventh tier. The wall was now nearly upon a level with my breast. I again paused, and holding the flambeaux over the masonwork, threw a few feeble rays upon the figure within.

A succession of loud and shrill screams, bursting suddenly from the throat of the chained form, seemed to thrust me violently back. For a brief moment I hesitated—I trembled. Unsheathing my rapier, I began to grope with it about the recess; but the thought of an instant reassured me. I placed my hand upon the solid fabric of the catacombs, and felt satisfied. I reapproached the wall. I replied to the yells of him who clamored. I re-echoed—I aided—I surpassed them in volume and in strength. I did this, and the clamorer grew still.

It was now midnight, and my task was drawing to a close. I had completed the eighth, ninth, and tenth tier. I had finished a portion of the last and the eleventh; there remained but a single stone to be fitted and plastered in. I struggled with its weight; I placed it partially in its destined position. But now there came from out the niche a low laugh that erected the hairs upon my head. It was succeeded by a sad voice which I had difficulty in recognizing as that of the noble Fortunato. The voice said—

"Ha! ha! ha!—he! he! he!—a very good joke indeed—an excellent jest. We will have many a rich laugh about it at the palazzo—he! he! he!—over our wine—he! he! he!"

"The Amontillado!" I said.

"He! he! he!—he! he! he!—yes, the Amontillado. But is it not getting late? Will not they be awaiting us at the palazzo, the Lady Fortunato and the rest? Let us be gone."

"Yes," I said, "let us be gone."

"*For the love of God, Montresor!*"

"Yes," I said, "for the love of God!"

But to these words I hearkened in vain for a reply. I grew impatient. I called aloud:

"Fortunato!"

No answer. I called again—

"Fortunato!"

No answer still. I thrust a torch through the remaining aperture and let it fall within. There came forth in return only a jingling of the bells. My heart grew sick—on account of the dampness of the catacombs. I hastened to make an end of my labor. I forced the last stone into its position; I plastered it up. Against the new masonry I re-erected the old rampart of bones. For the half of a century no mortal has disturbed them. *In pace requiescat!*

STUDY QUESTIONS for "The Cask of Amontillado"

COMPREHENSION

1. As noted in the chapter on narration, most stories contain conflict, or conflicts, that are internal, external, or both. What is the central conflict of this narrative? Is it internal or external?
2. What exactly is Amontillado? What makes it so valuable?
3. How does Montresor succeed in controlling or manipulating Fortunato?
4. What is the setting for this story? How is the setting appropriate to the event—or events—narrated in this story?

DEVELOPMENT AND ORGANIZATION

1. What is the inducer? Does it knock the protagonist's life out of it usual path, or is his universe already off track when the story begins?
2. There is strong evidence of a loop plot underneath this story. What is this evidence? Explain.
3. How has Montresor dealt with the conditions raised by the inducer? In which one of the three ways does the plot resolve? Is there any irony in the way the plot resolves?

STYLE AND TECHNIQUE

1. Where does Poe make especially effective use of descriptive detail?
2. What does dialogue contribute to this story? Would the story have been as effective without dialogue?
3. Discuss the characters of Montresor and Fortunato. How are they alike? How do they differ?
4. Can you find any examples of irony in this story? Where do you find examples of verbal irony? Do you find any examples of situational or dramatic irony? Discuss your answer.
5. What form of narration is used?
6. Reread the opening paragraph to this story. What does this paragraph reveal of Montresor? Does Montresor make any observations or comments that are not necessarily reliable—that is, not necessarily to be believed? Discuss your answer in some detail.

TEN-MINUTE TOPICS

1. Write a story which you put yourself in the place of a person taking the law into his/her own hands to solve or avenge a crime.
2. Write a story about finding one's way back to civilization when lost in the wilderness.
3. Write a story in which you take steps to hide a precious secret from another person.

GRANDMOTHER'S VETO

BY STEPHEN S. N. LIU

Her lifelong dream was to see her son again and be a grandmother. Now that her half-brother Chen Ming, a successful international-travel agent in Shanghai, had brought in her one-year visiting visa to America, she would leave the village in a few days. She glued her eyes on the photo which Chen Li (or Mike Chen in English), her only son, had sent to her last Christmas. It was a family portrait in color. Her two grandsons, Dave and Tim, aged twelve and sixteen, smiling at her; in his stylish garments, Chen Li looked elegant and dignified, standing beside his wife Helen, an attractive woman who was one of the finalists for Miss Chinatown in Los Angeles years ago. Chen Li left China before the Revolution. Some American missionaries in Hong Kong had arranged a scholarship for him to study in the USA. After a decade of hard work, he had completed his PhD at UCLA, had secured a civil engineering job with the city of Monterey Park, California, and had purchased a two-story house on the hill, north of the city. In Grandmother's eyes, Chen Li was still the awkward boy she had brought up on the farm, a very obedient child with a pleasing disposition.

For many hours a day, the seventy-six-year-old woman had been thinking (and worrying) about her trip to America which, in her vision, was a vast country with sky-high buildings and broad streets, magnificently bright and new. She would love America because it had protected her son and had given him a job and family. She couldn't sleep at night while the foreign country spread out before her eyes like an ocean of lights. She murmured the very name of Monterey Park, which seemed to have overwhelmed her soul with a magic spell.

She was up early that morning, with a luster of excitement in her eyes while she was on her way to the grave of her husband who, once a high school principal, had been physically abused by the Red Guards, Chairman Mao's killing machines. He plunged himself into the river during the last year of the Cultural Revolution, like hundreds and thousands of other leading educators and scholars in China. The hillside was barren in January, and the grave was half-hidden in dog-tail grasses. Sitting on the collapsed tombstone, she talked to her husband as though he were alive. "I must leave home, my old fellow," she said. "I'm going to see our son. It has been thirty-two years since he left us. You remember Chen Li, a good kid. He's now rich and happy. When I come back next year, I'll burn more paper coins for you. Perhaps your son and his family will come home with me. Good-bye, my old fellow. I wish you could go with me. I'm a little scared. . . ."

She rose to her feet and wiped her eyes. All of a sudden, a large bird, totally black, shrieked and lifted up its heavy wings from the scrubby rocks behind the grave. She saw its fierce, tawny eyes as it swayed over her head. Never had she seen such a bird in the field before. She hurried home. Everything in the cottage appeared more dear to her than ever: the clay stove where she had cooked her simple meals, the wooden bed she had shared with her husband, and the armchair she had sat in, sewing clothes for the Commune for nearly three decades.

Her sky-journey turned out to be a nightmare. For more than twelve hours she could not eat or sleep. She felt sick in the stomach as the plane dipped or tilted through the oozing clouds. Strange faces and languages made her uneasy. She imagined that she was being carried away by that weird bird she had seen at the hillside. She had hallucinations of falling down into the sea. She opened her eyes and trembled.

Chen Li met her at LA International Airport. She felt utterly dejected at the sight of her son. He looked much older than the image she remembered in the photo. His hair was going white in his early fifties. Two distinct dark circles framed his sunken eyes, as though he had not slept for days. He was a withered man, with his bones striving to attack his skin. They hugged each other and cried. It was Friday evening. The boys had to watch ballgames on TV, and their mother was doing her shopping at the Broadway Mall.

It was difficult for the two, mother and son, to start a conversation in the car. Finally Grandmother asked Chen Li if he had been ill. He explained that he had been working hard lately. Besides his engineering job, he was also in the real estate business. They talked intermittently as the traffic was incredibly heavy during rush hour. Monterey Park had now become a newly rising Chinatown in California. Most street signs were in Chinese; some of the police officers were ABC (America-born Chinese). Anyone who spoke English in Monterey Park would be an alien in those days. "I smell rotten potatoes, son," the old woman said as they climbed the steep road and left a city of lights behind.

"It's the odor from the city dumps, mother," Chen Li explained. "We have this offensive smell when the wind blows this way. People in town have to live with it. The smog is getting worse too. Lots of wealthy people and government officers from Hong Kong and Taiwan still manipulate their way to the States."

For the first week Grandmother got all excited about her new environment. She had never seen or lived in such a beautiful house before. Since her arrival, Chen Li had taken the family out to dine in the evenings. Helen had no desire or intention to cook meals for five people in the house. Trying to be thrifty, Grandmother volunteered to cook the dinners, but the boys made faces across the table. They talked aloud and spilled food from their mouths. Helen complained in English that Grandmother should have never cooked the pork chops, and that the fried eggs had no taste. She also grumbled about her husband's spending too much money on the old woman. When her parents came to visit them from San Francisco, Chen Li didn't buy any expensive gifts for them. She mentioned the new coat and new shoes for his mother. Listening to their angry voices in their bedroom, Grandmother had no idea what was going on. She couldn't understand a word of English.

Chen Li left the house for work early in the morning. Grandmother was all by herself in the living room when Helen came downstairs for a cup of coffee. Because she couldn't speak Mandarin, she said hello to the old lady in a flat tone, and then she went on attending her daily errands. After sending the boys to school, she drove to the Monterey Beauty Shop where she worked as a part-time hairdresser. She came home with her sons about three o'clock in the afternoon. The boys, all caparisoned like west-Texas cowboys, acted exactly like their mother. Unable to say anything in Chinese, they said hi to their grandmother and scurried into the living room to watch TV for hours. They usually left home just before dusk on their bicycles to visit their schoolmates in the vicinity.

"When you were a little boy," Grandmother said to Chen Li one evening, "you stayed home and studied. Now that you're the father, you must not let the boys waste their time on TV shows."

Chen Li grinned sheepishly and confessed that Helen had spoiled the kids, and that he couldn't do anything about it.

"If you don't have time to discipline the boys, I will," Grandmother assured him. "Remember what your father used to say: 'Bringing up a son without educating him is like bringing up an ass.' I can teach them some Chinese. I can show them table manners, and I'll try to cut short their TV hours."

Ironically enough, Chen Li had fallen asleep in the midst of his conversation with his mother. He came home tired each evening; his shoulders bent forward as if an invisible burden had been placed on his back. Grandmother shook her head and sighed as she watched him sinking into the sofa, with his cigarette butt still burning in the ashtray. The boys were out playing, and Helen stayed in her room upstairs. All was quiet but the incessant howling of the two German shepherds in the backyard near the swimming pool. Again, the boys had forgotten to feed the animals. The dogs had developed a habit of resting their forelegs on the shoulders of any person who came to feed them. They had nudged the boys into the pool to swim several times. Chen Li had warned his aged mother not to go near the feeding troughs by the water. Although Grandmother sensed the danger, she couldn't stand the hungry yelling of the animals, and she had secretly brought food to the dogs when there was nobody else in the house.

Since his real estate business was going very slowly, Chen Li usually returned home a little earlier in the evenings. He always looked worried and dejected. Grandmother blamed him for smoking too much. She didn't understand why her son didn't talk back to her after the first few weeks, nor did she know that Chen Li was physically exhausted because his wife, being fifteen years his junior, had an insatiable urge for sex. She was also a big spender, buying clothes and cosmetics, often complaining about her shortage of money. Grandmother would never inquire about her son's private life.

It was late on a Friday evening when two police officers appeared at the door with the boys. Chen Li's face flashed red as he talked and bowed to the officers. Helen became furious while her husband slapped the right cheek of Tim, their elder son. Later, Grandma wished to know what had happened to the children. Chen Li mumbled but finally told his mother that the boys had forgotten to pay while buying a Nintendo at the supermarket. The old lady frowned, asking, "Was that something like stealing stuff from a store?" Her last question was never answered as Chen Li left the living room with a burning cigarette in his hand.

Months passed. Grandmother was attacked by waves of loneliness. She ate little or nothing. Through half the night, she sat by the window and watched the city lights glittering through the smog like insomniac eyes. She missed the starry skies in the old country. She longed to see those simple, honest faces in the village. Occasionally she imagined that she was on her way to visit her husband at his grave. She had left him at the hillside for almost seven months, and she had too much to tell her old fellow. She often dreamed about her small cottage under the elms, but the street traffic or the sirens from a police car woke her from her spasmodic sleep. For days she had no appetite for the fast food Chen Li had brought home to save Helen from making a long face as she cooked the evening meals. He thought that his mother must have serious eating problems. He took her to a dentist and had three of her decayed teeth removed. He also had her visiting a Chinese doctor several times in Monterey Park. Nothing was wrong with his mother. And then came the unavoidable scene between the husband and wife. Helen was alarmed to see the medical bills coming through the mail, since Grandmother had no medical insurance.

One Saturday evening, Chen Li suggested eating out. Grandmother declined the offer. She preferred cooking her own rice porridge. Later, when the rest of the family returned from the restaurant, the boys, as usual, turned on the TV while their parents sat there in silence. Chen Li started smoking, ready for bed. Grandmother had done some work in the kitchen. She shambled toward her son and said to him in a calm voice that she wanted to go back to China. She told him that she had not been feeling right, that if she had to die she would like to be buried with her husband, and that Chen Li's uncle would take care of her burial in the village. Chen Li listened to her complaint absentmindedly. Helen moved closer and demanded an English translation. He ignored her request.

When the couple retired into their room that night Helen learned about Grandmother's problems and said to her husband, "We spent so much money to get her out of China. Now she wants to go back. Just ridiculous! I bet she'll be asking you to get her back to the US in a month. What's wrong with your mother? We've done everything for her, right?"

The next day when Chen Li came home from work his wife called him from upstairs to fix the window blinds. His mother stopped him in the living room. She reminded him of what she had said yesterday.

"You can't be too serious, mother," he said in a low voice. "It wouldn't be easy for you to come back to us again. Too much paperwork with the Chinese government."

"No, I'll not come back to the States," she uttered in a flash of despair. "I feel I'm living with a bunch of strangers. My grandsons don't know me. Your wife never tries to say anything to me. What kind of family have you got? You've never bothered to teach your children about manners. They have no respect for anybody, not even you. What will become of your sons when they grow up, rascals, shoplifters, trash, burdens for the American society? I can see that you're not happy, but I can't help you. I'm too old to do anything here. I want to die in China, not in your house. Please send me back. This is the last thing I want from you." With these words, she burst into tears.

Chen Li scratched his head and lighted up another cigarette. He muttered but didn't say anything. And then came the impatient voice of his wife. "I can't put back this damned thing, Mike. Will you please come up here and help?"

"I'll get back to you later, mother," Chen Li murmured and dragged his feet toward the stairway.

The old lady sulked in the chair and felt that her son had not listened to her distress. For several months she had been restless, often thinking about her husband who enjoyed a perfect sleep in his grave. She knew well that there were thousands of Chinese in Monterey Park, yet like her son, they were all too busy making US dollars and cents. Why should they care about an old woman's problems?

One afternoon, Chen Li and Helen had gone out to visit friends in Santa Monica, and the boys were bicycling with their schoolmates at the city park. The dogs began to make noises in the backyard. Grandmother rose from the chair and went out with a large can of dog food. The animals were glad to see her and shoved their furry heads against their benefactor. Grandmother had no strength to resist the coming weight this time. The next moment she was in the pool head and feet. She cried out for help only once. Without much struggle she yielded herself to the cold grip of death.

Three days later, she was cremated at the Western Paradise Mortuary. Remembering his mother's last request, Chen Li sent her ashes to his uncle in Shanghai and asked him to place the urn beside the grave of his father.

Life went on much the same in Monterey Park: the smell of rotten potatoes in the air, the smoke-gray smog, the traffic, and the anxious human faces in the hurrying crowd. . . . Without Grandmother's chiding, the boys had more time to watch their TV shows. The dogs were sent away to a friend. Chen Li had changed a little. He had become more impatient and more cynical. He refused to talk to anyone about his mother's accident. He didn't do well in his real estate business for months, and he cursed a lot, saying the four-letter words more often than he should. Just a week before Christmas, to Chen Li's surprise and dismay, his family doctor gladly announced that his wife was pregnant.

STUDY QUESTIONS for "Grandmother's Veto"

COMPREHENSION

1. Why is it important that we know that Grandmother originally planned to spend only one year with her son?
2. What are the central conflicts of this story? Does Grandmother experience an internal conflict? If so, what is the nature of that conflict? How does the external conflict contribute to the internal conflict?
3. What is the inducer, and what is the protagonist's response to it? In which of the three ways does the plot resolve?
4. What does Grandmother learn from her visit with her son in America? Why would she not want to live there for the rest of her life?

DEVELOPMENT AND ORGANIZATION

1. Of what importance to the story is the photo described in the opening paragraph? Is Liu using the photo ironically? Explain.
2. The image of water repeats in this story. What symbolic meaning does it have? What theme does it point to?
3. What do the story's two final paragraphs reveal about the impact of Grandmother's death upon Chen Li's family? What details are especially helpful in revealing the emotional impact of the Grandmother's drowning?
4. How does the story's setting affect the central conflicts? Does it make them better or worse? Explain.

STYLE AND TECHNIQUE

1. What point of view is used to tell the story: first person or third person? What is gained by presenting everything in the story from Grandmother's perspective?
2. How would you characterize Grandmother? What sort of person is she? What is important to her?
3. How would you characterize her son, Chen Li? What is his goal? What details and/or passages prove especially helpful in revealing his character?
4. How would you characterize Chen Li's wife, Helen? What motivates her?
5. Liu sets Grandmother, Chen Li, and Helen in a triangle that strongly affects the conflicts in this story. What are the connections between the characters? What are the tensions? Which characters do you perceive to be allies? Which are rivals? For what reasons? Explain.
6. Where does Liu use dialogue? What function does dialogue serve in this story?
7. Discuss the manner and style in which Liu relates Grandmother's death. Does Liu present Grandmother's drowning as a tragic or dramatic event? Why or why not?

TEN-MINUTE TOPICS

1. Write about a family member who feels isolated from the other members. Make sure you describe each of the family members and clearly illustrate why the main character feels his/her isolation. What motivates a family—either intentionally or unintentionally—to isolate this family member?
2. Write about a time when something long anticipated turns out to be something that does not meet those expectations. What happens? What goes wrong?
3. Describe an older family photo that you or someone you love has kept for many years. Why is this photo significant?

THE STORY OF AN HOUR

BY KATE CHOPIN

Knowing that Mrs. Mallard was afflicted with a heart trouble, great care was taken to break to her as gently as possible the news of her husband's death.

It was her sister Josephine who told her, in broken sentences; veiled hints that revealed in half concealing. Her husband's friend Richards was there, too, near her. It was he who had been in the newspaper office when intelligence of the railroad disaster was received, with Brently Mallard's name leading the list of "killed." He had only taken the time to assure himself of its truth by a second telegram, and had hastened to forestall any less careful, less tender friend in bearing the sad message.

She did not hear the story as many women have heard the same, with a paralyzed inability to accept its significance. She wept at once, with sudden, wild abandonment, in her sister's arms. When the storm of grief had spent itself she went away to her room alone. She would have no one follow her.

There stood, facing the open window, a comfortable, roomy armchair. Into this she sank, pressed down by a physical exhaustion that haunted her body and seemed to reach into her soul.

She could see in the open square before her house the tops of trees that were all aquiver with the new spring life. The delicious breath of rain was in the air. In the street below a peddler was crying his wares. The notes of a distant song which someone was singing reached her faintly, and countless sparrows were twittering in the eaves.

There were patches of blue sky showing here and there through the clouds that had met and piled one above the other in the west facing her window.

She sat with her head thrown back upon the cushion of the chair, quite motionless, except when a sob came up into her throat and shook her, as a child who has cried itself to sleep continues to sob in its dreams.

She was young, with a fair, calm face, whose lines bespoke repression and even a certain strength. But now there was a dull stare in her eyes, whose gaze was fixed away off yonder on one of those patches of blue sky. It was not a glance of reflection, but rather indicated a suspension of intelligent thought.

There was something coming to her and she was waiting for it, fearfully. What was it? She did not know; it was too subtle and elusive to name. But she felt it, creeping out of the sky, reaching toward her through the sounds, the scents, the color that filled the air.

Now her bosom rose and fell tumultuously. She was beginning to recognize this thing that was approaching to possess her, and she was striving to beat it back with her will—as powerless as her two white slender hands would have been. When she abandoned herself a little whispered word escaped her slightly parted lips. She said it over and over under her breath: "Free, free, free!" The vacant stare and the look of terror that had followed it went from her eyes. They stayed keen and bright. Her pulses beat fast, and the coursing blood warmed and relaxed every inch of her body.

She did not stop to ask if it were or were not a monstrous joy that held her. A clear and exalted perception enabled her to dismiss the suggestion as trivial. She knew that she would weep again when she saw the kind, tender hands folded in death; the face that had never looked save with love upon her, fixed and gray and dead. But she saw beyond that bitter moment a long procession of years to come that would belong to her absolutely. And she opened and spread her arms out to them in welcome.

There would be no one to live for during those coming years; she would live for herself. There would be no powerful will bending hers in that blind persistence with which men and women believe they have a right to impose a private will upon a fellow-creature. A kind intention or a cruel intention made the act seem no less a crime as she looked upon it in that brief moment of illumination.

And yet she had loved him—sometimes. Often she had not. What did it matter! What could love, the unsolved mystery, count for in the face of this possession of self-assertion which she suddenly recognized as the strongest impulse of her being!

"Free! Body and soul, free!" she kept whispering.

Josephine was kneeling before the closed door with her lips to the keyhole, imploring for admission. "Louise, open the door! I beg; open the door—you will make yourself ill. What are you doing, Louise? For heaven's sake open the door."

"Go away. I am not making myself ill." No; she was drinking in a very elixir of life through that open window.

Her fancy was running riot along those days ahead of her. Spring days, and summer days, and all sorts of days that would be her own. She breathed a quick prayer that life might be long. It was only yesterday she had thought with a shudder that life might be long.

She arose at length and opened the door to her sister's importunities. There was a feverish triumph in her eyes, and she carried herself unwittingly like a goddess of Victory. She clasped her sister's waist, and together they descended the stairs. Richards stood waiting for them at the bottom.

Someone was opening the front door with a latchkey. It was Brently Mallard who entered, a little travel-stained, composedly carrying his grip-sack and umbrella. He had been far from the scene of the accident, and did not even know there had been one. He stood amazed at Josephine's piercing cry; at Richards's quick motion to screen him from the view of his wife.

When the doctors came they said she had died of heart disease—of the joy that kills.

STUDY QUESTIONS for "The Story of an Hour"

COMPREHENSION

1. How does Mrs. Mallard take the news of her husband's death? Her reaction seems to unfold in stages; describe each one. What does her reaction communicate to the reader about her feelings for Brently Mallard?
2. What season provides the story's setting?
3. What does Mrs. Mallard open her arms to welcome?

DEVELOPMENT AND ORGANIZATION

1. List the concrete details Chopin uses to capture the world outside Mrs. Mallard's window.
2. How is Mrs. Mallard physically described? Does her mental state match her age? How so? How not?
3. At what level would you place the conflict faced by Mrs. Mallard: interior or exterior? Why?

STYLE AND TECHNIQUE

1. Why tell the story from a third-person and not a first-person point of view? What are the benefits and the drawbacks of this choice?
2. What is the significance of the story's title? What is gained and what is lost in that hour?
3. Does Chopin's use of the pronoun *she* to open so many of her paragraphs affect the story's movement? How so?
4. Chopin uses very little dialogue in this story. Why do you think so little would be used? Do you agree with this decision? If yes, why? If you think the story would benefit from more dialogue, explain why and where dialogue is needed.

TEN-MINUTE TOPICS

1. Compare and contrast the marriages of the Mallards (in "Story") and the Allens (in "Chrysanthemums").
2. Is this story's message dated? Do women and men continue to find themselves in this type of a relationship? Why? Why not?
3. Rewrite the story's last two paragraphs from either Brently's or Josephine's point of view.

THE CHRYSANTHEMUMS

BY JOHN STEINBECK

The high grey-flannel fog of winter closed off the Salinas Valley from the sky and from all the rest of the world. On every side it sat like a lid on the mountains and made of the great valley a closed pot. On the broad, level land floor the gang plows bit deep and left the black earth shining like metal where the shares had cut. On the foothill ranches across the Salinas River, the yellow stubble fields seemed to be bathed in pale cold sunshine, but there was no sunshine in the valley now in December. The thick willow scrub along the river flamed with sharp and positive yellow leaves.

It was a time of quiet and of waiting. The air was cold and tender. A light wind blew up from the southwest so that the farmers were mildly hopeful of a good rain before long; but fog and rain do not go together.

Across the river, on Henry Allen's foothill ranch there was little work to be done, for the hay was cut and stored and the orchards were plowed up to receive the rain deeply when it should come. The cattle on the higher slopes were becoming shaggy and rough-coated.

Elisa Allen, working in her flower garden, looked down across the yard and saw Henry, her husband, talking to two men in business suits. The three of them stood by the tractor shed, each man with one foot on the side of the little Ford-son. They smoked cigarettes and studied the machine as they talked.

Elisa watched them for a moment and then went back to her work. She was thirty-five. Her face was lean and strong and her eyes were as clear as water. Her figure looked blocked and heavy in her gardening costume, a man's black hat pulled low down over her eyes, clod-hopper shoes, a figured print dress almost completely covered by a big corduroy apron with four big pockets to hold the snips, the trowel and scratcher, the seeds and the knife she worked with. She wore heavy leather gloves to protect her hands while she worked.

She was cutting down the old year's chrysanthemum stalks with a pair of short and powerful scissors. She looked down toward the men by the tractor shed now and then. Her face was eager and mature and handsome; even her work with the scissors was overeager, over-powerful. The chrysanthemum stems seemed too small and easy for her energy.

She brushed a cloud of hair out of her eyes with the back of her glove, and left a smudge of earth on her cheek in doing it. Behind her stood the neat white farm house with red geraniums close-banked around it as high as the windows. It was a hard-swept looking little house, with hard-polished windows, and a clean mud-mat on the front steps.

Elisa cast another glance toward the tractor shed. The strangers were getting into their Ford coupe. She took off a glove and put her strong fingers down into the forest of new green chrysanthemum sprouts that were growing around the old roots. She spread the leaves and looked down among the close-growing stems. No aphids were there, no sowbugs or snails or cutworms. Her terrier fingers destroyed such pests before they could get started.

Elisa started at the sound of her husband's voice. He had come near quietly, and he leaned over the wire fence that protected her flower garden from cattle and dogs and chickens.

"At it again," he said. "You've got a strong new crop coming."

Elisa straightened her back and pulled on the gardening glove again. "Yes. They'll be strong this coming year." In her tone and on her face there was a little smugness.

"You've got a gift with things," Henry observed. "Some of those yellow chrysanthemums you had this year were ten inches across. I wish you'd work out in the orchard and raise some apples that big."

Her eyes sharpened. "Maybe I could do it, too. I've a gift with things, all right. My mother had it. She could stick anything in the ground and make it grow. She said it was having planters' hands that knew how to do it."

"Well, it sure works with flowers," he said.

"Henry, who were those men you were talking to?"

"Why, sure, that's what I came to tell you. They were from the Western Meat Company. I sold those thirty head of three-year-old steers. Got nearly my own price, too."

"Good," she said. "Good for you."

"And I thought," he continued, "I thought how it's Saturday afternoon, and we might go into Salinas for dinner at a restaurant, and then to a picture show—to celebrate, you see."

"Good," she repeated. "Oh, yes. That will be good."

Henry put on his joking tone. "There's fights tonight. How'd you like to go to the fights?"

"Oh, no," she said breathlessly. "No, I wouldn't like fights."

"Just fooling, Elisa. We'll go to a movie. Let's see. It's two now. I'm going to take Scotty and bring down those steers from the hill. It'll take us maybe two hours. We'll go in town about five and have dinner at the Cominos Hotel. Like that?"

"Of course I'll like it. It's good to eat away from home."

"All right, then. I'll go get up a couple of horses."

She said, "I'll have plenty of time to transplant some of these sets, I guess."

She heard her husband calling Scotty down by the barn. And a little later she saw the two men ride up the pale yellow hillside in search of the steers.

There was a little square sandy bed kept for rooting the chrysanthemums. With her trowel she turned the soil over and over, and smoothed it and patted it firm. Then she dug ten parallel trenches to receive the sets. Back at the chrysanthemum bed she pulled out the little crisp shoots, trimmed off the leaves of each one with her scissors and laid it on a small orderly pile.

A squeak of wheels and plod of hoofs came from the road. Elisa looked up. The country road ran along the dense bank of willows and cottonwoods that bordered the river, and up this road came a curious vehicle, curiously drawn. It was an old spring-wagon, with a round canvas top on it like the cover of a prairie schooner. It was drawn by an old bay horse and a little grey-and-white burro. A big stubble-bearded man sat between the cover flaps and drove the crawling team. Underneath the wagon, between the hind wheels, a lean and rangy mongrel dog walked sedately. Words were painted on the canvas in clumsy, crooked letters. "Pots, pans, knives, sisors, lawn mores, Fixed." Two rows of articles, and the triumphantly definitive "Fixed" below. The black paint had run down in little sharp points beneath each letter.

Elisa, squatting on the ground, watched to see the crazy, loose-jointed wagon pass by. But it didn't pass. It turned into the farm road in front of her house, crooked old wheels skirling and squeaking. The rangy dog darted from between the wheels and ran ahead. Instantly the two ranch shepherds flew out at him. Then all three stopped, and with stiff and quivering tails, with taut straight legs, with ambassadorial dignity, they slowly circled, sniffing daintily. The caravan pulled up to Elisa's wire fence and stopped. Now the newcomer dog, feeling outnumbered, lowered his tail and retired under the wagon with raised hackles and bared teeth.

The man on the wagon seat called out, "That's a bad dog in a fight when he gets started."

Elisa laughed. "I see he is. How soon does he generally get started?"

The man caught up her laughter and echoed it heartily. "Sometimes not for weeks and weeks," he said. He climbed stiffly down, over the wheel. The horse and the donkey drooped like unwatered flowers.

Elisa saw that he was a very big man. Although his hair and beard were greying, he did not look old. His worn black suit was wrinkled and spotted with grease. The laughter had disappeared from his face and eyes the moment his laughing voice ceased. His eyes were dark, and they were full of the brooding that gets in the eyes of teamsters and of sailors. The calloused hands he rested on the wire fence were cracked, and every crack was a black line. He took off his battered hat.

"I'm off my general road, ma'am," he said. "Does this dirt road cut over across the river to the Los Angeles highway?"

Elisa stood up and shoved the thick scissors in her apron pocket. "Well, yes, it does, but it winds around and then fords the river. I don't think your team could pull through the sand."

He replied with some asperity, "It might surprise you what them beasts can pull through."

"When they get started?" she asked.

He smiled for a second. "Yes. When they get started."

"Well," said Elisa, "I think you'll save time if you go back to the Salinas road and pick up the highway there."

He drew a big finger down the chicken wire and made it sing. "I ain't in any hurry, ma'am. I go from Seattle to San Diego and back every year. Takes all my time. About six months each way. I aim to follow nice weather."

Elisa took off her gloves and stuffed them in the apron pocket with the scissors. She touched the under edge of her man's hat, searching for fugitive hairs. "That sounds like a nice kind of a way to live," she said.

He leaned confidentially over the fence. "Maybe you noticed the writing on my wagon. I mend pots and sharpen knives and scissors. You got any of them things to do?"

"Oh, no," she said quickly. "Nothing like that." Her eyes hardened with resistance.

"Scissors is the worst thing," he explained. "Most people just ruin scissors trying to sharpen 'em, but I know how. I got a special tool. It's a little bobbit kind of thing, and patented. But it sure does the trick."

"No. My scissors are all sharp."

"All right, then. Take a pot," he continued earnestly, "a bent pot, or a pot with a hole. I can make it like new so you don't have to buy no new ones. That's a saving for you."

"No," she said shortly. "I tell you I have nothing like that for you to do."

His face fell to an exaggerated sadness. His voice took on a whining undertone. "I ain't had a thing to do today. Maybe I won't have no supper tonight. You see I'm off my regular road. I know folks on the highway clear from Seattle to San Diego. They save their things for me to sharpen up because they know I do it so good and save them money.

"I'm sorry," Elisa said irritably. "I haven't anything for you to do."

His eyes left her face and fell to searching the ground. They roamed about until they came to the chrysanthemum bed where she had been working. "What's them plants, ma'am?"

The irritation and resistance melted from Elisa's face. "Oh, those are chrysanthemums, giant whites and yellows. I raise them every year, bigger than anybody around here."

"Kind of a long-stemmed flower? Looks like a quick puff of colored smoke?" he asked.

"That's it. What a nice way to describe them."

"They smell kind of nasty till you get used to them," he said.

"It's a good bitter smell," she retorted, "not nasty at all."

He changed his tone quickly. "I like the smell myself."

"I had ten-inch blooms this year," she said.

The man leaned farther over the fence. "Look. I know a lady down the road a piece, has got the nicest garden you ever seen. Got nearly every kind of flower but no chrysanthemums. Last time I was mending a copper-bottom washtub for her (that's a hard job but I do it good), she said to me, 'If you ever run acrost some nice chrysanthemums I wish you'd try to get me a few seeds.' That's what she told me."

Elisa's eyes grew alert and eager. "She couldn't have known much about chrysanthemums. You *can* raise them from seed, but it's much easier to root the little sprouts you see there."

"Oh," he said. "I s'pose I can't take none to her, then."

"Why yes you can," Elisa cried. "I can put some in damp sand, and you can carry them right along with you. They'll take root in the pot if you keep them damp. And then she can transplant them."

"She'd sure like to have some, ma'am. You say they're nice ones?"

"Beautiful," she said. "Oh, beautiful." Her eyes shone. She tore off the battered hat and shook out her dark pretty hair. "I'll put them in a flower pot, and you can take them right with you. Come into the yard."

While the man came through the picket gate Elisa ran excitedly along the geranium-bordered path to the back of the house. And she returned carrying a big red flower pot. The gloves were forgotten now. She kneeled on the ground by the starting bed and dug up the sandy soil with her fingers and scooped it into the bright new flower pot. Then she picked up the little pile of shoots she had prepared. With her strong fingers she pressed them in the sand and tamped around them with her knuckles. The man stood over her. "I'll tell you what to do," she said. "You remember so you can tell the lady."

"Yes, I'll try to remember."

"Well, look. These will take root in about a month. Then she must set them out, about a foot apart in good rich earth like this, see?" She lifted a handful of dark soil for him to look at. "They'll grow fast and tall. Now remember this. In July tell her to cut them down, about eight inches from the ground."

"Before they bloom?" he asked.

"Yes, before they bloom." Her face was tight with eagerness. "They'll grow right up again. About the last of September the buds will start."

She stopped and seemed perplexed. "It's the budding that takes the most care," she said hesitantly. "I don't know how to tell you." She looked deep into his eyes, searchingly. Her mouth opened a little, and she seemed to be listening. "I'll try to tell you," she said. "Did you ever hear of planting hands?"

"Can't say I have, ma'am."

"Well, I can only tell you what it feels like. It's when you're picking off the buds you don't want. Everything goes right down into your fingertips. You watch your fingers work. They do it themselves. You can feel how it is. They pick and pick the buds. They never make a mistake. They're with the plant. Do you see? Your fingers and the plant. You can feel that, right up your arm. They know. They never make a mistake. You can feel it. When you're like that you can't do anything wrong. Do you see that? Can you understand that?"

She was kneeling on the ground looking up at him. Her breast swelled passionately.

The man's eyes narrowed. He looked away self-consciously. "Maybe I know," he said. "Sometimes in the night in the wagon there—"

Elisa's voice grew husky. She broke in on him. "I've never lived as you do, but I know what you mean. When the night is dark—why, the stars are sharp-pointed, and there's quiet. Why, you rise up and up! Every pointed star gets driven into your body. It's like that. Hot and sharp and—lovely."

Kneeling there, her hand went out toward his legs in the greasy black trousers. Her hesitant fingers almost touched the cloth. Then her hand dropped to the ground. She crouched low like a fawning dog.

He said, "It's nice, just like you say. Only when you don't have no dinner, it ain't."

She stood up then, very straight, and her face was ashamed. She held the flower pot out to him and placed it gently in his arms. "Here. Put it in your wagon, on the seat, where you can watch it. Maybe I can find something for you to do."

At the back of the house she dug in the can pile and found two old and battered aluminum saucepans. She carried them back and gave them to him. "Here, maybe you can fix these."

His manner changed. He became professional. "Good as new I can fix them." At the back of his wagon he set a little anvil, and out of an oily toolbox dug a small machine hammer. Elisa came through the gate to watch him while he pounded out the dents in the kettles. His mouth grew sure and knowing. At a difficult part of the work he sucked his under-lip.

"You sleep right in the wagon?" Elisa asked.

"Right in the wagon, ma'am. Rain or shine I'm dry as a cow in there."

"It must be nice," she said. "It must be very nice. I wish women could do such things."

"It ain't the right kind of a life for a woman."

Her upper lip raised a little, showing her teeth. "How do you know? How can you tell?" she said.

"I don't know, ma'am," he protested. "Of course I don't know. Now here's your kettles, done. You don't have to buy no new ones."

"How much?"

"Oh, fifty cents'll do. I keep my prices down and my work good. That's why I have all them satisfied customers up and down the highway."

Elisa brought him a fifty-cent piece from the house and dropped it in his hand. "You might be surprised to have a rival some time. I can sharpen scissors, too. And I can beat the dents out of little pots. I could show you what a woman might do."

He put his hammer back in the oily box and shoved the little anvil out of sight. "It would be a lonely life for a woman, ma'am, and a scary life, too, with animals creeping under the wagon all night." He climbed over the singletree, steadying himself with a hand on the burro's white rump. He settled himself in the seat, picked up the lines. "Thank you kindly, ma'am," he said. "I'll do like you told me; I'll go back and catch the Salinas road."

"Mind," she called, "if you're long in getting there, keep the sand damp."

"Sand, ma'am? . . . Sand? Oh, sure. You mean around the chrysanthemums. Sure I will." He clucked his tongue. The beasts leaned luxuriously into their collars. The mongrel dog took his place between the back wheels. The wagon turned and crawled out the entrance road and back the way it had come, along the river.

Elisa stood in front of her wire fence watching the slow progress of the caravan. Her shoulders were straight, her head thrown back, her eyes half-closed, so that the scene came vaguely into them. Her lips moved silently, forming the words "Good-bye—good-bye." Then she whispered, "That's a bright direction. There's a glowing there." The sound of her whisper startled her. She shook herself free and looked about to see whether anyone had been listening. Only the dogs had heard. They lifted their heads toward her from their sleeping in the dust, and then stretched out their chins and settled asleep again. Elisa turned and ran hurriedly into the house.

In the kitchen she reached behind the stove and felt the water tank. It was full of hot water from the noonday cooking. In the bathroom she tore off her soiled clothes and flung them into the corner. And then she scrubbed herself with a little block of pumice, legs and thighs, loins and chest and arms, until her skin was scratched and red. When she had dried herself she stood in front of a mirror in her bedroom and looked at her body. She tightened her stomach and threw out her chest. She turned and looked over her shoulder at her back.

After a while she began to dress, slowly. She put on her newest underclothing and her nicest stockings and the dress which was the symbol of her prettiness. She worked carefully on her hair, penciled her eyebrows and rouged her lips.

Before she was finished she heard the little thunder of hoofs and the shouts of Henry and his helper as they drove the red steers into the corral. She heard the gate bang shut and set herself for Henry's arrival.

His step sounded on the porch. He entered the house calling, "Elisa, where are you?"

"In my room, dressing. I'm not ready. There's hot water for your bath. Hurry up. It's getting late."

When she heard him splashing in the tub, Elisa laid his dark suit on the bed, and shirt and socks and tie beside it. She stood his polished shoes on the floor beside the bed. Then she went to the porch and sat primly and stiffly down. She looked toward the river road where the willow-line was still yellow with frosted leaves so that under the high grey fog they seemed a thin band of sunshine. This was the only color in the grey afternoon. She sat unmoving for a long time. Her eyes blinked rarely.

Henry came banging out of the door, shoving his tie inside his vest as he came. Elisa stiffened and her face grew tight. Henry stopped short and looked at her. "Why—why, Elisa. You look so nice!"

"Nice? You think I look nice? What do you mean by 'nice'?"

Henry blundered on. "I don't know. I mean you look different, strong and happy."

"I am strong? Yes, strong. What do you mean 'strong'?"

He looked bewildered. "You're playing some kind of a game," he said helplessly. "It's a kind of a play. You look strong enough to break a calf over your knee, happy enough to eat it like a watermelon."

For a second she lost her rigidity. "Henry! Don't talk like that. You didn't know what you said." She grew complete again. "I'm strong," she boasted. "I never knew before how strong."

Henry looked down toward the tractor shed, and when he brought his eyes back to her, they were his own again. "I'll get out the car. You can put on your coat while I'm starting."

Elisa went into the house. She heard him drive to the gate and idle down his motor, and then she took a long time to put on her hat. She pulled it here and pressed it there. When Henry turned the motor off she slipped into her coat and went out.

The little roadster bounced along on the dirt road by the river, raising the birds and driving the rabbits into the brush. Two cranes flapped heavily over the willow-line and dropped into the river-bed.

Far ahead on the road Elisa saw a dark speck. She knew.

She tried not to look as they passed it, but her eyes would not obey. She whispered to herself sadly, "He might have thrown them off the road. That wouldn't have been much trouble, not very much. But he kept the pot," she explained. "He had to keep the pot. That's why he couldn't get them off the road."

The roadster turned a bend and she saw the caravan ahead. She swung full around toward her husband so she could not see the little covered wagon and the mismatched team as the car passed them.

In a moment it was over. The thing was done. She did not look back. She said loudly, to be heard above the motor, "It will be good, tonight, a good dinner."

"Now you're changed again," Henry complained. He took one hand from the wheel and patted her knee. "I ought to take you in to dinner oftener. It would be good for both of us. We get so heavy out on the ranch."

"Henry," she asked, "could we have wine at dinner?"

"Sure we could. Say! That will be fine."

She was silent for a while; then she said, "Henry, at those prize fights, do the men hurt each other very much?"

"Sometimes a little, not often. Why?"

"Well, I've read how they break noses, and blood runs down their chests. I've read how the fighting gloves get heavy and soggy with blood."

He looked around at her. "What's the matter, Elisa? I didn't know you read things like that." He brought the car to a stop, then turned to the right over the Salinas River bridge.

"Do any women ever go to the fights?" she asked.

"Oh, sure, some. What's the matter, Elisa? Do you want to go? I don't think you'd like it, but I'll take you if you really want to go."

She relaxed limply in the seat. "Oh, no. No. I don't want to go. I'm sure I don't." Her face was turned away from him. "It will be enough if we can have wine. It will be plenty." She turned up her coat collar so he could not see that she was crying weakly— like an old woman.

STUDY QUESTIONS for "The Chrysanthemums"

COMPREHENSION

1. Where and in what month is the story set?
2. What are "planting hands"?
3. What route is the fix-it man traveling?

Development and Organization

1. Does Elisa look her age? Summarize how she is described throughout the story and look at specific details.
2. How does Henry Allen evolve in this story? Does he—like Elisa—experience change? What description shows his change or his stasis as a character?
3. Considering the time period (1930s), the characters' ages, and the setting of the story (a ranch), what seems to be missing from the Allens' lives? Does this lack figure into the symbols used in the story?

Style and Technique

1. Why does Steinbeck wait until paragraph four to introduce Elisa?
2. Why does Steinbeck give such time describing Elisa's gardening clothes and, later, her bathing scene? Be specific about what these scenes communicate to the reader about Elisa's sense of self.
3. Near the story's end, Steinbeck writes, "In a moment it was over." What does the "it" refer to? Is "it" truly over? Be specific.

Ten-Minute Topics

1. Is Elisa Allen stronger or weaker than Louise Mallard (in "The Story of an Hour")?
2. In what areas of your life do you wish you had greater freedom?
3. Why do humans enjoy sports that call upon their participants to engage in physical aggression?

YOUNG GOODMAN BROWN

BY NATHANIEL HAWTHORNE

Young Goodman Brown came forth at sunset into the street at Salem village; but put his head back, after crossing the threshold, to exchange a parting kiss with his young wife. And Faith, as the wife was aptly named, thrust her own pretty head into the street, letting the wind play with the pink ribbons of her cap while she called to Goodman Brown.

"Dearest heart," whispered she, softly and rather sadly, when her lips were close to his ear, "prithee put off your journey until sunrise and sleep in your own bed to-night. A lone woman is troubled with such dreams and such thoughts that she's afeard of herself sometimes. Pray tarry with me this night, dear husband, of all nights in the year."

"My love and my Faith," replied young Goodman Brown, "of all nights in the year, this one night must I tarry away from thee. My journey, as thou callest it, forth and back again, must needs be done 'twixt now and sunrise. What, my sweet, pretty wife, dost thou doubt me already, and we but three months married?"

"Then God bless you!" said Faith, with the pink ribbons; "and may you find all well when you come back."

"Amen!" cried Goodman Brown. "Say thy prayers, dear Faith, and go to bed at dusk, and no harm will come to thee."

So they parted; and the young man pursued his way until, being about to turn the corner by the meeting-house, he looked back and saw the head of Faith still peeping after him with a melancholy air, in spite of her pink ribbons.

"Poor little Faith!" thought he, for his heart smote him. "What a wretch am I to leave her on such an errand! She talks of dreams, too. Methought as she spoke there was trouble in her face, as if a dream had warned her what work is to be done tonight. But no, no; 'twould kill her to think it. Well, she's a blessed angel on earth; and after this one night I'll cling to her skirts and follow her to heaven."

With this excellent resolve for the future, Goodman Brown felt himself justified in making more haste on his present evil purpose. He had taken a dreary road, darkened by all the gloomiest trees of the forest, which barely stood aside to let the narrow path creep through, and closed immediately behind. It was all as lonely as could be; and there is this peculiarity in such a solitude, that the traveller knows not who may be concealed by the innumerable trunks and the thick boughs overhead; so that with lonely footsteps he may yet be passing through an unseen multitude.

"There may be a devilish Indian behind every tree," said Goodman Brown to himself; and he glanced fearfully behind him as he added, "What if the devil himself should be at my very elbow!"

His head being turned back, he passed a crook of the road, and, looking forward again, beheld the figure of a man, in grave and decent attire, seated at the foot of an old tree. He arose at Goodman Brown's approach and walked onward side by side with him.

"You are late, Goodman Brown," said he. "The clock of the Old South was striking as I came through Boston, and that is full fifteen minutes agone."

"Faith kept me back a while," replied the young man, with a tremor in his voice, caused by the sudden appearance of his companion, though not wholly unexpected.

It was now deep dusk in the forest, and deepest in that part of it where these two were journeying. As nearly as could be discerned, the second traveller was about fifty years old, apparently in the same rank of life as Goodman Brown, and bearing a considerable resemblance to him, though perhaps more in expression than features. Still they might have been taken for father and son. And yet, though the elder person was as simply clad as the younger, and as simple in manner too, he had an indescribable air of one who knew the world, and who would not have felt abashed at the governor's dinner table or in King William's court, were it possible that his affairs should call him thither. But the only thing about him that could be fixed upon as remarkable was his staff, which bore the likeness of a great black snake, so curiously wrought that it might almost be seen to twist and wriggle itself like a living serpent. This, of course, must have been an ocular deception, assisted by the uncertain light.

"Come, Goodman Brown," cried his fellow-traveller, "this is a dull pace for the beginning of a journey. Take my staff, if you are so soon weary."

"Friend," said the other, exchanging his slow pace for a full stop, "having kept covenant by meeting thee here, it is my purpose now to return whence I came. I have scruples touching the matter thou wot'st of."

"Sayest thou so?" replied he of the serpent, smiling apart. "Let us walk on, nevertheless, reasoning as we go; and if I convince thee not thou shalt turn back. We are but a little way in the forest yet."

"Too far! too far!" exclaimed the goodman, unconsciously resuming his walk. "My father never went into the woods on such an errand, nor his father before him. We have been a race of honest men and good Christians since the days of the martyrs; and shall I be the first of the name of Brown that ever took this path and kept—"

"Such company, thou wouldst say," observed the elder person, interpreting his pause. "Well said, Goodman Brown! I have been as well acquainted with your family as with ever a one among the Puritans; and that's no trifle to say. I helped your grandfather, the constable, when he lashed the Quaker woman so smartly through the streets of Salem; and it was I that brought your father a pitch-pine knot, kindled at my own hearth, to set fire to an Indian village, in King Philip's war. They were my good friends, both; and many a pleasant walk have we had along this path, and returned merrily after midnight. I would fain be friends with you for their sake."

"If it be as thou sayest," replied Goodman Brown, "I marvel they never spoke of these matters; or, verily, I marvel not, seeing that the least rumor of the sort would have driven them from New England. We are a people of prayer, and good works to boot, and abide no such wickedness."

"Wickedness or not," said the traveller with the twisted staff, "I have a very general acquaintance here in New England. The deacons of many a church have drunk the communion wine with me; the selectmen of divers towns make me their chairman; and a majority of the Great and General Court are firm supporters of my interest. The governor and I, too—But these are state secrets."

"Can this be so?" cried Goodman Brown, with a stare of amazement at his undisturbed companion. "Howbeit, I have nothing to do with the governor and council; they have their own ways, and are no rule for a simple husbandman like me. But, were I to go on with thee, how should I meet the eye of that good old man, our minister, at Salem village? Oh, his voice would make me tremble both Sabbath day and lecture day."

Thus far the elder traveller had listened with due gravity; but now burst into a fit of irrepressible mirth, shaking himself so violently that his snake-like staff actually seemed to wriggle in sympathy.

"Ha! ha! ha!" shouted he again and again; then composing himself, "Well, go on, Goodman Brown, go on; but, prithee, don't kill me with laughing."

"Well, then, to end the matter at once," said Goodman Brown, considerably nettled, "there is my wife, Faith. It would break her dear little heart; and I'd rather break my own."

"Nay, if that be the case," answered the other, "e'en go thy ways, Goodman Brown. I would not for twenty old women like the one hobbling before us that Faith should come to any harm."

As he spoke he pointed his staff at a female figure on the path, in whom Goodman Brown recognized a very pious and exemplary dame, who had taught him his catechism in youth, and was still his moral and spiritual adviser, jointly with the minister and Deacon Gookin.

"A marvel, truly, that Goody Cloyse should be so far in the wilderness at nightfall," said he. "But with your leave, friend, I shall take a cut through the woods until we have left this Christian woman behind. Being a stranger to you, she might ask whom I was consorting with and whither I was going."

"Be it so," said his fellow-traveller. "Betake you to the woods, and let me keep the path."

Accordingly the young man turned aside, but took care to watch his companion, who advanced softly along the road until he had come within a staff's length of the old dame. She, meanwhile, was making the best of her way, with singular speed for so aged a woman, and mumbling some indistinct words—a prayer, doubtless—as she went. The traveller put forth his staff and touched her withered neck with what seemed the serpent's tail.

"The devil!" screamed the pious old lady.

"Then Goody Cloyse knows her old friend?" observed the traveller, confronting her and leaning on his writhing stick.

"Ah, forsooth, and is it your worship indeed?" cried the good dame. "Yea, truly is it, and in the very image of my old gossip, Goodman Brown, the grandfather of the silly fellow that now is. But—would your worship believe it?—my broomstick hath strangely disappeared, stolen, as I suspect, by that unhanged witch, Goody Cory, and that, too, when I was all anointed with the juice of smallage, and cinquefoil, and wolf's bane—"

"Mingled with fine wheat and the fat of a new-born babe," said the shape of old Goodman Brown.

"Ah, your worship knows the recipe," cried the old lady, cackling aloud. "So, as I was saying, being all ready for the meeting, and no horse to ride on, I made up my mind to foot it; for they tell me there is a nice young man to be taken into communion to-night. But now your good worship will lend me your arm, and we shall be there in a twinkling."

"That can hardly be," answered her friend. "I may not spare you my arm, Goody Cloyse; but here is my staff, if you will."

So saying, he threw it down at her feet, where, perhaps, it assumed life, being one of the rods which its owner had formerly lent to the Egyptian magi. Of this fact, however, Goodman Brown could not take cognizance. He had cast up his eyes in astonishment, and, looking down again, beheld neither Goody Cloyse nor the serpentine staff, but his fellow-traveller alone, who waited for him as calmly as if nothing had happened.

"That old woman taught me my catechism," said the young man; and there was a world of meaning in this simple comment.

They continued to walk onward, while the elder traveller exhorted his companion to make good speed and persevere in the path, discoursing so aptly that his arguments seemed rather to spring up in the bosom of his auditor than to be suggested by himself. As they went, he plucked a branch of maple to serve for a walking stick, and began to strip it of the twigs and little boughs, which were wet with evening dew. The moment his fingers touched them they became strangely withered and dried up as with a week's sunshine. Thus the pair proceeded, at a good free pace, until suddenly, in a gloomy hollow of the road, Goodman Brown sat himself down on the stump of a tree and refused to go any farther.

"Friend," said he, stubbornly, "my mind is made up. Not another step will I budge on this errand. What if a wretched old woman do choose to go to the devil when I thought she was going to heaven: is that any reason why I should quit my dear Faith and go after her?"

"You will think better of this by and by," said his acquaintance, composedly. "Sit here and rest yourself a while; and when you feel like moving again, there is my staff to help you along."

Without more words, he threw his companion the maple stick, and was as speedily out of sight as if he had vanished into the deepening gloom. The young man sat a few moments by the roadside, applauding himself greatly, and thinking with how clear a conscience he should meet the minister in his morning walk, nor shrink from the eye of good old Deacon Gookin. And what calm sleep would be his that very night, which was to have been spent so wickedly, but so purely and sweetly now, in the arms of Faith! Amidst these pleasant and praiseworthy meditations, Goodman Brown heard the tramp of horses along the road, and deemed it advisable to conceal himself within the verge of the forest, conscious of the guilty purpose that had brought him thither, though now so happily turned from it.

On came the hoof tramps and the voices of the riders, two grave old voices, conversing soberly as they drew near. These mingled sounds appeared to pass along the road, within a few yards of the young man's hiding-place; but, owing doubtless to the depth of the gloom at that particular spot, neither the travellers nor their steeds were visible. Though their figures brushed the small boughs by the wayside, it could not be seen that they intercepted, even for a moment, the faint gleam from the strip of bright sky athwart which they must have passed. Goodman Brown alternately crouched and stood on tiptoe, pulling aside the branches and thrusting forth his head as far as he durst without discerning so much as a shadow. It vexed him the more, because he could have sworn, were such a thing possible, that he recognized the voices of the minister and Deacon Gookin, jogging along quietly, as they were wont to do, when bound to some ordination or ecclesiastical council. While yet within hearing, one of the riders stopped to pluck a switch.

"Of the two, reverend sir," said the voice like the deacon's, "I had rather miss an ordination dinner than to-night's meeting. They tell me that some of our community are to be here from Falmouth and beyond, and others from Connecticut and Rhode Island, besides several of the Indian powwows, who, after their fashion, know almost as much deviltry as the best of us. Moreover, there is a goodly young woman to be taken into communion."

"Mighty well, Deacon Gookin!" replied the solemn old tones of the minister. "Spur up, or we shall be late. Nothing can be done, you know, until I get on the ground."

The hoofs clattered again; and the voices, talking so strangely in the empty air, passed on through the forest, where no church had ever been gathered or solitary Christian prayed. Whither, then, could these holy men be journeying so deep into the heathen wilderness? Young Goodman Brown caught hold of a tree for support, being ready to sink down on the ground, faint and overburdened with the heavy sickness of his heart. He looked up to the sky, doubting whether there really was a heaven above him. Yet there was the blue arch, and the stars brightening in it.

"With heaven above and Faith below, I will yet stand firm against the devil!" cried Goodman Brown.

While he still gazed upward, into the deep arch of the firmament, and had lifted his hands to pray, a cloud, though no wind was stirring, hurried across the zenith and hid the brightening stars. The blue sky was still visible, except directly overhead, where this black mass of cloud was sweeping swiftly northward. Aloft in the air, as if from the depths of the cloud, came a confused and doubtful sound of voices. Once the listener fancied that he could distinguish the accents of towns-people of his own, men and women, both pious and ungodly, many of whom he had met at the communion table, and had seen others rioting at the tavern. The next moment, so indistinct were the sounds, he doubted whether he had heard aught but the murmur of the old forest, whispering without a wind. Then came a stronger swell of those familiar tones, heard daily in the sunshine, at Salem village, but never until now from a cloud of night. There was one voice, of a young woman, uttering lamentations, yet with an uncertain sorrow, and entreating for some favor, which, perhaps, it would grieve her to obtain. And all the unseen multitude, both saints and sinners, seemed to encourage her onward.

"Faith!" shouted Goodman Brown, in a voice of agony and desperation; and the echoes of the forest mocked him, crying—"Faith! Faith!" as if bewildered wretches were seeking her, all through the wilderness.

The cry of grief, rage, and terror, was yet piercing the night, when the unhappy husband held his breath for a response. There was a scream, drowned immediately in a louder murmur of voices, fading into far-off laughter, as the dark cloud swept away, leaving the clear and silent sky above Goodman Brown. But something fluttered lightly down through the air and caught on the branch of a tree. The young man seized it, and beheld a pink ribbon.

"My Faith is gone!" cried he, after one stupefied moment. "There is no good on earth; and sin is but a name. Come, devil! for to thee is this world given."

And maddened with despair, so that he laughed loud and long, did Goodman Brown grasp his staff and set forth again, at such a rate that he seemed to fly along the forest path rather than to walk or run. The road grew wilder and drearier and more faintly traced, and vanished at length, leaving him in the heart of the dark wilderness, still rushing onward with the instinct that guides mortal man to evil. The whole forest was peopled with frightful sounds; the creaking of the trees, the howling of wild beasts, and the yell of Indians; while, sometimes, the wind tolled like a distant church bell, and sometimes gave a broad roar around the traveller, as if all Nature were laughing him to scorn. But he was himself the chief horror of the scene, and shrank not from its other horrors.

"Ha! ha! ha!" roared Goodman Brown when the wind laughed at him. "Let us hear which will laugh loudest. Think not to frighten me with your deviltry. Come witch, come wizard, come Indian powwow, come devil himself, and here comes Goodman Brown. You may as well fear him as he fear you."

In truth, all through the haunted forest there could be nothing more frightful than the figure of Goodman Brown. On he flew among the black pines, brandishing his staff with frenzied gestures, now giving vent to an inspiration of horrid blasphemy, and now shouting forth such laughter as set all the echoes of the forest laughing like demons around him. The fiend in his own shape is less hideous than when he rages in the breast of man. Thus sped the demoniac on his course, until, quivering among the trees, he saw a red light before him, as when the felled trunks and branches of a clearing have been set on fire, and throw up their lurid blaze against the sky, at the hour of midnight. He paused, in a lull of the tempest that had driven him onward, and heard the swell of what seemed a hymn, rolling solemnly from a distance with the weight of many voices. He knew the tune; it was a familiar one in the choir of the village meeting-house. The verse died heavily away, and was lengthened by a chorus, not of human voices, but of all the sounds of the benighted wilderness pealing in awful harmony together. Goodman Brown cried out, and his cry was lost to his own ear by its unison with the cry of the desert.

In the interval of silence he stole forward until the light glared full upon his eyes. At one extremity of an open space, hemmed in by the dark wall of the forest, arose a rock, bearing some rude, natural resemblance either to an alter or a pulpit, and surrounded by four blazing pines, their tops aflame, their stems untouched, like candles at an evening meeting. The mass of foliage that had overgrown the summit of the rock was all on fire, blazing high into the night and fitfully illuminating the whole field. Each pendent twig and leafy festoon was in a blaze. As the red light arose and fell, a numerous congregation alternately shone forth, then disappeared in shadow, and again grew, as it were, out of the darkness, peopling the heart of the solitary woods at once.

"A grave and dark-clad company," quoth Goodman Brown.

In truth they were such. Among them, quivering to and fro between gloom and splendor, appeared faces that would be seen next day at the council board of the province, and others which, Sabbath after Sabbath, looked devoutly heavenward, and benignantly over the crowded pews, from the holiest pulpits in the land. Some affirm that the lady of the governor was there. At least there were high dames well known to her, and wives of honored husbands, and widows, a great multitude, and ancient maidens, all of excellent repute, and fair young girls, who trembled lest their mothers should espy them. Either the sudden gleams of light flashing over the obscure field bedazzled Goodman Brown, or he recognized a score of the church members of Salem village famous for their especial sanctity. Good old Deacon Gookin had arrived, and waited at the skirts of that venerable saint, his revered pastor. But, irreverently consorting with these grave, reputable, and pious people, these elders of the church, these chaste dames and dewy virgins, there were men of dissolute lives and women of spotted fame, wretches given over to all mean and filthy vice, and suspected even of horrid crimes. It was strange to see that the good shrank not from the wicked, nor were the sinners abashed by the saints. Scattered also among their pale-faced enemies were the Indian priests, or powwows, who had often scared their native forest with more hideous incantations than any known to English witchcraft.

"But where is Faith?" thought Goodman Brown; and, as hope came into his heart, he trembled.

Another verse of the hymn arose, a slow and mournful strain, such as the pious love, but joined to words which expressed all that our nature can conceive of sin, and darkly hinted at far more. Unfathomable to mere mortals is the lore of fiends. Verse after verse was sung; and still the chorus of the desert swelled between like the deepest tone of a mighty organ; and with the final peal of that dreadful anthem there came a sound, as if the roaring wind, the rushing streams, the howling beasts, and every other voice of the unconcerted wilderness were mingling and according with the voice of guilty man in homage to the prince of all. The four blazing pines threw up a loftier flame, and obscurely discovered shapes and visages of horror on the smoke wreaths above the impious assembly. At the same moment the fire on the rock shot redly forth and formed a glowing arch above its base, where now appeared a figure. With reverence be it spoken, the figure bore no slight similitude, both in garb and manner, to some grave divine of the New England churches.

"Bring forth the converts!" cried a voice that echoed through the field and rolled into the forest.

At the word, Goodman Brown stepped forth from the shadow of the trees and approached the congregation, with whom he felt a loathful brotherhood by the sympathy of all that was wicked in his heart. He could have well-nigh sworn that the shape of his own dead father beckoned him to advance, looking downward from a smoke wreath, while a woman, with dim features of despair, threw out her hand to warn him back. Was it his mother? But he had no power to retreat one step, nor to resist, even in thought, when the minister and good old Deacon Gookin seized his arms and led him to the blazing rock. Thither came also the slender form of a veiled female, led between Goody

Cloyse, that pious teacher of the catechism, and Martha Carrier, who had received the devil's promise to be queen of hell. A rampant hag was she. And there stood the proselytes beneath the canopy of fire.

"Welcome, my children," said the dark figure, "to the communion of your race. Ye have found thus young your nature and your destiny. My children, look behind you!"

They turned; and flashing forth, as it were, in a sheet of flame, the fiend worshippers were seen; the smile of welcome gleamed darkly on every visage.

"There," resumed the sable form, "are all whom ye have reverenced from youth. Ye deemed them holier than yourselves, and shrank from your own sin, contrasting it with their lives of righteousness and prayerful aspirations heavenward. Yet here are they all in my worshipping assembly. This night it shall be granted you to know their secret deeds: how hoary-bearded elders of the church have whispered wanton words to the young maids of their households; how many a woman, eager for widows' weeds, has given her husband a drink at bedtime and let him sleep his last sleep in her bosom; how beardless youths have made haste to inherit their fathers' wealth; and how fair damsels—blush not, sweet ones—have dug little graves in the garden, and bidden me, the sole guest to an infant's funeral. By the sympathy of your human hearts for sin ye shall scent out all the places—whether in church, bedchamber, street, field, or forest—where crime has been committed, and shall exult to behold the whole earth one stain of guilt, one mighty blood spot. Far more than this. It shall be yours to penetrate, in every bosom, the deep mystery of sin, the fountain of all wicked arts, and which inexhaustibly supplies more evil impulses than human power—than my power at its utmost—can make manifest in deeds. And now, my children, look upon each other."

They did so; and, by the blaze of the hell-kindled torches, the wretched man beheld his Faith, and the wife her husband, trembling before that unhallowed altar.

"Lo, there ye stand, my children," said the figure, in a deep and solemn tone, almost sad with its despairing awfulness, as if his once angelic nature could yet mourn for our miserable race. "Depending upon one another's hearts, ye had still hoped that virtue were not all a dream. Now are ye undeceived. Evil is the nature of mankind. Evil must be your only happiness. Welcome again, my children, to the communion of your race."

"Welcome," repeated the fiend worshippers, in one cry of despair and triumph.

And there they stood, the only pair, as it seemed, who were yet hesitating on the verge of wickedness in this dark world. A basin was hollowed, naturally, in the rock. Did it contain water, reddened by the lurid light? or was it blood? or, perchance, a liquid flame? Herein did the shape of evil dip his hand and prepare to lay the mark of baptism upon their foreheads, that they might be partakers of the mystery of sin, more conscious of the secret guilt of others, both in deed and thought, than they could now be of their own. The husband cast one look at his pale wife, and Faith at him. What polluted wretches would the next glance show them to each other, shuddering alike at what they disclosed and what they saw!

"Faith! Faith!" cried the husband, "look up to heaven, and resist the wicked one."

Whether Faith obeyed he knew not. Hardly had he spoken when he found himself amid calm night and solitude, listening to a roar of the wind which died heavily away through the forest. He staggered against the rock, and felt it chill and damp; while a hanging twig, that had been all on fire, besprinkled his cheek with the coldest dew.

The next morning young Goodman Brown came slowly into the street of Salem village, staring around him like a bewildered man. The good old minister was taking a walk along the graveyard to get an appetite for breakfast and meditate his sermon, and bestowed a blessing, as he passed, on Goodman Brown. He shrank from the venerable saint as if to avoid an anathema. Old Deacon Gookin was at domestic worship, and the holy words of his prayer were heard through the open window. "What God doth the wizard pray to?" quoth Goodman Brown. Goody Cloyse, that excellent old Christian, stood in the early sunshine at her own lattice, catechizing a little girl who had brought her a pint of morning's milk. Goodman Brown snatched away the child as from the grasp of the fiend himself. Turning the corner by the meeting-house, he spied the head of Faith, with the pink ribbons, gazing anxiously forth, and bursting into such joy at sight of him that she skipped along the street and almost kissed her husband before the whole village. But Goodman Brown looked sternly and sadly into her face, and passed on without a greeting.

Had Goodman Brown fallen asleep in the forest and only dreamed a wild dream of a witch-meeting?

Be it so if you will; but, alas! it was a dream of evil omen for young Goodman Brown. A stern, a sad, a darkly meditative, a distrustful, if not a desperate man did he become from the night of that fearful dream. On the Sabbath day, when the congregation were singing a holy psalm, he could not listen because an anthem of sin rushed loudly upon his ear and drowned all the blessed strain. When the minister spoke from the pulpit with power and fervid eloquence, and, with his hand on the open Bible, of the sacred truths of our religion, and of saint-like lives and triumphant deaths, and of future bliss or misery unutterable, then did Goodman Brown turn pale, dreading lest the roof should thunder down upon the gray blasphemer and his hearers. Often, waking suddenly at midnight, he shrank from the bosom of Faith; and at morning or eventide, when the family knelt down at prayer, he scowled and muttered to himself, and gazed sternly at his wife, and turned away. And when he had lived long, and was borne to his grave a hoary corpse, followed by Faith, an aged woman, and children and grandchildren, a goodly procession, besides neighbors not a few, they carved no hopeful verse upon his tombstone, for his dying hour was gloom.

STUDY QUESTIONS for "Young Goodman Brown"

COMPREHENSION

1. Hawthorne, an American writer, wrote this story toward the beginning of the nineteenth century, more than a century after the famous Salem Witchcraft Trials in which one of his ancestors, John Hawthorn, played a significant role in punishing people whom he suspected of participating in witchcraft. With this in mind, why do you think that Hawthorne—a writer who associated himself with the "transcendentalists"—wrote this piece in the first place?

2. Do you think that this story is intended as pure entertainment and escape? Why or why not?

3. Using this story as a basis, what views do you think Hawthorne held toward the Puritan community of the late seventeenth century?
4. Do you think Hawthorne supported or opposed Puritanism? Why or why not?
5. The New England Puritans believed that the Devil could enter one's dreams. What bearing does the fact have upon your understanding of the text?
6. Historically, how has the Devil been depicted by the church? Does knowledge of this increase your understanding of the nature of Young Goodman Brown's dilemma?
7. Why does Young Goodman Brown leave Faith?
8. Why has he agreed to a meeting with the Devil?
9. Of what does the Devil try to convince Young Goodman Brown? How does he go about winning Young Goodman Brown to his side?
10. Why might a Puritan think this agreed-upon meeting was a particularly stupid idea?

DEVELOPMENT AND ORGANIZATION

1. In most short stories, the protagonist undergoes a series of events that bring about a change in his or her situation, thought, or feeling. By the story's end, has Young Goodman Brown been changed by the events he has just witnessed? That is, is he thinking or feeling differently about himself and those around him? Explain your answer in some detail.
2. Most often the change in the protagonist is a response, or kind of response, to a conflict, internal, external, or both. What is the nature of Young Goodman Brown's conflict? Is it internal, external or both? What is the inducer that introduces this conflict?
3. Generally, if the reader can grasp the central conflict of the story, then he or she can articulate the story's theme. What is the theme of the story? Is Hawthorne simply making the point that humanity is evil? (If he is, then his story is little more than a parable.) Or could he be offering some insight into the psychology of the Puritan mind? If so, what is that insight?
4. Heavily influenced by the sixteenth-century Calvinists, Puritans believe in something labeled "the doctrine of the elect." That is, even before creation, God designated only certain individuals to be saved. How does this doctrine apply to Hawthorne's story? Does Young Goodman Brown discover that he is one of the elect? Explain.

STYLE AND TECHNIQUE

1. This story is also intended as an allegory. What is an allegory? How does an allegory differ from most other short stories?
2. What does Young Goodman Brown symbolize? What does his wife symbolize? Note the number of times he either refers to Faith or calls upon Faith.
3. What is faith?
4. Find a passage in which Hawthorne makes particularly effective use of concrete or descriptive detail. What is the intended effect upon the reader of the passage that you chose?

TEN-MINUTE TOPICS

1. Write about a dream that made you uneasy. What was the dream? What about it made you

uneasy? How did it affect you? Looking back on it, do you still feel the same way about the dream? What would be your response now if you had it again?

2. Write about a time you found—or lost—your own personal faith. What were the circumstances? What happened to change your mind? How has that decision shaped your life since?

3. Write about a time you've caught someone acting in a way you could not fathom them acting. What had been your opinion of this person before the action? What was the action? How did your opinion of this person change? Have you regained any of your former opinion of this person?

THE FLEA

BY JOHN DONNE

Mark but this flea, and mark in this,
How little that which thou deniest me is;
It suck'd me first, and now sucks thee,
And in this flea our two bloods mingled be.
Thou know'st that this cannot be said
A sin, nor shame, nor loss of maidenhead;
    Yet this enjoys before it woo,
    And pamper'd swells with one blood made of two;
    And this, alas! is more than we would do.

O stay, three lives in one flea spare,
Where we almost, yea, more than married are.
This flea is you and I, and this
Our marriage bed, and marriage temple is.
Though parents grudge, and you, we're met,
And cloister'd in these living walls of jet.
    Though use make you apt to kill me,
    Let not to that self-murder added be,
    And sacrilege, three sins in killing three.

Cruel and sudden, hast thou since
Purpled thy nail in blood of innocence?
Wherein could this flea guilty be,
Except in that drop which it suck'd from thee?
Yet thou triumph'st, and say'st that thou
Find'st not thyself nor me the weaker now.
    'Tis true; then learn how false fears be;
    Just so much honour, when thou yield'st to me,
    Will waste, as this flea's death took life from thee.

STUDY QUESTIONS for "The Flea"

COMPREHENSION

1. To whom is the speaker of this poem talking? What is his purpose for addressing this audience?
2. What is the audience's response to the proposition being made by the speaker? Why does the speaker call this response "cruel and sudden"?
3. What final argument does the speaker make to his audience?

DEVELOPMENT AND ORGANIZATION

1. What does Donne mean by the words *mark, pamper'd, stay, cloister'd, use,* and *honour?*
2. What syllogism rests behind the speaker's argument? What main method of development does the speaker use to support this argument, and where does this development appear? Is the premise of his argument sound? The conclusion? Why or why not?
3. The chapter on argumentation recommends taking the arguments of the opposing view into account. Does the speaker do so? If yes, what does the audience say in defense?

STYLE AND TECHNIQUE

1. The central image of this poem is a flea. What symbolism surrounds this image? How does this symbolism fit with the speaker's purpose?
2. Donne deliberately indents (and rhymes) the last three lines of each stanza. Why does he do so? Look closely at the meaning of these lines and compare it to what the speaker says in the rest of each stanza.
3. What metaphors does the poem establish? Do they seem strange or outlandish to you? Why or why not?
4. "The Flea" is an example of a closed-form poem. What makes it so? Look specifically at the line and stanza lengths, the syllable patterns, and the rhyme scheme.
5. Donne deliberately allows only the speaker's voice in this poem. Why does he not allow the audience to speak directly?

TEN-MINUTE TOPICS

1. Four readings in this book focus on insects (and spiders). After reading all of them, write your own poem about an insect (or other bug).
2. Write a poem to another person in which you ask him or her to do something for you. You could ask for something as mundane as taking out the trash or for something as intimate as the matter of "The Flea."
3. If you had overheard the conversation in "The Flea" taking place between two people, what would your response be? Do you think the speaker makes his case effectively? Do you agree with the response of the audience?

ODE TO A NIGHTINGALE

BY JOHN KEATS

My heart aches, and a drowsy numbness pains
    My sense, as though of hemlock I had drunk,
Or emptied some dull opiate to the drains
    One minute past, and Lethe-wards had sunk:
'Tis not through envy of thy happy lot,
      But being too happy in thine happiness,—
          That thou, light-winged Dryad of the trees
            In some melodious plot
      Of beechen green, and shadows numberless,
          Singest of summer in full-throated ease.

O, for a draught of vintage! that hath been
    Cool'd a long age in the deep-delved earth,
Tasting of Flora and the country green,
    Dance, and Provençal song, and sunburnt mirth!
O for a beaker full of the warm South,
      Full of the true, the blushful Hippocrene,
          With beaded bubbles winking at the brim,
            And purple-stained mouth;
      That I might drink, and leave the world unseen,
          And with thee fade away into the forest dim:

Fade far away, dissolve, and quite forget
    What thou among the leaves hast never known,
The weariness, the fever, and the fret
    Here, where men sit and hear each other groan;
Where palsy shakes a few, sad, last gray hairs,
      Where youth grows pale, and spectre-thin, and dies;
          Where but to think is to be full of sorrow
            And leaden-eyed despairs,
      Where Beauty cannot keep her lustrous eyes,
          Or new Love pine at them beyond to-morrow.

Away! away! for I will fly to thee,
    Not charioted by Bacchus and his pards,
But on the viewless wings of Poesy,
    Though the dull brain perplexes and retards:
Already with thee! tender is the night,
      And haply the Queen-Moon is on her throne,

Cluster'd around by all her starry Fays;
    But here there is no light,
Save what from heaven is with the breezes blown
    Through verdurous glooms and winding mossy ways.

I cannot see what flowers are at my feet,
    Nor what soft incense hangs upon the boughs,
But, in embalmed darkness, guess each sweet
    Wherewith the seasonable month endows
The grass, the thicket, and the fruit-tree wild;
    White hawthorn, and the pastoral eglantine;
        Fast fading violets cover'd up in leaves;
            And mid-May's eldest child,
The coming musk-rose, full of dewy wine,
    The murmurous haunt of flies on summer eves.

Darkling I listen; and, for many a time
    I have been half in love with easeful Death,
Call'd him soft names in many a mused rhyme,
    To take into the air my quiet breath;
        Now more than ever seems it rich to die,
    To cease upon the midnight with no pain,
        While thou art pouring forth thy soul abroad
            In such an ecstasy!
Still wouldst thou sing, and I have ears in vain—
    To thy high requiem become a sod.

Thou wast not born for death, immortal Bird!
    No hungry generations tread thee down;
The voice I hear this passing night was heard
    In ancient days by emperor and clown:
Perhaps the self-same song that found a path
    Through the sad heart of Ruth, when, sick for home,
        She stood in tears amid the alien corn;
            The same that oft-times hath
Charm'd magic casements, opening on the foam
    Of perilous seas, in faery lands forlorn.

Forlorn! the very word is like a bell
    To toll me back from thee to my sole self!
Adieu! the fancy cannot cheat so well
    As she is fam'd to do, deceiving elf.
Adieu! adieu! thy plaintive anthem fades

Past the near meadows, over the still stream,
    Up the hill-side; and now 'tis buried deep
        In the next valley-glades:
Was it a vision, or a waking dream?
    Fled is that music:—Do I wake or sleep?

STUDY QUESTIONS for "Ode to a Nightingale"

COMPREHENSION

1. What is a nightingale? Why would Keats be addressing it in this poem?
2. Compare and contrast this ode to the one written by Steven Wagoner earlier in this book.
3. For most of us, understanding poetry is difficult. However, one of the ways to break down the barrier between ourselves and the poet is to paraphrase the poem—that is, to put the poem in our own words. With this in mind, try to paraphrase each stanza. As you do so, you'll probably need a dictionary to look up the meanings of words with which you are not familiar. In Keats's poem, these would include *hemlock* (line 2), *opiate* (3), *Lethe* (4), *Dryad* (6), *vintage* (11), and so on.
4. John Keats is considered one of the leading writers in the British Romantic Movement (1780-1830). The Romantic poets were characterized by a number of things: they sought in their writings to convey strong feelings; they demonstrate, over and over, a reverence for nature that verges on a form of worship; they believed in the power of the creative imagination, that inborn ability that allowed the poet to transcend the purely physical realm and to articulate the presence and the truths of higher realms of being.
   a. To begin, what feeling, or feelings, is Keats trying to convey in this poem? What feeling is he trying to articulate in the first two stanzas?
   b. What is it that inspires such ecstasy in the poet? What words and phrases prove most helpful in conveying his ecstasy?
   c. What is Keats's view of death? Is it similar to the contemporary view of death? For Keats, is death annihilation?
   d. What state of being is Keats trying to describe in stanzas four and five?
   e. In much of his poetry, Keats alludes to his belief in something called "negative capability." By "negative capability," the poet maintains an almost completely passive state that allows him or her to perceive experiences that are at times contrary (death in life, light in darkness) to reason. Logically, one cannot really transcend the physical world in which everything can be explained in terms of natural cause and effect. However, poetry allows the writer to transcend logic. What experiences does Keats convey in this poem that seem contradictory? What are the words that convey the contradictions? Which experiences seem to place the poet in a higher realm of being? What is that realm? What are the words Keats places in the poem that show us that the speaker has transcended the physical realm?

DEVELOPMENT AND ORGANIZATION

1. John Keats typically overwhelms the reader with imagery—words that appeal to sight, sound, taste, touch and/or smell. Why does he do this? What do you think he is trying to achieve?
2. Why does the poet address the bird directly? What does the bird represent? In what sense is the bird immortal?
3. What are the setting and situation for the poem?

STYLE AND TECHNIQUE

1. The lines in the poem start in different places, not all of them flush to the lefthand margin of the page. What is the impression that the lines first make upon you? Which lines seem to be grouped together? Does Keats center any meanings or images in each of the groupings?
2. Keats drops certain letters in the poem and uses unusual spellings for others. Which words have these changes? What effect do these changes have on the poem?
3. Which words in the poem rhyme? Put a similar letter after each word that rhymes to find the poem's rhyme scheme. For example, the word "pains" in line one rhymes with "drains" in line three; "drunk" in line two rhymes with "sunk" in line four. So the rhyme scheme for the first four lines looks like this:

> . . . pains A
> . . . drunk B
> . . . drains A
> . . . sunk B

TEN-MINUTE TOPICS

1. Write a poem in which you address something in the natural world around you. Try to use your five senses, and try to convey your own state of mind.
2. Write a poem in which you take your reader from an everyday setting to a fantastical setting, either in another universe or inside the realm of dream. What is the everyday place like? What is the fantastic place like? What connects the two realms? How does one travel from one to the other? Are there any dangers on the trip? Can one get back to the everyday world from the fantastical?

THE BALLAD OF THE HARP-WEAVER

BY EDNA ST. VINCENT MILLAY

"Son," said my mother,
  When I was knee-high,
"You've need of clothes to cover you,
  And not a rag have I.

"There's nothing in the house
  To make a boy breeches,
Nor shears to cut a cloth with
  Nor thread to take stitches.

"There's nothing in the house
  But a loaf-end of rye,
And a harp with a woman's head
  Nobody will buy,"
  And she began to cry.

That was in the early fall.
  When came the late fall,
"Son," she said, "the sight of you
  Makes your mother's blood crawl,—

"Little skinny shoulder-blades
  Sticking through your clothes!
And where you'll get a jacket from
  God above knows.

"It's lucky for me, lad,
  Your daddy's in the ground,
And can't see the way I let
  His son go around!"
  And she made a queer sound.

That was in the late fall.
  When the winter came,
I'd not a pair of breeches
  Nor a shirt to my name.

I couldn't go to school,
  Or out of doors to play.
And all the other little boys
  Passed our way.

"Son," said my mother,
  "Come, climb into my lap,
And I'll chafe your little bones
  While you take a nap."

And, oh, but we were silly
  For half an hour or more,
Me with my long legs
  Dragging on the floor,

A-rock-rock-rocking
  To a mother-goose rhyme!
Oh, but we were happy
  For half an hour's time!

But there was I, a great boy,
  And what would folks say
To hear my mother singing me
  To sleep all day,
  In such a daft way?

Men say the winter
  Was bad that year;
Fuel was scarce,
  And food was dear.

A wind with a wolf's head
  Howled about our door,
And we burned up the chairs
  And sat upon the floor.

All that was left us
  Was a chair we couldn't break,
And the harp with a woman's head
  Nobody would take,
  For song or pity's sake.

The night before Christmas
  I cried with the cold,
I cried myself to sleep
  Like a two-year-old.

And in the deep night
  I felt my mother rise,
And stare down upon me
  With love in her eyes.

I saw my mother sitting
  On the one good chair,
A light falling on her
  From I couldn't tell where,

Looking nineteen,
  And not a day older,
And the harp with a woman's head
  Leaned against her shoulder.

Her thin fingers, moving
  In the thin, tall strings,
Were weav-weav-weaving
  Wonderful things.

Many bright threads,
  From where I couldn't see,
Were running through the harp-strings
  Rapidly,

And gold threads whistling
  Through my mother's hand.
I saw the web grow,
  And the pattern expand.

She wove a child's jacket,
  And when it was done
She laid it on the floor
  And wove another one.

She wove a red cloak
  So regal to see,
"She's made it for a king's son,"
  I said, "and not for me."
  But I knew it was for me.

She wove a pair of breeches
  Quicker than that!
She wove a pair of boots
  And a little cocked hat.

She wove a pair of mittens,
  She wove a little blouse,
She wove all night
  In the still, cold house.

She sang as she worked,
  And the harp-strings spoke;
Her voice never faltered,
  And the thread never broke.
  And when I awoke,—

There sat my mother
  With the harp against her shoulder
Looking nineteen
  And not a day older,

A smile about her lips,
  And a light about her head,
And her hands in the harp-strings
  Frozen dead.

And piled up beside her
  And toppling to the skies,
Were the clothes of a king's son,
  Just my size.

STUDY QUESTIONS for "The Ballad of the Harp-Weaver"

COMPREHENSION

1. Why can't the mother clothe her son?
2. Where is the son's father?
3. How do mother and son stay warm?
4. What topples "to the skies"? Why is this item and its description significant?

DEVELOPMENT AND ORGANIZATION

1. Who (or what) is the "harp-weaver"? How is the harp-weaver's presence alluded to throughout the poem? What does the harp-weaver symbolize? What does the harp-weaver create?
2. How much time (approximately) elapses in the ballad?
3. What physical details does Millay use to describe the mother and son?

STYLE AND TECHNIQUE

1. Though called a ballad, the poem varies from the ballad form described in the headnotes to this chapter. In what ways does the poem vary (look especially at the line and syllable patterns)? What do the differences add to the poem?
2. From whose point of view is the poem told?
3. At what point in the poem does Millay stop using dialogue? Why do you suppose she does this?

TEN-MINUTE TOPICS

1. Write your own ballad.
2. Discuss the sacrifices made as a parent or a caregiver.
3. Think of an object you associate with a loved one. In what ways does that object symbolize the individual and your experience with him or her?

A MAN WITH POCKETS

BY ALBERTO RÍOS

1

Putting something in his pockets began simply enough.
A young man: first it was a black comb.

A new brown wallet followed, his own house key,
Some spare change, a small knife—

The gift of an eighteenth birthday, the last way left
His parents could say, *Take care of yourself.*

These were not any longer the quartz and igneous rocks,
The green-backed, still-moving beetles,

The chewing gum prizes saved of childhood.
These were new pockets, bigger pants, and new ideas.

The things in his pockets grew up as he grew up.
The key soon enough imagined its need for a key chain,

And not simply something plain. Perhaps a companion key,
As well, the back shed's key, that grizzle-toothed brass finger.

The small knife, everyone agreed, would be elegant in a sheath,
A nice, three-color plastic-lace braid hanging from it.

2

The wallet set up an entire business of its own, quickly
Under its own management and with no board of directors:

It gathered cards for all manner of transaction and recognition,
Allowance and identification, direction and appointment.

It gathered photographs and coupons, paper money at last,
And everything else that might be prodded into folding.

The pockets looked like the cheeks of a chipmunk
And were big enough to give him the aspect of a pontoon boat.

On most days he began to walk more slowly,
But on windy days nobody could keep up with him.

He started to look for pants with more pockets,
Or rather, he *had* to look for them.

A handkerchief, which he never used, some balled-up tissues
He thought he would use but didn't use, either.

Sometimes a small book, or his lunch, a sandwich,
Some cookies, and some potato chips.

3

His new pockets filled just as quickly as the old ones.
He could never wear shorts.

And finally he could not sit.
He tried, but it was easier not to.

And then it was easier not to walk so much at all.
Instead, people came to him.

They came at first to offer consolation, to assure him
It was not unusual, this richness of circumstance, really.

But consolation was soon followed by reward,
Unexpected—a knife-sharpener, a new pair of socks,

All the things he had and which they needed.
And they were curious things, not things

Readily available anywhere else, not in stores,
Certainly. These were the things found in drawers,

Discarded at first, or saved for later,
Then suddenly and altogether necessary.

4

He could not walk but he gave flight to so many others,
A lightness of spirit at having found something

Irretrievably lost otherwise. He gave happiness
Where others had thought to give it to him.

This was the bargain, then, that he made with the world.
He would keep the small things at his side

In exchange for the big things not seeing him,
not needing him, not paying him any attentions.

And it was a kind of life, free of tigers and danger,
But love, too, free of that and not entirely satisfying.

A bargain was a bargain, however, and his life was calm.
It was a full-enough life, a way to move, a way of breathing

Without moving. He became something else,
Not himself. A place, a garden, a store,

Everything but what he had been—a little boy
Believing in the necessary things of the world.

STUDY QUESTIONS for "A Man with Pockets"

COMPREHENSION

1. Who gave the man his wallet?
2. What kind of pants does the man look for, and why?
3. What is the "bargain" that the man makes "with the world"?
4. What does the man's life lack? What does it contain?

DEVELOPMENT AND ORGANIZATION

1. What is the purpose behind organizing the poem into four sections? What is the focus of each section?
2. How does the man's perception of the world change as he ages?
3. How do the images and symbols of each section connect to and develop from those of the others?

STYLE AND TECHNIQUE

1. Why does the poem use a third-person point of view?
2. How many lines make up each of the stanzas? Why is this an effective form?
3. How does Ríos use personification in the poem?

Ten-Minute Topics

1. What do the things we own say about who we are? (Think about small-scale items like those used in the poem.)
2. Write your own poem, imitating the form and intent of this one. Start with the title "A Man (or Girl) with ___."

MODES TABLES

Here are more examples of the modes of development and support discussed in this book. The first table below provides explanations for each of the modes and some humorous examples. The second table provides more serious examples.

TABLE ONE

Mode	Example
Description	"Teachers wear out of date clothing styles, they squint, they wear glasses, they're always wearing some strange hairdo, and they always look tired and pale as if they were sick all the time. . . ." These details help paint a picture so that your readers can see the teachers for themselves.
Narration	"When I was in sixth grade, I had a teacher for math who had a humongous nose and crooked teeth. . . ." Here you are relating a personal experience with an ugly teacher that you had. You are assuming that your audience has also met ugly teachers and that your experiences with your teachers were similar.
Example	"An example of an ugly teacher as opposed to a well-groomed teacher is one who never bothers to coordinate his clothes or otherwise care for his appearance. . . ."
Process	"Teachers start their day making themselves ugly by visiting the dentist to have their teeth drilled. Then they roll in the mud. . . ." Step by step, you show how a teacher becomes ugly. This task is similar to writing a how-to manual or a recipe, where you show all of the stages followed and tools needed to finish a project.
Comparison and Contrast	"Compared to construction workers, teachers . . ." Here you are comparing two groups of people to show that the traits of one are better or worse that the traits of the other.
Cause and Effect	"Teachers are ugly because of their gene pool, their upbringing, and their training. . . ." Here you are trying to find a reason for why this has come about—teachers are ugly as an effect of something else.
Classification	"There are three types of ugly teachers: the physically unattractive type, the earsplitting-voice type, and the hideous-personality type. . . ." Here, you split the group into different types, the way you would label species in a Biology class, and then provide a detailed description of each type.
Division	"A close examination of the ugly teacher reveals many parts that add up to the whole. . . ." Here, you are going to break a single teacher's traits into component parts.

Definition	"An ugly teacher is someone who loves to inflict pain on people trapped within classrooms. . . ." Defining an object or an idea doesn't simply mean going to the dictionary and copying what that says. Every time you use a word you give it a different spin, and you should let your readers know from time to time just what defines an idea for you.
Analogy	"Like teachers, frogs are ugly. Frogs have buggy eyes, their skin is slimy, they live underwater in muddy holes and eat worms and flies. . . ." You are relating the teachers to something else you think is similar (in this case nonhuman), and by describing the aspects or traits of the similar object, you are in effect describing teachers.
Reporting	"At a press conference today, the secretary for the Department of Education announced that teachers are ugly. . . ." Here you report on a speech that you eyewitnessed.
Argument (deductive)	"All teachers are ugly; Joe is a teacher; therefore, Joe is ugly." Here you argue a conclusion based upon a premise that must be, for the most part, correct. Deductive arguments fail (1) if the premises are untrue, and/or (2) if the conclusion does not follow from the premise. The direction of deduction is general axiom to particular case.
Argument (inductive)	"Teacher A is ugly, teacher B is ugly . . . teacher Z is ugly. Therefore we can hypothesize that all teachers are ugly." In this case, you are moving from specific proofs toward a general hypothesis. As with the deductive argument, the inductive argument fails if the premise, here based upon observations, is untrue or based upon too small a sample, or if the conclusion does not follow from the premise.
Quotations/ Citing Authorities/ Statistics	"According to *Time* magazine, teachers are uglier as a group than employees in other fields. . . . The secretary of education announced Thursday that teachers were uglier than counselors and principals. . . . Statistics compiled by the US government show . . ." You are supporting your claims with information provided by sources or studies that are knowledgeable in the field and accepted as authorities.

TABLE TWO

Mode	Example
Description	"The popular vacation spot of Cancun has a long white sandy beach, turquoise seas, and large coconut palms. . . ."
Narration	"When my wife and I went on our honeymoon, we visited Lake Tahoe for two weeks of skiing. . . ."

Example	"An example of a historic vacation spot would be Philadelphia. There visitors find the Liberty Bell. . . ."
Process	"To go on vacation, the first thing you must do is consider which destinations fit your interests, then you must save money, and then you must shop for airfare and hotel rates. . . ."
Comparison and Contrast	"Las Vegas, compared to Atlantic City . . ."
Cause and Effect	"Freight ship vacations on the rivers of Europe have become popular because of the moderate costs, the constantly changing sites, and most importantly, the novelty. . . ."
Classification	"Three main types of vacations are the family vacation, the honeymoon, and the weekend getaway. . . ."
Division	"To be successful, the honeymoon vacation requires several key ingredients. . . ."
Definition	"A vacation is a trip taken to ease the stress and the burdens of day-to-day life. . . ."
Analogy	"Vacations are like dessert. Work days are the meat and potatoes of our existence. Occasionally, we have time after the main course for something sweet. . . ."
Reporting (interview)	"John Smith, the CEO of Smith Accounting, has said, 'Vacations are important to the wellbeing of our employees. . . .'"
Argument (deductive)	"All people like vacations; John and Jane are people; therefore, John and Jane like vacations."
Argument (inductive)	"LeRoy broke his leg while on vacation; Suki got food poisoning while on vacation . . . Andy had his wallet stolen while on vacation. Therefore we can hypothesize that vacations can be dangerous."
Quotations/ Citing Authorities/ Statistics	"Research done by the Psychology Institute at Harvard University reveals that four out of five adult Americans take vacations to relieve stress."

Suggested exercise: Create your own humorous chart for the modes. Some possible topics may be frivolous lawsuits, annoying habits, outlandish fashion statements, and bad television shows.

READER RESPONSE SHEET

If you are in a class that uses peer editing—trading papers in a small group in class and offering each other feedback—here is a check sheet that will help you comment on your classmates' papers. Write out this list on a separate sheet of paper, fill in your responses, and give them to the writer when you are done.

Title of Essay:

Writer's Name:

Cite the essay as if it were to appear on a works cited page (MLA format):

1. What is the writer's purpose in writing this essay? Is that purpose conveyed in an implied or explicit thesis? If the thesis is explicit, please copy it down here. If it is implied, state it in your own words.

2. What tone does the writer adopt in this essay? How does the tone affect you as a reader? Does the writer adopt this tone to fit a persona he or she is trying to project? What persona is the writer trying to project?

3. What is the essay's primary issue? Where is this issue made clear?

4. Name two audiences who would most benefit from reading this essay. What stake does each audience have in the essay's issue?

5. How does this essay—or its subject matter—relate to you and your life experience?

6. What types of transitions does the writer use (refer to the discussion found in chapter one)? Copy those transitions found in the space below and identify the paragraph number where each is found.

7. Determine the overall organizational pattern used for the essay—refer to the blueprints found in chapter one and the paradigms found at the end of the successive chapters' headnotes. Explain your perception of the organization in the space provided below.

8. Pick four intriguing sentences from this essay. Copy them down in the space below. Name the parts of speech contained in the sentences. If you cannot identify a word form, refer to a grammar handbook or a dictionary. Can you name the phrase types that create each sentence? What type of information does each sentence bring to light?

9. What types of rhetorical strategies—the means by which the writer validates the thesis—are employed in the essay?

10. Has the writer used development and support that adequately explains the issue to the intended audience? Does the writer fulfill the reader's expectations for what is to appear in this essay? Where are there places that the writer could expand/develop more completely to meet the needs of the audience?

GLOSSARY OF IMPORTANT TERMS

Abstract—The opposite of *concrete*. The word can be nearly the equivalent of *general*, but for clarity it is useful to distinguish an abstraction from a general word. An abstract word refers to a *quality* of something else—a quality that cannot exist alone, but only in connection with something else. The word *horse* is rather general, but it is concrete. A horse's *strength*, on the other hand, is abstract. It is an entirely different thing from the strength of an oak tree, or the strength of a smell, or the strength of a conviction. In the last case, we have an abstract word modifying another abstract word. Nearly any word ending in *-ism*, *-ness*, *-tion*, *-ment*, or *-ity* is abstract. A helpful way to think of an abstract word is to consider it an adjective (such as *strong*, *polite*, or *courageous*) that has been converted by an act of the intellect into a noun (such as *strength*, *politeness*, or *courage*). In general, beware of using too many abstract words in your writing unless you provide plenty of concrete support.

Anecdote—An anecdote is a brief story or narration that we incorporate into an essay to support a general statement. For instance, to illustrate the need to know how to fix a flat tire, we might tell the anecdote of a friend who waited many hours in the desert for someone to come along and fix her flat tire.

Argumentation—Argumentation is the fourth mode of the essay. In an argumentative essay, the writer seeks to convince readers to accept his position in a debatable issue by using reasons and proofs. Two common forms of argumentative strategies are *induction* and *deduction*. Often argumentative essays require research.

Audience—The term refers to the people or to the person to whom you address your essay. Your audience may influence the selection and arrangement of details in your essay. For instance, say that you are writing an essay on the disintegration of the traditional family unit. Writing to a group of fundamentalist Christians, you might cite many Biblical passages with which they may be familiar. If, on the other hand, you were addressing this essay to a group of sociologists, you might use case studies and facts and statistics that would not be so interesting to the church group.

Body—The body is generally in the middle of the essay, between the introduction and the conclusion. It is here, in the narrative essay, that we develop the action and conflicts leading to the climax. In a description essay, we build up sensory details. In an expository essay, we use one or more of the techniques studied in this book—e.g., comparison and contrast, process, definition—to develop the thesis. In an argumentative essay, we use the body for developing proof to support the essay's central proposition or claim.

Character—an actor in a story that has a distinct personality and influences the outcome of the plot. A *major character* has much influence, and a *minor character* has little or no influence.

Cliché—A cliché is a once clever expression now ineffective because of overuse. Examples of these trite expressions include "chills running up and down my spine," "sharp as a tack," "neat as a pin," "nipped in the bud," "old as the hills," "the grass is always greener on the other side of the fence," and so on. Avoid using them.

Closed Form—Closed Form categorizes poetry that strictly adheres to a pattern of rhyme, syllable count, word or line repetition, or stanza length.

Coherence—Coherence is one of the qualities that instructors look for in essays. An essay is coherent when, sentence by sentence and paragraph by paragraph, it clearly follows a logical chain of development and organization originating with the issue. When that issue governs the topic sentences of individual paragraphs, and those topic sentences in turn govern each individual sentence within the paragraph, the essay will be unified by a single controlling idea. To write a coherent essay, use transitions and make sure your topic sentences relate to your thesis. See also **Unity**.

Cohesion—Cohesion is a quality that governs the flow of a sequence of sentences. In the sequence, each sentence should open with information learned in a previous sentence and end with information that is new or unknown to the reader. This information, however, must relate to the essay's issue, or the essay will lack coherence. Consider the following passage: "I like doughnuts. The best doughnuts in town are sold at Connie's Bakery. Connie's Bakery stands on the corner of Main Street and First Avenue. First Avenue was torn up in the recent downtown development. The development took a long time." The sentences are cohesive because each opens with information learned in a previous sentence, but they are incoherent because they do not focus on the issue raised in the first (topic) sentence: the speaker's fondness for doughnuts.

Conclusion—The final part of an essay, the conclusion may consist of one or more paragraphs in which, in the case of description, the writer may summarize the dominant impression he has been trying to convey through the use of concrete images; in which, in the case of narration, he brings the story to a close; and in which, in the case of exposition, argumentation, or literary analysis, he summarizes and/or restates the thesis and/or takes a broader view of the topic. However, in writing your concluding paragraph never introduce a new idea, an idea that has not been developed and supported in the essay's body.

Concrete—The term *concrete* refers to those descriptive words and details that appeal to the five senses: sight, sound, taste, touch, and smell. Effective writing employs concrete language.

Connotation—As opposed to the denotation, or dictionary meaning of a word, connotation refers to the nondictionary, associative meaning of a word. For instance, the term *red* denotes a color but may suggest or connote anger; the term *doubloon*, while denoting a Spanish gold coin, may conjure images of pirates, the high seas, and adventure.

Deduction—See **Syllogism**.

Denotation—As opposed to connotation, denotation refers to the dictionary meaning of a word. Thus, the term *doubloon*, according to the *Random House Dictionary*, denotes "a former gold coin of Spain and South America."

Description—The descriptive essay is the first of the four essay modes. In a description, the writer selects and arranges concrete details to convey an impression (or impressions) of the subject described.

Development—Also known as detail, complexity, diversity, or density, development must be present for an essay to say something significant. It consists of facts, examples, descriptive passages—anything that allows the reader to share something of the writer's experience of an idea, not merely the bare idea stated abstractly. A writer cannot validate a thesis without proper development.

Essay—If you learn nothing else from this text, you should learn what an essay is. Ways of organizing our impressions, thoughts, and experiences, essays may be broken into four modes: *description*, *narration*, *exposition*, and *argumentation* (count the literary analysis as exposition). Regardless of the essay type, we must make sure that our essay has an introduction, a body, and a conclusion, all held together by a single dominant impression, in the case of description; a plot, in the case of narration; a central idea, in the case of exposition; or a central proposition, in the case of argumentation.

Evidence—Evidence refers to the proof that supports your central claim, accusation, or proposition. Listerine, for instance, could cite no evidence to support its claim that its products helped cure dandruff. Similarly, before we find a man guilty of a crime, we must find proof or evidence—fingerprints, documents, eyewitnesses, etc.—that indicate his guilt. Evidence comes through the essay's development and support, including facts, statistics, quotes, examples, etc.

Exposition—The third mode of essay writing, the exposition, or expository essay, is intended to explain or inform. To do so, we may make use of one of the expository techniques covered in this text: example, comparison and contrast, process, and so on.

Figures of Speech—A departure from the literal meanings of words, figures of speech are used to convey even more vivid images or impressions of the topic about which we are writing. One kind of figure of speech, a *metaphor*, is a direct comparison between two objects not in the same category and states that one object is another. "The moon was a ghostly galleon" is a familiar metaphor in which the poet Noyes equates the moon with a ship. Other metaphors include "The mouth of the righteous is a fountain of life" and "Pleasant words are a honeycomb, / Sweet to the soul and healing to the bosom." A *simile* is another figure of speech comparing two objects not in the same category but making use of such terms as *like*, *as*, and *so*. Thus, "Bill was so skinny he looked like a snake that had frozen" is a simile comparing Bill with a frozen snake. Other similes include "All of our righteous acts are as filthy rags" and "Reckless words pierce like a sword." A third figure of speech worth noting is *personification*, the attributing of human qualities to nonhuman objects. The sentence "The trees marched up the hill in a straight line" is an example of personification because trees cannot literally march. Another example of personification is "Wisdom has built her house. / She has hewn her seven pillars"; on a literal level, wisdom cannot build or hew—these are human activities. Two more figures of speech are *synecdoche* and *metonymy*, both of which rely on substitution. Synecdoche means a part substitutes for the whole, or a whole for the part: "All hands on deck!" substitutes *hands* (part) for *sailors* (whole); "I bought a new set of wheels" substitutes *wheels* (part) for *car* (whole); "Los Angeles won the World Series" substitutes *Los Angeles* (the entire city) for the *Angels* or *Dodgers* (the baseball team). Metonymy means substituting a term closely associated with another: "The White House issued a statement" substitutes *White House* (residence) for *president* (resident; person making statement); "The fish rose from the deep" substitutes *deep* (attribute) for *ocean* (object with depth; home of fish); "All reports go to the corner office" substitutes *corner office* (workspace of important worker) for *boss* (important worker).

General—Referring to many individuals or individual objects, opposite of specific. Generality is a relative matter; a word that is general in one context may be specific in another. For example, the word *dog* is general in relation to *Weimaraner* but specific in relation to *mammal*. General statements in essays have the same effect on the reader as abstractions; without specific, concrete reference points, they sound vague. Thus, the statement, "I am proud of my car" is quite general and vague. The following, though still general, is more specific: "I am proud of my Toyota." And this statement is the most specific, and thus least general, of all: "I am proud of my 2012 Toyota Camry."

Illustration—Illustration is simply another word for example.

Image—A word or series of words appealing to the senses, an image is made of concrete detail and, at times, figures of speech. The following description is filled with concrete images (italics): "A few miles south of Soledad, the Salinas River drops close to the hillside and runs *deep and green*. The *water is warm*, too, for it has *slipped twinkling* over the *yellow sands* in the sunlight before reaching the *narrow pool*."

Induction—Induction is the process of arriving at a general conclusion/proposition on the basis of specific proof or evidence. If, for instance, after sampling twelve green apples and finding them all sour we reach the conclusion that green apples are sour, we would be using induction.

Introduction—The opening part of an essay consisting of one or more paragraphs. In a descriptive essay, the introduction introduces the subject to be described and establishes mood. In a narration, the introduction generally captures the reader's interest, introduces the main character(s), establishes point of view, and sometimes sets mood or tone. In expository and argumentative writing, the introduction captures reader interest, introduces the topic, establishes tone, and generally but not always states the thesis. In a literary analysis, the introduction names the author and title of the work to which the writer is responding, states the work's premise, focuses on a literary element, and offers a thesis that explains how the element functions in the work. A boring introduction diminishes reader interest. It is often wise to write your introductory paragraph last, with a complete knowledge of the essay's contents.

Irony—Irony is a device often used for humorous or surprise effect. We may be acquainted with *verbal irony*, which can verge on sarcasm, when we say one thing but mean quite the opposite. If we say, "Boy, I really enjoyed that class" and mean just the opposite, we have employed verbal irony. Often we have seen *situational irony* at work. An ironic situation is one in which appearance and reality, expectation and fulfillment are at odds. Thus, in a murder mystery, all surface clues may point to the butler as the murderer; this is appearance, and we expect the butler to be found guilty. Irony enters in when it is revealed that the maid is, in reality, the guilty one. *Dramatic irony* means that the audience knows information that the characters do not: a wife disparages her husband to a friend on the phone when the audience sees the husband overhearing the conversation. *Cosmic irony* occurs when the universe seems to work against everything a character does: it rains every day that a woman plans a picnic for her family.

Issue—Issue denotes a narrowed-down topic, one that meets the subject matter and length requirements of an essay. To arrive at an issue, the writer must use multiple levels of prewriting and invention. For example, if your instructor asks you to write an essay on controversial legal decisions, you will need to spend a considerable amount of time brainstorming, clustering, free-writing, and researching before you arrive at a workable issue. In this instance, you may have moved from controversial legal decisions to the not-guilty verdict in the O. J. Simpson murder trial. The relationship between writer, issue, audience, and purpose is essential to the development of a suitable thesis for an essay.

Logical Fallacies—These are fallacies or errors in reasoning and may most often appear in our argumentative essays. Below is a list of some of the more frequently occurring logical fallacies.

1. *False Analogy*—consists of comparing two things which, though seemingly alike, are really very different (e.g., We have pure-food and -drug laws, so why can't we have laws to keep moviemakers from giving us filth?).
2. *Argument in a Circle*—consists of offering a restatement of the main assertion as a reason for accepting that assertion (e.g., "There is only one argument that can be made to one who rejects the authority of the Bible, namely that the Bible is true." —William Jennings Bryan).
3. *Presumed Cause and Effect*, or *Post Hoc ergo Propter Hoc*—consists of citing two events and insisting that because one happened first, one caused the other (e.g., Young people joined Occupy Wall Street because they were brought up in permissive households).
4. *Non Sequitur*—consists of asserting that one fact has led or must inevitably lead to a particular consequence; literally means "It does not follow" (e.g., If gay marriage becomes law, then more straight people will lose health benefits at work).
5. *Begging the Question*—consists of the writer's assuming to be true what it is his responsibility to prove, of building his argument upon an undemonstrated claim (e.g., The stance that the president's socialist healthcare plan will cost the nation billions of dollars builds on the unproved claim that the plan is indeed socialistic).
6. *Argumentum ad Hominem*—consists of attacking the opposition rather than addressing the issue at hand (e.g., A critic attacks Tea Party members for being insensitive to the poor rather than examining their stance on reducing government spending).
7. *Argument by Extension* or *Red Herring*—consists of extending the issue in question, or adding distractions, until one is arguing a different subject altogether (e.g., Commissioner Sue Jones can't be convicted of embezzlement because the district attorney who is prosecuting her is a wife-beater and hates all women; the DA is therefore unqualified to handle this case).
8. *Either-Or*, or *False Dilemma*—consists of distorting the issue by insisting that only two alternatives exist (e.g., The abortion issue boils down to a simple choice between the American family and murder).
9. *Hasty Generalization*—consists of making a general assumption without considering enough facts (e.g., All Vroom-Vroom cars are worthless junk because one Vroom-Vroom car blew a tire).
10. *Argumentum ad Populum*, or *Argument by Consensus*—rests on the assumption that a statement is true because a majority of people believe it (e.g., We should all watch *The Best TV Show Ever!* because it's the most popular show on television).

Lyric Poetry—Poetry that centers on an image or series of images is called lyric poetry.

Metaphor—See **Figures of Speech**.

Mood—An atmosphere created by a written work that evokes an emotion in the reader. Mood is usually created by a combination of setting and tone.

Narration—(1) One of the modes of the essay, narration tells a story. However, narration may be used to develop description, exposition, or argumentation. (2) In storytelling and literary analysis, narration is related to point of view. Asking what type of narration is used in a story is roughly equivalent to asking what point of view is used.

Narrative Poetry—Poetry that tells a story is called narrative poetry.

Narrator—A special persona adopted by an author or writer to tell a story.

Open Form—Opposed to closed-form poems, open-form poetry that does not strictly adhere to any patterns. Also known as *free verse*.

Paragraph—A series of sentences that work as a unit within a larger prose work. Each new paragraph is set off by an indentation of the first line. In an essay, certain paragraphs can be identified by function: an introductory paragraph (or paragraphs) should capture reader attention, introduce the topic, establish tone, and state the thesis; body paragraphs should support the thesis, each paragraph containing a topic sentence supported by details; and a conclusion, made of one or more paragraphs, should summarize the main ideas of the body, state or restate the thesis, take a broader view of the topic, or follow one of the other strategies listed earlier in the paradigms.

Parallelism—Parallelism is a stylistic device by which ideas of equal importance are expressed in similar grammatical form. The most famous example of parallel sentences may be "I came, I saw, I conquered." The sentences are exactly parallel—or similar—in structure. Eighteenth-century English literary giant Samuel Johnson offers us some of the best examples of parallelism in the language: "We are all prompted by the same motives, all deceived by the same fallacies, all animated by hope, obstructed by danger, entangled by desire, and seduced by pleasure" (taken from *Rambler* essay #60).

Person—The term *person* refers to the pronoun case in which an essay is written. The author of the essay or narrative written in the first person will make frequent use of the pronouns *I, we, me, my, us, our*. An author who writes an essay or story in third person makes use of the third-person pronouns *he, she, him, her, they, them*, and so on.

Persona—Literally, a mask. Used now to mean an assumed personality separate from the personality of the writer. A persona is commonly used to produce an ironic effect. Benjamin Franklin pretended to be a callous, bloodthirsty German count in "Me Sale of the Hessians," an essay designed to discredit the British use of Hessian mercenaries against the Americans. Jonathan Swift pretended to be a man who approved of cannibalism in "A Modest Proposal," probably the most famous use of a persona in all English literature.

Personification—See **Figures of Speech**.

Plot—The structure of events in a story. A plot begins with an *inducer*, which brings conflict to the life of the story's *protagonist*, and ends when the protagonist somehow resolves that conflict. Following the Aristotelian model, the plot saves its most exciting or tension-inducing event for late in the story, usually the moment when the protagonist is closest to achieving or losing his goal.

Point of View—The perspective through which a story is told, point of view describes the narrator's distance from the story and the pronouns used to label the characters. Point of view is categorized as either *first-person*, *second-person*, or *third-person*.

Premise—The term *premise* refers to the basic assumption upon which a line of reasoning—or an entire argument for that matter—is based. One of the central premises of The Declaration of Independence, for instance, is that all men are created equal and entitled to life, liberty, and the pursuit of happiness.

Proposition—A proposition is the central claim—or thesis, if you will—around which an argument is based.

Protagonist—The main character in a story.

Purpose—Every piece of writing has a purpose—an intended outcome. Essays are typically written to achieve one of four outcomes: to teach, to inform, to entertain, or to persuade. The essay's purpose is tied to the writer's relationship with her target audience and chosen issue.

Rhetorical Question—A rhetorical question is one that is invented to provide thought but not to be answered. In our speech and writing we make use of rhetorical questions, such as the following: "Who wouldn't be proud of such a son?" or "What could be better than to spend Christmas Eve with family and friends?"

Satire—Satire is a form of writing that pokes fun at people, institutions, and ideas. J. Patrick Coolican's "Hey, Reno: Cry It Out with a Tire Fire and a Keg" makes fun of the city and citizens of Reno. Russell Baker in "The Plot against People" satirizes scientific method.

Setting—The setting of a story (or of a narrative essay) is the time and place in which the characters (including the narrator) act. The setting is not only a backdrop but also the boundary imposed on the characters: they cannot act in a way not suitable to the setting.

Simile—See **Figures of Speech**.

Slang—A favorite form of speech for most of us, slang is characterized by informal vocabulary, metaphorical lines, even at times "street talk."

Stanza—A group of lines in a poem comparable to a paragraph in prose.

Story—A story is a sequence of events, usually shaped by a plot and told by a narrator.

Style—The particular manner in which one writes. Samuel Johnson's style, for instance, is very formal, marked by formal vocabulary and complex sentence structure.

Syllogism—The basic unit of logic used in deductive reasoning, a syllogism contains a major premise, a minor premise, and a conclusion, as in the following example:

> Major premise: All men are mortal.
> Minor premise: Mike is a man.
> Conclusion: Mike is mortal.

Symbol—An object used to stand for something else. The flag, for instance, symbolizes the country it represents, the dove symbolizes peace, and the Star of David symbolizes Judaism.

Theme—The main idea or message conveyed by a narrative, often what one can conclude based on the actions of the characters or the narrator. For instance, the theme of Langston Hughes's "Salvation" is that pressure from others may lead us to actions that we may later regret. Themes are not what the essay is about, but what the essay says about a certain idea. For example, in Brent Staples's essay "Black Men and Public Space" racism is not the theme. What his essay says about racism—that black men, intentionally or not, alter public space—is the theme. Themes are created through repetition and emphasis. A good piece of writing may contain multiple themes.

Thesis—The most important part of an essay, the thesis expresses the main idea to which all other elements of the essay are subordinate. The thesis may be stated in one or more sentences, or it may be implied. Embodied in the thesis are *issue, audience, writer,* and *purpose.*

Tone—The attitude that the writer takes towards his/her subject matter. Thus, the author's tone in an essay written to protest the dumping of nuclear waste just outside the city limits may be one of outrage. But the term *tone* can also refer to the writer's attitude towards and relationship with his/her reading audience.

Transitions—Transitions are devices used to connect sentences with sentences, paragraphs with paragraphs. We should be aware of two kinds of transitions: the repetition of a key word or idea (or a synonym or a pronoun substituting for that idea); and traditional expressions such as *furthermore, additionally, for instance, finally,* and so on. Transitions create important bridges between ideas within an essay, making the essay a whole entity rather than a series of disjointed paragraphs.

Unity—Unity is a quality that should be a part of every essay and paragraph. In a tightly unified essay, every detail in that essay should in some way support the thesis. In a unified paragraph, every detail should support the topic sentence. Details that fail to support the thesis of an essay or the topic of a paragraph should be eliminated. See also **Coherence**.

Writer—The writer, the essay's author, can adopt any number of personas, serious or not, in order to present his issue to his audience. You have many roles to fill in your life, and you can work as one of them as an essay writer. You could be a concerned parent, an angry taxpayer, an avid football fan. Your persona should have a vested interest in the issue being discussed and should demonstrate a credible understanding of the essay's issue. In part, your essay's merit will be judged based upon how well you present your voice and your knowledge in the essay.

INDEX BY AUTHORS

INDEX BY TITLES